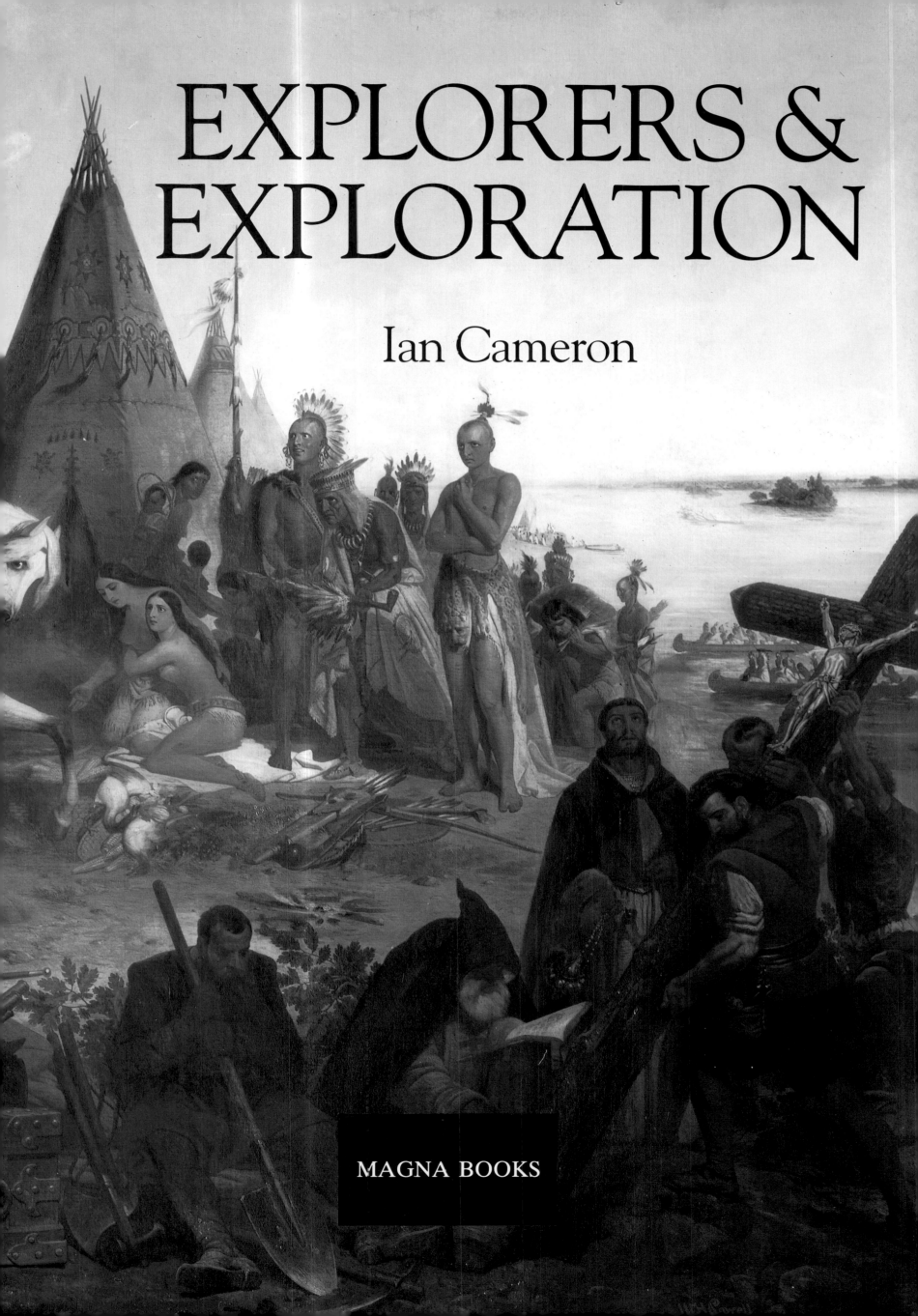

EXPLORERS & EXPLORATION

Ian Cameron

MAGNA BOOKS

Published by Magna Books
Magna Road
Wigston
Leicester LE8 2ZH

Produced by Bison Books Ltd
Kimbolton House
117a Fulham Road
London SW3 6RL

ISBN 1-85422-148-5

Printed in Hong Kong

Page 1: 'A Man of the Sandwich Islands in a Mask' is the original
caption for this engraving based on a drawing made by John
Webber in the course of Cook's third voyage.

Page 2-3: De Soto's 'discovery' of the Mississippi, as seen by the
19th century artist William Powell.

This page: Dumont D'Urville's ships *Astrolabe* and *Zelée* in the
Antarctic ice in 1840.

Contents

Introduction   8

1. Prehistoric and Early Explorers   12

2. Exploration by Sea   26

3. Europe and Asia   70

4. Africa   96

5. Central and North America   124

6. South America   172

7. Australasia   200

8. The Arctic   228

9. The Antarctic   252

10. Underwater Exploration   276
    by Gerald O'Brien

11. Space Exploration   286
    by Tim Furniss

Select Bibliography   300

Index and Acknowledgments   301

'An endless procession passes before us of struggling figures, some erect and powerful, others weak, bent and dying of hunger, cold or scurvy, but all gazing forward to where their goal might be found. What were these men seeking? They were setting out to explore the unknown . . . In every part of the world in every age this quest for knowledge has driven man forward. And so long as the human ear can listen for the breaking of waves on an unknown shore, so long as the human eye can try to follow the northern lights, and so long as human thought can reach out towards distant worlds in space, so long will fascination of the unknown carry man forward. When man loses this thirst for knowledge he will no longer be man.'

Fridtjof Nansen

Introduction

We are all explorers. Even those of us who seldom leave home are forever making journeys of discovery as we come across something new. Our emergence from the womb, our first crawl, our first love affair, our first job, all are acts of exploration; and since human beings have been indulging in these activities from time immemorial, it follows that the instinct to explore is a characteristic as old as the race itself.

The first explorers were therefore the first men, our ancestors *Homo sapiens*, who are thought to have evolved from primates some one and one half million years ago on the plains of Africa. About 300,000 years ago our ancestors left the African plains and began to spread throughout the Earth; and their reasons for making this move were almost certainly the reasons that have prompted exploration from that day to this: curiosity and the wish to improve their lot.

Curiosity is a basic human trait — don't we all want to know what lies behind a locked door or an enigmatic smile? Equally basic is the wish to find a better hunting-ground or a better job, a quest often given impetus by the fact that our neighbors' grass so often looks greener than our own. Such basic motives would have been enough to account for mankind's initial exploration of the Earth.

However, as human beings become more sophisticated, so their reasons for wanting to explore become more complex. In particular basic curiosity developed into the wish-to-acquire-knowledge-for-its-own-sake. As long ago as the 10th century the Scandinavian author of the *King's Mirror* wrote:

If you wish to know why men journey to far places, often at great danger to themselves, it is the threefold nature of man that draws him thither. One part of him is the desire for fame, another part is the desire for wealth, and the third part is the desire for knowledge.

This wish to acquire knowledge has, in the last thousand years, been the motive behind most of the truly great feats of exploration. It has also given an exploratory gloss to many military and commercial undertakings. Several major explorers were soldiers (such as Alexander the Great), and several major voyages and journeys were made by traders who, like Flecker's pilgrim, could claim

We travel not for trafficking alone:
By hotter winds our hearts are fanned:
For lust of knowing what should not be known
We take the golden road to Samarkand.

'Lust of knowing' is not, however, the only attribute explorers have needed. They have frequently needed great powers of endurance, and have always needed courage.

It isn't easy for the present generation to visualize how arduous and dangerous it was to travel before the advent of mechanized transport. Today we can board a Jumbo and circle the world in 24 hours; only 500 years ago it took Magellan's expedition 1090 days to circle the world, and out of his crew of 277 only 19 survived. Nearly all explorers have had to face privation — heat and cold, sick-

ness, exhaustion, hunger and thirst. Not much more than 100 years ago the explorer Giles was close to dying in the Australian outback when he spotted a baby wallaby: 'I pounced on it,' he wrote, 'and ate it living, raw, dying — fur, skin, bones, skull and all.' Nearly all explorers have also had to face dangers, either from the terrain they traversed or the people they met. 150 years ago the explorer Laing, trying to reach Timbuktu, was captured by the Tuareg who 'shot him, stabbed him and left him for dead, with gashes all over his body, his right hand almost severed, his jaw broken, and ear cut off and his scalp slashed open in five places.' Miraculously Laing recovered and went on to reach Timbuktu, only to be recaptured. This time the Tuareg made no mistake; they strangled him with their turbans, then hacked off his head.

These qualities of curiosity, toughness and courage are apparent in an incident which encapsulates the essence of exploration . . . In 1253 Friar William of Rubruck set out to make contact with the 'Great Khan of Tartary' whose peripatetic capital was believed to lie east of Mongolia. After traveling for 3000 miles through the deserts of central Asia, Rubruck was taken, none too gently, to an

Below: Louis Antoine de Bougainville commanded the first French circumnavigation of the world in 1766-69.

Far left: A print from a 1537 book by the geographer Giovanni de Sacrobosco. Exploration is symbolized by the (inaccurate) globe maps and the carracks in the background.

Left: W. Woodham Graham, probably the first person to climb in the Himalaya 'purely for pleasure.'

Below: Wilfred Thesiger (center) with a group of Arab companions. Thesiger traveled widely in the Sahara and the Arabian deserts.

audience with the Khan. He was bundled into a huge tent, 30-feet in diameter, its entrance hung with mares' teats and cows' udders, its wall whitened with powdered bone and its roof supported by pillars lacquered with gold. 'Do not be afraid,' the Khan said to him 'If I was afraid,' the friar replied, 'I would not be here.'

Explorers like Rubruck have helped to push back the frontiers of the unknown. Their exploits have added to our understanding of the world we live in. The story is our heritage.

Opposite, top left: The great navigator Captain James Cook.

Opposite, top right: One of exploring's most bitter controversies, Robert Peary and Frederick Cook dispute the credit for being first to the North Pole.

Opposite, bottom: The German naturalist and traveler Alexander von Humboldt.

Top left: Edward John Eyre, one of the great explorers of Australia.

Above & top: Exploration and the development of astronomical and navigational instruments often went hand in hand. These illustrations taken from a 16th century manuscript include a cross-staff (above), first used at sea by the Portuguese around that time.

Left: A fabulous gold mask of the Inca sun god Inti.

Prehistoric and Early Explorers

The desert lay lifeless under the sun, but at a rock-pool in the oasis a group of primates were cooling themselves in the shallows. Watching them, crouched behind rocks, were newcomers to this part of the desert, a species never seen there before, a pair of *Homo erectus* hunters. The *Homo erectus* were hungry. In their hands were clubs of stone.

A sudden dash, a flurry of blows, and the youngest of the primates was dead. The rest of the group, screaming with rage and terror, fled into the desert, and the hunters were left with their kill. The oasis, by right of conquest, was theirs. Man had discovered another part of his planet.

Such incidents must have been commonplace as, from abut 250,000 BC onward, our ancestors fanned out from their heartland in Africa to occupy the Earth. From skeletons and artefacts it is possible to plot and date their migrations. The first *Homo erectus* were creatures of the tropics. Before they could survive in temperate let alone polar regions they needed to be able to make clothes, build shelters and control fire. By about 275,000 BC they had acquired these skills, and were pushing north from Africa into the seaboard of present-day Palestine and the Lebanon. From here some headed west into Europe – the Dordogne valleys and the Guadaljara plateaux are littered with their skeletons – and some headed east into Asia, one wave passing to the south of the Himalaya and one to the north. By about 200,000 BC they had reached Peking (where their skeletons have been found 160 feet deep in the limestone caves of Choukoutien) and Java (where in the plains around Modjokorto and Wodjak skeletons of *Homo erectus*, *Solo* man and Pleistocene man have been recently unearthed.) Another 150,000 years were to pass before our ancestors found their way out of Eurasia. Then, not much more than 30,000 years ago, when the Earth was in the grip of the most recent ice-age and sea-levels were low, nomadic hunter-gatherers crossed from Asia to America by a land bridge over what is now the Bering Strait, and from New Guinea to Australia by a land bridge over what is now the Torres Strait. By 10,000 BC these hunter-gatherers had penetrated as far south as Tierra del Fuego and Tasmania, and with the exception of a few islands in the Pacific, man had occupied all the habitable parts of the Earth.

These early migrations were remarkable achievements. Indeed when some Stone Age family moved into

Above: A reconstructed skull of homo erectus.

Left: Stone Age family preparing a meal in front of their cave. A painting by Paul Jamin.

Previous page: An early Egyptian/Phoenician trading galley passing through the Red Sea.

territory no human being had before set foot in, these were arguably the greatest moments of all in the history of exploration. They were, however unrecorded moments. We can estimate approximately when they took place, and we can visualize some of the difficulties and dangers these Stone Age explorers faced – they would have had to travel entirely on foot without scientific aids, and the Earth in those days was more heavily forested and its fauna more numerous and aggressive than today. We cannot, however, reconstruct their feats in detail. Such reconstruction only becomes possible with the invention of writing.

Writing evolved in present-day Iraq about 6000 years ago, and Sumerian cuneiform tablets lead us to believe that about this time exploratory-cum-trading voyages were taking place between the deltas of the Tigris and the Indus. The cuneiform tablets, however, contain so little information that these early Sumerian voyages must be regarded as conjectural. Not till we come to another millenium and another continent do we have enough evidence to reconstruct the journeys of some of those early explorers in detail. Then *circa* 3000 BC, the Egyptians began to record the exploits of their travelers in bas-relief and hieroglyphics.

From the time of the Egyptians onward it is possible to tell the story of exploration as a continuous narrative, bearing in mind that what explorers have been doing over the last 5000 years is not so much discovering new territory as bringing one group of people into contact with another. The idea that our planet was 'discovered' by Europeans during a great burst of post-renaissance traveling is very wide of the mark; for wherever explorers like Columbus went they found that someone had been there before them. In the 20th century Europeans climbed the 'unknown' Andes, only to find Inca altars on the highest peaks; in the 19th century European seamen died searching for an 'undiscovered' North West Passage along whose shores nomadic Eskimos had been living for millenia; in the 18th century Cook landed on 'the remotest island on Earth' (Easter Island), only to find there gigantic statues left by a previous civilization; in the 13th century Marco Polo traveled to 'barbaric Cathay' in search of silk, and found on the opposite side of the world a civilization as advanced and ancient as his own. Even the ancient Egyptians who made the first journey ever to be recorded in detail (the expedition to Punt) found at their journey's end not only gold, incense, ebony and ivory, but a civilized people who received them with pomp and traded with them with scrupulous honesty.

Explorers down through the ages may occasionally have discovered new territory; sometimes they discovered new people, but what they discovered most often of all is the truth of the saying that 'there is no new thing under the sun.'

The Egyptians (c. 3000 BC – 1000 BC)

Above: The first writing: Sumerian cuneiform tablets from the Tigris valley, *circa* 4000 BC.

The story of recorded exploration begins on the Nile.

The Nile is an ideal river for waterborne traffic because the current flows down it from south to north and the prevailing wind blows up it from north to south. A people with the know-how to build the pyramids soon found a way of utilizing these conditions, and by 3000 BC the Egyptians were constructing long low ships with collapsible masts which could be rowed downstream with the current and sailed upstream with the wind. These vessels were ideal for river traffic, but were virtually useless in the open sea; being built of brittle and unyielding palm-wood, they could not stand the pounding of waves and tended literally to fall apart at the seams. However, in about 2600 BC the Egyptians sent a coastal expedition to Byblos in the Lebanon where the Phoenicians were beginning to emerge as effective if unpopular traders – 'they are,' wrote a temple priest, 'miserable Asiatics; evil is the place they live in, with many trees and bad water.' However, among the Phoenicians' 'many trees' were the famous cedars of Lebanon, and we know from cargo-manifests that cedarwood was one of the items brought back to the Nile, where it provided the Egyptians not only

with oil for embalming but also with first-class timber for ship-building. By about 2500 BC Pharaoh Sahure had a number of seaworthy ships; there is evidence that he sent three of them to search for Punt.

Punt, according to legend, was the home of both the gods and the Egyptians' earliest ancestors: a land said to be abounding in gold, silver, ebony, ivory and above all incense. The latter was of particular interest to Sahure, for incense was as great a desideratum in ancient Egypt as were spices in medieval Europe; one temple alone (that of Amon in Thebes) burned over 300,000 bushels a year. Scholars are uncertain of the exact whereabouts of Punt. Locations have been suggested as close to the Nile as

Aden on the coast of the Red Sea, and (risibly) as far from the Nile as Tumbes on the coast of Peru; but bearing in mind the length of time the ships were away, the cargo brought back, and the physiognomy of the people of Punt as depicted on frescoes, the most probable site is present-day Mozambique.

The Egyptians made three expeditions to Punt: the first under Pharaoh Sahure *circa* 2500 BC, the second under Pharaoh Mentuhotep *circa* 2000 BC, and the third under Queen Hatshepsut *circa* 1492 BC. For the last of these we have sufficient evidence to reconstruct the voyage in detail.

Queen Hatshepsut is known to have been beautiful,

able and ambitious – 'the first great lady in history.' She came to power in 1501 BC, only to find that her father's wars had left Egypt devoid of both incense and gold. It was to replenish the royal coffers with these much-needed commodities that she decided to send an expedition to Punt. This was a major undertaking, and it was several years before five specially-strengthened ships and about 130 specially selected crew were ready to leave Coptos. The fleet rowed through the canal which in those days connected the Nile to the Red Sea, and in the summer of 1493 BC stood south into the unknown.

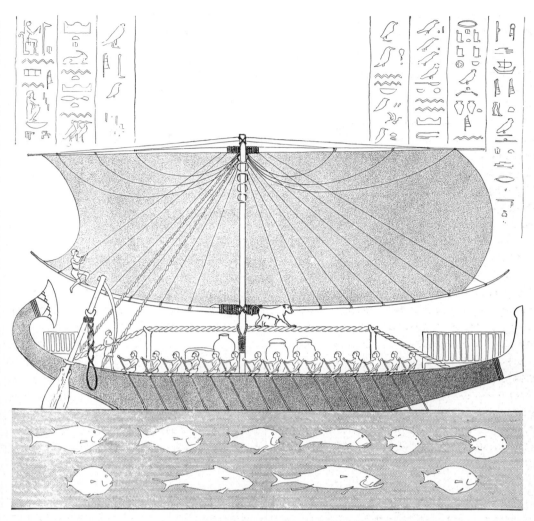

The expedition was commanded by a man about whom we know only his name, Nehsi. Nehsi kept no log or diary, so our only sources of information about his voyage are temple frescoes and the writing of subsequent historians. From the frescoes we can estimate that the Egyptian ships were roughly 100 feet in length, 22 feet in beam and 90 tons in weight; they were built of cedarwood, were rowed by about 22 oarsmen and had a single mast and sail supported by a veritable spider's web of rigging. They had little storage space and no navigational aids, which points to the fact that the voyage must have been coastal, with the ships seldom if ever venturing out of sight of land, and the crew landing frequently to top up with water and food. It would have taken them a month to clear the Red Sea, and perhaps as long again to round Cape Guardafui, the Horn of Africa. Then, with the northeast monsoon and the North Equatorial Current to help them they would have enjoyed an easy passage south down one of the most beautiful shorelines on Earth, the coast of present-day Somalia, Kenya and Tanzania.

How far south they went is a matter of conjecture, but a possible destination is Sofala at the mouth of the River Save.

There are several reasons for identifying Punt as Sofala. The cargo brought back is listed as 'gold, silver, frankincense, 31 myrrh trees, ebony, ivory, antimony, leopard skins, long-tailed apes and a southern panther alive', and all these could have been found in the neighborhood of Sofala. Temple frescoes depict the people of Punt as living in reed-huts built on stilts; the Save delta is marshland, and to this day the local inhabitants live in stilted reed-huts. Another fresco shows the king and queen of Punt and their retinue; some people think that the sturdy limbs and exaggerated buttocks of the queen suggest she was deformed; however a more likely explanation is that she was a Khoikhoi (or Hottentot) – a people known, in prehistoric times, to have lived near Sofala.

Nehsi and his men spent several months in Punt, careening their ships, making contact with the local rulers, and almost certainly visiting the nearby Zimbabwe gold-fields, where Egyptian and Phoenician artefacts have been found. Relations between the people of Egypt and the people of Punt seem to have been friendly, with none of the burning and looting which in millenia to come so often characterized the coming of European explorers. In all the tablets and frescoes which commemorate Hatshepsut's expedition there is no hint of a weapon raised in anger.

The homeward voyage would have been more difficult than the outward, for the ships were heavily laden, and both wind and current were against them. Their single sail would have been useless now, and the crew must had had to row for month after month into head-wind and head-sea under a tropic sun. They would have been lucky to average nine miles a day. But at last, after a voyage of nearly three years and 9000 miles, they returned in triumph to the Nile.

'All five ships,' we are told, 'were laden with the fabulous treasures of Punt . . . never was the like brought back to any monarch since the world began.' There were processions, banquets, speeches and sacrificial offerings; the achievements of Nehsi and his crew were recorded in fresco and on papyrus, and Hatshepsut proclaimed a two-day public holiday and paid her father the greatest compliment she could think of – she planted the 31 myrrh trees round his tomb. 'See, I have made him a Punt in his garden. It is big enough for him to walk in.'

Time cannot erase the feeling that something very much worth while had been accomplished, and one won-ders why, if the voyage was so successful, it was never re-peated.

The answer would seem to be that the Egyptians were basically a stay-at-home people who depended on the Nile – 'the mother of all (their) wants' – whose ebb and flow was the be-all and end-all of their lives. They con-sidered it ungrateful and therefore impious to leave the Nile, and their three expeditions to Punt must be re-garded as one-off, untypical ventures. Indeed in the long run the people who benefited most from the voyages to Punt were probably not the Egyptians, but their neigh-bors the Phoenicians.

The Phoenicians (c. 2500 BC – AD 1)

The Phoenician were a dark-skinned Semitic people who, about 2750 BC, moved into the coastal region of what is now Israel and the Lebanon. Hostile neighbors prevented them from expanding by land, so they expanded by sea, redistributing by ship the treasures which reached them by caravan. They became traders *par exellence*, first cornering the seaborne traffic of the Mediterranean, then extending their voyages to the Black Sea, the Red Sea, the Atlantic coast of Europe and the west coast of Africa. Gradually over the centuries they built up the world's first maritime empire.

The key to their success was their ships. The Phoen-icians were great adapters. The took Egyptian hiero-glyphics and turned them into an alphabet; they took Egyptian techniques of weaving and dyeing, improved them, and built up their great cloth emporiums of Tyre and Sidon; and they took the design of Egyptian hulls and the rig of Arab sails and combined them to create the world's first ocean-going merchant fleet. Phoenician ships were larger than those which Nehsi had taken to Punt; scholars put their average length at 120 feet, their beam a little under 30 feet, their draft at 7 feet and their weight at over 350 tons; they were decked-in (giving plenty of room for cargo), and had a single sail, free of rig-ging. With this easily-worked sail and with their oars, the Phoenicians were able to anticipate the boast of Eliza-bethan seamen that there was 'no sea unnavigable, no land unattainable.'

Everyone agrees they were magnificent seamen, but when it comes to reconstructing their exploits there is a difficulty. Because they were essentially traders anxious to preserve their trading monopoly, the Phoenicians were secretive and kept no records. Indeed they falsified their sailing orders, destroyed their cargo ledgers, and, to dis-courage competitors, disseminated fo'c'sle yarns of ves-sels being crushed and eaten by sea serpents or blown off the rim of the world. The story goes that one Phoenician captain, rather than let a competitor follow him on a trad-ing mission, deliberately ran his vessel aground. Our knowledge of the Phoenicians has therefore come down to us only at second hand through the eyes of subsequent (mostly Greek) historians; and it is from Herodotus' *His-tories* that we have to reconstruct what was undoubtedly the Phoenicians' greatest exploit, their circumnavigation of Africa.

Herodotus writes:

Libya (*as Africa was then called*) is known to be surrounded by sea on all sides, save for that small part which borders Asia. The first man to prove this was Pharaoh Necho II of Egypt who equipped an expedition of Phoenician ships and commanded them to sail into the Southern (*Indian*) Ocean, to round Libya and return to Egypt through the Pillars of Heracles (*the Straits of Gibraltar.*)

So, Herodotus tells us, the Phoenicians set out, and

Whenever it was autumn they landed, tilled the fields, and waited for the harvest in whatever part of Libya they happened to be; when they had harvested the corn they sailed on. After two years they came to the Pillars of Heracles and in the third year returned to Egypt. When they got back they related a story which I cannot believe – namely that as they rounded the southern tip of Libya they beheld the midday sun on their right-hand-side.

This account may be brief, but several factors point to it being true. Herodotus was a meticulous historian writing soon after the event, and he recorded the circumnaviga-tion not as a tall story but as fact. The direction of the voyage (east to west) and its time-table (three years) fit the capabilities of contemporary ships. Phoenician maps are almost unique in showing sea to the south of Africa – most other maps show 'Libya' joined to a mythical Great Southern Continent – and it is hard to see how the Phoenicians could have known that Africa was to all in-tents and purposes an island unless they had sailed round it. Finally there is Herodotus's reference to the sun; for incredible as it must have seemed to the ancients, when Necho's men rounded the Cape of Good Hope, being in the southern hemisphere, they would indeed have seen the mid-day sun on their right. Thus the very fact which made the voyage incredible to the ancients makes it credible to us.

Assuming we believe Herodotus, the Phoenicians would have left Kosseir in the summer of 600 BC. For four or five months, like the Egyptians a millennium before

Below: A bireme, as depicted in an Assyrian sculpture of *c.* 700 BC.

Right: A romantic interpretation of Herodotus reading from his *Histories* to the Greeks.

them, they would have enjoyed an easy passage down the east coast of Africa, before putting into Sofala, the last outpost, for Europeans, of the known world. Here they would have reprovisioned, before heading into the Mozambique Channel. This was the moment of truth. No ship from Europe had ever before ventured into the Mozambique Channel and returned; for in the narrow seaway between Africa and Madagascar the North East Monsoon and the Mozambique current form a race of water which sweeps vessels inexorably south. As Necho's crew were swirled down-channel at a rate of something like 10 knots they must have realized they had no hope of returning to Egypt by the way they had come; they had to circumnavigate 'Libya' or die. South of the Mozambique Channel the cliffs would have grown steadily higher, the nights colder, the squalls more violent and the seas heavier; and we can imagine the Phoenicians' relief as the coastline turned first west and then north. We can picture them creeping thankfully between Table Mountain (then an island) and the shore, then heading north for what they obviously hoped would be a quick passage home. However, the most difficult part of their journey was still to come.

Soon after rounding the Cape of Good Hope they must have landed to sow their grain – scholars have suggested Saint Helena Bay as a possible site; this is certainly good crop-growing country, and if the Phoenicians had sown in May (599) they could have harvested and been back in their ships by October. As they again headed north, 'Libya' became increasingly barren; soon they would have been skirting the Namib Desert, one of the driest places on Earth, and it was fortunate for them that on this part of their voyage they would have been helped on their way by both the Benguela Current and the south east trades. By the end of 599 they would have been approaching a very different littoral, the lush and heavily-forested Congo; and now, as they entered the Gulf of Guinea, their troubles started; for, for the first time since leaving Kosseir, both wind and current were against them. The next nine months must have been purgatory, as they struggled to make headway against the adverse Guinea Drift and north east trades. With their sail useless, they would have had to rely entirely on their oars; and we can imagine them rowing week after week and month after month, literally for their lives, as sweating under a tropic sun and weakened by fever and dysentery, they inched their way round the bulge of Africa. By midsummer it would have been time for them to land and for the second time sow corn. A likely site would have been Senegal, where the soil is sufficiently fertile for them once again to have harvested within five months. And soon after resuming their journey, they would have come at last to a familiar shore: the Sahara. They joy at re-

Above: Phoenician ships and soldiers fighting, a drawing based on reliefs found at Konyunik and believed to depict a war between Tyre and the Assyrians.

turning to the world they knew must have been past belief. For never before and seldom since have explorers taken so spectacular a leap into the unknown, and survived.

The last part of their journey, via the Pillars of Heracles and the north coast of Africa, must have been an anticlimax. Their home-coming seems to have been an anticlimax too; for they arrived back in the middle of a war, and without any of the gold or incense which would have made their expedition a popular success. So the men who had traveled farther than men from Europe had ever traveled before went quietly to their homes and were forgotten – a fact which highlights the Phoenicians' one great failing as explorers. The Greeks would have recorded so great a voyage for science; the Romans would have recorded it for posterity; but the Phoenicians, being interested only in trade, regarded it as a failure and forgot it.

The Phoenicians were magnificent practical seamen who voyaged far beyond the confines of the Mediterranean – 2000 years were to pass before other ships from Europe traveled as far. Yet because they had no 'lust of knowing' their stature as explorers is suspect. At the bar of history they have been hoist with their own petard, their obsession with secrecy.

The Greeks (*c.* 1000 BC – AD 1)

Soon after 2000 BC a pastoral people migrated from the Danube basin to the Greek peninsula. Finding their new home was too arid to provide sufficient farming-land to meet their needs, they took to the sea and established city-colonies, first in the Aegean Islands, then along the coasts of Asia Minor and the Black Sea, and finally throughout the Mediterranean. They became rivals of the Phoenicians, much of whose empire they gradually assimilated. As explorers these Greeks or Hellenes, had one quality which the Phoenicians lacked: they had a love of knowledge for its own sake – on their military campaigns they took botanists to collect plants, and on their voyages

astronomers to study the stars. They recorded their achievements, both in carefully-researched histories and in great works of literature like *The Illiad* and *The Odyssey*.

By land, their greatest feats of exploration stemmed from their military campaigns. The journeys of Cyrus, Xenophon, Craterus, Nearchus and above all Alexander the Great were basically journeys of conquest, with exploration a by-product (albeit an important one) of subjugation.

By sea, in contrast, their great feats were peaceful and scientific: the founding of city-states which took root on

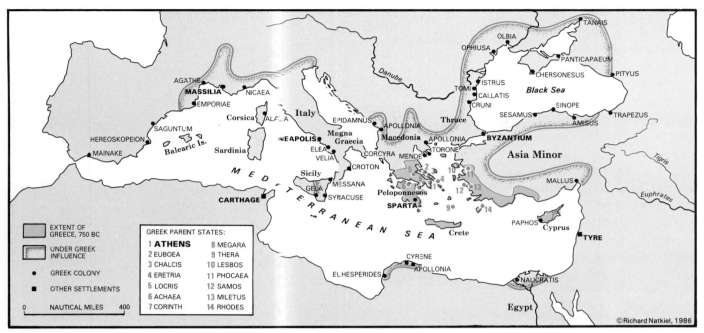

Left: The Greek empire *circa* 750 BC, showing the extent of their trading voyages and explorations.

Below: Xenophon sighting the Black Sea on his return from Persia.

Bottom: A wall painting of Alexander the Great at the battle of Issus.

remote coastlines, and the voyages of men like Pytheas of Marseilles – a scholar-astronomer who penetrated deep into the Atlantic in search not of trade, but of knowledge.

The Campaigns of Alexander the Great
(*c.* 334 – 323 BC)

Alexander, the son of King Philip II of Macedonia, was born in 356 BC. Between the ages of 13 and 15 he was tutored by Aristotle, a fact which undoubtedly fostered his interest in empirical concepts and never-failing curiosity. When he was 20 his father was assassinated, and Alexander inherited both his kingdom and his long-standing feud with Persia. In 334 BC he crossed the Dardanelles with 30,000 infantry and 5,000 cavalry, and in a series of brilliant campaigns conquered present-day Syria, Lebanon, Israel and Egypt. Then, in pursuit of the Persian King Darius, he led his army first through the Persian heartland of the Tigris and Euphrates, and then into the remote regions of central Asia, where his exploits were both exploratory and military.

He penetrated as far north as the River Jaxartes where he found Tashkent, as far east as the approaches to the Pamirs where he founded Leninabad, and as far south as the delta of the Indus where he found Karachi, thus making Europeans aware of several hundred thousand square miles of territory hitherto unknown to them. Two of his greatest achievements were leading his army over the Hindu Kush and down the Indus.

The name Hindu Kush means 'Hindu Killer', this westerly spur of the Himalaya deriving its name from the fact that 'many of the slaves brought to us (in Arabia) from India die while crossing the mountains on account of the snow and the cold.' For Alexander to have taken his army over the range in summer would have been a remarkable achievement. He did it in winter. In November 330, as his troops moved into the foothills north of Kandahar, the thinness of the air was already causing his men sickness, dizzyness and shortage of breath. Early in 329 they paused beneath the summit ridge to found the misnamed Alexandria-in-the-Caucasus – an unlikely oasis of Greek culture in an improbable Afghan valley – then came the moment of truth, the crossing of the 11,600-foot Khaiwak Pass. It must have been a nightmare journey, with the snow deep, the cold intense, food scarce and fuel non-existent. The men, struggling through drifts up to their armpits, suffered from exhaustion, snowblindness and frostbite; in their thousands they were frozen solid to the rocks as they leaned against them. The horses

and pack asses fared even worse; nine out of ten died, but at least their bodies, eaten raw because there was no fuel to cook them, provided the troops with food. Alexander lost more men and more animals crossing the Hindu Kush than in all his subsequent campaigns in central Asia. But he achieved his objective, surprising the Persians who believed him to be still on the opposite side of the mountains, driving them in confusion over the River Oxus and capturing their leader.

A couple of years later, after a campaign at the approaches to the Himalaya, he decided to float his army down the Indus to the sea. This was another formidable undertaking, involving the building of a fleet in hostile territory and its passage down a river which is notoriously hazardous. The historian Arrian writes:

Where the rivers (*Indus and Jhelum*) converge, are swift currents through a narrow passage, with terrific whirlpools where the water surges and boils. So great was the roar of the water that the oarsmen were struck dumb with terror. Many ships were swirled downriver out of control; two were wrecked with the loss of most of their crews.

When, a month later, the ships neared the mouth of the Indus, an even greater peril awaited them. For the Indus delta is scoured by some of the fiercest tides on Earth – a rise and fall of 40 feet in a couple of hours is not uncommon.

When the tide ebbed, the entire fleet was left stranded, which caused Alexander's men (*who came from the near tideless Mediterranean*) much bewilderment. This bewilderment turned to terror as the tide rushed in again, so that the ships were refloated, flung together, dashed against the shore and staved in.

Alexander had to rebuild virtually his entire fleet.

It is said that as he lay dying, three years later in Babylon, Alexandria sighed for new worlds to conquer. The story may be apocryphal, but it sums up both his character and his achievements. He was one of those gifted, charismatic figures who alter history. As well as leading his army for more than 20,000 miles thorough territory largely unknown to Europeans, he founded 70 major cities, and disseminated Hellenic culture throughout much of present-day Turkey, Iraq, Iran, Afghanistan, Pakistan and Kazakhstan. For a brief moment he made Europe and Asia one. And it was not the least of his qualities that he brought to his travels an inquisitive mind, and a desire to garner, record and share knowledge. He was among the first explorers to take specialists (like naturalists and anthropologists) with him, the first to take 'steppers' to pace out and calculate the distances he traveled, and the first to make scientific maps and keep scientific diaries. Although best known as a great conqueror, he was also a great explorer.

The Voyage of Pytheas to Great Britain and Ultima Thule (*c.* 310 – 304 BC)

The Greeks may not have been such proficient seamen as the Phoenicians – the center of their world was usually a city not a ship – but in one important respect they were more accomplished – they were better navigators.

Helmsmen probably started steering by the stars almost as soon as ships put to sea; but the Greeks were the first people to raise astral navigation to a science, the first to pinpoint true north, and the first to be able to calculate latitude. Most of their voyages were coastal trading ventures, bringing to their none-too-fertile homeland grain and fish from the Black Sea, ivory from Egypt, cop-

Above: Alexander the Great in combat with the ruler of the Kipchaks: an Indian miniature by Mir Khusrau Dehlavi.

per from Sardinia, silver from Asia Minor, and timber from Cyprus and the Lebanon. We do, however, have evidence of one outstanding deep-water voyage which had scientific objectives, that of Pytheas of Marseilles.

Pytheas was an academic – the first man to fix the position of the celestial pole, and the originator of an extremely accurate method of determining latitude by using a calibrated sundial. He left Marseilles in the spring of 310 BC, and after five years came back with stories of his adventures which a Mediterranean people could not believe. Pytheas was branded a 'charlatan', an 'arch-falsifier' and a 'weaver of fables'. Only recently has it been realized that every one of his so-called 'tall stories' has a credible scientific explanation. From the few fragments of his work *The Ocean* which have survived, we can piece together the story of his voyage.

The first hazards he had to face were Phoenician warships blockading the Straits of Gibraltar. These he avoided by hugging the shore and sailing only by night and by midsummer 310 BC his vessel had rounded Cape St Vincent and was heading into the little-known waters of the North Atlantic. After sailing for several weeks out of sight of land he came to 'a small island off the coast of a peninsula, where we landed and found that the longest day was exactly 16 hours.' This landfall was probably the Isle d'Oeussant (Ushant to later British seamen) off Brittany, a supposition strengthened by the fact that Pytheas brought back an extremely accurate map of the Breton peninsula. He then crossed the Channel to Land's End in Cornwall, where he spent several weeks observing tin being mined, smelted, hammered into ingots and 'carted across the sand in wagons to a small island known as Ictis.' Many Greeks were sceptical of Pytheas's account of the tin industry, especially his descriptions of how the metal was smelted and carted by wagon to an offshore island. Yet the truth of what he wrote is borne out by the fact that you can to this day see remains of the ancient Britons' smelting pits and the ruts which have been left by their wagon-wheels on the rocks below Ictis (Saint Michael's Mount.)

His account of Britain provoked even greater incredulity. It was not so much his cartography that was questioned, as his description of the islands' inhabitants, climate and natural phenomena.

The inhabitants are said to have sprung from the soil, and are simple and primitive. They thresh their corn indoors in barns and store the ears underground. They do not drink wine, but a fermented liquor called curmi which is made from barley . . . As we progressed north, all cultivated grain and fruits and all domestic animals disappeared, and the inhabitants were reduced to living on roots . . . Here we found the longest day to have 17 hours of daylight . . . here to have 18 hours of daylight . . . and here 19 hours . . . In places around the coast, the tide rises and falls by 50 feet, and waves run 100 feet high.

All this was beyond belief to people who lived in the sun-drenched and tideless Mediterranean, where waves of ten feet were rare and the days had a more or less uniform 12 hours of daylight. Yet we can now see that all Pytheas' observations have a basis of truth. In the Shetlands the longest day in midsummer is 19 hours; in the Bristol Channel the tide can indeed ebb 50 feet, and in the Pentland Firth between Scotland and the Orkney Islands waves of 90 feet have often been recorded and indeed within living memory a freak wave is known to have swept over the 200-foot cliffs of Stroma.

Somewhere north of the Shetlands Pytheas eventually came to a land which he called Ultima Thule, a name symbolizing remoteness and inaccessibility. He described Thule as 'an island about 6 days sail to the north of Britain': one obvious possibility is Iceland, another is Norway, which was then thought to be an island. 'Here,' he wrote, 'the sun is above the horizon for 22 hours out of 24, and even at midnight there is sufficient light to read by.' This sounded highly improbable to the Greeks, who were even more sceptical of Pytheas's claim that when he tried to sail north from the island he was brought up short by a congealed or 'jellyfish' sea. The historian Strabo writes:

Pytheas tells us that one day's sail from Thule is the sluggish or congealed sea. In these regions he says there is no longer any distinction between land, sea and air, but a mixture of all three like jellyfish which binds everything together and can be traversed neither on foot nor by boat; and this he saw with his own eyes – or so he would have us believe!

A jellyfish-like barrier of land, sea and air does indeed sound a tall story; but here again Pytheas may not have been exaggerating. For a day's sail to the north of Iceland he might well have come in contact with the edge of the Arctic pack-ice. As the Norwegian explorer Fridtjof Nansen has explained,

What Pytheas saw was almost certainly ice-sludge which is formed along the edge of pack-ice which has been ground to a pulp by the action of waves. The expression "can be traversed neither on foot nor by boat" is exactly applicable to this ice-sludge. If we add that fog is often found near the edge of the ice, then the remark that land, sea and air are merged together is not ridiculous but very graphic.

Another scholar-explorer to support Pytheas is Frank Debenham, Emeritus Professor of Geography at the University of Cambridge:

When ice forms on water it has a thin flexible skin, and is broken up by waves into small segments called pancake ice . . . this does indeed look as if the sea is covered in jellyfish.

After leaving Ultima Thule Pytheas returned, via the Baltic to Marseilles, only to find he was neither the first explorer nor the last to be ridiculed for telling the truth. His stories of a sun that never set, a sea that froze and waves of 100 feet were not believed, and for 2000 years he was regarded as the Munchhausen of the classical world. Only recently has it been appreciated that he was a great explorer, the first man to bring to the Mediterranean a cornucopia of accurate information about the little-known world of northern Europe.

The Egyptians and Phoenicians may have traveled as far as the Greeks and to equally exotic locations. But men like Alexander and Pytheas brought a new approach to their travels. They calculated the distances they covered; they fixed the latitude of the countries they visited, and they recorded information about the people and phenomena with whom they made contact. They had that 'lust of knowing' which transforms the drudgery of travel into the exhilaration of exploration. They were the first scientific – you might almost say the first modern – explorers.

Below: A sixth century Greek ship, depicted on a piece of pottery.

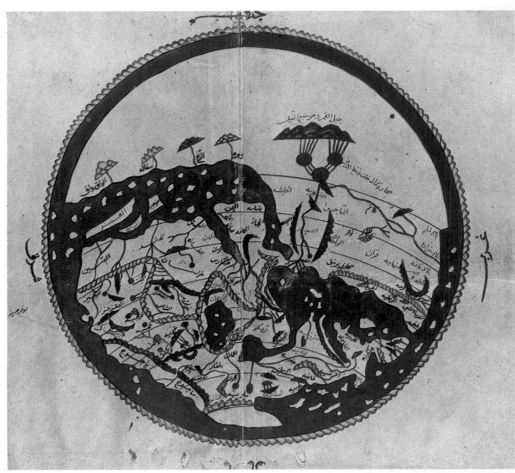

The Arabs (c. AD 1 – 500)

Long before ships from Europe entered the Indian Ocean, the Arabs in their *dhows* had established trade-routes between Africa and India. At first their voyages were coastal – the flimsy-looking but seaworthy dhows skirting the shores of present day Somalia, Saudi Arabia, the Oman, Iran and Pakistan – and took the better part of a year. Then came an important discovery, described in a first-century seaman's manual, *The Periplus of the Erythraean Sea*.

The pilot Hippalus, by observing the location of the ports and the conditions of wind and sea, discovered how to lay his course direct across the (*Indian*) ocean. And from his day on, vessels bound for India have kept not to the shore, but at the time of the south-westerly monsoon have headed boldly out to sea, throwing the ship's head considerably to the south. So the southwest monsoon came to be known as the Hippalus, after the name of him who first made the direct passage.

A round voyage which had previously taken more than two years was suddenly reduced to a couple of months. This was an enormous stimulus to trade. For then, as now, time was money and insurance heavy; merchants who had hesitated to finance a long voyage via a hazardous shore, with levies extorted at the necessarily fre-

quent ports of call, looked more favorably on a short voyage *via* the open sea. Within a generation of Hippalus's discovery, trade in the Indian Ocean had increased tenfold. A further boost was provided *circa* AD 120 when the merchant Alexander pioneered a similarly direct passage across the Bay of Bengal, from the east coast of India to Malaysia.

In the halcyon years of the *pax Romana* Arab dhows and Mediterranean merchantmen – many of them far larger than Columbus's *Santa Maria* – were engaged in peaceful and extensive two-way trading: cloth, glass, gold, silver and coral from the west being exchanged for silk, ivory, jewels and spices from the east. According to cargo ledgers there was also a flourishing two-way traffic in 'singing boys' and 'beautiful maidens for the harem.'

This trade was eventually disrupted by the barbarian invasions which brought about the collapse of both the Roman and Chinese empires. It is, however, a proven fact that 1500 years before the so called 'discovery' of India by Vasco de Gama, Arab dhows and Roman merchantmen were voyaging extensively between the Red Sea, India and Malaysia. Merchants like Hippalus and Alexander were great if little-known explorers whose discoveries had important consequences in three continents.

Above left: 'A Ship crossing the Persian Gulf': detail from the 13th century *Maqamat* by Al Hariri.

Above: A 12th century world map by the Arab cartographer Al Idrisi. North is at the bottom. The holy city of Mecca is in the center. The ocean, surrounding the known world is in blue.

The Chinese (c. 140 BC – AD 1440)

The Chinese have been spasmodic explorers, at times energetically pioneering trade routes between Asia and Europe, and sailing boldly round the southern tip of Africa and possibly round the southern tip of Australia, at other times withdrawing from the outside world behind their symbolic great wall – a fact which emphasizes that highly-civilized people who live in lush surroundings have less incentive to travel than those who live on bleak littorals. The great explorers of the world have been not the cultured and luxury-loving Egyptians, Chinese and

Renaissance Italians, but the more Spartan Phoenicians, Vikings and 15th century Portuguese. Nonetheless in certain eras the Chinese made extensive and important discoveries, both by land and by sea.

By land, imperial envoys of the Han dynasty made long and arduous journeys through central Asia, the most important being those of Chang Ch'ien who, between 138 and 109 BC, pioneered the silk road from Peking to Samarkand, a caravan-route which was to provide a tenuous link between east and west for almost 2000 years. (For this and other Chinese journeys by land see Chapter 3, The Exploration of Eurasia.) By the beginning of the first century BC Chinese merchants were established in the Persian Gulf and the Red Sea, and during the reign of the Emperor Augustus (27 BC – AD 14) a Chinese envoy lived in Rome. It is clear from Han literature and maps that the Chinese of this period had a considerable knowledge of Europe – also of Indonesia and Africa – a fact which again makes nonsense of the old-fashioned belief that the world was 'discovered' by post-Renaissance Europeans.

By sea the commitment of the Chinese to exploration has been spasmodic; for they, like the ancient Egyptians were essentially a stay-at-home people, whose fertile heartland provided most of their material needs, and whose religion (in particular Confucianism) encouraged an inward-looking way of life. For long periods contact with the outside or barbarian world was frowned on, and commerce was left in the hands of the Arabs, Malays and Indians. It was only in the comparatively brief spells when their empire was ruled by an expansion-minded dynasty that the Chinese took to the sea; on these occasions, however their exploration was on the grand scale.

The cradles of Chinese seafaring were the mouths of the Chang Jiang, Xun Jiang and Huang He Rivers. By the fifth century BC long narrow sampans (*ghe ca tom*) were emerging from the major river deltas to engage in coastal trade, and these sampans evolved gradually into sturdy seagoing junks (*twago*), which reached Japan by the third century BC and the east coast of India by the second. Initially voyaging was mainly coastal; however, by the third century AD Chinese junks were cutting across the Indian Ocean to trade direct with Africa. In the harbors of Mogadishu, Kilwa and Sofala archaeologists have found vast quantities of Chinese hardware (coins, porcelain, silk and jade) while contemporary paintings show large numbers of junks at anchor off the African coast. These vessels are described as 'square-sterned, well armed against pirates and able to carry as many as 500 persons': this would make them a good deal larger than contemporary vessels from Europe – a fact corroborated by Marco Polo who, on his visit to Khublai Khan, was shown over huge vessels of more than 1000 tons, with five raked masts, rudders of 450 square feet and luxuriously furnished cabins. The Chinese put to sea in style.

Their seafaring reached its apogee early in the 15th century with the seven expeditions of Cheng Ho.

The ostensible objective of these expeditions was to track down a deposed emperor who was believed to have sought refuge abroad. This, however, was probably no more than an excuse for showing the flag and demonstrating Chinese puissance to the outside barbarian world; for never before and seldom since have official visits been made over so wide an area on so lavish a scale. The first expedition (1405-7) visited Thailand, Singapore, Java and Sumatra. The second (1407-9) skirted the east and west coasts of India and the island of Sri Lanka. The third (1409-11) voyaged extensively throughout Indonesia, and some scholars believe that at least one ship was blown off course by a storm and rounded Australia; for an early-15th century Chinese vase is engraved with an animal that is unmistakably a kangaroo and a remarkably accurate outline of the Australian continent. On the fourth expedition (1413-15) the main fleet sailed into the Persian Gulf and the Red Sea, while a subsidiary flotilla followed the coast of Africa. Since this flotilla brought back accurate maps of both the east and west coasts of Africa, it seems likely that they rounded the Cape of Good Hope and stood some distance into the Atlantic. An interesting feature of these maps is that nearly all of them

Left: A 16th century Chinese junk in Java, an engraving from a Dutch book published in 1597, *Navigato ac Itenerarium* by Jan Huygen van Linschoten.

show a great lake in the middle of Africa, with rivers flowing out of it to both the north and south. This has led to the theory that they anticipated their European counterparts by several hundred years in discovering the source of the Nile. The fifth and sixth expeditions (1417-19) and (1421-22) traversed the Pacific seaboard, from Japan in the north to Brunei in the south. While after the seventh expedition (1431-33) it was written:

Cheng Ho took note of the distances covered, the diversity of customs and the difference in morals. Every country that was visited acknowledged the suzerainty of the emperor and agreed to pay tribute, and by the time the last ships returned to Suchow Chinese knowledge of the world had been increased by 20 realms.

As surprising as the range of these expeditions was their size. All sources agree that the first (which was by no means the largest) consisted of 62 ships and 37,000 men: but that the estimated number of ships involved was well over 1000 and the total number of men over 120,000. Among the latter were not only scholars, linguists, doctors and astronomers, but a host of technicians with such esoteric skills as crafting jade and breeding peacocks. No contemporary European nation could have launched and sustained so ambitious a program of exploration.

It used to be taught that Vasco da Gama discovered India in 1498. Yet the Chinese had been trading with India for one thousand years before da Gama was born. We are so accustomed to interpreting history through Mediterranean eyes (from a Greek-cum-Roman viewpoint) that it is easy to underestimate the achievements of non-European nations like the Chinese.

Below: Chinese trade-routes of the 15th century, showing the coastlines known to Ming seamen, and the extent of Cheng Ho's (Zheng He's) voyages.

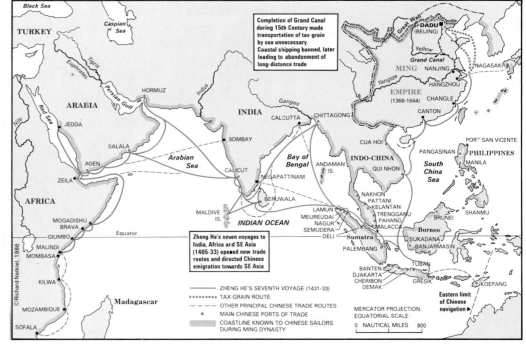

Exploration by Sea

The surface of the Earth consists of more water than land: 71 percent of it is ocean and 29 percent of it continent. Voyages have therefore been every bit as important as land journeys in the history of exploration. Indeed seamen have added more to our knowledge of the world than landsmen; it would be difficult to name three land-explorers whose discoveries were comparable with those of Columbus, Magellan and Cook.

The sea, however, is not our natural environment, and the exploration of it has always posed problems.

The first problem was that natural phenomena often excluded sailing-ships from certain parts of the ocean. Even the highest mountains (the Himalaya) have passes through them, and even the driest desert (the Sahara) is crisscrossed by trade routes; but in several of the world's seaways winds and currents combine so fiercely that a sailing ship is able to move in one direction only; hence once it has passed a certain point it can never return – at least not by the same route. In other seaways (such as the Doldrums and the Sargasso Sea) there is not enough wind for a sailing ship to move at all; while surrounding the Arctic and Antarctic are vast fields of impenetrable ice. In the days of sail exploration was hampered by these 'no go' areas: sealanes into which many may have entered but few returned.

Another problem was navigation. It is easier to find one's way by land than by sea. Travelers by land nearly always have some feature – a river or mountain – to help establish their position; travelers by sea on the other hand can easily sail for weeks on end without sighting any feature at all. A dead-reckoning plot is easier to keep on land than at sea, because one's speed and direction over water are hard to judge. Celestial observations can, it is true, be made equally easily from ship or camp; but it is

Left: A 14th century miniature from John de Mandeville's *Travels* showing a ship equipped with a compass.

only in the last couple of centuries that this has been a reliable aid to navigation. (From the days of the ancient Greeks seamen may have been able roughly to fix their position north-and-south by the stars; but until they knew the true size of the Earth their position east-and-west could only be guessed at. When Columbus arrived in the Caribbean he thought he was off the coast of Asia – and that was 9000 miles out. When Magellan arrived in the Pacific he expected any moment to sight Indonesia – and that was 10,000 miles out.) As a corollary to this,

Previous page: 16th century Portuguese ships of the type used on voyages to India.

Below: An untitled world map, printed in Ulm in 1486 by Johann Reger.

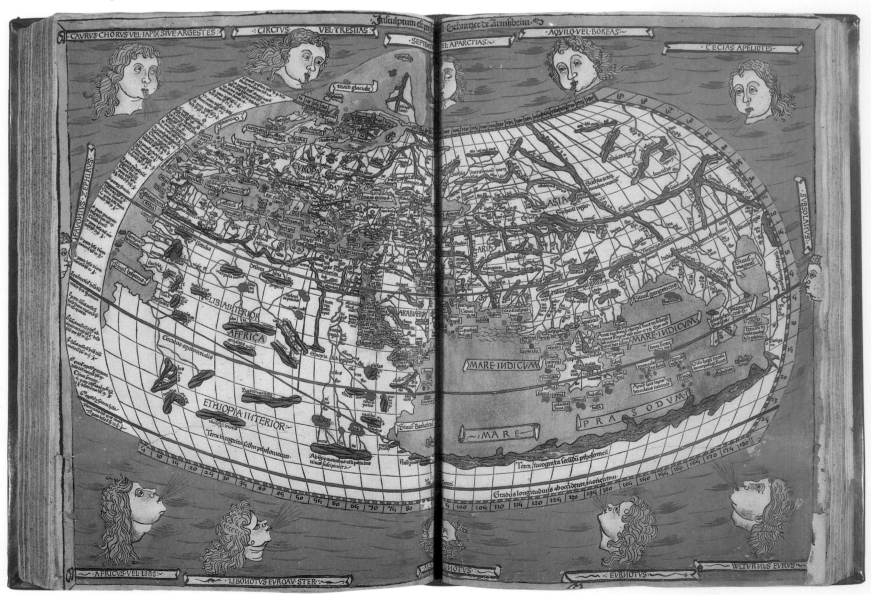

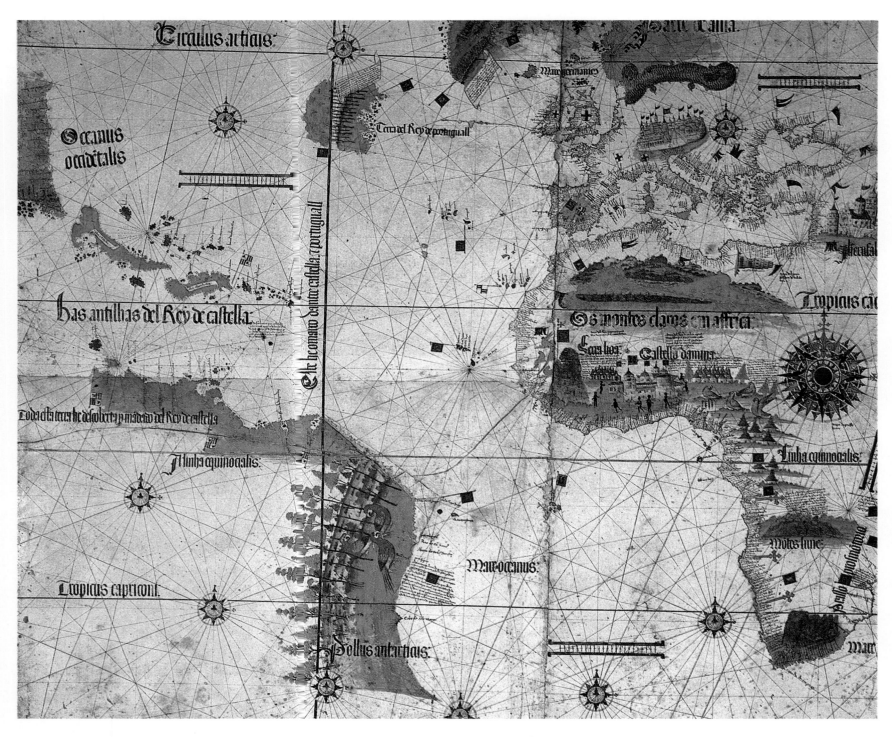

explorers could often produce quite accurate outlines of this or that fragment of coast, but were unable to fit these outlines into an overall map of the world.

The last and most intransigent problem was that an explorer could only go where his ship could sail.

Few vessels, prior to the beginning of this century, were built specifically for exploration. The explorers' ships were those in everyday use at the time. It is not therefore surprising that the most successful explorers have been found among those peoples whose livelihood depended on their vessels – the Polynesians, the Phoenicians, the Vikings, the people of the Iberian Peninsula and the British.

The most successful ships built by these seafaring people all had three characteristics in common. They were seaworthy: although their seaworthiness was achieved in many different ways – Polynesian pahis survived in bad weather by letting the sea soak *through* their hulls, Portuguese caravels survived by having watertight hulls which kept the sea *out*. They were roomy – Phoenician traders were larger and could carry more men and provisions than some of the ships that sailed with Magellan on his voyage round the world. And they were all maneuverable, able in particular to make headway against the wind – the Phoenicians and Vikings achieved this by using oars as well as sails, the Portuguese achieved it by using a novel (lateen) rig for their sails.

Great ships spawn great discoveries; and the story of exploration by sea is basically the story of successive bursts of voyaging made possible by vessels of outstanding construction and design. The first of these great vessels were the Polynesian pahis.

Above: An anonymous hand-colored parchment, *circa* 1502, smuggled out of Portugal. It shows the line set up by the Treaty of Tordesillas (1494) dividing the new lands claimed by Portugal and Spain. It will be seen that the recently discovered Newfoundland has been displaced some 15 degrees East to bring it under Portuguese suzerainty.

The Polynesians (*c.* 1500 BC – *c.* 1200 AD)

It is often said, to quote an old edition of the *Encyclopaedia Britannica* that deep water voyaging began with the Vikings. Yet long before Viking longships were island-hopping across the North Atlantic, and even before Phoenician traders were nosing through the Straits of Gibraltar, Polynesian pahis were sailing for thousands of miles through the vast reaches of the central Pacific.

What evidence do we have that these voyages took place? What prompted them? And how did a people who were neither literate nor numerate achieve such fantastic feats?

Polynesia consists of a huge triangle – more than 99 percent of it sea – with its apexes at New Zealand, Hawaii and Easter Island. This is an area larger than the USSR, and one would have expected it to be populated by a variety of ethnic groups. However, when Europeans first entered the Pacific they found that all the inhabitants of Polynesia had the same appearance, characteristics and culture and much the same language. They were one people. 'Is it not remarkable,' wrote Cook, 'that this same Nation should have spread themselves over all the islands of this vast ocean?'

Since the Polynesians had no written language, there is no literary evidence of how they came to occupy the various atolls and archipelagos. However, oral traditions are strong, and the archaeological evidence irrefutable.

The Polynesians originated in Southeast Asia. About 1500 BC, possibly as the result of a population explosion, they left the mainland and began to migrate eastward through Indonesia. By about 1300 BC they had reached Fiji – then the edge of the known world. From Fiji, some headed north into Melanesia, and some east into the Pacific. Peter Bellwood, a leading authority on Pacific pre-history, writes:

The people who settled in Melanesia became absorbed into the local populations, and only a few racial and ethnographic traces of them survive today. The voyagers who entered Polynesia had a very different history; they entered a huge island world devoid of men, and founded the societies which we now call Polynesia. The present Polynesians are direct descendants of these intrepid voyagers of 3500 years ago.

We know roughly when the various islands were settled: Figi c. 1300 BC, Tonga c. 1000 BC, Samoa c. 900 BC, the Marquesas c. AD 350, Easter Island and Hawaii c. AD 700, the Society Islands c. AD 900, New Zealand c. AD 1100.

There is no doubt about what the Polynesians did. How they did it is more open to question. There are two theories as to how they arrived on their Pacific islands. One that they arrived by purposeful migration; the other that they arrived by drift and by chance.

A lot of romantic nonsense used to be written about Polynesian voyaging: 'Fired by the lust of adventure and the desire to see new lands, canoe after canoe set out . . . undeterred by fear of storm or shipwreck.' The truth is another story. The Polynesians had no wish to leave their islands, and every reason to fear storm and shipwreck; they had neither compasses nor sextants; they could not determine longitude; they could not measure displacement caused by currents and winds, and in bad weather they quickly became disorientated and lost. In view of these shortcomings a New Zealand scholar, Andrew Sharp, put forward the theory that the Pacific islands were settled by accidental or drift voyages.

These pages: Drawings and paintings of the Polynesians by European travelers, (Wallis, *above* and *below*, Webber, *right*; and Wilkes, *below right*). The Polynesians sailed vast distances to populate the islands of the Pacific. Their boats (opposite) were relatively small but wonderfully seaworthy.

Accidental voyagers had a hundred generations, with scores of involuntary incidents in each generation, in which to hit the archipelagos. Most accidental voyagers were no doubt overwhelmed by storm or exposure, or were carried to islands already populated. Of those who came to an uninhabited island, most would be men who had been carried away while fishing or going on forays against neighboring islands. The great events in the prehistory of the Pacific were when an isolated canoe with women aboard happened for the first time on a new island group. In the early days this would be a very infrequent event, since the population was fragmentary ... But when it did happen, the seed of human continuity and increase throughout that island group was sown ... As the population grew, other involuntary voyagers were launched into the Pacific wastes, most to die, a very occasional handful to carry their seed to a new island.

This undoubtedly, is how most Pacific Islands were populated.

Most, but not all. For practical seamen have found, and computer analysis of winds and currents has confirmed, that it is virtually impossible to drift by chance from central Polynesia to Hawaii, New Zealand or Easter Island; one has to make a conscious effort to sail there. It would therefore seem that at least some visits to some islands must have been premeditated.

Such voyages – sailing out of sight of land for thousands of miles for weeks on end – would have demanded exceptionally fine seamanship and navigation. Could the Polynesians have done it?

They had the ships. For fishing and inshore sailing they used vaas and vaa-ties: outriggers about 25 feet in length with a single sail. For ocean sailing they used

pahis: twin-hulled, twin-masted vessels about 80 feet in length which could either be sailed or rowed. Pahis may have *looked* ramshackle, but in fact they were amazingly resilient, their loose construction enabling them to soak up punishment under which a more rigidly-built vessel would have disintegrated. They had a unique ability to stay afloat. They were also remarkably fast and maneuverable. 'I do declare,' wrote Cook, 'they can outsail us!'

They had adequate provisions for long voyages and space in their *pahis* to store them. They would have taken with them fresh meat (pigs, dogs and chickens), and a cornucopia of fresh vegetables (coconut, tara, sweet potatoes and yam). Such a diet would have been rich in vitamin C; and the scurvy which decimated European crews was unknown to the Polynesians.

They had the men. Of all the people of Earth the Polynesians alone live in a world that is sea-orientated rather than land-orientated – there are 500 parts of ocean in Polynesia to every one part of land. Living in such an environment they developed unique seafaring skills. As the Aborigine knows his desert and the hunter-gatherer his rain forest, so they came to know their ocean. They could interpret fish and bird behavior, swell patterns and cloud patterns, underwater phosphorescence and mirages; for it was only by understanding such phenomena that they survived. They would have made a more than competent deep-water crew.

But could they navigate? They had no maps, no charts, no instruments – not even a compass – and it used to be thought that purposeful long-distance voyages must therefore have been beyond them. Modern research and (more importantly) modern voyaging suggest otherwise.

It was claimed that the Polynesians 'used the stars as their guide.' But how they did this has only recently been understood.

They steer, wrote *Ellis and Firth* by a star path . . . A star path is a succession of stars, on the same bearing as the island for which they are heading, and towards which the bow of their canoe is pointed. Each star is used (in turn) as a guide when it is low in the heavens; as it rises it is discarded and their course is reset by the next to rise in the star path. One after another these stars rise and are followed till dawn.

This is a system totally different from the European. A Westerner sees the stars as stationary; he is interested in them only in that split second at which he uses his instruments to take a bearing on them. A Polynesian sees them as ever-moving; he lines up on the 'star pit' out of which they rise, one after another. The latter system is less accurate and more dependent on the weather, and one had to know where one is starting from and going to. But within these limitations, it works.

This has been proved, in recent years, by voyages carried out by pahis designed to traditional specifications, built of traditional materials, and relying entirely on traditional skills: that is to say their crew have denied themselves all modern or external aids, have navigated entirely by the star path system, and have carried only provisions which would have been available to Polynesian voyagers 1500 years ago. In 1969 the *Isbjorn* sailed in this way from the Carolines to the Marianas. In 1976 the *Taratai* sailed from the Gilbert Islands to Fiji. And a few years later the *Hokule'a* sailed from Hawaii to Tahiti.

Such voyages have helped to reaffirm the Polynesians' achievements. We may never know exactly how much of their voyaging was accidental and how much deliberate; but what they achieved is beyond question. By populating virtually every habitable island in the central Pacific they became the most widely-spread ethnic race on Earth. They were great seafarers. And great explorers.

Above: The bleak and icy cliffs of Cape York, Greenland, visited by Irish curraghs in the 6th century and Viking longboats in the 10th.

Right: An allegorical illustration from *The Voyage of St Brendan*.

The Irish (c. 500 – 900)

The Irish love a good story, and the exploits of their legendary folk-heroes are recorded in travelers' tales known as *immarama*. According to *immarama*, 7th and 8th century Irish explorers ventured as far afield as the American mid-west, the South American altiplano, and even the islands of the Pacific. This is a myth.

However, the adventures of one Irish folk-hero, Saint Brendan, would seem to be firmly rooted in fact.

Saint Brendan lived in the 6th century, and is known to have founded monasteries in Galway, the Hebrides and Brittany. According to a religious tract known as the *Navigatio Sancti Brendani* he was also involved in a voyage deep into the Atlantic in the course of which his curragh visited islands as far apart as the Faroes, the Azores, the Bahamas, Iceland, Greenland and Jan Mayen; also the Newfoundland fog banks. This *sounds* a tall story. However, if we study the *Navigatio* we find that it never pretends to describe a single voyage carried out by a single person; it is a miscellanea of voyages which, for literary effectiveness, have been linked to the semi-legendary Saint Brendan, in much the same way that a number of early Greek adventures became attributed to the folk-hero Odysseus. Seen in this light, the *Navigatio* contains passages which are difficult to account for unless one accepts that they are descriptions of places actually been to and phenomena actually seen – been to and seen not in the course of one continuous voyage, but in the course of many voyages spread over many years.

The *Navigatio* starts with a description of Saint Brendan choosing his crew and building his boat. We are told

that he selected 14 men to accompany him, set up camp on the Dingle Peninsula, and built a curragh . . .

They used iron tools. The curragh itself, however, had no metal in it, but consisted of a wood and wickerwork frame covered with cow-hides which had been tanned in oak bark; its seams were tarred . . . They took with them provisions for 40 days, including butter to grease the hides, and put to sea.

The voyage began with a succession of calms and storms – most of them lasting the biblical 40 days – then Saint Brendan and his crew came to 'an island inhabited by sheep of the most extraordinary size, and full of streams in which were a multitude of brown fish, delicious to eat.' They spent the winter here, and in the spring moved on to another and smaller island a few miles to the west. This smaller island was 'grassy, full of purple flowers and populated by vast numbers of white birds, one of which spoke to the saint and advised him to return home.' These islands were almost certainly Streymoy and Vagar in the Faroes. For the name Faroes is derived from the Danish *faar* = sheep; and these animals have always flourished in the Faroes, growing exceptionally large because of the nutritious grass. On Streymoy, the largest of the group, there are streams full of brown trout. Vagar, lying a little to the west, is covered in grass and heather and is a famous bird sanctuary, harboring in particular the all-white skua, kittiwake and Arctic tern. These birds may not have talked to Saint Brendan, but they could have given him advice; for by observing their migrations he would have inferred that there was no land for some

distance to the north – hence the prudence of his heading for home.

The next part of the *Navigatio* describes a long voyage south, with the crew fasting in order to eke out their provisions. Eventually they came to an island with a balmy climate. Here they spent Christmas. They then drifted for several weeks 'in divers directions' until they were cast up on a rocky island, rich in vegetation and springs. However, the spring-water turned out to be bad, and those who drank it were taken ill. They left this 'island of bad water' and after three days heading westward became becalmed in an area where the sea was 'like a thick curdled mass'. Their curragh, we are told, became ensnared. The sun was hot, the swell heavy, and with neither wind nor current to help them the crew despaired of every being able to extricate themselves. However, after 20 days they at last broke out by using their oars. It is possible that the first island was Madeira. It is probable that the second was Sao Miguel in the Azores, which is about the only island in the central Atlantic which has springs of bad water, tainted with sulfur and iron. And it seems obvious that the curdled sea was Sargasso.

All this would indicate that Irish curraghs sailed at least as far north as the Faroes and as far west as the

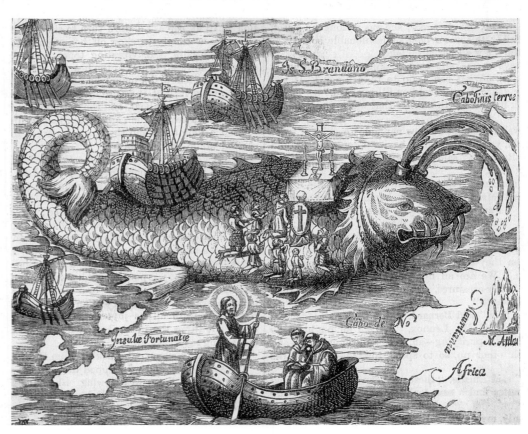

Azores. The next part of the *Navigatio* suggests they sailed farther.

We are told that Saint Brendan and his men sighted an island which they described as 'completely flat, almost level with the sea and without rivers or trees.' Offshore they found

the ocean so transparent that it looked as though they could touch even its greatest depths with their hands, and the fishes were visible in great numbers, like flocks of sheep at pasture, swimming nose to tail. Saint Brendan said Mass, and his crew entreated him to speak quietly, lest the monsters of the deep might be provoked to attack them . . . For eight days, even with a favorable wind and all sail, they were scarce able to cross this pellucid sea.

There follows a description of their landing on another island, where they were amazed by

the wonderful fragrance of the air, like a house stored with pomegranates, the beautiful birds and the great fountains springing everywhere from the fertile soil . . .

This description does not fit any European waters. It is, however, an exact description of a coral sea – for it is coral dust which makes the water so clear. The only extensive coral sea in the Atlantic is the Caribbean; and to confirm the curragh's whereabouts, the circling 'monsters of the deep' were obviously not the harmless dolphin and porpoise of the east Atlantic (for the crew were not frightened of these), but the larger and fiercer barracuda, sailfish and swordfish of the Caribbean. Further evidence

that Saint Brendan had indeed reached the West Indies is that his description of the first island exactly fits Long Island in the Bahamas, and his description of the second exactly fits Jamaica – whose name stems from the Arawak *Xaymaca* = a multitude to waters.

These descriptions have the hallmark of first-hand observation. It is hard to see how they could have been written by anyone other than a member of a crew which did indeed reach the Caribbean.

The latter part of the *Navigatio* contains some sensational passages. We are told that Saint Brendan first sighted

an immense building in the sea, tall, bright, bejewelled as a crystal temple, *then a* high black mountain rising sheer out of the water, its base wreathed in mist, its summit shooting banners of flame into the sky. *Next they came to* an island inhabited by giant smiths, one of whom came up from his underground workshop and attacked them by flinging masses of burning slag at their curragh.

They fled; but their troubles were not over; for they were pursued by a ferocious whale. Saint Brendan prayed, and another monster 'with huge bristles, tusks like a boar and a bewhiskered mouth – a veritable sea cat huge as an ox,' rose out of the sea, attacked the whale and killed it. Soon after this they landed on an island where they were detained by blizzards and 'plagued night and day by stinging devils.' Finally they found themselves 'blanketed in thick vapor which was pressed tight against the water and so dense they could see only the distance of an oar.'

Above: Rolling Atlantic breakers pound the shore of Jamaica, an island probably visited by the Irish explorer St Brendan in the 7th century.

All this used to be the butt of historians. Yet the beje-welled temple could have been an iceberg, the black mountain could have been Jan Mayen, the island of smiths could have been an Icelandic volcano in eruption described by someone who knew the classical myth of Etna and the Cyclopean forge; the sea cat could have been a walrus, the stinging devils mosquitoes, and the banks of vapor the Newfoundland fog belt.

The *Navigatio* would therefore seem to be a literary *tour de force* based on fact, its author having collected authentic stories of seamanship and woven them into a tapestry which for a long time was too exotic for posterity to accept, but which was made up nonetheless of the strands of truth.

We may never know either the details or the full extent of the voyages of Irish curraghs; but it seems highly probable that they pioneered those sea lanes between the Old World and the New which were used a couple of centuries later by the Vikings.

Above: In the Lee of the Iceberg, by William Bradford. This clearly shows the threat a looming iceberg posed to a ship powered only by sails, something mentioned in the 7th century *Navigatio.*

The Vikings (c. 800 – 1100)

The word Viking comes from the Norse *vikingt* = a pirate or raider, and by common usage the name is now given to the Scandinavian adventurers who, between the 9th and 11th centuries, left their homeland to plunder trade or settle along the coastline of Northern Europe and the islands of the North Atlantic.

The popular image of a Viking is that of a fierce, hel-meted warrior looting a church, and maybe going on to indulge in a bit of pillage and rape. Initially, this may have been a fair picture. Loot, however, is an ephemeral source of wealth, and the *leitmotiv* of Viking voyaging soon shifted from looting to trading and colonizing. It was as traders and colonizers that they became – almost by accident – explorers.

We know both the motive for their exploration, and the means by which they achieved it.

It was the barren nature of their homeland that made the Vikings take to the sea. Most of Norway is bleak and mountainous, with only a few narrow strips of land suitable for cultivation. Most of Sweden and Denmark and virtually all of Finland was, in the days of the Vikings, heavily forested; while throughout northern Scandinavia the long cold winters precluded prosperous settlement.

Such a land was able to support only a limited number of people and could provide only limited opportunities for acquiring wealth. An increasing population and the law of primogeniture led to a situation in which the younger and/or unfavored sons of families found wealth and land easier to come by abroad than at home. Many Swedes headed east into Kievan Russia. Many Norwegians and Danes headed west into the Atlantic but they would not have got far if it had not been for their excellent ships.

Viking *drakars* (i.e. warships) and *knorrs* (i.e. cargo vessels) were beautiful, versatile and seaworthy. Beautiful because they had a classic design: simple, well-proportioned and uncluttered – the hallmarks of the thoroughbred in any field. Versatile, because with their single square and easily-worked sail and their 20 to 30 oars they could make headway both with the wind and against it. Seaworthy, because although their construction was relatively light, it was also supple and strong, enabling them to ride the punch of the sea rather than fight it. An ocean-going longship would have been roughly 90 feet long, 20 feet wide and 30 to 40 tons in weight; it would have had a draft of about 3½ feet, and a crew of between forty-five and fifty-five.

Left: The versatile lines of a Viking longship of the 8th century. Powered by both oars and sail, the longships could make headway both with the wind and against it.

In such ships the Vikings voyaged far to the north of the Arctic Circle and 'beyond the sunset and the paths of all the western stars' to the mainland of America.

To start with their voyages could not be classed as exploratory, for they were raiding countries both populated and (for their day) civilized. They first landed in England in 793 at Lindisfarne (Holy Island) off the coast of Northumberland, 'destroying God's church with plunder and slaughter.' A few years later they sacked the Scottish monastery at Iona, before passing on to Ireland where in 841 they established a fortified camp at Dublin. They then moved to France where they 'conquered all in their path', and Spain where they received short shrift from the Moors.

Soon, all along the Atlantic coast of Europe, except the Iberian peninsula, Viking raiding was giving way to settlement; while at the same time colonies were being established on the far-flung islands of the North Atlantic. It was their voyages to these islands which were, in the context of exploration, the Vikings' greatest achievement.

They island-hopped from the Old World to the New: settling in the Orkneys and Shetlands c. 880, the Faroes c. 825 and Iceland c. 860. Then came their two greatest discoveries: Greenland in 982 and America in 1003.

Greenland was discovered by Eric the Red, whose nickname stemmed not only from his ginger beard but also his fiery temper. In 981 he became involved in a blood-feud, killed two of the sons of a local chief, and was banished from Iceland for three years. Most men would have taken their ship and their followers back to Europe. Eric, however, headed west, hoping to find the coastline allegedly sighted some years earlier by a seaman named Gunnbjorn who had been blown off-course in a storm. After several weeks' battling against headwinds and heavy seas, he sighted the ice-covered skerries off the east coast of Greenland. This is a desolate shore, devoid of life; but on rounding Cape Farewell (the southernmost tip of Greenland) Eric came to a more promising littoral, the deeply indented fjords around present-day Julianehab. This was terrain every bit as attractive as the lava-bound hinterland of Iceland. His discoveries, however,

Above: A Viking vessel drawn up on land for use as a habitation.

Left: Principal Viking trade routes by land and by sea.

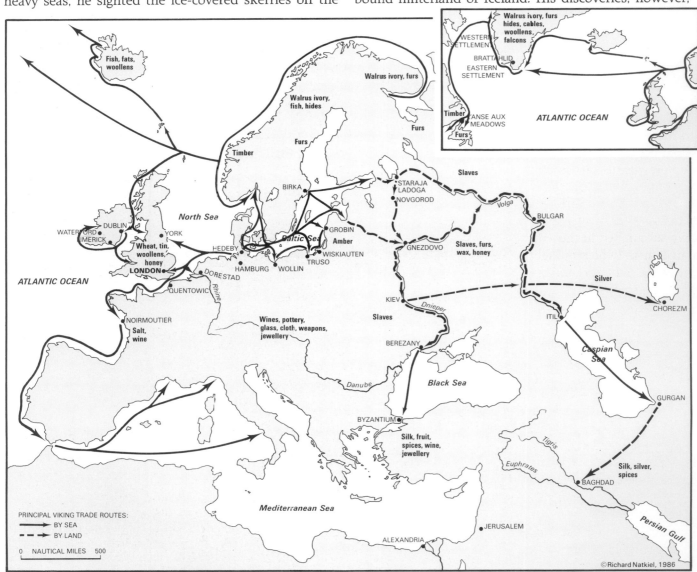

PRINCIPAL VIKING TRADE ROUTES:
→ BY SEA
--→ BY LAND
0 NAUTICAL MILES 500

©Richard Natkiel, 1986

Eventually they came to the land which Bjarni had sighted last. They lowered their boat and rowed ashore. They found no grass, only ice-covered mountains, and between mountains and sea a wilderness like a field of stones. So they called the place Helluland (*Land of the Flat Stones*).

Scholars have identified this as Baffin Island. After a few days on a southerly heading

they came to another land, and again rowed ashore. The country here was flat, low-lying, heavily forested and fringed by fine beaches of white sand. Leif called it Markland (*Land of the Woods*).

This scholars agree, was almost certainly south Labrador. After sailing south for an unspecified period, Leif Eriksson put ashore for the third time, apparently in idyllic surroundings.

. . . a small river came tumbling into the sea from a lake . . . the tide ebbed and flowed strongly . . . there were salmon in both river and lake . . . the dew on the grass was sweet like honey . . . the land was so fertile they felt sure that no cattle-fodder would be needed. (*Here they build a house and settled down for the winter.*) . . . there was so little frost that the grass hardly withered . . . and Tyrher said "I have found something new: vines and grapes." And Leif decided to call the country Vineland in memory of Tyrher's discovery.

Vineland, with its frost free winters and wild grapes, has been sought by many a scholar, from both armchair and boat. Its location is still uncertain; and efforts to pinpoint it have been hindered rather than helped by the publication in 1965 of The Vineland Map. For many scholars

Left: Viking raiders landing on the coast of France.

Below: A romantic interpretation of the discovery of Greenland by Eric the Red.

had only just begun; for in one of the most remarkable voyages ever made, he pushed north up the coast of Greenland for almost 1000 miles, discovering another area of potential settlement around present-day Godthab, and wintering, frozen into the ice, well north of the Arctic Circle.

He returned to Iceland at the end of 3 years with tales of 'Groenland' (the Green Land), saying that 'people would be more likely to go to a new country if it had an attractive name.' For this, he has been dubbed a romancer; but in fact his description of Greenland was not unreasonable. He himself came back in 985 with 25 ships and built a farmhouse in Eriksfjord where he lived happily for the rest of his life. In their heyday the Greenland settlements boasted 4000 inhabitants, 300 farms, dozens of churches and a cathedral. For almost 500 years the colonists traded with Europe, exporting furs, sealskin, hides, woolen goods, walrus and narwhal ivory, falcons and even polar bears. They only succumbed in the 15th century to a dramatic change in climate (which brought the seals south and with the seals the Eskimos) and the Black Death. Far from being a failure, the Greenland settlements flourished; they also served as the final stepping stone to America.

The first sighting of America by a European of which we have firm evidence was made by Bjarni Herjolsson. In 986, while voyaging to Eriksfjord, Bjarni was blown southwestward by a storm and three times sighted a coastline which, he was convinced, was *not* Greenland. Emerging from banks of fog, he sighted first 'a shore without mountains and well timbered', then (after a couple of days' heading north) 'a flat country covered with woods,' and a couple of days after that 'a land of ice and stones that was good for nothing.' When he finally struggled back to Greenland, he told Erik the Red's son, Leif Eriksson of his discoveries, and in due course Leif set out to try and retrace Bjarni's route in reverse. That most reliable of Sagas, the *Flateyiarbok*, tells us:

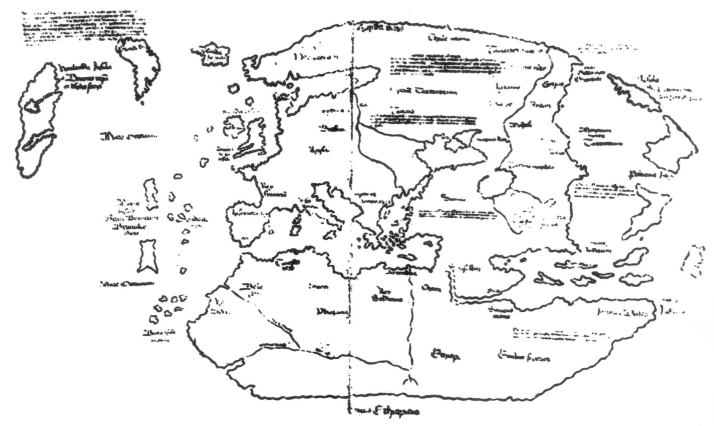

Left: The Vineland Map, supposedly drawn *circa* 1440, showing Greenland and America (top left) as islands.

Below: A ship design accompanies sun and serpent symbols in this early (*c.* 500 AD) Danish picture stone.

believe the map to be a forgery – partly because of a 20th century pigmentation in the ink, and partly because Greenland is shown as an island, a fact which was discovered only 100 years ago. One possible location for Vineland is Cape Cod in Massachusetts. A more probable one is L'Anse aux Meadows in Newfoundland, where the ruins of a Norse house and a number of Norse artefacts have recently been discovered.

The exact whereabouts of Vineland may still be in doubt. However, there is no doubt at all that it was somewhere on the east American seaboard, or that the Vikings landed and wintered there in 1003. They were enchanted with the land they had discovered, and glowing reports of 'Vineland and the Good' were soon circulating throughout the northern settlements.

Why, one wonders, was discovery not followed by colonization? After all, substantial Viking settlements were established by their voyagers in Britain and Ireland and in northern France despite the resistance of the local population. The name of the Normandy region (the land of the north men) still commemorates this presence.

The fact is that the Vikings tried very hard to colonize North America, but were thwarted partly by distance and, more decisively, by the Skraeling or Indians. The Sagas are explicit on this. We are told that in 1012 'Karlsefari set out with 160 men, 5 women and many domestic animals, determined to settle in Vineland'; but after four years, during which he endured repeated attacks by the Skraeling, he gave up, 'for it seemed obvious that although the land was attractive they could live there only in fear and with constant warfare.' Leif's younger brother had even less luck. He sighted a headland of great beauty and fertility. 'Here,' he said, 'I will build my home' – not, it should be noted my 'house' but my 'home'. A couple of days later, killed by an Indian arrow, he was buried on the headland where he had hoped to live. An end symbolic of the Vikings' efforts to bridge the gap between the Old World and the New.

The basic reason for the Vikings' failure to capitalize on their discovery was that, like all early explorers, they lacked the fire-power to overcome the people whose lands they found their way to. They met them on more or less equal terms: one club was very like another club, the Skraelings' arrows were a match for the Vikings' swords.

It was another story a few centuries later. For by the time the next progeny of classic ships sparked off the next burst of deep-sea voyaging, the explorers' weapons had become more sophisticated. From the 16 h century onward whenever European explorers landed on shores hitherto-unknown to them, it did not matter if the indigenous people welcomed them or not. Whatever the Europeans wanted – provisions, loot, slaves or land – they took it by right of their arquebus, muskets and ships' cannon.

The Portuguese (c. 1400 – 1550)

The era that used to be known as the Dark Ages – the six or seven hundred years between the collapse of the Roman Empire and the dawn of the Renaissance – was not a good time for exploration. For much of the period Europe was submerged by a succession of invasions-cum-migrations which were given a cutting edge by differences of religion. Christian Europe came under siege from Saracens and Berbers in the south, and from Magyars and Ottoman Turks in the east. People were too busy trying to stay alive to have time to explore.

And just as these migratory invasions were subsiding, Europe suffered an even greater disruption. It has been estimated that between 1347 and 1351 one person in three died of bubonic plague. The Black Death, as the plague was called, is thought to have originated in China. It was disseminated by the fleas which are parasitic on black rats. These rats arrived *via* silk-road caravans in the Crimea, thence *via* Venetian and Genoese vessels to the ports of the Mediterranean, and from here they percolated to just about every community in Europe. Whole villages were wiped out. Even the remote settlements in Greenland were decimated. And Europe was never the same again. Labor, formerly so plentiful, became suddenly scarce; the old feudal order (which had been based on cheap and subservient labor) began to break up, and a new middle class of merchants and bankers to emerge. This new middle class had everything to gain from trade, and hence from exploration.

There was, however, a problem. By land, trade and exploration were impossible to the south because of the barrier of the Sahara, and impossible to the east because of the blockade of militant Islam. While by sea European ships were not yet sufficiently seaworthy to venture into the 'no go' areas of the Atlantic. In the north Atlantic they might be able to hop from island to island; but in the central reaches they became ensnared in the Sargasso Sea, and in the south they were swirled away by the combined impetus of the north east trades and the north equatorial (or Canary) current. And if one wonders why vessels did not work their way south by hugging the coast of Africa, the answer is that for a thousand years they tried to, but never managed to pass Cape Bojador and return.

Cape Bojador, on the coast of the Spanish Sahara, may not look a very formidable barrier. However, a reef runs seaward from it for more than a dozen miles; this forces vessels away from the coast and into open water, and here wind and current pick them up and swirl them away into the ancients' 'Sea of Darkness': a limbo from which there was no return because sailing ships, in those days, could not sail against the wind.

What made the golden age of exploration possible was the development of a ship, the Portuguese caravel able to make headway against the wind. What made this golden age a reality was the vision of one man, Henry the Navigator, who sent his caravels into the unknown to roll back the map of the world.

Caravels have been described as 'brilliant composites'. For their hull they used the flush-oak carvel planking of Iberian river-boats, for steering they used the axled rudder of Baltic cogs, and for sails they used the lateen rig of Arab dhows. It was the grafting of oriental sails on to a European hull which made them so seaworthy and maneuverable; in particular, their simple and easily-worked triangular sails enabled them to make headway as much as 50 degrees into the wind. 'I see no reason,' wrote the Venetian navigator Cadamosto, 'why these ships should not go anywhere in the world.'

Henry the Navigator was born in Oporto in 1394, the third surviving son of John I of Portugal and Philippa, the daughter of John of Gaunt of England. He is one of the great figures of history: part-saint, part-scientist, and totally involved in a love affair with the sea. At Sagres, a bleak headland on the southwest tip of Portugal, he created a naval academy: building a shipyard, an observatory and a school of navigation and pilotage where he accumulated a library of maps, charts and instruments. This academy attracted a team of all the nautical talents – the Jews of Mallorca famous as mapmakers, shipwrights from the Tagus, Loire and Rhine, mariners from as far apart as the Red Sea and the Baltic, and scientists from half-a-dozen countries who were skilled in the use of lodestone, windrose and astrolabe. Henry's dream was that of a militant Christendom, enriched by seaborne trade, extending its domain beyond the confines of Europe into the unknown corners of the world. In pursuit of this dream he sent his caravels into the Atlantic.

In the central reaches of the ocean, Madeira, the Cape Verde Islands and the Azores were swiftly and profitably colonized. But in the south Henry's hopes continued to founder on the reef of Bojador. Between 1415 and 1433 no fewer than twenty expeditions headed down the African coast; but not one ship ventured beyond the much-feared cape. Until this barrier was breached, Henry's dream of trading with Africa and India remained a chimera.

Below: Diagram of a 15th century Portuguese caravel. Caravels combined the hull of the west with the lateen-type sails of the east, and were the first European vessels able to sail against the wind.

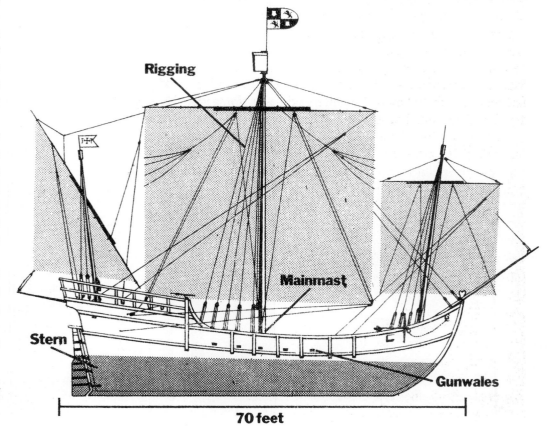

Rigging

Mainmast

Stern

Gunwales

70 feet

In 1433 a caravel commanded by Gil Eannes stood south from Sagres. Eannes was born in Lagos, a member of the petty nobility of Portugal who provided Henry with most of his sea captains, much as the West Country squirearchy of England provided Elizabeth I with most of hers. His ship was small; probably not more than 60 feet in length and 60 tons in weight. It had a crew of about 25, and the currently-evolving lateen rigged sails. To start with their voyage was routine. Keeping close inshore, they passed first through a blood-red sea – discolored by the red sand and mud spewed out by the Tensift River – then through a bottle-green sea – discolored by the coarse grey sand of this part of the Sahara. Soon they were level with the Canaries. Most ships would now have stood west to where, among the islands, a combination of trade and piracy would have brought easy pickings. But Eannes, inspite of the murmurings of his crew, continued to hug the coast, until at last they saw ahead of them the edge of the known world: Cape Bojador.

Bojador is a bizarre headland. The wind off the Sahara is like the blast from a furnace. The shore is barren, and the sea looks as though it is boiling; for where the northwesterly swell piles up against the rock-bound coast the water seethes and bursts-up as if from blowholes in what look like fountains of boiling spray. Not an easy place for a sailing ship to survive in. But beyond the headland were horrors thought to be infinitely worse.

In the days of Henry the Navigator fear of the unknown was endemic. The more ignorant of Eannes' crew believed that to the south of Bojador the sun was so fierce that it would burn them black, make the sea boil and melt the pitch in their seams. Great monsters, it was thought, lay waiting in the ocean to devour them; and if by chance they survived these hazards they were still cer-

Above: Henry the Navigator, the 15th century Portuguese prince who founded Portugal's great tradition of maritime discovery. This is a miniature from Enea de Azuraza's *Cronica de Guine*, and is probably the best likeness of the prince.

Far left: Gil Eannes, one of the greatest 15th century explorers, commemorated on a Portuguese stamp.

Left: Bartolemeu Dias, the first man to sail around the Cape of Good Hope.

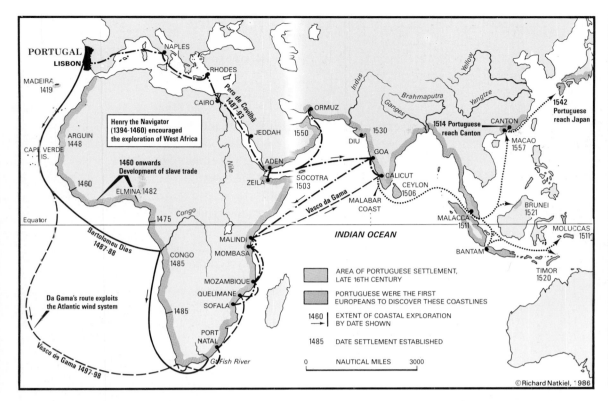

Above left: The routes of 15th century Portuguese explorers.

Above: Vasco da Gama (c. 1469-1524), who not only successfully navigated the Cape of Good Hope, but went on to sail to India, pioneering what became an immensely profitable trade route to the Far East.

tain to be swept to oblivion by the great race of water which poured endlessly off the rim of the Earth. The better-informed of the crew were equally terrified; for they believed that if they ventured south of Bojador wind and current would swirl them away – as it had swirled away every ship before them – into sea lanes from which there could be no return. As Eannes stood parallel to the reef and out to sea, it is easy to imagine how his men felt.

We are told that he headed out to see for 'a day and a night, in light wind and poor visibility.' The moment of truth came when he judged they must be clear of the reef, and altered course to try and claw his way back to the land. And the lateen rig did not let him down. Slowly but surely, against both wind and current, the caravel inched her way inshore, until the coast of the Sahara again loomed out of the mist.

Ernle Bradford, the biographer of Henry the Navigator, describes their historic landfall.

As they ran in, the sailors gathered in the bow, shading their eyes. Slowly the coast came into view. It looked at first the same coast as they had seen before. But as they drew nearer, they saw there was one great difference. They looked south and saw that the land ran on, flat, sandy and shining under the sun with no cape breaking its sweep. They looked north and saw that they had passed the impassable! They had rounded Cape Bojador! . . . It was as if a wall had fallen down, as if a barrier that had held man back for centuries had been breached. More than a cape was passed that day by Gil Eannes A whole era of superstition fell away.

A few miles south of Bojador Eannes was rowed ashore. Nothing moved. There was no sign of life. As far as the eye could see the desert lay seared and sterile under a sadic sun. Then, near the crest of one of the dunes, Eannes noticed a faint shadow. He clambered up to it, and saw, nestling in the shade of a sandstone ledge, a cluster of tiny plants. And, what was more, plants that were familiar: the starlike flowers known in the Algarve as the roses of Saint Mary. He picked them, boxed them up, and took them back to Prince Henry.

After that few people ever believed again that the world ended at Cape Bojador – or indeed at any other headland. The horizon became not a barrier but a challenge, and mariners began to boast that 'no shore was unattainable, no sea unnavigable.'

The rounding of Bojador sparked off a spate of exploratory voyages which soon unveiled the extent of Africa. In 1444 Nuno Tristao reached Senegal; in 1457 Diogo Gomes reached Sierra Leone; in 1472 Fernao do Peo reached the River Niger, and in 1482 Diego Cao reached the Congo. These were forerunners of the two great Portuguese voyages which rounded the tip of Africa and opened up a sea route to India and the Spice Islands of the east.

In 1487 Bartolemeu Dias set out with three ships. He soon reached Cape Cross in present-day Namibia, the farthest south that Henry's caravels had yet penetrated. From now on he had both the south east trades and the Benguela Current against him, and for several months he made little headway. Eventually he stood away from the shore and into the unknown reaches of the Atlantic. Here a succession of storms first drove his caravels as far south as the 40th parallel – farther south than men from Europe had ever been – then, in the 'roaring forties,' he picked up that great belt of winds which blow non-stop around the Earth, and his caravels were swept east. The seas were enormous; ice formed on the open decks; his men suffered terribly from cold. Struggling back to the north, Dias at last sighted a coastline which, to his surprise stretched away to the northeast. He landed first at Mossel Bay and a few days later at the mouth of the Great Fish River. Although he did not realize it at the time, he had rounded the tip of Africa, and the route to India and the Spice Islands lay waiting to be discovered.

A decade later Vasco da Gama discovered it.

He set out in 1497 with four ships – well provisioned – and well armed – and a crew of 170. His expedition was a great one, both in the distance it covered and the discoveries it made; but it was also a catalog of disasters and lost opportunities. It took him 96 days to reach the Cape, the position of which he calculated with commendable accuracy. It was on the east coast of Africa that his troubles began. His initial contact with the indigenous people was friendly. However, it was not long before there were misunderstandings. The Portuguese 'fired off a number of bombards, killing several natives. (They) then erected the Cross of Christ on a headland, but this was immediately destroyed' – a pattern to be repeated many times in the next two-and-a-half centuries. Heading north up the coast of present-day Mozambique, da Gama soon came to an area under Muslim control; for Arab dhows from the Red Sea and the Gulf had been trading here from time immemorial. The Portuguese were not

company in combat or through scurvy. He proved that it was possible to sail from Europe, via the southmost tip of Africa, to India and beyond, thus inaugurating one of the busiest trade routes in the world.

At much the same time as da Gama was landing in India, another Portuguese – Pedro Alvares Cabral – was landing in Brazil and exploring 2000 miles of the coast of South America. Voyages to the Pacific, Indonesia and China followed; and in an amazingly short space of time Portuguese seamen had made known to Europeans three-quarters of the coastlines of the world.

However, the effort was more than a small nation could sustain.

My country, oh my country, (*lamented a contemporary chronicler*). Too heavy is the task that has been laid on your shoulders. Day after day I watch the ships leaving your shores filled always with your best and bravest men. And too many do not return . . . Who then is left to till the fields, to harvest the grapes, to keep the enemy on our frontiers at bay?

The dream of Henry the Navigator was about to become reality; but it was not only, or ever principally, the Portuguese who were beneficiaries.

Left: Vasco da Gama being received by Indian emmissaries.

Below: Da Gama and his men are received by the Indian prince they knew as Samorin, in 1498.

welcome. In spite of a facade of friendship, the Arabs refused them the water and provisions that would have prevented their dying of scurvy, and tried to lure them ashore by showing them drawings said to be of the Holy Ghost. Suspecting a trap, da Gama kidnapped local pilots and set course for India. After a three week voyage he made an historic landfall a little north of Calicut. His ships remained in India for three months; but here too they were not welcome, for the Arab merchants who had been trading with India for more than a millenium not surprisingly regarded them as interlopers.

This was the start of a feud between the Portuguese and the Arabs which, for cruelty and ferocity, has few equals in history. Da Gama was guilty of flogging, torturing and murdering Arabs. The next Portuguese to arrive on the scene, Albuquerque went further.

To enhance the terror of his name he always separated Arabs from the other inhabitants of a captured city, and cut off the right hands of the men, and the noses and ears of the women. He spared only the prettiest of the girls, whom he reserved as personal gifts for men of influence. At Goa he outdid himself in cruelty, ordering the massacre of every Arab man, woman and child, including newborn babes. This massacre occupied the Portuguese soldiers for three days of non-stop slaughter, during which they killed more than 8000 people. Alburquerque boasted of these exploits to King Manuel in his official report, giving thanks to the Almighty for His aid.

Da Gama returned to Portugal after a voyage of two years and more than 15,000 miles, having lost half his ships'

The Spaniards (c. 1480 – 1620)

While Portuguese caravels stood mainly southeastward – to Africa and India – Spanish galleons stood mainly southwestward – to the Caribbean, South and Central America and the Pacific.

Spain, at the end of the 15th century, was well placed to take advantage of the upsurge in exploration and trade. Geographically, the countries of the Iberian peninsula had a headstart over their northern and Mediterranean rivals. Economically, Spain was in urgent need of trade, because her agricultural prosperity was at a low ebb – her soil eroded by the *mesta* system of sheep grazing. While even more importantly a large percentage of her population suddenly found themselves at a loose end because of the ending of their 800 year crusade against the Moors.

It was this crusade which forged the character of the Spanish people and made them the sort of explorers they were. From roughly 710 to 1492 the people of Spain had waged a bitter and almost non-stop war against the people of Islam who occupied the south part of the Iberian peninsula. 'Every male Spaniard was a fighting machine, born to the saddle and the sword, burning with religious fervor, and utterly devoted to freeing his homeland from the Infidel.' The qualities they admired were endurance, courage, pride honor and chivalry. Fighting was what they were good at. However, in 1492 the last Moorish stronghold in Spain, Granada, fell to the Christians; the last Moorish troops were evacuated to North Africa, and suddenly there was no one left for the Spaniards to fight. By one of the more significant coincidences of history, the year Granada fell was also the year Columbus discovered a sea route to and from America. Soon the men who had fought the Moors were heading overseas to seek new Infidels to do battle with. They became conquistadors.

This background explains the bigoted brutality of many Spanish explorers. It explains – but does not excuse – the fact that an arquebusier could kill a native nursing mother simply to prove he was a good shot, and then justify his act by saying 'what matter if the heathen are consigned to hell today since they will go there in any case tomorrow.' Non-Christians they regarded as subhuman.

The ships used by Spanish explorers were mostly carracks, a larger, slimmer and more sophisticated version of the caravel. A typical carrack would have been about 120 feet long and 30 feet wide, with a square stern and a beakhead extending anything up to 25 feet for'ard of its keel. It would have had four masts, easily-worked lateen-type sails and high bulwarks. It would also have had gun ports. And cannon.

Its crew would probably have been cosmopolitan; for the Spaniards were not at home on the sea, and many of their expeditions – including the two greatest — were commanded by foreigners. Columbus came from Genoa, Magellan from Portugal.

If asked to name the world's greatest explorer most people would probably say Columbus. Yet Christopher Columbus was not an attractive character; Eric Newby describes him as 'vain, arrogant, boastful, ambitious for wealth and power, and deceitful.' He failed to recognize the significance of his discoveries, insisting to the end of his days that he had arrived off the coast not of a new continent but of Asia. He ended up by being arrested and sent back to Europe in disgrace and in chains. He died a disillusioned and broken man. His achievements do not

seem, on the face of it, commensurate with his reputation.

His first expedition (1492-93) consisted of three small ships: the *Santa Maria, Pinta* and *Niña*. They left Spain on August 3rd, reprovisioned in the Canaries, and after a voyage of 70 days sighted an island which has been identified as Watling Island in the Bahamas. Columbus's first contact with the Carib Indians was friendly; parrots, cotton and reed-spears being exchanged for red capes, glass beads and bells. He went on to sight and land on other islands, notably Cuba and Haiti, leaving a garrison on the latter, before setting sail *via* a northerly course for Europe, which he reached on March 4th.

His second expedition (1493-96) consisted of three galleons, 14 caravels and 1200 soldiers farmers and missionaries, its objective being both exploration and settlement. It soon became obvious that Columbus was better at setting a course than founding a colony. There were disputes, mutinies, a shortage of food and constant battles with the Caribs whom Columbus regarded as

Below: A woodcut impression of Columbus' first fleet; from left to right, the *Santa Maria, Pinta* and *Niña.*

Bottom: A Spanish galleon. Note that this vessel is depicted with square rig on the main and fore masts and lateen rig on the mizzen mast. Some doubt exists regarding the exact layout of the ships used by Columbus.

potential slaves and shipped back to Seville. His discoveries this time included Dominica, several of the Leeward Islands and the south coast of Cuba, which he mistook for China.

His third expedition (1498-1500) consisted of six vessels manned mainly by freed criminals – for on his first two voyages conditions had been bad and mortality high. He discovered Trinidad and sighted, for the first time, the mainland of America. His landfall was the coast of present-day Venezuela: a beautiful but unhealthy shore where he claimed to have found 'rivers of gold nuggets of such quality it was a marvel.' He judged correctly (by the size of the rivers) that the land he had found was of continental proportions, but continued to insist it was part of Asia.

His fourth and last expedition (1502-04) was the most demanding and the least successful. His four ships were poorly provisioned and manned. The weather was appalling. 'The fury of the heavens gave me no rest,' he wrote; 'rain, thunder and lightning were near-continuous, and it seemed as though the end of the world was at hand.' He discovered Martinique, which he thought must be Japan, and Honduras, which he thought must be Indo-China. He tried to found a colony but failed, and after a long voyage attended by almost every disaster imaginable, returned to Seville a disappointed and dying man.

This does not, on the face of it, seem to justify his reputation as the world's number one explorer. And his reputation would indeed appear to be based on the outcome of his voyages rather than on the voyages themselves. For Columbus not only sighted a New World, he discovered a way both to it and back from it: outward-bound *via* the northeast trades to the south of the Sargasso, and homeward-bound *via* the westerlies to the north of the Sargasso; and this for nearly 500 years has been the classic route between the Old World and the New. In the wake of the *Santa Maria* there has sailed a whole genealogy of

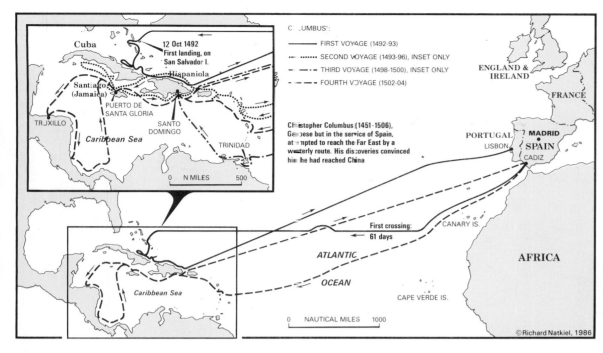

vessels – treasure galleons, slavers, traders and unshine cruises. Other explorers sailed farther, suffered greater hardships, faced greater dangers and discovered more extensive coastlines; but few journeys have had such immediate and important consequences as those of Columbus.

In this he was the antithesis of Magellan.

Fernão de Magalhaes was born in 1480 in Portugal. His parents were members of the petty nobility of Minho, and, like many boys with his background, he was educated at court: a court which, under the influence of Henry the Navigator, was uniquely orientated to seafaring. The young Magellan studied cartography, astronomy and celestial navigation; he worked in a shipyard, and eventually sailed as a *sobresaliente* (supernumerary) for service in the east. By the time he was 30 he was in command of a caravel, had been wounded three times and had voyaged as far afield as Ternate and Malacca in the Spice Islands. He was a first-rate practical seaman.

Returning to Portugal in 1516, he sought backing for a voyage to the Spice Islands by sailing not east *via* the tip of Africa, but west *via* a strait which reportedly cut through the mainland of America and linked the Atlantic to the recently-sighted ocean beyond. He tried to interest the king of Portugal in his idea, but was snubbed; for Portugal was by now sated with discoveries and reluctant to embark on new ventures. Magellan had recently married a Spanish girl; so, helped by her family, he put his idea to the king of Spain. Charles of Spain was more perspicacious than Manuel of Portugal. He recognized a good man and a good idea. And on August 10th, 1519 Magellan led a mini-armada – five ships and 277 men – into the Atlantic.

The greatest voyage in the history of exploration was under way.

Magellan's circumnavigation of the world was a saga of dangers faced, hardships endured, wonders seen and discoveries made. Within a fortnight of setting out there was an incipient mutiny – for the Spanish captains resented being under the command of a Portuguese. Off the coast of Africa the ships were scattered by a storm, rolling so violently that their yardarms feathered the sea. They became becalmed in the Sargasso – 'the tropic sun

Top, far left: An early impression of Columbus' landing on Hispaniola.

Above left: Columbus' four voyages to the New World.

Above: A woodcut portrait of the explorer by Tobias Stimmer.

Far left: Columbus explains his scheme to reach Asia by sailing west across the Atlantic to members of the Spanish royal court.

Below left: Columbus carries the flag of the Catholic Kings to the New World.

blazed down on them, the tar melted in their seams, their ships' timbers split, their food turned putrid.' After an idyllic run down the coast of South America, they enjoyed a saturnalia in Rio de Janeiro – 'the women,' wrote Magellan's diarist Pigafetta, 'wear no clothes except their hair, and in exchange for a knife or an axe we could obtain two or even three of these delightful daughters of Eve, so perfect and well shaped in every way.' Standing south past the estuary of the Plate (which, to their disappointment turned out to be the mouth of a river and not the sought-for strait) they came to seas where no ship from Europe had been before. For eight weeks the fleet was battered by winds of hurricane strength, bludgeoned by huge waves, lashed by hail and sleet and weighed down with ice. Three times they were scattered; the *Victoria* ran aground, the *Santiago* was dismasted, the *San Antonio* sprang a leak and all but foundered. The Spanish captains had no stomach for this: 'The fool is obsessed with his search for a strait,' one of them is said to have shouted. 'On the flame of his ambition he will crucify us all!'

They sought shelter for the winter in the bleak harbor of Saint Julian. Here there was another mutiny, which began with the Spanish captains plotting to hang Magellan in chains, but ended with one of them killed in the fighting, one beheaded and one marooned. In the spring Magellan, now in firm command of his armada, renewed his search for a strait. And in October 1520, on the periphery of the sub-Antarctic, he found it, his ships being swept by storm and by chance into what looked like the mouth of a river. The river, however, led unexpectedly to

a lake and the lake to a succession of narrow fjordlike waterways. For close on three hundred miles Magellan picked his way through these tortuous straits (which today bear his name,) before emerging into an unknown ocean which he christened the *Mar Pacifico*.

His ships' companies reckoned their voyage was almost over and that in a few days they would sight the Spice Islands – in fact it had barely begun. For week after week they headed north-westward with no sign of land, and soon began to have an inkling of the vastness of the ocean they had discovered. Their supplies dwindled, and as they neared the tropics what little food they had turned putrid while their water became scum-coated and yellow. Soon men began to die of that plague of 16th and 17th century seamen: scurvy. They were near the end of their tether when they at last sighted an atoll: Puka-puka in the Tuamotus. Here they found sufficient fresh water and food to give them temporary respite. After convalescing for a week they again headed northwest, thinking they were approaching the archipelagos which were known to fringe the coast of southeast Asia. They were wrong. Far from having crossed the Pacific, they had traversed barely a third of it.

Their voyage became more and more terrible.

They were athwart the Equator now, and the heat of the sun metamorphosed the sea-birds and fish they had salted on Puka-puka to a turmoil of worms – worms they were soon reduced to pounding to pulp and eating. When their last biscuit had gone, they scraped the maggots out of the casks, mashed them and served them as gruel. They made cakes out of sawdust soaked with the urine of rats – the rats themselves,

Above and right: These four sketches show the routes of Columbus's voyages of 1492, 1493, 1498 and 1502.

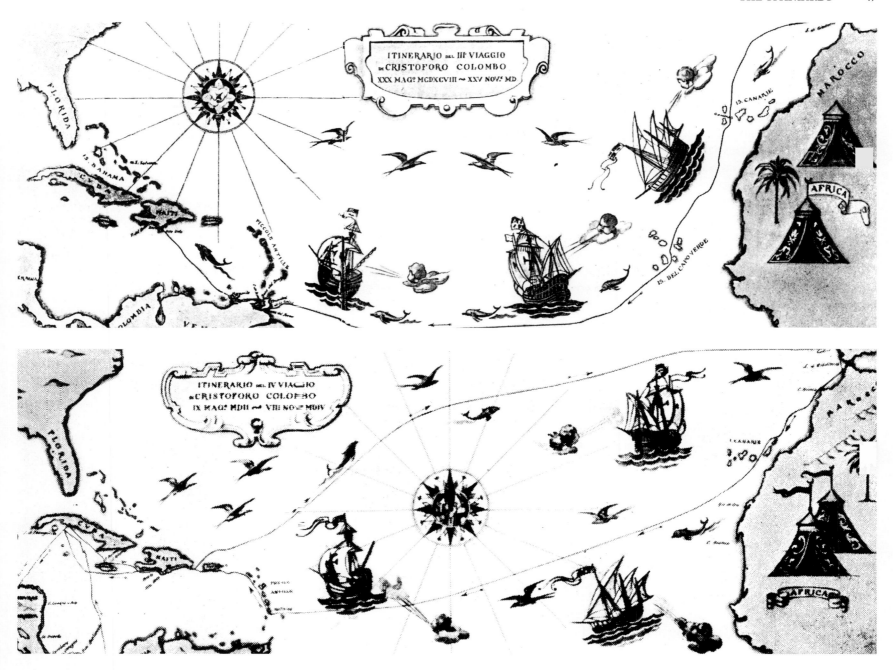

Left: Ferdinand Magellan, 1480-1521, during the first circumnavigation of the globe, 1519-22. This engraving shows him encountering a variety of strange sea animals, none of which seem quite as frightening as the hardships he really encountered.

as delicacies, had long since been hunted to extinction. They unwound the leather from their masts, soaked it, boiled it and ate it.

Men lay curled up on deck, too weak to move, dying of scurvy, malnutrition and exposure. There was not a single crumb of food left in any of Magellan's ships, when they drifted on to Guam in the Marianas.

Magellan had done what no man had ever done before. He had crossed the Pacific.

The rest of his voyage was anticlimax. And tragedy.

After convalescing in the Marianas, the fleet moved on to the Philippines. Here they spent several months amassing vast quantities of gold and converting the people to Christianity. In the course of his proselytizing Magellan became involved in a feud between two local chiefs. He was lured ashore, ambushed and killed – the Spanish captains watching with satisfaction and refusing to come to his aid. Most historians have been critical of Magellan's behavior in the Philippines, and it is true that his proselytizing cost him his life; but it is also true that Spanish culture and the Catholic faith have endured for four-and-one-half centuries in the Philippines, which is today the only nation in Asia that is predominantly Christian.

The chaos which followed Magellan's death indicates his stature as a commander; for his once proud armada now drifted from disaster to disaster. The Spanish captains walked into a trap and were massacred; his ships were driven from the Philippines; they took to piracy (several officers keeping a harem of Muslim women); some vessels were scuttled, some were wrecked and one was captured by the Portuguese and her crew hanged as pirates. Eventually, after a voyage of almost exactly three years, a handful of survivors struggled back to Spain. Five ships and 277 men had set out; only one ship and 19 men returned; but they had done what no-one had ever done before; they had circumnavigated the world.

Magellan added a vast new ocean to the Spanish crown; but the route by which he reached it and crossed it was so long and difficult that it was many years before Spain derived much benefit from his discoveries. However, in 1565 the brig *San Lucas*, sailing to the north of Japan to pick up favorable winds and currents, discovered a route across the Pacific from west to east; and with voyages across the new-found ocean now possible in both directions, trade increased and so in consequence did voyages of exploration.

In 1567 and again in 1595 Alvaro de Mendaña led major expeditions across the Pacific, discovering the Ellis Islands, the Solomons and the Marquesas, but leaving in his wake a trail of death and destruction –

After spending a fortnight in the Marquesas during which it has been estimated that more than 250 Polynesians were killed, the fleet stood west, leaving on Fatu-Hiva three savagely mutilated Marquesian bodies and three beautifully carved wooden crosses – symbols of the tragic gulf between Spanish intention and achievement.

Mendaña's chief pilot, Pedro Fernandez de Quiros, was appalled at this treatment of the peaceful Polynesians. He sought permission to led an expedition of his own, his objectives being firstly to discover *Terra Australis Incognita* (the Unknown Southern Continent) which was believed to lie in the southwest Pacific, and secondly to convert the people of the lands thus discovered to Christianity. It took him nearly a decade to get his project off the ground. For Spain in 1600 was in much the same position as Portugal in 1500; sated with discoveries and more

anxious to hang on to the territory she already had than to accumulate more. However, in 1605 three ships set out from Peru – 'our men dressed in sackcloth and on their knees in prayer. For withour desire to spread the True Faith and enrich the Crown of Spain, all things seemed possible to us.'

Quiros is often regarded as an impractical visionary who achieved less than he aspired to. There is some truth in this. On the other hand he was a fine seaman, his dream of treating the Polynesians well and converting them to Christianity was a noble one, and he and his second-in-command Luis de Torres made discoveries which enabled cartographers to delineate skein after skein of archipelagos throughout 100,000 square miles of previously unmapped ocean. Within four months of leaving Callao they had found Ducie and Henderson Islands, many atolls in the Tuamotus, several of the Cook Islands, the Duff group and the larger of the New Hebrides. And

Below: Magellan's achievement was a tribute not only to his skills as a navigator, but also to his ability as a commander. In addition to the usual hazards of storms, sailing uncharted waters, and enduring scurvy Magellan survived two mutinies from his mainly Spanish crew who objected to serving under a Portuguese captain.

FERDINAND MAGELLANUS.

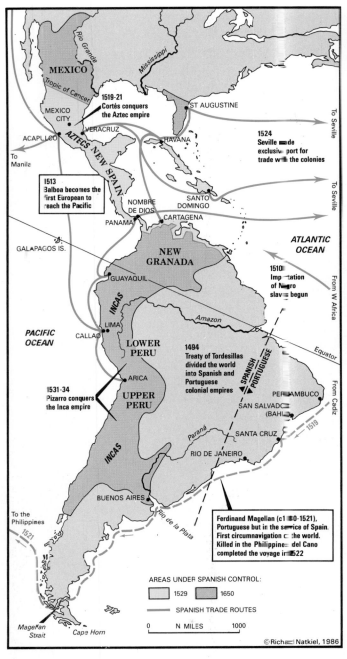

north appear to form a continuous coastline. He landed on Espiritu Santo, where he laid the foundations of a city (the New Jerusalem) and indulged in a surfeit of ceremonies and processions. Most of his crew, however, were more interested in finding El Dorado than founding Jerusalem. In search of gold they captured and killed several Melanesians; there was continual skirmishing, and Quiros decided to move on. As his ships left harbor they were scattered by violent storms. Quiros was taken ill, as a result of eating poisonous fish known as *fargos*, and obliged to return to South America. Torres, meanwhile, went on to discover Papua-New Guinea and the strait between that island and Australia which bears his name on modern maps.

Quiros tried to raise funds for another expedition; but the authorities were not interested, and he died disillusioned and in poverty in 1614. With him died the heroic age of Spain.

By the early 17th century the countries of the Iberian peninsula were fully occupied with exploiting the discoveries they had already made; the mantle of exploration therefore passed to the more dynamic and enterprising nations of northern Europe: the Dutch, the French and the British.

Above: Magellan's ship, the *Victoria*. He set out with five ships and 277 men in August 1519; three years later, only one ship and 19 men limped back to Spain to tell the tale.

Left: Spanish and Portuguese exploration of South America in the 16th and 17th centuries.

on each occasion Quiros managed to establish good relations with the island people.

Early in May 1606 his fleet sighted 'a massive and lofty chain of mountains, their peaks wreathed in cloud'. Quiros thought he had come at last to 'that great continent wherein lie countless millions of heathen awaiting salvation.' What he had come to in fact was Vanuatu (the New Hebrides) whose islands when approached from the

The Dutch (*c.* 1580 – 1700)

The Dutch have the sea ever on their doorstep; much of their land has been reclaimed from it, and few places in Holland are out of sight of a coastline, river or canal. During their struggle for independence from Spain (1559-1648) half the emerging Dutch nation took to the sea; they became known as the Sea Beggars, tough mobile privateers who by 1600 were operating over 10,000 warships and merchantmen. Trade was their lifeblood, and in search of trade their jachts and fluyts explored coastlines as far apart as Arctic Russia, South Australia and Japan.

In 1602 the *Vereenighe Oostindische Compagnie* (the Dutch East India Company) was founded, its objective being to finance the wars of independence. It became arguably the most powerful trading conglomerate in history. Under a succession of able governors-general it drove the Portuguese and the British out of Indonesia, and established a virtual monopoly in supplying Europe with the produce – in particular the spices – of the East.

The Company's priority, however, was trade rather than discovery; it is therefore not surprising that of the three greatest Dutch explorers – Barents, Le Maire and Tasman – only the last was a Company employee.

Willem Barents sailed in search of a North East Passage in 1596. He became frozen-in off the coast of Novaya Zamlya, but managed to survive the winter by building a shelter out of the timber of his crushed ships. His niche in history is among the explorers of the Arctic (*see* chapter 8.)

Jakob Le Maire and Willem Schouten were entrepreneurs. They resented the stranglehold that the Company was exerting, and were determined to find a route to the Spice Islands that was not under Company control. Le Maire had read reports of Drake's circumnavigation of the world (1577-80), and was convinced there must be a westerly route into the Pacific other than *via* the difficult and tortuous Straits of Magellan. In search of this route the *Eendracht* and *Hoorn* left Holland on June 14th, 1615.

In August, held up by contrary winds, they landed in Sierra Liona, a country of crocodiles, buffalos, birds that bark like a dog and lemons . . . we made contact with the blacks and obtained by barter 25,000 lemons.

There is a surprising inference in this: that as early as 1615 the Dutch knew that lemons cured scurvy. A little to the north of the Straits of Magellan they beached their vessels for careening. One method of careening is to remove the weed and barnacle by burning; and it was while they were doing this that the flames, to their horror, got out of control and the *Hoorn* became a total loss. So it was the *Eendracht* alone which, early in 1616, approached the southernmost tip of Tierra del Fuego. These were unknown waters, where no ship had ever sailed before. The *Eendracht* passed through the channel between Staten Island (named after the Dutch parliament, The States General) and Cape Horn (named after the ship they had lost),

with heavy seas from the west, and large numbers of penguins and whales . . . ahead the water was clear blue which made us think we were coming to the Great South Sea (*the Pacific*) whereat we were glad, holding that a way had been discovered by us hitherto unknown to man, as we afterwards found to be the truth.

This was a major feat of exploration, opening up a new and easier route to the Pacific.

In the course of the next nine months, as the *Eendracht* headed for Batavia, Le Maire made a number of minor discoveries: three more atolls in the Tuamotus, Boscawen and Keppel Islands, several of the Bismarck

Archipelago and the north coast of Papua-New Guinea. They had frequent skirmishes with the people of the islands on which they landed:

The natives (*wrote Le Maire*) were very afraid of us, and were in constant fear that we would kill them and take their land . . . when their king told them that we would soon leave there was much rejoicing.

They reached Batavia after a voyage of 18 months and 40,000 miles, having lost only three men. This was a fine feat of seamanship; but Le Maire got neither thanks nor credit for it. The Company, afraid that he might be instrumental in breaking their monopoly, had him arrested and shipped back to Holland in disgrace. He died on the voyage home: it is said of a broken heart.

Not surprisingly future Dutch explorers toed the Company line, and the next major voyages – those of Tasman – were carried out in Company ships under Company orders.

On 12 August 1642 Abel Janszoon Tasman left Batavia with instructions to 'find the remaining parts of the terrestial globe'; in particular to delineate the Great Southern Continent, whose west coast had been briefly sighted by Dutch ships *en route* to Batavia. Tasman's achievements were less heroic than his expectations. He first took his ships, the *Heemskerk* and *Zeehaen* to Mauritius, and from here stood south into the unknown. The weather was appalling: heavy seas, bitter cold, high winds and fog. He sighted seaweed and fragments of trees – almost certainly from Kerguelen Island – but with more discretion than valor backed off, saying the weather was 'too bad to search for an unknown coast.' For week after week his ships were swept east, their rigging coated with ice, their decks plastered with snow. Then on 25 November they sighted 'a barren coast, against which the sea beat boisterously.' They made a brief landing, 'heard from the woods the shrill noise of people singing, whereat through fear we came back on board . . . and stood seaward.' A couple of weeks later they again sighted land – a large elevated country . . . on the shore stood men of enormous stature, armed with huge clubs; they shouted loudly with rough voices.' Again Tasman backed off, making only one half-hearted and unsuccessful attempt to put ashore. Standing north, he next discovered an archipelago to be known as The Friendly Islands. Here he received an enthusiastic welcome.

We were most cordially entertained, some women taking off their clothes and bartering them for nails, others indicating that they wished to have sexual intercourse . . . Truly they are a peaceful people, but excessively lascivious and wanton.

Below: The Dutch trading emporium of Batavia in Indonesia: from a copper engraving *circa* 1682.

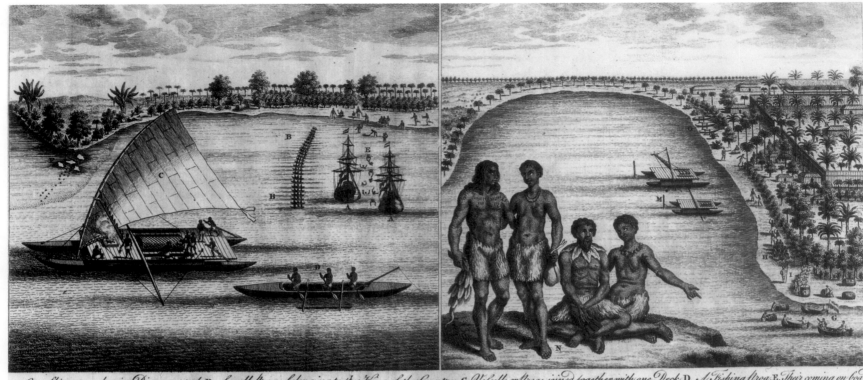

A. *Our Ships at anchor in Diemens road.* B. *Small ftroas belonging to the King of the Country.* C. *Veffells or ftroas joined together with one Deck.* D. *A Fishing ftroa.* E. *Their coming on board with Coco Nuts &c.* F. *The Kings residence.* G. *The place where our Boats lay when they went to Water.* H. *The place where they came to meet Our people with flags of Truce.* I. *The place where Our*

They returned to Batavia via the Ringgolds (north of Fiji), New Ireland and the Moluccas.

Tasman had made the first sighting by a European of Tasmania, New Zealand and Tonga; he had proved that Australia did not extend southward towards the Pole, and he had treated the indigenous people kindly – during his whole voyage not a shot had been fired in anger. On the other hand he had, as the Company put it, 'been remiss in failing to investigate the nature and extent of the lands he had discovered.'

He was sent on a second voyage (1644-45) with orders to delineate the north extent of Australia. He managed to follow the coast from the Gulf of Carpentaria to Shark Bay, but failed to find the Torres Strait (between the northeast tip of Australia and Papua-New Guinea) or to discover anything that might encourage trade. His failure prompted the Company to comment that 'future voyages of discovery would be entrusted to more vigilant and courageous persons.'

Tasman was certainly more cautious than heroic. Nevertheless his track took him for long distances through seas where no-one had ever sailed before; he delineated the rough outline of Australia; and it was hardly his fault that the discoveries he made led to little increase in the trade that was the be-all and end-all of Dutch voyaging.

Above: Amsterdam Island in the Pacific, visited by Tasman in 1643.

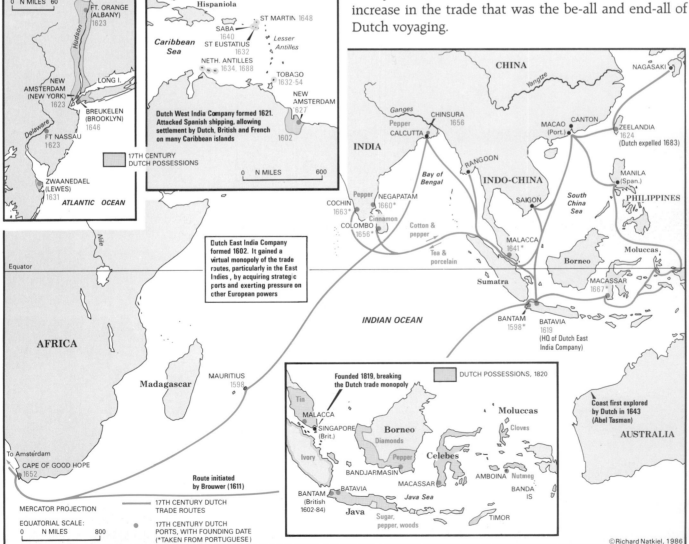

Left: Dutch 17th century trading routes, with insets of Dutch possessions in North America, the Caribbean and Indonesia.

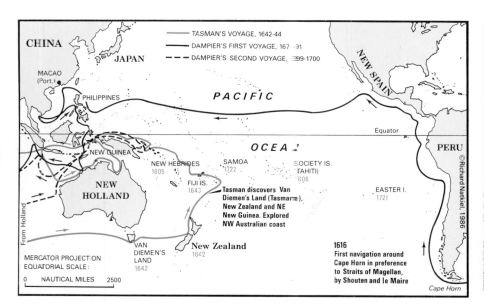

The French (c. 1530 – 1770)

French explorers were first to sight a number of islands in the Atlantic, Pacific and Indian Oceans, and among the first to sight the coasts of Canada, Australia and Antarctica. Most French voyages, however, were individual enterprises and lacked the government support given to (say) Spanish voyages to South America or Dutch voyages to Indonesia; for, over long periods, France's commitments in Europe precluded her interest in ventures overseas. Only in two places – Canada and the Pacific – were the exploits of French explorers of lasting consequence.

It was the French who opened up Canada.

In 1494 John Cabot brought back to Europe reports of 'vast shoals of fish as dense as the weed of the Sargasso';

he had discovered the Grand Banks off Newfoundland. English and French fishing vessels quickly descended on these rich pastures, and it was not long before the fishermen discovered that the best way of getting their catch back to Europe was to take it ashore, dry it and salt it. Isolated fish-processing factories sprang up along the coast of Newfoundland. Contact was made with the local Indians; and these Indians, in exchange for metal tools and weapons, offered the fishermen a *quid pro quo* which was to help bring about the birth of a nation: fur, and in particular the fur of the beaver.

Forty years after Cabot's discovery, Jacques Cartier made three voyages to Canada with the dual objective of

Above left: The Pacific voyages of Tasman and Dampier.

Above: A contemporary engraving of Dutch East India Company merchantmen.

Left: A romantic view of John and Sebastian Cabot's 'discovery' of America.

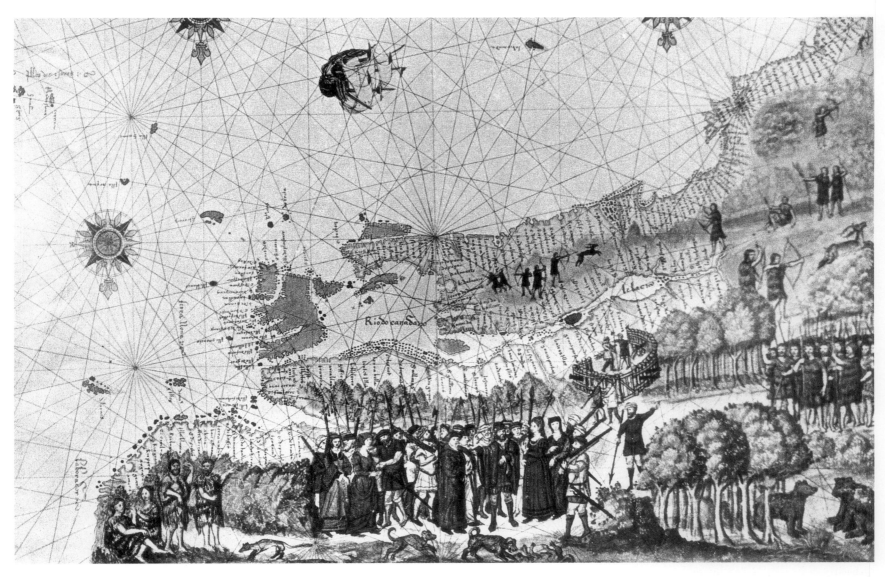

Top, far left: French settlers led by Jacques Cartier disembark at Charlebourg-Royal in 1542: from a map by Vallard.

Left: A portrait of Cartier, after a painting by P. Gandon.

expanding the fur trade and searching for a strait said to 'reach far into the sunset.'

On his first voyage (1534) he made a landfall off the north coast of Newfoundland, discovered the Belle Isle Strait (between Newfoundland and Labrador) and entered the estuary of the Saint Lawrence, which he mistook for a bay. He found the soil 'horrible and rugged rock – I think this must be the land God gave to Cain' – and the people 'the sorriest in the world.' On his second voyage (1535-6) his three ships penetrated 800 miles up the Saint Lawrence River. This was a fine piece of exploration: for winds were unhelpful, currents strong and rapids frequent, while in winter the river was choked with ice. Cartier and 34 of his ships' company struggled as far west as the Indian citadel of Hochelago (present-day Montreal) where he was welcomed by a gathering of over 1000 Hurons. Retreating to present-day Quebec, he spent the winter 'frozen into the ice, and suffering greatly from cold and scurvy.' His third voyage (1541-42) was less successful. He tried to found a colony miles upriver from Quebec; but conditions were too harsh and it was abandoned.

These three voyages delineated the waterway – the Saint Lawrence – which was to play a major role in opening up North America to European settlers, and they ensured that the first of these settlers would be French. Sixty years later Champlain was to build an empire on the foundations Cartier laid.

In the Pacific the French were late-arrivers. Bougainville, Le Perouse, D'Entrecasteaux, Baudin and Freycinet all made voyages which added to scientific knowledge, but only the first-mentioned made a significant geographical discovery – Bougainville was almost certainly the first European (on June 6th, 1768) to sight the east coast of Australia.

Bougainville also has another claim to fame. He and his naturalist Commerson were responsible for resuscitating and giving credence to one of the most enduring myths in history: the myth of the Noble Savage.

On April 2nd, 1768 Bougainville landed in Tahiti. He spent only 11 days on the island, and on his return to France wrote a bestselling book *Voyage autour du mond par la fregate du roi La Boudeuse et la flûte L'Etoile,* a

Below, far left: A Tasmanian called Ouriaga as sketched by Nicolas Petit who accompanied Baudin on his voyage.

Center left: Sketches by Lesueur of the Banded kangaroo and the Short-legged emu, both of which are now extinct.

comparatively short section of which dealt with Tahiti and its people. He had obviously fallen in love with them.

As we walked over the grass, dotted here and there with fine fruit trees and intersected by streams, I thought I had been transported to paradise. Everywhere we went, we found hospitality, peace, innocent joy and every appearance of happiness . . . Soon our men were walking about the island alone and unarmed, and were invited into the islanders' homes and offered food and young girls.

It seemed to the French intelligentsia that Bougainville had stumbled across a people living in a time warp: a people who belonged to

the real youth of the world, that idyllic stage in homo sapiens' evolution when family love had been added to the basic instincts of survival and reproduction, and human beings lived in small communal units free from the sins of possessiveness and greed.

The legend of Adam and Eve was updated; and in the words of Beaglehole, that doyen of Pacific historians,

there now rose up something new and incomparably exciting, Man in the state of nature; the Noble Savage entered the study and the drawing room of Europe in naked majesty to shake the preconceptions of morals and of politics.

The Spaniards had regarded the people of the Pacific as heathen awaiting the flames of perdition; the Dutch had regarded them as objects to be exploited. The French may have been wrong in regarding them as Noble Savages, but the concept brought a welcome touch of humanity and idealism to the story of exploration.

The British (c. 1570 – 1780)

Although the British have a reputation as seafarers, comparatively few of the world's coastlines outside the Arctic and Antarctic were discovered by British ships. The *forte* of the British was colonization rather than exploration. They established strategic bases in Canada (which was discovered by the French), Australia and New Zealand (discovered by the Dutch), India and South Africa (discovered by the Portuguese) and the southern states of America (discovered by the Spaniards); and they retained these bases and used them as springboards fo empire-building by the firepower of their warships. In the long term British settlers reaped where Portuguese Spanish and Dutch explorers had sowed.

One of the few British seamen who did make major geographical discoveries was Drake.

Sir Francis Drake is usually remembered for singeing the beard of the king of Spain and for finishing his game of bowls before defeating the Armada. However he was also the first man to command a successful circumnavigation of the world (Magellan died *en route*), his discoveries were important and the value of the treasure he brought back unprecedented.

He set out in 1577 with five ships and 164 men, officially to search for *Terra Australis*, unofficially – but with the blessing of Queen Elizabeth – to plunder Spanish ports and Spanish treasure ships in the Pacific. Emerging from the Straits of Magellan, his fleet was scattered by a succession of storms which raged for 52 days, bludgeoned the *Marigold* to destruction, and drove the *Pelican* southeastward beyond the tip of Tierra del Fuego:

Swept toward the Pole Antarctic, as a pelican alone in the wilderness, with the most mad seas, a lee shore, and contrary and intolerable winds . . . we came at last to the uttermost cape of these lands (*Cape Horn*) which stands near 56 degrees, beyond which there is no main (*land*), but the Atlantic Ocean and the South Sea meet in a most large and free scope.

Top left: 'La Nouvelle France,' as depicted in a mid 16th century map from Guillaume le Testu's *Cosmographie Universelle.* Newfoundland is shown incorrectly as a group of three islands.

Far left: Louis Antoine de Bougainville: a colored engraving after Boilly.

Left: Sir Francis Drake, the first man to command a successful circumnavigation of the world and return alive.

Drake was the first person to realize that there was a way into the Pacific *via* the southernmost tip of America.

He went on to plunder the coasts of present day Chile and Peru. Here there were rich pickings, one treasure ship alone, the *Cacafuego*, yielding gold pesos which today would be valued at over $10,000,000. He then made his way along the American seaboard as far north as California – which he named New Albion because its cliffs reminded him of the white cliffs of Dover – before crossing the Pacific and returning home *via* the Moluccas and the Cape of Good Hope. Never before or since have ships brought back such a fabulous cargo of gold, silver, spices, jewels and silks. Those who had invested in his voyage got a return of 5000 percent, and the monetarist J.M. Keynes writes:

The booty brought back by Drake may be considered the fountain of British overseas investment. Out of the proceeds, Elizabeth paid off the whole of her foreign debt, and invested the balance in the Levant Company. Out of the profits of the Levant Company was formed the East India Company on which rested the foundation of England's trade overseas.

A very different and far greater explorer was Cook.

James Cook was born at Marton in Yorkshire on October 27th, 1728, the second child of a Scottish farm laborer. At the age of 18 he signed as deckhand aboard a brig carrying coal from Newcastle to London, and by hard work and common sense taught himself pilotage, navigation, surveying and astronomy, at the same time working his way up the lower-deck hierarchy to the rank of mate. When he was 25 he was offered a ship of his own; but to everyone's surprise he turned the offer down and enlisted as an ordinary seaman in the Royal Navy. Here again he worked his way up from the lower-deck, and again (on his 29th birthday) was offered command of a ship, the *Pembroke*. The *Pembroke* was ordered to Canada, and here Cook discovered his *métier*: surveying. His survey of the Traverse Rapids on the Saint Lawrence led to the British capture of Quebec, and he went on to chart the coasts of Labrador and Newfoundland with unprecedented accuracy; he also wrote a treatise on the eclipse of sun, which he sent to the Royal Society. This had important consequences; for when it was decided to send a warship to the southern hemisphere ostensibly to observe the transit of the planet Venus but secretly to search for and survey the Great Southern Continent, Cook was ideally qualified and was offered the command.

He led three great expeditions to the Pacific.

On his first voyage (1768-71) in command of the 368-ton bark *Endeavour* and a crew of 94, he left Plymouth in August, and having surveyed the area of Cape Horn entered the Pacific in January 1769. After a passage of 127 days he arrived at Tahiti, where the transit of Venus was to be observed, with his crew in good health and free from scurvy. This was a remarkable achievement. For scurvy in those days was the bane of long distance voyaging: it was commonplace for a ship's company to suffer a death rate of 50 percent or sometimes even 70 percent.

Above: 'Poulaho, King of the Friendly Islands, drinking Kava.' This engraving, based on a drawing by Webber, depicts a scene witnessed during Cook's third voyage.

Below: The voyages of Drake and Cabot.

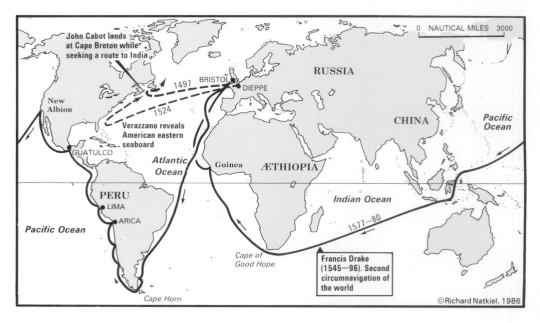

Above: Cook's *Endeavour* enters Botany Bay.

'No pen can describe the misery of life in our ships,' wrote Roggeween after losing most of his crew while crossing the Pacific.

Some became so emaciated that they looked like walking corpses and death blew them out like so many candles. Others became very fat, blown up like balloons; these were so afflicted with dysentery that they passed nothing but blood except for two or three days before they died when their excrement was like grey sulphur – and this was a sure sign that their hour had come. All were overcome by melancholy, and even those, like myself, who were not seriously ill, were left weak and enfeebled. My teeth were loose in my gums which were swollen to the thickness of a thumb and my body was covered with red, yellow green and blue swellings, the size of hazelnuts.

Scurvy was caused by a lack of the vitamin C found in fresh vegetables, and was exacerbated by the dreadful conditions below-deck: poor ventilation, overcrowding, stinking bilge water and minimal sanitary facilities. Cook had suffered these conditions himself, and was determined no crew of his would go through the misery and squalor that he had been through. He divided his ship's company into three watches instead of the usual two, to ensure they had plenty of sleep. He initiated a novel diet, 'sauerkraut and lemon preserve' which, as we now know, was rich in vitamin C. And he insisted on high standards of hygiene: daily baths, clothing and bedding brought on deck every three days for airing, and the *Endeavour*

'cured weekly with fires and smoked clean with vinegar and gunpowder.' There was some discontent at first at so strict a routine. 'Every day is Sunday' (i.e. a captain's round's day) 'with Mr Cook!' one of his crew complained. But a clean bill of health justified his revolutionary regime.

Like the French a year earlier, Cook and his men were enamored with Tahiti – they felt 'imparadised'. They spent three idyllic months on the island recording the passage of Venus, then headed south in search of *Terra Australis*.

In October 1769 they sighted New Zealand, which had not been visited by a ship from Europe since Tasman first saw the islands more than a century earlier. Cook spent six months charting the coast of New Zealand with meticulous accuracy and establishing friendly relations with the Maoris. Then he continued his search, and in April 1770 sighted an unknown shore: the east coast of Australia. 'It seems,' he wrote, 'an agreeable land, with hills covered in parts with trees and bushes and interspersed with tracts of sand.' He landed in Botany Bay – so called because his botanist Banks found in the hinterland a cornucopia of plants hitherto unknown to science. Standing north up the coast of present-day Queensland, the *Endeavour* was soon in difficulties: first holed by coral and beached, then nearly swept to destruction on the Great

and after following the ice for several thousand miles in appalling conditions, he headed for the Pacific islands where his ships spent the winter.

Next season he carried out the same sort of ice-edge cruise in the Pacific. Conditions were terrible; and as *Resolution* and *Adventure* approached the Antarctic Circle the word 'ice' appears in almost every line of Cook's Diary.

THURSDAY 16th DECEMBER: weather dark, gloomy and very cold. Our Sails and Rigging hung with Ice and Icikles . . . SATURDAY 18th: Moderate breezes; thick Foggy weather with Snow and Sleet which froze to the Rigging as it fell, so that everything was cased with Ice . . . TUESDAY 21st. A strong gale attend'd with thick Fogg; our Rigging so loaded with Ice we could scarce get our top-sails down to a double-reef . . . FRIDAY 24th: Wind northerly a strong gale with thick Sleet and Snow which froze to our Rigging. Our ropes became like wire, our sails like plates of metal. I have never seen so much Ice. The whole World was covered in it.

On January 30th, 1774 Cook reached his farthest south – 71° 11'. It was impossible to go farther. There was clearly no 'Land of Brazil Woods, Elephants and Gold' in the Pacific, and his ships again retreated to the islands for the winter.

In the summer of 1775, after putting ashore at Tierra del Fuego to collect fresh vegetables, Cook stood into the southernmost reaches of the Atlantic. By now *Resolution* had been sailing virtually non-stop for 2½ years; she was on her way home, her crew eager to get back to their families. Yet it was here that Cook made the only positive

Left: James Cook (1728-1779), one of the foremost British mariners and explorers. He did more than any other navigator to add to our knowledge of the Pacific and Southern Ocean.

Below: Harrison's marine chronometer, invented in the mid eighteenth century. This, more than any other invention, made navigation a great deal more accurate, and naval expeditions, beginning with Cook's, far less haphazard.

Barrier Reef; but by fine seamanship Cook managed to work his way along the Reef and through the Torres Strait which divides Australia from New Guinea, until he came to familiar waters among the Spice Islands. In October 1770 he dropped anchor in Batavia. Nine months later he was back in England.

This was a great voyage. Cook brought back to Europe the first factual account of the Polynesians. He circumnavigated and delineated New Zealand. He discovered and surveyed the east coast of Australia. He confirmed the existence of a seaway between Australia and New Guinea. And, perhaps most important of all, he proved that scurvy could be conquered.

His second voyage (1772-75) is often considered the greatest ever made – personally I would place it second only to Magellan's.

He left England on July 13th, 1772 with two ships, the 460-ton *Resolution* and the 335-ton *Adventure*: his orders to search again for the Great Southern Continent, that 'Land of Brazil Wood, Elephants and Gold' which, it was still believed, must exist in the southern hemisphere to counterbalance the landmass of Eurasia in the northern. In search of this mythical land Cook circumnavigated the world at high latitude, carrying out three great 'ice edge cruises,' in the Indian, Pacific and Atlantic Oceans.

After reprovisioning at Cape Town – now so popular a port of call that it was known as the 'Tavern of the Seas' – he headed southeast into the Indian Ocean. The weather was bad; and in much the same latitude as London Cook ran into ice.

Steer'd along the edge of the pack, he wrote, until we found ourselves quite surrounded by ice which extended in all directions as far as the eye could see. There were High mountains of ice within the field, also Whales, Penguins and other Birds.

On January 17th, 1773 the *Resolution* and *Adventure* became the first ships ever to cross the Antarctic Circle; but there was no way Cook could penetrate farther south,

discoveries of the voyage: the volcanic cones of the South Sandwich Islands, and the ice-coated island of South Georgia:

a terrain savage and horroable, the rocks raising their lofty summits till they were lost in cloud, the Vallies buried in everlasting snow . . . Who would have thought that an island situated at the same latitude as England should in the Height of Summer, be wholly covered many fathoms deep in frozen Snow. Yet this island alone could not have produced a ten-thousandth part of the Ice we met with in the previous years of our voyage . . . I THEREFORE FIRMLY BELIEVE THERE MUST BE LAND NEAR THE POLE TO WHICH THIS VAST QUANTITY OF ICE ADHERES, ALTHOUGH SUCH LAND MUST LIE QUITE WITHIN THE POLAR CIRCLE AND BE INACCESSIBLE.

A few months later, after a voyage of 1114 days and 70,000 miles (almost three times round the world), *Resolution* was back in England; not one of her crew had succumbed to scurvy.

This was another great expedition. Before it, every map of the world showed (incorrectly) a legendary land occupying more than half the southern hemisphere. After it, every map of the world showed (correctly) a vast ocean covering most of the southern hemisphere, with the mythical Great Southern Continent reduced to a far smaller ice-girt land-mass lying 'quite within the Polar Circile.'

Cook had replaced myth with reality.

His third voyage (1776-1780) was his longest – over 4 years – and his most extensive – taking him to all five continents and all five oceans. He left England in February with two ships, *Resolution* and *Discovery*: his orders to search for another chimera, the seaway which it was still believed might link the Atlantic and Pacific Oceans *via* the north coast of Canada. This was an old desideratum given a new twist by the fact that Cook was going to attempt the passage from west to east, by entering it *via* the Pacific.

The first 18 months of his voyage were uneventful. He surveyed Kerguelen, in the Indian Ocean, paid his fifth

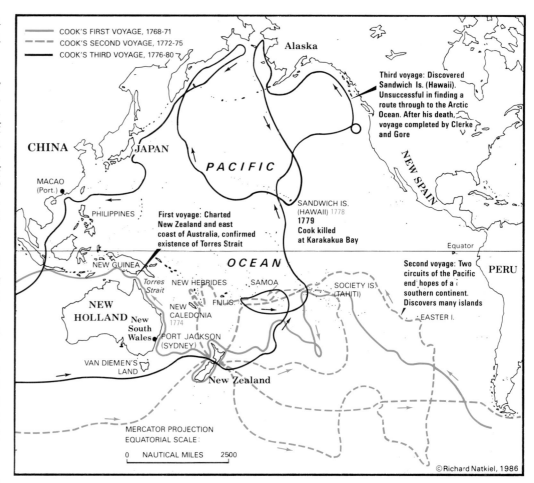

visit to New Zealand – a country and people he came increasingly to eulogize – and revisited Tonga and Tahiti. Although it was only ten years since the first meaningful contact between Polynesians and Europeans there were already signs that the islanders' traditional way of life was under threat. Cook, a humane and clearsighted man, wrote in his Diary:

We debauch their morals and introduce among them wants and diseases which they never before knew and which serve only to disturb that happy tranquility they and their foreFathers had enjoyed.

Above: The routes of Cook's three voyages.

Below: Cook's men shooting walrus or, as the contemporary caption would have it, sea horses.

For the gentle Polynesians the writing was already on the wall.

Early in 1778 *Resolution* and *Discovery* stood into the North Pacific, a world virtually unknown to Europeans. On January 20 they discovered the archipelago of Hawaii – Oahu, Kauai, Niihau, Kaula and Lehua – their precipitous cliffs pounded by great waves. A safe anchorage could not be found; landings were brief and hazardous; and after establishing friendly relations with the islanders, Cook headed for Drake's New Albion.

He sighted the coast of America on March 7, 1778, near the mouth of the Alsea River in Oregon. The weather was bad; and as he worked his way north Cook missed the great strait which reaches inland to present-day Vancouver, and the first safe anchorage he could find was in Nootka Sound. Here he spent a month, repairing his ships and getting to know the land and its people.

There are, he wrote, high hills and deep vallies, for the most part cloathed with large timber, such as Spruce fir and white Cedar. The inland mountains are covered with Snow; the Clemate is, however, infinitely milder than on the East coast of America (in) the same latitude. *Of the people he wrote*: They showed neither fear nor mistrust, but seemed inoffensive and display'd great readiness to trade . . . In disposition good natured, but quick to resent what they looked upon as an insult.

They lived in huge rambling wooden buildings, surrounded by gutted and drying fish, and the pelts of bear, wolf, deer, sea otter and seal. It was a different world to the islands of the Pacific: the land rugged rather than gentle, the climate bracing rather than balmy, the people tough rather than attractive, the girls shy rather than pro-

Left: Cook's ships anchored in Nootka Sound, Vancouver Island; a painting by Webber.

Below left: 'The arrival of the *Discovery* and *Resolution* in Kamchatka, April, 1779: an aquatint by Stadler.

Below: 'The death of Captain Cook,' a 19th century painting.

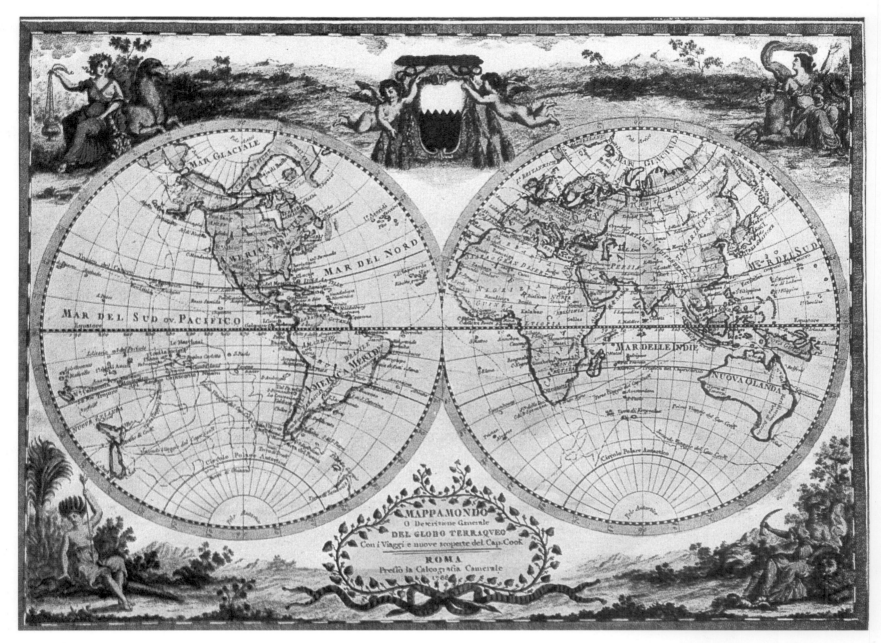

vocative, and their lifestyle chaotic and dirty rather than well ordered and clean. But the Indians had a disorganised confidence, good nature and vitality, and during the whole of Cook's visit not a shot was fired in anger.

On April 27 *Resolution* and *Discovery* again stood north, following the coastline first of British Columbia then Alaska. Cook did not find the entrance to the mythical strait which was supposed to link the Pacific to the Atlantic; he did, however, meticulously survey a huge coastline which up to then had been visited by only the occasional ship from Russia. And what a coastline it was, extending for over 3500 miles (roughly the width of the Atlantic). In the south are a mass of fjords and islands; in the center the great half-sunken range of the Aleutians extends into the Pacific; in the north a shore of lunar desolation is fringed with ice. Almost everywhere the coast is pounded by heavy seas, rainfall is heavy, and banks of swirling fog ubiquitous. It was often difficult to distinguish snowfield from cloudbank, and island from mainland. 'Thick fog and foul wind,' wrote Clerke (Cook's second-in-command) 'are disagreeable intruders to people tracing a Coast.' To fix the position of one particularly obscure headland Cook had to take no fewer than 43 bearings on it. But at last, passing through the strait which the Russian Vitus Bering had discovered 50 years earlier he emerged into the more sheltered Arctic Ocean. For several weeks he explored the area but found his way everywhere blocked by an impenetrable field of ice.

'Its seaward edge no more than 10 or 12 feet high, but becoming ever higher and more rugged to the northward.' There was no flaw in its defenses, no hope of his ships breaking through it. Cook therefore returned through the Bering Strait, intending to winter in Hawaii.

On an island at the mouth of the strait, the Aleuts looked like opposing the Europeans' landing. Cook told his men under no circumstances to fire 'and walked up to the Natives alone, without a single thing in his hand, thus quite disarming them.' Unlike many previous explorers he treated the people he met as human beings; which makes what happened next the more tragic.

On his return to Hawaii Cook was welcomed as the god-from-another-world. However, a petty dispute broke out; an island chief was accidentally killed, and Cook and a handful of his men found themselves cut off from their boat and were hacked to death. 'The Indians rushed forward, held him under the water and beat his head with a stone, while others struck him with clubs; then they hauled him over the rocks, using every barbarity to his body.' His remains were carried inland, his skull beaten to pieces, his body burned and his bones given to the priests. An ironic end for a gifted and humane man who cared deeply for the people of the ocean which he delineated with such meticulous skill.

Charles Darwin wrote his epitaph: 'he added a hemisphere to the civilized world.'

The Russians (*c.* 1720 – 1860)

Until the early 18th century Russia was a federation of feudal kingdoms with no interest in or knowledge of the sea. It was Peter the Great (1672-1725) who turned his country into a modern seafaring nation, founding the Imperial Navy and creating out of marshland and desolation two great ice-free ports: St. Petersburg in the Baltic and Petropavlovsk in the North Pacific, his 'windows to the world'. However, by the time Russian vessels ventured into the oceans, most of the world's coastlines were already being parcelled out among the nations of Europe.

Russian exploration was therefore restricted to the two areas still unknown: the North Pacific and the Antarctic.

In 1719 Peter sent two explorers, Evreinov and Luzhin, to delineate his vast but little-known Pacific territories. They discovered the site for an ice-free port on the desolate Kamchatka Peninsula, but failed to discover whether Asia and America were joined together. To settle this point, and to survey the unknown Pacific coast of North America, Peter sent Vitus Bering on two great voyages of discovery.

Left, top: Mappamondo, Calcrografia Camerale, Rome, 1786. The routes followed by Cook are traced on this Italian map, and the cartographic effect of his discoveries is immediately clear. The east coasts of Australia and New Zealand and northwestern Canada and Alaska are accurately shown for the first time.

Below left: Orbis Terrarum, by Ortelius, 1564. This shows the fabled Northwest Passage and the great southern continent, both more accurately investigated by Cook.

Below: The harbor of New Archangel in Sitka, Alaska, founded by members of Peter the Great's navy in the eighteenth century, from a drawing by Lisiansky, 1805.

Bering was Danish – there being no experienced Russian-born officers in the newly-formed Imperial Navy. The difficulties facing him were enormous. He left St. Petersburg in 1725, and had to haul his equipment and stores across 6000 miles of Eurasian steppe, then fell timber, drag it over the snow by sledge, and build his ship the *St. Gabriel* in a port which consisted of 'no more than a couple of dozen rude dwellings.' It was 1728 before he was heading north up the coast of present-day Koryakskiy Khrebet and through the strait between Asia and America which now bears his name. He crossed the Arctic Circle and managed to force his way to 67° 18′ N before thickening sea ice threatened to hem the *St. Gabriel* in, and he was forced to retreat. He returned to Russia with an accurate map of the coast of northeast Asia, having proved that Asia and America were divided by a strait which in summer was free of ice. He had, however, failed to sight let alone survey America, and with this objective he and his second in command Chirikov set out some 12 years later from Petropavlovsk.

Their voyage was part of an ambitious program which involved surveying Russia's entire Arctic coastline, charting the Kurils and Japan, and locating the coast of northwest America and opening it up to the Russian traders. Chirikov and Bering were soon separated by bad weather. The former, on July 15th, 1741, 'sighted some very high mountains, their summits covered in snow, their lower slopes with trees ... This,' Chirikov wrote, 'must be America'. He was right, his landfall almost certainly being Prince of Wales Island in southern Alaska. He sent his two longboats inshore to reconnoiter, but they disappeared – probably lost in a tide-race. Without his boats Chirikov could neither land nor reprovision, and he very prudently headed for home. Skirting the Aleutians, which he sighted at intervals through a miasma of sleet and fog, he managed to struggle back to Petropavlovsk. It had been a difficult voyage. Several of his crew had died of scurvy and many of those who survived were so weak they could hardly stand.

But his tribulations were nothing compared with those of his commander.

Bering sighted land a couple of days later than Chirikov and a couple of hundred miles farther north. '17 July,' his Diary reads, 'saw a chain of high snow-covered mountains, among them a great volcano.' His landfall must have been Kayak Island, behind which lies the 18,000-foot volcano Mount Elias. He spent only ten hours ashore, collecting plants and rock samples, then set course for Kamchatka: a decision which must have seemed over-cautious at the time, but which events were to justify. The course he set took him a little to the south of Chirikov's, and he ran into even worse weather. His ship, the diminutive *St. Peter*, was battered by high winds and heavy seas and came close to foundering. His crew, short of food and water, grew progressively weaker; soon they were dying of scurvy. In desperation they ran the *St. Peter* aground on an island, Beringa, hoping to find sufficient food and water to survive the winter. They hacked pits out of the frozen sand, covered them with driftwood and blankets, and brought the sick ashore.

Some, *wrote their naturalist Steller*, died as they were carried into the cold air, others died on the beach. The shoreline became a terrible sight. Before our dead could be buried, they were mutilated by the foxes who became so bold as to devour the helpless living ... Men were continually dying, and there was no-one strong enough to drag away the corpses. Nor could the living move away from the dead. We all remained mixed up together in a circle with a fire in the center ... Bering was dying, and we could do nothing to help him. As he lay half-buried in the sand in the hollow that had been dug for him, he begged to be left this way for warmth. He died on 8 December.

Below: 'Vitus Bering perishes in the ice-bound seas'. A contemporary painting which has the facts all wrong – only one ship was involved and it was run ashore on a flat beach without an iceberg in sight – but which nevertheless evokes the horror of the Russians' fate.

Above: A composite engraving of the exotic fauna hunted in the Arctic: whale, narwhal, polar bear, reindeer, walrus and seal.

Somehow, about half of the crew survived; and with the coming of spring they collected driftwood from the *St. Peter* – which had broken up in the winter storms – built a completely new vessel and half-sailed half-drifted into 'the long-desired haven of Petropavlovsk.' Few ships' companies have ever suffered such privations and survived.

Bering's voyages delineated the rough outline of the North Pacific, and established Russian suzerainty over this little-known *cul-de-sac* of the world. In the wake of the *St. Gabriel* and the *St. Peter* came not only a whole series of Russian vessels – the expeditions of Krusenstern

(1803-06), Kotzbue (1815-18) and Lutke (1826-9) – but also the *pomyshenniki*, the hunters-cum-fur-traders of the Russian American Company. For more than 100 years the wealth of Alaska and the Aleutians – the fish, timber, gold and in particular the furs -augmented the coffers not of the New World but the Old; Alaska became a department of Imperial Russia, known simply as Russian America; not until the purchase of 1867 did this bleakly beautiful part of the world come under American control. So from the Russian point of view it could be said that the crew of the *St. Peter* who died in such terrible circumstances on Beringa did not die in vain.

The Americans (*c.* 1780 – 1880)

As early as the 15th century the rulers of several European kingdoms were sponsoring voyages of exploration. In contrast, it was the middle of the 19th century before the first officially sponsored US maritime expedition – that of Charles Wilkes – got under way; for Americans were too busy rolling back their own land frontier to feel the need to seek others. By the mid 19th century most of the world's coastlines outside the Arctic and Antarctic had been delineated. America's national expeditions have therefore been largely confined to the Polar regions (*see* Chapters 8 and 9), and to the depths of the oceans and space (*see* Chapters 10 and 11.)

Individual and commercial expeditions are another story.

Few places in the world have such a strong and distinguished tradition of sea-faring as New England. From the time of the founding fathers to the present day, vessels from ports like Boston, Nantucket, New Bedford and

Stonington have been wresting from the ocean a harvest which has brought prosperity to the seaboard of northeast America. By the mid-18th century New England sloops and brigs were voyaging not only throughout the North Atlantic but deep into the Arctic in search of fish, walrus, narwhals, whales and seals. The two latter were especially profitable; for the ever-multiplying machines of the industrial revolution needed animal oil to keep them lubricated, while improved techniques in the fur trade led to a growing demand for seal-skin. However, about the middle of the 18th century the New England fishing fleet was faced with disaster; it had been too successful; the whales and seals of the North Atlantic disappeared, for they had been hunted virtually to extermination. Yankee vessels were therefore obliged to seek alternative killing grounds, and in pursuit of their elusive quarry they sailed literally to the farthest ends of the Earth.

Whale-ships rounded Cape Horn and combed the Indian and Pacific Oceans, discovering not only many new species of whales, but a multitude of remote islands, some almost as far south as the Antarctic Circle, some as far north as the Bering Strait. These whale-ships not only carried out some of the longest and most dangerous commercial voyages ever made, they brought prosperity to two places which badly needed a stimulus. In the early 1800s the number of whalers in Australia exceeded the number of convicts and settlers combined. While in the mid 1800s the annual visits of the New England fleet brought enormous benefits to ports like San Francisco and Vancouver – as late as 1870 more than a hundred New England vessels a year were using these ports on their way to and from the Bering Strait.

It would, however be fair to say that whalers were exploiters rather than explorers, and their discoveries were limited to a number of isolated islands.

Sealers, on the other hand, made important discoveries.

Drake had reported seals on the beaches of Tierra del Fuego as early as 1578, but, for a couple of centuries, distance and the most tempestuous seas on Earth precluded their being hunted. Then in the 1770s fishermen from New England began to work their way down the coast of South America. Within the span of a generation (between 1780 and 1810) they killed over 4 million seals, first on the beaches of the mainland, then, as their quarry became overhunted and scarce, on the offshore islands. It was here, south of Cape Horn, that they discovered skein after skein of sub-Antarctic archipelagos – the South Orkneys and South Shetlands – the stepping stones to Antarctica.

It is impossible to say which sealers discovered which islands and when. For in conditions as difficult as anywhere on Earth – heavy seas, strong winds and ever-shifting banks of mist and fields of ice – landfalls were hard to identify. Also New England skippers tended to play down their discoveries, burn their records and make few entries in their logs. For sealing was a secretive business; 'wholesale massacre on a deserted shore, with a new-found rookery like a vein of gold, its whereabouts too precious and too easily exhausted to be divulged.' There is, however, no doubt that New England sealers worked their way south through these ice-encrusted archipelagos until they sighted the Great Southern Continent for which explorers had been searching for more than 300 years. And not only sighted it, landed on it.

It used to be thought that the first men to set foot on the mainland on Antarctica were members of one of the big national expeditions all of which claimed to have 'discovered' the continent in 1841. However, a much better claim can be made for the crew of the New Haven brig *Cecilia* in 1821.

The South Shetlands, in the summer of 1820-21, were a rendezvous for large numbers of sealers. The Stonington fleet dropped anchor in the flooded crater of Deception Island. A contingent from Australia landed on Livingston Island, and when the *Cecilia* tried to join them 'warned off their rival with Guns, Pistoles and Swords'. John Davis, skipper of the *Cecilia*, wrote: 'Concluded it best to go on a cruise to find new lands, as the seal is done for here.' On January 30th, 1821 Davis headed south into unknown waters. Next afternoon he sighted 'a low new-discovered island,' where he managed to land. When the sun put in a brief appearance, Davis was able to fix his latitude: 63° 25′ S: and from this and from his description of the island it seems certain his landfall was Low or Jameson Island. In the course of the next week the crew of the *Cecilia* killed over 1000 seals. Then on February 6th, they again headed into the unknown. Their course was

Below: 'The island of Woahoo in the Pacific,' visited by the whaler C.E. Bensell in 1821.

southeast, and in the rays of the dying sun they sighted a small island almost dead ahead; this must have been the diminutive Hoseason which lies some 30 miles to the southeast of Low Island. The *Cecilia* continued on a course of southeast throughout the night, pasing Hoseason and making at dawn a spectacular discovery.

Wednesday 7th February 1821, *Davis wrote in his log*. Commences with open Cloudy Weather and Light winds a Standing for a Large Body of Land in that direction S.E. At 10 A.M. close in with it, out Boat and Sent her on Shore to look for Seal. At 11 A.M. Boat returned, but (had) found no Seal. At noon our latitude 64° 01′ South. Stood up a Large Bay, the Land high and covered intirely with snow . . . I think this Land to be a continent.

Since the *Cecilia*'s starting point and course are known, and since her last fix places her almost alongside the Antarctic Peninsula, there seems little doubt that her crew sighted and landed on the mainland, probably in Hughes Bay at the entrance to the Gerlache Strait.

This was a fitting climax to the New England sealers' 20-odd years of voyaging in some of the most dangerous waters on Earth. It was also a unique achievement. Other explorers claiming to be first to set foot on other undiscovered shores, were in fact nearly always landing in countries already occupied by indigenous people. But when the *Cecilia*'s longboat grounded in Hughes Bay and her crew scrambled ashore, they were the first humans ever to set foot on the virgin continent of Antarctica.

Above: A New England whaler off the Cape of Good Hope, a contemporary painting.

Left: Samoan dancers performing before Charles Wilkes, a contemporary engraving.

Europe and Asia

Although our ancestors originated in Africa, most early civilizations sprang up in Eurasia: the Sumerian on the Tigris, the Minoan in Crete the Herappan on the Indus, and the Shang in China. These were the first of a succession of cultures which have ebbed and flowed throughout Eurasia over the last 5000 years; and the civilizations of the south and east were as old and as advanced as those of the west. The exploration of Eurasia has therefore involved forays from three different epicentres, expansion from the south being restricted by the physical barrier of the Himalaya, expansion from the east being restricted by China's periodic withdrawals from the world behind her symbolic Great Wall, and expansion from the west being restricted by the fact that Islamic peoples controlled the trade routes of the Middle East and created a no go area for Europeans.

With such a background it is not surprising that the exploration of Eurasia has been complex and inspired at different times by different motives – conquest, trade, proselytizing, the desire to gain knowledge. Nor is it surprising that the explorers of this huge and culturally sophisticated landmass have needed different traits from the explorers of, say, the polar icecaps or the Australian outback. For they have needed to establish a rapport with the people of cultures other than their own. They have needed to be diplomats – a characteristic shared by men as apparently disparate as Alexander the Great, Hsuan-Tsang, Marco Polo, Edmund Hillary and Wilfred Thesiger.

Among the earliest explorers of Eurasia were Alexander from the west and Chang Ch'ien from the east (*see* Chapter 1). Then came the Romans.

The Romans (*c.* 100 BC – AD 400)

The Romans were a practical people. They were interested in exploration only when it helped to safeguard or enrich their empire. Yet the very act of creating so vast an empire as the Roman involved journeys of discovery. For in its heyday Rome controlled an area which stretched from Hadrian's Wall in the north to Aswan in the south, and from Lisbon in the west to the Persian Gulf in the east. It would not be too fanciful to regard the legionaries who campaigned on and guarded these far-flung frontiers as explorers.

In Britain Hadrian's Wall is usually thought of as the limit of Roman occupation. However, several legions are known to have campaigned farther north, building another wall (the Antonine) between present-day Edinburgh and Glasgow, establishing a fort at Inehtuthill (north of Perth) and carrying out a punitive raid in the Grampians. One wonders what auxiliary troops from say North Africa or the Middle East thought of this northern wilderness? They at any rate must have regarded themselves as men who had ventured on to the rim of the world.

In Africa (*see* Chapter 4) Roman legions crossed the Atlas Mountains and penetrated deep into the Sahara, possibly to Lake Chad. They also ascended the Nile as far as Khartoum, and campaigned in Ethiopia.

In the Middle East it is known that one of Augustus's

Previous page: The north face of Everest, a photograph taken by the first Chinese expedition to climb the mountain.

Below: One of the most northerly outposts of the Roman empire, the fort at Ardoch, Scotland. The very act of creating such a huge empire involved exploration; the chilly wilds of Scotland must have seemed very alien indeed to troops from North Africa.

Left: A Roman troop ship, with its soldiers about to step off into the unknown of another foreign land.

generals, Aelius Gallus, was ordered to pacify Arabia Felix (present-day Yemen), probably with a view to consolidating the incense trade. Gallus set out from the shore of the Red Sea in 25 BC with 10,000 men; but more than half his army died of hunger and thirst in the desert – one of history's least-successful attempts at exploration.

In Persia the Romans established fortified towns as far east as Amida on the Tigris and Garni in Soviet Armenia; while their legions are believed to have campaigned around Baku on the shore of the Caspian, where a Flavian centurion from Melitene carved his name on a rock face. It is a far cry from the Aegean to the Caspian, and here again the legionaries must have felt that they had penetrated to the very ends of the Earth.

The Romans succeeded in pushing back the frontiers of the Mediterranean world and bringing under the aegis of their *pax Romana* a vast number of disparate people over a wide area of territory. It would, however, be true to say that their *forte* was empire-building rather than exploration.

The Pilgrimage of Hsuan Tsang (629 – 645)

About the time that Roman legions were defending the last bastions of their empire against nomads from central Asia, a Chinese scholar-priest was venturing among these same nomads in one of the most remarkable solo journeys ever made.

Hsuan Tsang, anxious to study the fountainhead of Buddhism at first hand, decided to travel from China to India by land and by himself: a journey of incredible difficulty and danger which had never been attempted before. He set out from the Great Wall of China in 629.

His route took him first across the Takla Makan depression.

Here, are no birds in the sky, no beasts on the ground, no vegetation and no water. By night goblins burn torches numerous as the stars. By day winds whip up the most terrible sand-storms.

He ran out of water, and had nothing to eat or drink for four days before stumbling fortuitously into an oasis. Recuperating, he narrowly escaped being killed by bandits, before joining a caravan which was trying to cross the Tien Shan.

These mountains are steep and treacherous. They reach to the skies. Ever since the beginning of the world snow has been falling on them, and this snow has been converted to ice which

Below: Mongolian 'yurts' – tents of warm white felt covered with canvas – have retained the same design for 1000 years.

Far left: The Great Wall of China was originally built before the third century BC but it was substantially repaired and extended by the first Ch'in emperor from AD 221.

Left: The spread of Buddhism from its origins in India had originally been *via* the trade routes traveled in the opposite direction by Hsuan Tsang.

never melts and whose glare is blinding. Even heavy fur-lined clothes cannot prevent the wind and the cold from freezing the body.

In a nightmare crossing of the Tien Shan 14 of his travelling companions were frozen to death. North of the mountains Hsuan found himself in a world of bleak hills, deep valleys and never-ending grassland: home of the nomadic Mongols, whose kingdom is the back of a horse and whose magnificent *yurts* (felt tents) were 'so rich in furs and so decorated with gold that they dazzled the eye.' Hsuan Tsang enjoyed the Mongols' hospitality for the better part of a year before reaching and following the traditional trade route from Samarkand to the Oxus, from the Oxus to Balkh, the 'Mother of Cities', and from Balkh over the high passes of the Hindu Kush and into the headwaters of the Indus. This was another difficult part of his journey.

Perilous were the roads and dark the gorges. Here were ledges hanging in mid-air and bridges suspended across fearful abysses. The pilgrim had at times to swing down a rock-face by ropes, and other times traverse the face of the rock by a path less than a foot wide.

But at last, four years after leaving the Great Wall, Hsuan descended into the flood plain of the Ganges.

He spent twelve years in the sub-continent of India, travelling from the Himalaya in the north to Sri Lanka in the south, and being involved in enough adventures, escapes and religious confrontations to fill a volume. Eventually he returned *via* the Hindu Kush and the Pamirs to his native China, 'laden with many gold and silver statues, 150 relics of the true Buddha and 657 learned books.' This was one of the longest and most difficult journeys ever made, both in distance covered and time taken. Not without justification is Hsuan Tsang known in the east as the 'prince of pilgrims.'

The Viking Traders (*c.* 900 – 1100)

Our image of the Vikings as pillagers by sea, is so firmly rooted it is often overlooked that they were also traders by land, traveling *via* the rivers of the USSR as far afield as the Black, Caspian and Aral Seas.

By the end of the 9th century small trading centers had sprung up round the shores of the Baltic – Hedeby in Denmark, Birka in Sweden, Grobin in Latvia and Wollin

in Poland – and by the end of the 10th century these had burgeoned into flourishing ports, the termini of a regular long-distance trade route between east and west. The Vikings provided furs, amber, walrus-ivory, weapons and slaves – it is an indication of the status and wealth of the cultures involved that it was the white-skinned Europeans who were slaves and the darker-skinned Asiatics

Left: A restoration of the Oseberg Viking longship now in a museum in Oslo.

purchasers – in return they received silks, gold and in particular silver. This silver was converted into brooches, pendants and rings: the so-called 'hack silver' which was the basis of the Vikings' currency. One indication of the scale of the trade is that over 90,000 Arab coins have been found in Scandinavia, and over 150,000 items of hack silver. An even more telling indication is the comment by a contemporary cleric that in 1070 the largest and most prosperous town in Europe was Wollin on the the Oder.

Two routes were used by the Viking river-boats. The northern started at present-day Leningrad and led up the River Neva and into Lake Ladoga. From here it was possible to voyage via a series of rivers and lakes to the navigable reaches of the Volga and the great emporium of Bolgar, where caravans from the east met river boats from the west. Some Vikings stopped here; but the majority continued some 1000 miles down river to the Caspian and Aral Seas, where they were not averse to seizing by pillage what they could not obtain by trade. The southern route started at Riga, Wollin or Truso and progressed via a complex succession of river crossings to Kiev (then ruled by a Scandinavian monarchy): from here it was an easy journey down the Dnieper to Odessa on the Black Sea and thence by boat to Byzantium – which the Vikings on more than one occasion besieged.

For a couple of centuries Viking river boats and rafts plied this esoteric two-way traffic between the Baltic and the inland seas of Eurasia. Then events in the east wrote *finis* to a series of journeys as remarkable as they are little-known.

Genghiz Khan and Tamerlane (*c.* 1200 – 1400)

If one defines an explorer as someone who travels great distances through desolate terrain unknown to them, then the horsemen of the Mongol armies were among the greatest of explorers. For they swept almost the length and breadth of Eurasia, from Korea to Vienna and from the Arctic Ocean to the Persian Gulf; they even attempted seaborne invasions of Java and Japan. The greatest of their leaders were Genghiz Khan and Tamerlane.

It is hard to say what motivated the Mongols in their stupendous wanderings. The immediate reason for their campaigns was that Genghiz Khan persuaded the tribes of Mongolia to stop fighting one another and unite to fight non-Mongols; and the immediate reason for their success was that they used the horse as a weapon of war more effectively than anyone before or since. A more fundamental reason may have been that their heartland was suffering from a worsening climate, with lack of rain progressively reducing the area of land available for pasture. Perhaps a more fundamental reason still was that the Mongols were a dying breed. Ten thousand years ago about 95 percent of the world population was nomadic; today less than one half of 1 percent are nomads. The Mongols may have realized that their way of life was under threat. They saw wealth being concentrated more and more in cities, and a lifestyle that they wanted no part of they destroyed: destroyed with the frenzy of those who know that time is not on their side.

In 1208 Genghiz Khan invaded China with over 100,000 horsemen. The Great Wall was breached. The cities of the Ch'in empire were captured one by one, looted and razed to the ground. In 1215 Peking surrendered.

Every man, woman and child within the capital was put to the sword, *wrote an eye-witness.* It was the most prolonged and glorious slaughter.

The city was then burned to the ground, and the ashes raked level so that not even the outline of a building could be traced. The cost of this invasion in people killed and displaced, damage inflicted and tribute demanded was crippling. Having 'purified' the Buddhists, Genghiz

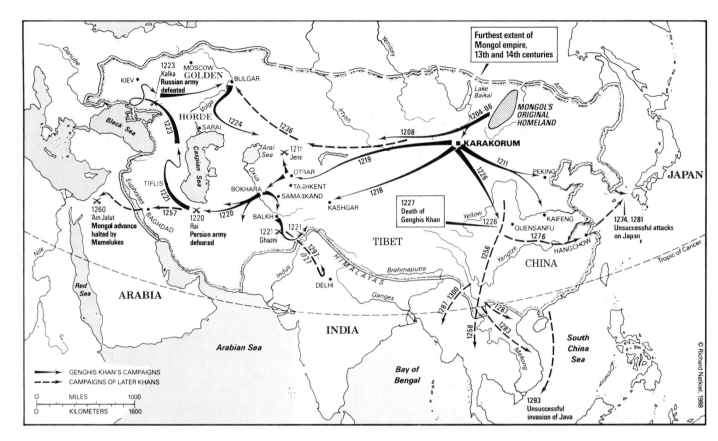

Left: The extent of the Mongol empire in the 13th and 14th centuries.

Below: The Mongols attack Kiev.

Bottom left: A Mongol warrior plaiting the tail of his horse.

Bottom: The ruins of Shahr-i-gholghola, sacked by the Mongols in 1222.

Khan turned his attention to the Muslims. In 1219 he led more than 200,000 horsemen, known as the Golden Horde, west through the Takla Makan. What had happened in the plains of China was now repeated in the steppe of Asia. One by one the great cities of the Muslim world – Bukhara, Balkh, Samarkand and Baghdad – fell to the Horde whose prowess in war has seldom been equaled and never surpassed.

They came, they uprooted, they burned, they slew, they despoiled, they departed, *lamented a contemporary chronicler.* Our splendors are effaced from the earth as writing from paper, our palaces have become the abode of the owl and the raven.

Genghiz Khan died in 1227, having in less than 20 years carved out for himself an empire three times the size of Alexander's.

His sons extended his conquests deep into Europe, annihilating the Russians at Kiev and Novgorod, the Poles at Liegwitz and the Hungarians at Mohi. By the end of the 13th century Mongol armies were campaigning in the Ural Mountains, the Sinai Desert, the Korean Peninsula, and on the shores of Java and Japan. Their final and most bloodthirsty campaign was in India.

In 1398 Tamerlane led his army into the Hindu Kush: 'I have come,' he said, 'to lead a campaign to the death

against the infidel, to purify their land from idolatry and to seize their riches, since plunder taken in war is as lawful to our people as mother's milk.' Over 20,000 of his men died of cold, exposure and exhaustion in the snow-blocked passes of the Hindu Kush; but the remainder, when they had struggled through to the plains, decimated the Indian armies. After one of the bloodiest battles in history, Delhi surrendered. The city was immediately set on fire and the population massacred – 'it was clearly the will of God', wrote Tamerlane, 'that disaster should fall on a place of such evil.' With the Indian army annihilated, the rich towns of the plains were systematically looted and their inhabitants killed. Places associated with the Hindu faith were singled out for particularly savage treatment: 'On the banks of this abominable river (the Ganges), every man, woman child and living creature was consigned to the fires of hell.' At the end of six months' plundering Tamerlane needed 40,000 pack-mules to carry his loot as he retreated through the Afghan passes, leaving in his wake a world in ruins –

Above: Tamerlane. When he died in 1405 he was in the process of preparing a massive attack on Ming China.

Above left: Tamerlane's warriors make a cairn from the severed heads of their enemies.

Left: 'Their cities have wheels, their kingdom is the back of a horse': a Mongol community in transit over the steppe.

Left: Mongol warriors assembling for the invasion of Japan: from a Japanese scroll, *circa* 1293.

crops burned, irrigation-systems shattered, towns reduced to rubble, upward of 5 million dead, and a legacy of chaos, famine and disease from which it took the people of India a century to recover.

Although the Mongols did little actual exploring they had a considerable effect on the human geography of Eurasia: disrupting the established way of life, moving huge numbers of people over huge distances, and helping to create ethnic minorities which are still a cause of friction today.

The Travels of Marco Polo (1271 – 1295)

Everyone has heard of Marco Polo; yet his little known father and uncle, Maffeo and Nicolo, made an earlier and even more remarkable journey to China between 1260 and 1269. It is Marco's name which is remembered today largely because, when the Polos got back from their second journey, their adventures were written up by a highly competent 'ghost writer' into one of the classics of exploration, *Description of the World*. From this we can follow their adventures step by step.

They set out from Italy in 1271 and took nearly a year to reach Ormuz on the Persian Gulf. From here they had planned to travel to China by sea; but disconcerted by the ramshackle appearance of the Arab dhows, 'held together with loose cords and a few wooden nails,' they decided instead to head for Kaiping by land *via* the mountains of central Asia. They had the happy knack, during their journey, of noticing and recording interesting facts about the places they passed through and the people they met.

After crossing the deserts of Persia, 'where the wells are few and far between, and what little water there is is brackish and green as grass', they came to the Valley of the Assassins. Here, Marco would have us believe,

were the most beautiful gardens in the world, criss-crossed by conduits flowing with wine, milk and honey; and in the garden fair damsels willing to minister to every desire, also young boys being instructed in the art of murder.

It sounds a tall story, until Marco goes on to explain that the boys were given cannabis in increasingly heavy doses until they became addicted, could not tell fact from fantasy, and were willing to commit murder to obtain more.

The Arabic for cannabis is *Hash-hish*: hence the name of the Assassins – an organization which probably murdered more people in the 13th century than have the Mafia in the 20th.

Crossing into present-day Afghanistan, the Polos came to Balkh.

Below: The Assassin fortress of Masyaf.

Here, *wrote Marco*, there used to be many fine palaces and mansions of marble, but these now lie in ruins. Grass grows in the streets, and wild goats graze in the deserted fields.

- evidence of the lasting efforts of Genghiz Khan's spoliation. In the upper reaches of the Oxus they observed that the men had a predilection for women with large buttocks:

She is considered the most glorious who is stoutest below the girdle. The girls therefore pad out their breeches with up to 300 feet of cotton or silk, thick-pleated and scented with musk.

Of the Pamirs Marco wrote:

On top of these ranges are broad plains with a great abundance of grass, few trees and springs of the purest water. This is said to be the highest place in the world. It is so high, you see no birds flying, fire burns with a pale flame and gives off so little heat you may put your hand in it, and there are huge sheep with horns six palms in length.

At the time these too were regarded as tall stories. However, in recent years ornithologists have confirmed that no birds hover over the upper slopes of the Pamirs; mountaineers have confirmed that the lack of oxygen renders flames ineffective, while zoologists have confirmed that the horns of the giant sheep, *ovis poli*, do indeed measure 'six palms in length.'

In the autumn of 1273 the Polos descended from the Pamir into the plains of Sinkiang, a desert-area laced with occasional oases. Here they joined the Silk Road as it skirts the Takla Makan depression. This was an old and

Left: A Chinese impression of Mongol cavalry outside fortifications, possibly representing the Great Wall.

Below: Vessels of the Kublai Khan in 13th century China.

much-traveled route; but Marco recorded many interesting new facts about it. In Yarkand he noticed that 'many of the inhabitants have a strange swelling on the side of their neck'; it has recently been discovered that impurities in their water make the people particularly susceptible to goiter. In Tun-Luang he found 'secret places full of idols'; this was the site of the Cave of the Thousand Buddhas which 600 years later yielded so rich a harvest to the archaeologist Aurel Stein. As they approached the Great Wall they were told that

in these parts if a stranger comes to a man's house, that man will straightway leave his home and his family and will not return until the stranger has gone. This custom is said to ensure wealth, good crops and healthy children.

Four years after leaving Venice the Polos were escorted, with much pomp and ceremony, into the Kublai Khan's summer palace in Kaiping. For Marco's father and uncle this was the end of a great adventure. For the 20-year-old youngster it was the start of an even greater one; for he was to spend the next 17 years in the service of the Khan.

Above: A 13th century caravan crossing the desert: from the *Carla Catalana*.

Left: The Polos pay homage to one of the potentates encountered on their epic journey.

The years that Marco spent in China were of greater significance than the journey he made to get there. For the Khan got to know him, like him and trust him; and soon he was sending him on diplomatic missions the length and breadth of his kingdom, from Korea to the Malay peninsula. While carrying out these missions Marco got to know China and the Chinese better than any European had ever known them before. And how he must have marveled at the shops and buildings, larger than any in Europe, the paper currency, the sophisticated printing-presses, the burning of coal and the cornucopia of jewels and jade, gold and silver, silks and spices. Here, he must have realized, was a civilization every bit as old and advanced as his own.

And this was the message he brought back to Europe.

In 1292 the Khan allowed the Polos to leave, giving them 14 ships, a retinue of 600 men and one last mission: to escort a Chinese princess to Trebizond to enable her to marry a Persian prince. It is an indication of the hazards of 13th century travel that the journey – via Sumatra and Sri Lanka – took over two years and only 18 out of the 600 survived.

In Europe Marco's account of his adventures was widely read but not always believed; for the wonders he had seen were too exotic for sceptics, and he was accused of exaggerating and dubbed *el Milione*. As he lay dying his friends begged him to recant the lies he had told, but he replied simply: 'Of the wonders I saw I have not told you the half.' Time has proved him right. For it is now realized that his so-called 'tall stories' – his garden of dreams, his flames that gave off no heat and his huge-horned sheep were not fantasy but fact. It is also realized that in the words of the historian H.A.L. Fisher 'Marco's story brought about an intellectual revolution in Europe quite as important as that great expansion of human knowledge which two centuries later proceeded from the discoveries of Columbus.'

Few explorers have done more to disseminate real knowledge.

Above: Harvesting peppers in Madagascar, an illustration from Marco Polo's *Book of Wonders*. Twenty years after his epic journey, Polo dictated an account of his travels to a fellow inmate of Genoa prison.

Left: Marco Polo's route to the east, 1271-75.

Below: The Polo family leave the court of Kublai Khan, 1292. Marco had worked for the great emperor for 17 years.

The Jesuit Explorers: Goes (1603 – 07), and Grueber and D'Orville (1661 – 63)

Marco Polo's travels may have temporarily stimulated trade between East and West *via* the Silk Road; but it was not long before the rise of the militant Ottoman Turks made travel through the Middle East virtually impossible for Christians. Contact between the two civilizations was again lost; lost so completely that by the end of the 16th century Europeans were not even certain whether the China reached by Portuguese seamen was the same country as the Cathay which had been reached centuries earlier by the Polos.

There was, however, still contact between India and China; and reports kept filtering through to the Indian sub-continent that pockets of Nestorian Christians were eking out a precarious existence in the mountains of central Asia. Typical of these reports was the story told to the Jesuit missionaries in Goa by an itinerant merchant:

There lives in Cathay a Khan some of whose people are Mohammedans and some Isavitae (*followers of Jesus*) . . . the latter indulge in ceremonies which involve wearing white robes, ritual singing, the use of incense, the taking of communion and the worship of one God.

The Jesuits decided to send an emissary to China to see if this was so; and the man they chose was Bento de Goes, a 42 year old priest, born in Spain.

Goes left Agra in January, 1603 disguised as an Armenian trader; and the fact that he was obliged to travel in disguise highlights a problem which was to bedevil the exploration of central Asia over the next 300 years. Europeans were *persona non grata*. So to the difficulty of the terrain was added the hostility of the people.

The caravan which Goes joined soon came under attack from the tribes of the Hindu Kush who obviously felt, like Tamerlane, that 'plunder was lawful as mother's milk.' They had to hire an escort of 400 troops to protect them, and took nearly 6 months to struggle through to Kabul. At this point most of Goes' traveling companions gave up and returned to India; but the priest crossed the Hindu Kush *via* the Parwan Pass (which had been used 2000 years earlier by Alexander), and headed into the little-known Pamirs. Here his horses died of cold, and 'the uncongenial state of the atmosphere made it almost impossible to breathe, hence we felt oppressed beyond endurance and gasped continuously for breath.' He found that in several villages the people had brown hair, blue eyes and a fair complexion. 'They are called Calcias, which means "ravens driven high into the mountains."' Some anthropologists believe the Calcias were descendants of the troops of Alexander the Great. Eventually he arrived in Yarkand, a trading emporium controlled by the Chinese where 'the women wore no veils and hid from no man.' He spent almost a year there; though it should be pointed out it was not the charms of the ladies that detained him but the cupidity of the Chinese officials, who refused him permission to join an east-bound caravan until he had paid a succession of hefty bribes. However, by the winter of 1604-5 he was heading round the periphery of the Takla Makan depression: a bleakly beautiful world through which his caravan would have moved in a silence so absolute it could almost be felt. To the north, south and west great mountains rose out of a sea of sand, sometimes half hidden by loess – clouds of dust-particles which hung defying gravity in mid-air. It is this loess which gives Asia its imagery of yellow: yellow

dust settling on yellow soil, seeping into yellow rivers that empty into a Yellow Sea. This was difficult terrain. Goes' companions were difficult too; for they had seen through his disguise and allowed him a place in their caravan only on sufferance. At every oasis there were scruples to be overcome, delays to be endured, officials to be bribed. But at last he reached the Great Wall of China. This, however, was as far as he got. He died – almost certainly poisoned – on 10 April 1607, his traveling companions at once seizing his money and burning his diary.

Goes was the first European to travel by land from India to China. He found no Nestorian Christians, but his journey did help to re-establish the links between East and West and to prove that Cathay and China were one.

An even more arduous journey was undertaken by Fathers Grueber and D'Orville, who traveled from Peking to Agra not by the usual caravan routes, but by cutting directly across the Tibetan plateau and the Nepal Himalaya.

The Jesuit Johann Grueber was a brilliant theologian and mathematician. He was also tough as the proverbial

Below: Contact between China and the west was regained in the 16th century. The Jesuits lost no time in sending missionaries to Cathay. This picture shows a Jesuit priest (note his Chinese robes) in the Peking Observatory, *c.* 1660.

old boots. He needed to be; for his journey was one of the most physically demanding ever made. Together with his companion, the self-effacing Albert D'Orville, he left Peking early in 1661, passed through the Great Wall and headed southwest into the little-known 'Tartar Desert'. Skirting the Koko Nor, the largest lake in Tibet, the Fathers came to a world of lunar desolation, where range after range of featureless mountains lay strewn across their path like the waves of a petrified sea: 'an impossibly barren land,' wrote Grueber, 'whose bleak hillsides are broken only by the occasional cluster of *yurts*, home of the predatory Mongols.' They crossed the highest of the ranges, the Kun Lun, by a 15,000 foot pass and found themselves in the central plateau of Tibet. This too was forbidding terrain, a landscape of desiccated rock lashed by unremitting wind where even the deepest valleys were 10,000 feet above sea level. Eight months after leaving Peking they struggled through to that Mecca of travelers, the forbidden city of Lhasa, where no European had set foot for 300 years.

How one wishes Grueber had written more about the everyday life of the people of Lhasa and less about their religion. He did, it is true, make one or two sketches of the city, and was the first European to describe the Tibetans' ubiquitous prayer-wheels and the blessing associated with the turning of them, *Om mani padme hum* (Hail, oh jewel in the lotus!) Most of his diary, however, consists of an esoteric dissertation on Buddhist dogma. This he ended with the words,

It is amazing how their religion agrees with the Romish. They too celebrate the Mass with bread and wine, they too give extreme unction, bless those who marry, pray for the sick, form processions, sing in choirs, honor the relics of idols, have monasteries and nunneries, observe fasts, undergo pennances,

consecrate holy men and send out missionaries who live in poverty and travel barefoot.

Grueber had solved the mystery of the 'Nestorians' said to be in hiding among the mountains. Travelers had mistaken Buddhist ceremonies for Christian services.

The Fathers spent 6 weeks in Lhasa, then headed south for the Himalaya. Soon they found themselves facing the formidable massif of Cho-Oyo and Everest. It was winter; the only pass was deep in snow; 'the air,' wrote Grueber, 'was so rarified it became almost impossible for us to breathe.' Somehow they struggled through, very likely being the first Europeans to sight the

Above left: Mount Kailas in Tibet, the Hindus' holy mountain, source of the 4 major rivers of India.

Below: Prayer wheels in a Buddhist temple in Lhasa.

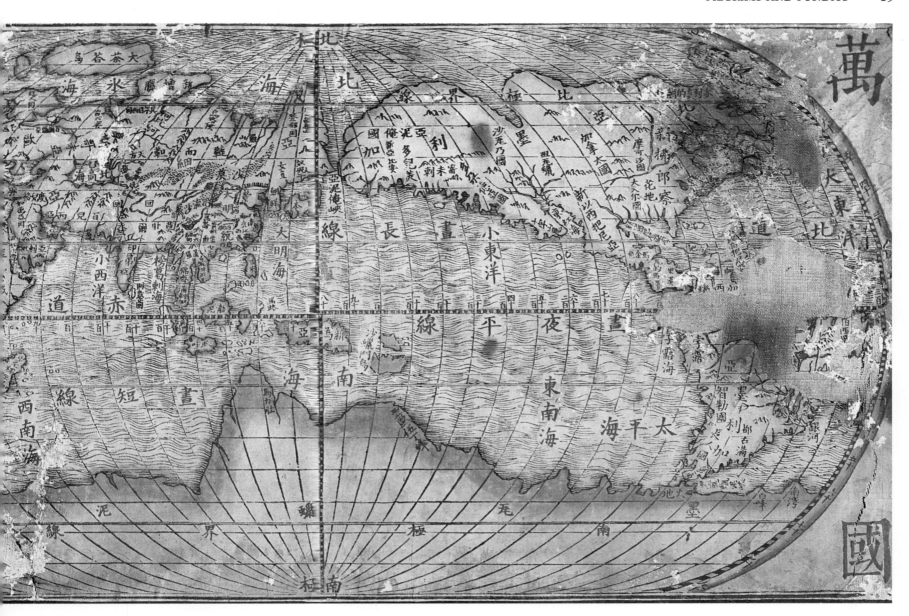

Above: A mid 17th century map drawn by a Chinese artist under the direction of the Jesuit missionary Matteo Ricci.

summit of Everest. Emerging into the gorge of the Bhotia-Kosi, they would have had to traverse a succession of hair-raising paths and bridges before emerging into the plains of India.

Almost exactly a year after leaving Peking they entered the Jesuit mission in Agra, where the patient and uncomplaining D'Orville quietly died, 'altogether worn out by the privations he had endured.' Grueber continued his journey alone, his arrival at the Vatican in 1663 ending an impressive if little-known feat of exploration.

Pilgrims (*c.* 500 BC) and Pundits (*c.* AD 1860)

Grueber was the first European to cross the Himalaya from north to south; but a couple of millennia earlier the range had been crossed by Indian pilgrims from south to north. The idea that the mountains of central Asia were explored solely by Europeans and comparatively recently is very wide of the mark.

In many parts of the world our ancestors were afraid of mountains, regarding them as the home of evil spirits. This, however, was never the way the people of Pakistan and India thought of the Himalaya. They realized that their existence depended on the rivers which flowed from the mountain snows, and regarded the great peaks with veneration. Paths that led up to them they lined with shrines, their upper reaches they adorned with prayer-flags, their summits they worshipped as gods. Year after year they flocked to the Himalaya as pilgrims, plunging into the snows with the same ecstasy as they plunged into the sacred waters of the Ganges. And one peak they regarded as their holiest of holies, Mount Kailas. The choice was significant.

Here is what Hindu legend (*The Mahabharata*) says of Kailas.

It is the monarch of all mountains, a never-tiring worker for the common good . . . It is covered with lush forests; its rivers are sweet as ambrosia and adorned with lotus. On its upper slopes is the assembly hall of Brahma, from whose ever-flowing fountains pours the elixir of life.

Yet those who visit Kailas today describe it as a beautifully-shaped but relatively small mountain, well to the north of the main range of the Himalaya; there isn't a tree within miles of it, let alone a forest, a lotus or a fountain. And if one asks why Hindu pilgrims should have singled out this remote and apparently unremarkable peak for special veneration there can be only one answer. They realized that Kailas was the fountainhead from which stemmed the great rivers of the Indo-Ganetic plain. For on the slopes of Kailas, or within a few miles of them, rise the four major rivers of India: the Indus, Sutlej, Ganges and Brahmaputra. The inference is inescapable: that Hindu pilgrims had followed these rivers through the Himalaya to their source on the Tibetan plateau. How else could the writer of *The Mahabharata* have realized that Kailas was the fountainhead from which the life-bringing rivers flowed south into the plains?

Two thousand years later other men from the Indian sub-continent were again pushing north into the plateaux of central Asia, but their motives were very different from those of the pilgrims.

India was one of the first parts of the world to be accurately surveyed. The Great Trigonometrical Survey of India was a Herculean undertaking, described as 'perhaps the greatest geographical achievement on any continent in any age'; it took over 50 years and over 10 million man-hours to complete, and was the basis on which the rest of Asia was subsequently delineated. By the 1850s teams of surveyors were pushing into the Himalaya, setting up their observation-tables on peak after peak to enable them to fix by triangulation the height and position of the jumble of peaks ahead. Most teams consisted of one or two European-born officers and three or four native-born *Khalasis*. And their achievements as mountaineers – let alone surveyors – are almost beyond belief. At a time when seasoned climbers in the European Alps were having difficulty attaining the summits of peaks of 12,000 feet, *Khalasis* in the Himalaya and Karakoram were regularly reaching the top of far more difficult peaks of 20,000 feet – their highest-ever climb was probably made in 1869 when an unknown *Khalasi* struggled with his theodolite to the summit of Shilla (23,050 feet.)

In the early 1860s the survey was dealt an apparent death blow. The countries to the north of India – Afghanistan, Tibet, Bhutan and Nepal – closed their frontiers. British surveyors became *persona non grata*; one of them, William Johnson, who ventured over the border to try and map the Kun Lun, triggered off an international incident.

The British, however, were loath to terminate their Survey. This was partly because of a genuine desire to put *terra incognita* on the map, and partly because they wanted to know just how effective a barrier the mountains would be against a possible Russian or Chinese invasion from the north. The head of the Survey, Thomas Montgomerie, therefore decided to send disguised and specially-trained *Khalasis* beyond the frontier to make secret observations. These men were trained to walk at a uniform 2000 paces per mile, counting and recording each step, and to determine latitude at night by using a sextant and quicksilver. If caught, they faced at best ill-treatment and imprisonment, at worst torture and death. Montgomerie describes some of the tricks of their trade.

Above: The Pundit Rai Bahadur Kishen Singh. Note the rosary counting aid he is holding.

Left: Mount Kailas, the holy mountain for Buddhists and Hindus. From its slopes rise the four great rivers of the Indian sub-continent, the Indus, Sutlej, Ganges and Brahmaputra.

Right: Pundit Nain Singh, the most important of the native surveyors who took part in the Great Trigonometrical Survey of India during the 19th century.

Noticing the frequent use made by Tibetans of the rosary and prayer-wheel, I recommended my Pundits (*as the native-born explorers were called*) to carry both. It was essential that when they were counting their paces they should not be interrupted. Pundit Nain Singh found it best to march at the back of a caravan, and when people did come up to him, the sight of his prayer-wheel was enough to stop them addressing him. For when he saw anyone approaching, he at once began to whirl his wheel round, and since all good Buddhists doing this are supposed to be in religious contemplation, he was seldom disturbed. The prayer-wheel he used looked like an ordinary hand one; but inside, instead of the usual prayer Om mani padme hum, were slips of paper for recording bearings. The Pundits' rosaries, instead of the usual 108 beads had 100, every tenth bead being larger than the others. At every 100th pace a bead was dropped; each large bead to fall therefore represented 1000 paces or half a mile . . . Quicksilver is difficult to carry; but Nain Singh managed to hide some of his in a cocoa-nut, and the rest in cowrie shells sealed with wax.

The most important of the Pundits' journeys was that of Nain Singh, and the most astonishing that of Kinthup.

Nain Singh was given the job of pinpointing and collecting information on Lhasa. In 1865 he joined a caravan as it was leaving Sikkim for the forbidden city, and at once started counting his paces. It is 1580 miles from Sikkim to Lhasa; that is to say in the course of his journey Nain Sing took 3,160,000 steps, every one of which he counted and recorded. Once in the city, he fixed its position with accuracy, then set about collecting data on such diverse subjects as housing, religious rituals, the composition of the Tibetan army, crop production and imports and exports. At the end of 18 months he returned to Montgomerie with more information about Lhasa than had been gleaned by all the previous European visitors to the city put together. For this and other journeys he was awarded that most prestigious of explorers' accolades the Gold Medal of the Royal Geographical Society, 'thus publicly marking our appreciation of the noble qualities of loyalty, courage and endurance, by the display of which he has added so largely to our knowledge of Asia.'

Kinthup (his first name is not known) was given the job of tracing the course of the Brahmaputra. It was suspected that the Tsangpo which rose near Kailas and flowed east past Lhasa *might* be the same river as the Brahmaputra which, some 1000 miles to the southeast

flowed into the Bay of Bengal. There was, however, a gap of some 150 miles where both rivers were too tumultuous to be followed: a no-go area of rapids, waterfalls, deep gorges and the heaviest rainfall on Earth where the plateau of Tibet abuts the plains of Arunachal. A captain in the Royal Engineers came up with the suggestion that a number of specially marked logs should be floated down the Tsangpo, and a watch kept for them on the Brahmaputra. Kinthup was given the task of cutting and throwing in the logs.

He managed to get into Tibet disguised as the servant of a Mongolian lama. The lama seems to have had a more enjoyable time in Tibet than the pundit. We are told that in Lhasa 'he feasted with his colleagues in a monastery non-stop for six days'; that on their way to the Tsangpo 'he fell in love with the wife of his host and could in no way be persuaded to continue the journey'; and that when they ran out of money, he sold Kinthup into slavery in exchange for a horse, on which he rode off and was never seen again. After 7 months of drudgery Kinthup escaped, and, still determined to carry out his mission, began to work his way down the Tsangpo. It was a terrible journey. The passes were deep in snow; the wind was so violent he could make headway against it only by crawling on hands and knees; at night he slept in caves or fissures in the rocks. He was captured again, spent another five months as a slave in a monastery, then, under the pretext of making a pilgrimage, was granted a few weeks' absence. He returned to the Tsangpo, cut and notched 500 logs and hid them in a cave. He did not throw them into the river because it was now nearly two years since he had left Sikkim and well past the date that

Above: A Buddhist prayer wheel, carried by many of the Indian participants in the survey of India.

Below: 'Buddha's all-seeing eyes', Bodhnath, Nepal.

a watch for the logs would be kept. Returning to the monastery he did another spell of servitude; then, under the pretext of making a second pilgrimage, he journeyed secretly to Lhasa, sought out an official who was returning to Sikkim and gave him a letter to the Surveyor-General, undertaking to 'throw 50 logs per day into the Tsangpo between the 5th and the 15th of the tenth month of the Tibetan year.' He completed his term of slavery, made his way back to the cave and threw in his logs as promised; then after a journey of incredible diffi-culty, managed to make his way back to India after an absence of more than 1500 days.

Kinthup was the archetypal Pundit, the epitome of those unselfish, unrewarded men – so anonymous that they were often known only by their initials – who risked their lives for a cause they did not wholly understand and for a country other than their own. Even today and even in India and Pakistan their exploits are little known; yet in all the history of exploration there have been few finer achievements.

Explorers of the Steppe: Atkinson (c. 1851), Semyonov (c. 1855), the Fedchenkos (c. 1865), Przhevalski (c. 1875)

By the middle of the 19th century the Russians were rolling back their frontier as fast as the Americans, a century earlier, had rolled back theirs; 500 square miles a day were coming under the Tsar's suzerainty. It was of course Russian explorers who did most to open up central Asia; but they had a little-known precursor, the artist Thomas Atkinson.

Atkinson had no education, and at the age of 9 was working in a stone-mason's yard in Yorkshire. He became a skilled mason and a competent artist, and in the 1840s was sent to Hamburg to help with the restoration of an historic church. Here he met Von Humboldt who told him that 'if he wanted to see great stonework he should visit the Creator's most magnificent edifices in central Asia.' Atkinson managed to get an audience with the Tsar, who was so impressed with him that he gave him a pass to travel as his guest the length of breadth of Russia. Armed with this pass, an artist's easel and paints and not much else, Atkinson and his wife set out in 1850 on a little-known journey.

My sole objective, he wrote, was to sketch the scenery – then scarcely known in Europe . . . In 7 years I travelled some 39,500 miles, visiting places unknown to Marco Polo and the Jesuit Priests.

This, to quote the Russian explorer Semyonov, was 'an extraordinary achievement, unprecedented in the exploration of Asia.' One feels that the Atkinsons deserve to be better known, especially since their travels were characterized by courage, human warmth, and a very real love of the country they traveled through and the people they met. It is pleasant too, to record that they seem thoroughly to have enjoyed themselves – in all the literature of travel there are few more entertaining incidents than that of Mrs. Atkinson putting the male-chauvinist Kirghiz warriors in their place by refusing to give them tea until their wives had had a cup first.

A more conventional figure was Peter Semyonov who in the 1850s explored the Tien Shan, the Celestial Mountains of Chinese mythology, which lie to the north of the Takla Makan. In 1856 he arrived in the area with a force of 50 Cossack cavalry; for his expedition was not only scientific, but was intended also to show the flag and assert Moscow's authority over the Kara Kirghiz tribesmen. Semyonov made two great journeys into the Tien Shan, being the first person to study any part of it scientifically. The climax of his second and greater expedition was crossing the Zauka Pass . . .

So great was our difficulty in breathing that we could spend only a few minutes at the highest point, but at last we attained our objective and stood gazing down on a scene of unexpected beauty: a vast plain, dotted with green ice-encrusted lakes, and of so great an elevation that the mountain peaks which rose from it appeared as mere hillocks. We were now in the very heart of Asia, nearer to Delhi than Omsk, nearer the Indian Ocean than the Arctic, and midway between the Pacific and the Black Sea . . . The fire that we lit crackled fitfully and gave off no heat. Yet all around us, peeping out of the snow, were Alpine flowers of the most brilliant color.

It is typical of Semyonov that he went on to classify the Alpines. It was his *forte* as an explorer that wherever he went he collected scientific data on flora, fauna, rock-structure, climate and orography. By bringing this modern approach to the exploration of one of the least-known ranges in the world, he well deserves the title given him by the Tsar, Peter Petrovich Semenov-Tyan-Shanskiy (Semyonov of the Tien Shan.)

Alexis and Olga Fedchenko did for the Pamir what Semyonov did for the Tien Shan. In the mid 1860s they explored the upper reaches of the Zarafshan (near present-day Leninabad) and traced the river to its source. They then went on to explore the huge ice-choked valleys of the northern Pamir, where they discovered some of the largest glaciers in the world outside the polar circles. It was not, however, the glaciers which interested the Tsar, but the Fedchenkos' reports of coal, iron, marble

Left: Nicholas Przhevalski, 1839-88, the Russian explorer who made important journeys into Mongolia, Turkestan and Tibet.

and gold, and their discovery that this little-known part of central Asia was by no means as barren as had been expected.

In the occasional valley, *wrote Alexis*, every particle of soil is put to good use, and the whole area is a mosaic of fields of cotton, wheat, barley and millet, fed by an extensive system of aryks (*irrigation channels*) – we followed one for no fewer than 47 miles.

The Fedchenkos were not major explorers, for much of the terrain they traversed was already populated, and they collected comparatively little scientific data. They did, however, help to bring under the suzerainty of the Tsar an area which had been thought poor but which proved rich – Uzbekistan is now arguably the most prosperous republic in the USSR.

Semyonov and the Fedchenkos explored terrain which became part of Russia; an even greater explorer explored terrain which was eventually to become part of China. Between 1870 and 1888 Nicholas Przhevalski led four great expeditions into the deserts of the Takla Makan and the plateaux of Tibet.

The whole of central Asia, *he wrote*, between the mountains of Siberia to the north and the Himalayas of India to the south, is terra incognita; of its geology, climate, flora and fauna we are almost totally ignorant. This, it seemed to me, would be a most rewarding area for research; although I was soon to discover that its scientific attractions were counterbalanced by the appalling difficulty of the terrain – wind-lashed deserts devoid of water, and temperatures alternating between burning heat and searing cold – not to mention a suspicious and barbarous population.

Few expeditions have endured such privations over so long a period as Przhevalski's. Year after year his camels plodded over featureless plains of sand and desiccated

Above: The bleak terrain on the approaches to Mount Kongur in Xinjiang Province in western China. Przhevalski led four expeditions into this area.

Left: The remote Shimshal region of northern Pakistan, visited by the British explorer Younghusband in the late 19th century, partly through unjustified fears that it offered a practical route for a Russian invasion of India.

plateaux of rock, swept by winds against which it was at times impossible to stand. They ran out of fuel and food – 'were obliged to cut up and burn a saddle to make ourselves a little tea which was all we had that day.' Their clothes disintegrated – 'having no boots, we had to resort to sewing bits of yak hide on to our tattered leggings.' Yet Przhevalski and his men not only survived, they charted the terrain through which they trekked with meticulous accuracy *and* collected a wealth of scientific data; '1000 specimens of birds, 3000 insects, and 4000 plants, including many new to science.' Fittingly Przhevalski was buried (at his request)in his explorers' kit on the shore of Lake Issyk-kul, looking out over the tableland of central Asia where he had spent the better part of his life.

Hunters and Climbers

Hunting and exploration have often gone hand in hand. In Africa Livingstone made some of his earliest and greatest journeys in the company of big-game hunters, and Samuel Baker would probably never have set foot in the continent if it hadn't been for his 'joy of the chase'. In Asia Przhevalski could not have survived on the Tibetan plateau if he had not hunted and killed yak; while the first European to set foot in parts of the Himalaya and Hindu Kush may well have been an officer on leave seeking the heads of antelope, tiger or bear to add to his trophies.

Hunting may have been a useful adjunct to exploring, but it seldom if ever inspired great feats of exploration. Climbing, on the other hand, was the driving force which took men and women to some of the highest and remotest places on Earth.

Climbing is a modern pastime. Our ancestors feared and hated the mountains, thinking of them initially as the abode of demons and dragons, and subsequently as symbolic bastions of evil – 'a world of death which God, by curse, created evil.' The idea of climbing for pleasure originated only about 200 years ago in the European Alps. By the middle of the 19th century most of the European Alps had been climbed, and mountaineers were obliged to seek more distant heights to conquer. An obvious desideratum for them was central Asia, where the highest and most magnificent peaks on Earth are grouped together in six gargantuan ranges: the Himalaya, Hindu Kush, Karakoram, Pamirs, Tien Shan and Kun Lun.

The first person to climb in central Asia 'purely for my own pleasure' was the Englishman WW Graham who in 1883 reached the summit of the Forked Peak (20,340 feet) not far from Kanchenjunga. There followed a succession of expeditions into the mountains, with teams of anything between two and four-hundred men and women locating, reconnoitering and attempting to climb the

Above, far left: Many of Nepal's hillsides are terraced to make better use of the steep terrain.

Above: Namche Bazaar in Solu Khumbu, the Sherpa capital. Nearly all Everest expeditions taking the Nepalese route go through this important town.

Far left: The Himalaya, with Everest in the center, as seen in a distant view.

Left: One of the holiest places in the Hindu world, Pashupatinath in Kathmandu. The holy Bagmati River runs through the town, and non-Hindus are banned from visiting the area to the left of this picture.

great peaks. These climbers often penetrated into the most inaccessible places, where non-climbers would have had no reason to venture. It is doubtful, for example, if anyone early this century would have made a detailed study of the north face of Everest unless they had wanted to climb the mountain. Yet in 1921 the leader of the British attempt on the summit could write:

All approaches to Everest from the north, northwest and east have been carefully reconnoitred, and a possible route to the top was found via the Rongbuk Glacier and the northeast ridge. Some 13,000 square miles of new country was surveyed and mapped, a large number of birds and mammals were collected, the geology of the region was worked out and photographs taken of a country previously quite unknown.

This was a pattern repeated many times on many mountains in the Himalaya and their adjoining ranges. Although not usually regarded as explorers, mountaineers made a considerable contribution to the exploration of central Asia.

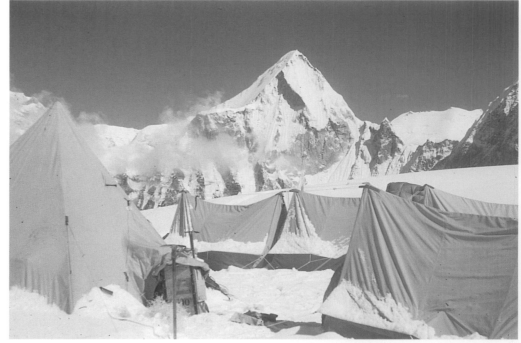

The Naturalists

By the end of the 19th century few blank spaces remained on the map outside the Polar Circles, and the heroic age of exploration – with arduous treks on foot, by camel or with man-drawn sledge – gave way to the scientific age – with explorers collecting data on flora, fauna, geomorphology, orography and climate etc. It was no longer enough for an explorer to cross a desert, hack through a forest or stand on a peak; he needed to know what rocks the desert was made of, why the forest was so impenetrable, what forces had raised the peak so high.

In the vanguard of these modern explorers have been the naturalists. Much of their work has been done in rain forests – the Earth's richest and most fragile eco-system – and the jungles of South East Asia have been a particularly fruitful area for research.

Borneo is the world's third largest island. It lies astride the equator and in the path of two annual monsoons, and more than 90 percent of it is covered with rain forest. Human beings have lived here for over 50,000 years, but it was only in the mid 19th century that they began to examine their environment scientifically, with British and Dutch colonial officials like St. John and Korthals

Top: The mighty K2. At 28,253 feet (8611m) K2 is the highest mountain in the Karakoram and the second highest in the world. Its name is derived from the 19th century British surveyors who provisionally listed it as only the second-highest peak in the Karakoram. Its temporary designation has now become its most usual name.

Above: Camp IV, established during the successful 1953 expedition which finally conquered Everest.

Above: Machapuchare, the 'fish-tail' mountain, first climbed in the 1950s. It is now out of bounds to climbers because the villagers living beneath it regard it as a holy peak.

Left: Everest, the highest mountain in the world at 29,028 feet (8828m). The route of the 1953 expedition followed the skyline ridge on the right.

making collections of plants and birds. They were joined in 1854 by one of the world's leading naturalists. Alfred Wallace had spent nearly ten years studying insects in the Amazon, but had lost his entire collection when the ship in which he was returning to England caught fire and sank. He came to south-east Asia to rebuild his collection, and it was here that he had his famous 'flash of light' which enabled him – at the same time as Darwin – to publish the theory of evolution by natural selection. He was followed, towards the end of the 19th century, by a number of ornithologists who studied the exotic and idiosyncratic birds of the forest; but it was not until 1932 that the first large-scale expedition penetrated to the heart of the island. Then Tom Harrisson's Oxford University expedition spent three months making an ecological investigation of Mount Kalulong, obtaining specimens of over 50 reptiles, 350 mammals, 1000 birds, 2500 plants and 25,000 insects and invertebrates. For Harrisson this was the start of a love affair with Borneo, where he and his wife were to spend the rest of their lives working to help the creatures – in particular the orang-utans – for whose survival they cared so deeply.

The Oxford expedition was the precursor of the more important Royal Geographical Society expedition of 1977-8 to Mulu.

Mulu is an area of limestone mountains – their lower slopes thickly covered with rain forest, their upper with mist forest – which lies near the junction of Brunei, Sabah and Sarawak in northeast Borneo. The Society's ostensible reason for going there was to prepare a plan for the Sarawak government to turn Malu into a National Park; but its more fundamental reason was to make a study in depth of the rain forest; for, to quote the expedition leader Robin Hanbury-Tenison, 'to preserve (or come to that to want to preserve) a rain forest it is essential to know it and understand it.' So 115 scientists, including the world's leading authorities in their discipline, spent 15 months in Mulu getting to know their environment.

Geomorphologists studied the karren, huge limestone pinnacles rising steeple-high out of the riot of vegetation. Ornithologists identified and ringed birds like the exotic hornbills and dancing pheasants. Botanists studied the trees and found that a typical acre supported 268 trees representing 136 species (a similar area of temperate forest would support no more than 100 trees of some 15 to 18 species.) While a team of specialists examined the forest's system of recycling, and came up with some surprising conclusions.

Laymen who stare in awe at the huge trees and riotous vegetation of a rain forest often imagine that so much growth must spring from a rich soil. This is not the case. The soils which support rain forests are weak and poor – too poor for agricul-

Left: Tom Harrisson, one of the early conservationists, who devoted much of his life to safeguarding the orang-utans of Borneo.

ture. They generate growth by a complex and delicately balanced system of recycling: a system in which leaf and twig fall, precipitation, mycelium, and the action of animals, termites and invertebrates all play their part in constantly breaking down and decomposing material and making it again available as a nutrient. This is a delicate system, vulnerable to disruption . . . and once disrupted it is almost impossible to regenerate a self-balancing environment.

At the end of 15 months the scientists had collected sufficient data to make a well-informed analysis of what a rain forest was, how it functioned, and how and why it should be preserved.

Those who went to Mulu thought it 'a wonderful experience'; they had a good time; they suffered minimal hardship and little danger, and it might be thought that their achievements were insignificant compared, say, to Hsuan Tsang's or Przhevalski's. But this is not so. They were *bona fide* explorers carrying out *bona fide* exploration: cerebral rather than physical, but none the less important. They may have marched to the beat of a different drum to Hsuan Tsang and Przhevalski, but they marched in the same direction and with the same purpose: reaching into the unknown to bring back knowledge.

Explorers of the Arabian Deserts: Doughty (*c.* 1875) and Thesiger (*c.* 1950)

One of the last parts of non-Arctic Eurasia to be explored was the Arabian Desert, and in particular the Empty Quarter, that 'Abode of Emptiness' which lies south of the Persian Gulf and east of the Red Sea.

Arabia is a land of searing heat by day and bitter cold by night, violent wind and an almost total absence of water: difficult terrain to explore. And to the difficulty of the terrain has been added the hostility of the people. For Arabia is the heartland of the Muslim world; until comparatively recently unbelievers caught in Mecca or

Medina were 'offered the choice of circumcision or death,' and Christians trying to explore the country were obliged to travel in disguise.

The first European who is known to have explored Arabia (apart from the luckless Gallus whose efforts cost some 5000 of his troops their lives) was Pedro de Covilhao, a Portuguese spy who spoke Arabic. In the course of his travels he landed in 1487 at Jiddah, shaved his head, disguised himself as a pilgrim and managed to visit Mecca – a more hazardous venture it would be hard to

imagine. In the course of the next 300 years the only Europeans to reach the Holy City were either in disguise or in slavery: Varthema got there posing as a Mameluke guard, Pitts as a slave forced by torture to become a Muslim, Seetzan disguised as a dervish, Burckhardt as a genuine convert. In the early 19th century a number of minor scientific-cum-military expeditions explored the south coast and its hinterland, where the British were anxious to establish coaling stations for their ships *en route* to India; during these expeditions the Hadharamawt and the Rub'al Khali were roughly surveyed by Wellsted and von Wrede. Then in the late 19th century there arrived in Arabia an explorer who was important on two counts.

Charles Doughty made no attempt to hide his faith or his nationality, but was accepted by the Bedouin for what he was – a European and a Christian. And he was a gifted writer, whose works helped to bridge the gulf which divided the Christian world from the Muslim. In *Arabia Deserta* he described his journey first by camel caravan from Damascus to Mecca, and then with the nomadic Bedouin northeast into the geographical heart of Arabia. His prose encapsulates the harsh beauty of the desert: 'rock partridges were everywhere in this high granite country, smelling in the sun of the resinous sweetness of southern wood.' It encapsulates also the character of the desert people: their generosity and intolerance, piety and pride, and their never-failing *camaraderie*. With the publication of *Arabia Deserta* Europeans were given the chance to understand at least something of a world that had previously been closed to them.

An explorer who was not only accepted by the desert people but who chose to follow their way of life was Wilfred Thesiger.

Thesiger was born in Addis Ababa and educated at Eton and Magdalen College Oxford; the first fact is more significant than the second, for all his life he was an *aficionado* of deserts and desert people. In the 1930s he traveled with Denakil tribesmen in the desolate and little-known highlands of Ethiopia, and explored the Tibesti Mountains in the Sahara. In 1946 he was asked by the United Nations to visit the Empty Quarter to study locust movements. No European had ever lived in this waterless wilderness; but Thesiger spent four years there (1947-50) crossing and recrossing the desert with a group of Bedu tribesmen, finding the harsh terrain a physical challenge and the companionship of the Bedu an inspiration. 'I was humbled,' he wrote 'by these illiterate herdsmen who possessed, in greater measure than I, generosity, courage,

endurance and patience.' Subsequently he spent 3 years with the Marsh Arabs, again living as one of them and finding their way of life more to his liking than that of the West.

Memories of my visit to the Marshes, *he wrote*, have never left me: firelight on a half-turned face, the crying of geese, duck flighting in to feed, a boy's voice singing somewhere in the dark, canoes moving in procession down a waterway, the setting sun seen crimson through the smoke of burning reedbeds . . . Stars reflected in dark water, the croaking of frogs, peace and continuity, the stillness of a world that has never known an engine. Once again I experienced a longing to share this life, and to be more than a mere spectator.

Thesiger has been called the last of the great oldfashioned explorers; this is true in as much as he was one of the last people to tread where no European had trod before. But he is also among the first of the modern explorers: men and women who in increasing number are seeking the lonely places of the Earth and finding there peace-of-mind and a way of life more rewarding than the preoccupation of the Western world with the acquisition of trivia.

Above left: Mecca, the holy city of the Muslim world, showing the sacred Kaaba.

Above: Wilfred Thesiger, *aficionado* of deserts and desert people.

Left: Charles Doughty, whose classic work *Arabia Deserta* extolled the camaraderie of the nomadic Bedouin.

Africa

Africa was the cradle of the human race and the continent abuts the Mediterranean where many of the earliest civilizations evolved. One might have expected it to be among the first parts of the world to be explored. Yet only 150 years ago large areas of Africa were a blank on the map. There are two reasons for this. For millennia the Sahara Desert prevented the continent being explored by land, while a combination of difficult winds and currents prevented it being explored by sea.

The Sahara covers over 9,000,000 square kilometers – an area greater than the USA. It is made up of vast waterless plains of gravel and sand which stretch from the Atlantic Ocean to the Indian and become increasingly arid as one travels south. A more effective barrier to exploration would be hard to imagine.

Winds and currents were an equally effective deterrent. In the early days of sail, ships which stood south down the coast of Africa were unable to get back to Europe. For in the Atlantic Ocean the North East Trade Winds and the Canary Current combined to swirl vessels into the Sargasso Sea; while in the Indian Ocean the North East Monsoons and the Agulhas Current combined to sweep them into the roaring forties. These, for ships unable to sail against the wind, were no-go areas. Not until the evolution in the 15th century of the Portuguese caravel were Europeans able to voyage down the coast of Africa and return. Prior to the 15th century exploration was therefore limited to the occasional venture inland from the north coast, or was carried out by non-Europeans.

'The Glory that was Greece and the Grandeur that was Rome.'

The Greeks and Romans both had empires on the north coast of Africa. The Greeks, in search of more land and in particular more food-producing land, founded colonies along the shores of present-day Egypt, Libya and Tunisia; these eventually became independent city-states (like Carthage) which fell under the domination of Rome.

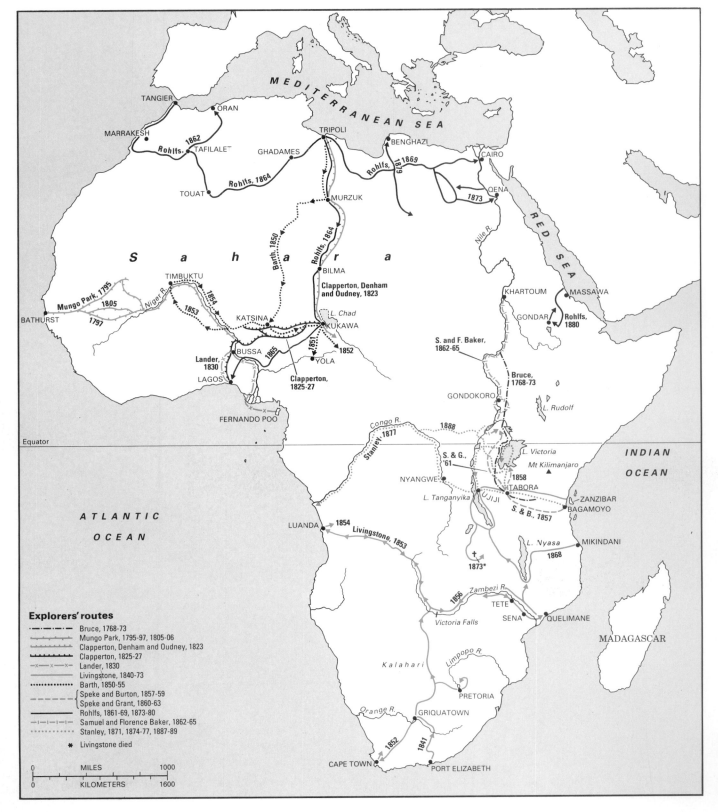

Explorers' routes

- Bruce, 1768-73
- Mungo Park, 1795-97, 1805-06
- Clapperton, Denham and Oudney, 1823
- Clapperton, 1825-27
- Lander, 1830
- Livingstone, 1840-73
- Barth, 1850-55
- Speke and Burton, 1857-59
- Speke and Grant, 1860-63
- Rohlfs, 1861-69, 1873-80
- Samuel and Florence Baker, 1862-65
- Stanley, 1871, 1874-77, 1887-89
- * Livingstone died

Previous page: The glorious panorama of Victoria Falls.

Left: Major journeys in the European exploration of Africa.

Left: The extent of the Roman Empire under Diocletian.

ROMAN EMPIRE UNDER DIOCLETIAN
BOUNDARIES OF DIOCESES
ROMAN CAMPS

In its heyday the Roman empire in Africa stretched from Elephantine (near Aswan) on the Nile, to Sala (near Rabat) on the Atlantic coast of Morocco. From these outposts, occasional forays were made into the unknown.

In 25 BC Roman legions under Petronius were involved in a punitive expedition against the Queen of Ethiopia. This led to the mapping of the Nile as far as the Fourth Cataract, where the river cuts through the Baiyuda Desert. In about 55 AD the Emperor Nero planned a more ambitious venture, ordering an expedition led by two unknown centurions to discover the source of the Nile. They made a brave attempt, following the river for more than 600 miles before they were halted by

a region of vast marshes, where plants and mud and water are so intermingled that one cannot force a way through either on foot or by boat.

They had reached the Sudd: the papyrus-swamps of the Middle Nile which no European was to see again until the 18th century.

In another part of Africa another centurion, Maternus, made an even longer journey. In 19 BC the Roman Governor of Tunisia, while campaigning on the desert, reached the oasis of Ghadamis. From here we are told that Julius Maternus made 'a four months journey to the south, with camels, to the region of Agisymba, where at a great lake the rhinoceroses foregather.' We are not able to identify Agisymba; but the only great lake south of Tunisia where there were likely to have been rhinoceros is Lake Chad. It therefore seems likely that Maternus traveled for more than 1000 miles, through the Tibesti Mountains, to a lake which no European was to sight again until the 18th century.

From the western outposts of their empire the Romans made at least one major foray into the unknown. In 42 AD Suetonius Paulinus led a punitive expedition against

Left: The temple of Jupiter, Juno and Minerva in the Roman Capitol at Dougga in Tunisia, one of the best-preserved Roman settlements in north Africa.

the Moors which took him through the Atlas Mountains to the River Ger – probably the Souss, which flows into the Atlantic at Agadir. Here he reported 'vast numbers of birds' – doubtless the swallows, skuas, tern and storks which call in to feed in this part of Morocco on their migration south. Also 'vast woods of scented timber' – doubtless the stands of larch and juniper which flourish in this periphery of the Sahara.

If one wonders why the Romans' successors did not make greater efforts to push south, one reason seems to be that the North African seaboard suffered a decline in importance and prosperity; it degenerated from an area where people put down roots to a corridor through which nomadic people traveled: a migratory route for Vandals from the northwest, Berbers from the southwest, and successive waves of Arabs from the east. These nomadic people often had with them great flocks of goats which browsed away the scanty vegetation, eroded the soil and allowed the desert to take over areas which in Roman times had been a mosaic of cornfields and olive groves. Today the ruins of cities like Leptis Magna, with their magnificent aqueducts, theaters, basilica, libraries and multitudinous public baths rise out of a sea of sand. By the Middle Ages the towns of the north Sahara were less prosperous than those of the south.

Above: An Egyptian cargo vessel depicted in a 1st century Roman mosaic. Demand in the Roman world for exotic African goods helped to develop contacts between the civilizations.

Top left: The ruins of the Roman town of Volubilis in Morocco show the former grandeur of the Roman presence here.

Below left: The Arab city of Constantine as it appeared to 18th century European visitors.

The Travels of Ibn Battuta (1352 – 1353)

The first and greatest non-African explorers of the Sahara were Arab merchants of the Middle Ages who pioneered trade routes across the desert long before Europeans set foot in it. One of the last of these great Arab travelers was Ibn Battuta, and his journey across the Sahara reveals how much was known about the desert in the Middle Ages and how prosperous it was.

Battuta was the most far-ranging traveler-by-land in history. He was born in 1304 in Tangier, and between 1325 and 1355 he visited almost every corner of the known world, from the Volga in the north to Sumatra in the south, and from Marrakesh in the west to Peking in the east. In 1352 he set out on one of the last of his journeys, across the Sahara.

I bought camels, *he wrote*, and four months' forage for them, and set off through the desert for the distant Land of the Negroes . . . After 25 days we came to Taghaza, an unattractive village where the water is brackish, there are no trees, and the houses are built of blocks of salt. This salt is found lying in thick slabs, as though tool-squared, on the surface of the desert. Negroes often come here and take away the salt, which serves in their country as a currency.

Leaving Taghaza, Battuta joined a caravan which plodded south for 12 days through featureless desert,

passing the skeletons of several previous travellers and their camels who had died of thirst . . . There is no visible track here – nothing but sand blown hither and thither by the wind . . . This part of the desert is haunted by demons, and if a man is

Left: An 18th century battle with corsairs in Algiers harbor, from Chatelaine's *Atlas Historique*. The slave trading activities of the corsairs discouraged contact between north Africa and Europe until the 19th century.

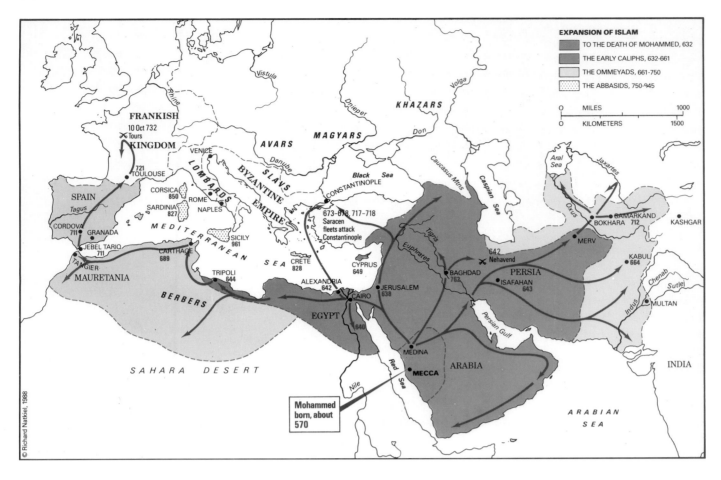

© Richard Natkiel, 1988

Left: The expansion of Islam which established Muslim civilizations north and south of the Sahara. Contact with the Muslim world's scientists and astronomers brought new techniques in navigation and shipbuilding to northern Europe's explorers and traders.

alone they make sport of him and so disorder his mind that he loses his way and perishes.

Eventually they came to Tasarahla, where they rested for a week beside subterranean springs before finding a guide to take them on the final stage of their journey to Iwalatan in southeast Mauritania. Here Battuta made contact with the people he called Negroes.

His first impression was not favorable. 'They have poor manners,' he wrote, 'and show a great contempt for the people of other races.' This underlines the fact that the peoples of the south Sahara thought of themselves as a cut above their neighbors. And with good reason. For whereas Eurasia in the 14th century was suffering a recession, due largely to the Black Death, the kingdoms of the southern Sahara were enjoying a boom. Mali, Songhai and the Hausa States were, in those days, famous throughout the Islamic and Christian worlds for their wealth and culture. Their capitals were great walled cities, thronged with merchants and university students. When their kings traveled abroad they outdid their European counterparts in the magnificence of their retinue. (In 1324 when the king of Mali went on a pilgrimage to Mecca he took with him so much gold that the currencies of the Middle East emporiums had to be devalued.) Nor was this wealth the monopoly of a royal *élite*. To quote Battuta: 'The inhabitants of these cities live by trade. Each year they travel to Egypt, and bring back the finest fabrics and wares. They live in luxury and ease, vying with one another in the number of their slaves.' He sums up the source of their wealth in a single sentence: 'in their country are many gold mines.'

The gold mines in fact were not in the Sahara, but along what used to be known as The Gold Coast. And what fantastic mines they were, providing over two-thirds of the gold then in circulation in the Old World. This gold could not be transported by sea, since vessels were unable to make the passage from the Gold Coast to Europe because of adverse currents and winds; it had therefore to be transported by land, by camel-caravans – which exported gold, slaves and the produce of the forest, and imported salt, linen and weapons. These car-

van routes were the arteries through which flowed the wealth of the Sahara kingdoms.

Battuta spent nearly two years in these kingdoms, visiting Mali, 'the principal city of the Negrolands'; Jenne, 'where the university has many scholars and poets,' and Timbuktu, 'where many times each year caravans of up to 4000 camels would arrive from Egypt.' He returned to Tangier in 1355.

Battuta may have been a traveler rather than an explorer, but his journeys shed light on little-known parts of the world.

Left: René Caillie's drawing of Timbuktu, 1830. The square sandstone buildings had probably changed little since the days of Ibn Battuta.

The Mystery of the Niger and Timbuktu

At the end of the 18th century Africa was still, for Europeans, 'the dark continent,' a land of mystery; and one river and one town epitomised this aura of mystery: the Niger and Timbuktu.

The Niger lay only a couple of thousand miles from the capitals of Europe; yet as late as 1800 neither its source, its course nor its outlet to the sea was known; many people thought it flowed into the Nile. In 1795 a young naval doctor, Mungo Park, set out to try and follow the river from source to mouth. As a white Christian travelling through Muslim territory, he was asking for trouble. Within a couple of months of setting out from the Gambia every one of his companions had either deserted or died. Park, however, was not short of courage, and he struggled on alone, harrassed, spat at, robbed, humiliated and eventually flung into prison. After 3 months he escaped, at last reached the Niger and followed it downstream for some 100 miles. By this time he was penniless, starving and racked by malaria and dysentery. He would almost certainly have died if he had not been befriended by a slave-trader, who restored him to health and escorted him back to the Gambia. Park had suffered much and achieved little. Ten years later he was back again, this time with a motley entourage of 45 servicemen, most of whom had joined his expedition in the hope of earning a free discharge. Everything went wrong. They set out from the Gambia at the wrong time of year, with the temperature 130°F and the troops in their heavy red uniforms fainting in the heat; their pack-asses were stung to death by bees; their guides were flogged to death by tribal chiefs; they were attacked by lions in the day, and wild dogs in the night; as they swam the swollen rivers they were dragged under by crocodiles. By the time they reached the Niger, their numbers had been reduced from 45 to 12. And their troubles were not over. More men died of fever, and the canoes which they bought with the last of their money turned out to be rotten and foundered. Eventually the survivors – Park, four soldiers and two native guides – attempted to float downriver. They got as far as the Bussa Rapids; but here, a later report tells us,

they were showered with missiles and poisoned arrows . . . They fired at their attackers until their ammunition was expended; then, locking themselves in each other's arms, they sprang into the water, sank, and were never seen again.

In 1822 another expedition, led by Clapperton, Oudney and Denham set out for the Niger, this time approaching the river from the north. Their efforts were more disputatious than successful. The leaders quarreled, Denham accusing Clapperton of having homosexual relations with their native servants. They split up, and made individual journeys in the region of Lake Chad, which no European had sighted since Julius Maternus in the first century BC. Their exploits helped open up a little-known part of the Sahara, but did little to solve the mystery of the Niger.

The river was eventually delineated by Richard Lander, the son of a Cornish innkeeper whom Clapperton had employed as his valet. Clapperton was making another attempt to follow the Niger in 1826 when he contracted malaria; Lander had nursed him and held him in his arms as he lay dying on the riverbank at Sokoto, and four years later the gentleman's gentleman returned to Africa determined to fulfil his dead master's dream. By now it had been established that the Niger rose in the coastal mountains of Guinea, flowed east along the periphery of the Sahara, then swung south through present-day Nigeria; but no-one knew where it entered the sea. Lander and his brother approached their objective by a new

Below: Mungo Park. After his first African journey Park published *Travels in the Interior of Africa*, and tried to settle as a doctor in his native Scotland. However, he was not happy and returned to Africa for a second and fatal attempt to trace the course of the Niger.

Below left: Hugh Clapperton, 1788-1827. Like Mungo Park, Clapperton was a Scot and he too published a *Narrative* of his first journey while the events of his second were described by Lander.

route. They headed inland from the Slave Coast until they came to a great river; they followed this river upstream until they had identified it beyond doubt as the Niger, then reversing course they followed it downstream to its mouth. It was a tough journey, to some extent relieved by the exotic beauty of the scenery –

Magnificent festoons of creeping plants, forever green, hung from the tops of even the tallest trees, and, dropping to the water's edge, formed an immense natural grotto through which we paddled.

The river did not give up its secrets easily – their canoes were capsized by hippopotamuses and sunk by storms; they were attacked by crocodiles, threatened with poisoned arrows and captured and held to ransom by Ibo tribesmen – but at last they emerged through one of the many channels of the Niger delta, and were picked up by the slave-trader *Thomas* and given passage to England.

This was an important piece of exploration, carried out, in the words of the Admiralty, 'by a man who was very humble but very intelligent.' And, the Admiralty might have added, very brave.

At much the same time as an English valet was putting the Niger on the map an equally improbable explorer, a French baker, was doing the same for Timbuktu.

Rumors about Timbuktu had been circulating in Europe for a millennium; its libraries were said to contain priceless manuscripts and its houses to be roofed with gold; yet no European had ever set foot in the city and lived. A Scottish army officer, Alexander Laing, tried to get there in a caravan from Tripoli, disguised as a Moorish trader; however, he was recognized by the Tuareg tribesmen of the desert, who shot stabbed and left him for dead, 'with gashes all over his body, his right hand

Left: A contemporary engraving of Clapperton in Nigeria.

almost severed, his jaw broken, an ear cut off, and his scalp slashed open in five places.' Somehow he survived, and was carried by Moors who took pity on him into Timbuktu. Recovering, he tried to get back to Europe, but was again recognized by the Tuareg, who this time made no mistake. They strangled him with their turbans, then hacked off his head.

René Caillie prepared better and fared better. The 6th son of a French baker from Mauzé, he was a frail-looking

Below: Hippopotamuses in a Nigerian river, one of the hazards which Lander had to overcome on his journey.

Far left: The German traveler Heinrich Barth made important travels in central Africa in a British government-sponsored expedition in the 1850s.

Left: A mosque in present-day Timbuktu in Mali. The building, however, was part of a university famous throughout the Arab world in the 15th and 16th centuries.

young man with sorrowful eyes, an air of patient resignation, uneducated, unskilled and painfully shy. He arrived in Senegal in 1816, 'determined to make myself famous by some important discovery.' For 10 years he took part in various expeditions, all of which came to grief in the forests, swamps and unhealthy hinterland of West Africa; then, hearing that the Geographical Society of Paris were offering a 10,000 franc reward to the first person to bring back a description of Timbuktu, he decided to make the city his goal.

His preparations were eminently sensible. He spent a year living among the Brakna Moors, learning their customs and language; he bought and studied the Koran; and he invented a plausible cover-story: that he had been born in Egypt of Arab parents, taken to France as a baby by troops of Napoleon's army, and was now trying to get back to the country of his birth *via* Timbuktu. He set out in April 1827. The going was difficult: first over the steep coastal mountains of Guinea, then through endless swamps where he became disorientated and lost. At last he reached the Niger, only to succumb to scurvy.

Violent pains in my mouth warned me I had this dreadful disease. My palate became bare, the bone peeling away in layers; my teeth dropped out of their sockets. For a fortnight I was without sleep, and in such agony I feared the pain might damage my brain . . . but a kind old mother brought me rice-water twice a day, and after 6 weeks I began to feel better.

Early in 1828 he joined a caravan bound for Jenne – 'a pleasant town, its people well-dressed, lively and intelligent.' Here he exchanged the last of his valuables for the local currency – cowrie-shells – and bought a place in one of the huge ramshackle canoes trading downriver to Timbuktu. After a nightmare journey – threatened by pillaging Tuaregs and nearly suffocating to death as he hid under bales of cotton – he at last reached the city of his dreams. 'Never,' he wrote, 'have I felt deeper emotion or deeper satisfaction. But I dared not show my feelings. To God alone did I confide my joy.'

Timbuktu, however, turned out to be very different from the exotic emporium of popular imagination.

It consists of a huddle of small houses, most of them built of mud, set in the middle of a vast and featureless expanse of sand. Everything was enveloped in silence; not even the song of a bird could be heard.

There were no houses roofed with gold, no libraries filled with priceless manuscripts; only the occasional caravan of camels bringing wares which were unloaded into dusty storerooms waiting to be taken away by other caravans of camels. Timbuktu, Caillie realized, was a place wealth often passed through but seldom remained.

Below: René Auguste Caillie won a 10,000 franc prize from the Geographical Society of Paris for his dangerous journey.

Left: The town of Kirina in Mali, seen in a present-day photograph, was one of the principal centers of the empire of Sundiata visited by Ibn Battuta.

His homeward journey was another epic of endurance. He joined a caravan bound for Tripoli: 1400 camels and 400 slaves. Month after month the sun blazed down on them; sandstorms enveloped them; the Tuareg robbed them; they ran out of food and water, and were reduced to sucking their blood and drinking their urine. But at least they reached Tripoli and Caillie managed to struggle back to Tangier and eventually to France.

He enjoyed a brief spell of popular acclaim, but it was not long before doubts were raised about the authenticity of his story. If he had come back with reports of vaults of gold he would probably have been believed; but because he described Timbuktu as it was and not as it was thought to be, he was doubted. It was only after the great Saharan journeys of the German Heinrich Barth (1850-55) that the truth of everything Caillie had reported was confirmed. By then the luckless Frenchman had died, penniless and forgotten.

The Great Trek (1835 – 40)

In North Africa exploration was gradual, with the people of Eurasia slowly penetrating the Sahara, trading, mingling and often intermarrying with the original negroid inhabitants. In South Africa, in contrast, exploration was as sudden as the explosion of a gun, with a whole nation fanning out in a spur-of-the-moment migration across the veld.

Throughout the 18th century Cape Town was a flourishing Dutch colony: a port-of-call known as 'The Tavern of the Seas' because it provided fresh meat, fruit and vegetables to ships' companies *en route* to the east. The Dutch colonists – like everyone else in those days – took what land they needed by *force majeure* and reduced the indigenous people to subservience. By the early 19th century the colony consisted of roughly equal numbers of white Dutch farmers and black Bantu slaves, compressed into a relatively small area within 250 miles of Cape Town. This thriving community was handed over as part of the spoils of the Napoleonic Wars to the British, who soon brought in legislation which struck at the very root of the Dutch farmers' prosperity. They abolished slavery.

This, to the Dutch, was unjustified interference with their traditional way of life. If they were not allowed to own slaves *inside* the British colony, they would own them *outside*. They got together their cattle and sheep, loaded their belongings on to their wagons, and headed into the unknown.

This mass migration, known as the Great Trek, began in 1835, reached its climax in 1836 and continued into the 1840s. A few families set out alone, but most banded together into wagon-trains of about 100 white men, women and children and as many black servants: the idea being to form a group large enough to defend itself but not so large it could not live off the land through which it passed. So a whole nation headed north:

Trekking forever over never-ending grass,
They had no home except the tented wagon,
And the great plain and the great sky,
And silence.

Among the first and greatest of these *Voortrekkers* were the Trichardts.

The Trichardts teamed up with the Van Rensburgs, the two families making a group of about 80 white people (more than half of them children); they traveled in 11 wagons and took with them 500 cattle and 2000 sheep and goats. In the autumn of 1835 they crossed the Orange River and headed north over a seemingly endless plain. They advanced slowly – no more than 5 or 6 kilometers a day – with their animals grazing *en route*. After 6 months they reached the approaches to the Drakensberg Mountains. This, the Trichardts decided, was the promised land: good pasture, plenty of game and a long way from the British: here they would build a new life.

Left: Table Bay at the Cape of Good Hope as seen in the late 18th century by artist W Hodges.

The Van Rensburgs, however, decided to push even farther afield. This was a mistake. They ran into a Zulu war impi and were massacred.

The Zulus gave the Great Trek an unexpected dimension of danger. When the *Voortrekkers* had set out they were not anticipating opposition – less than a dozen of the Trichardts and Van Rensburgs even carried guns. However, in the coastal region of present-day Natal, the charismatic tribal leader Shaka had transformed the Zulus into one of the most highly-disciplined and highly successful war-machines the world has ever known: 'a cross between the Spartans of ancient Greece and the Panzer divisions of Hitler's Germany.' Hungry for more land, the Zulus began to march south at the same time as the *Voortrekkers* began to push north. They met head on, transforming the Great Trek from a pastoral migration to a racial war.

The Trichardts were soon in difficulty. They tried very

Below: A sketch by W H Coetzee of the Trichardts' wagons at Wit Rivier Poort during their trek in 1837.

Left: Dutch farmers returning from a hunting trip, by Samuel Daniell.

hard to put down roots building houses, schools and a church, and laying out gardens and irrigation channels. But after a couple of years they began to run short of essentials, in particular gunpowder for their rifles; their clothes disintegrated, their cattle succumbed to the tsetse fly, and what had happened to the Van Rensburgs made them feel very much out on a limb. They decided to head for the coast, where they had been told the land was good, there were Portuguese settlements, and they would feel less isolated. Across their path lay a seemingly unsurmountable barrier: the Drakensbergs.

All *Voortrekkers* who crossed this rugged 11,000-foot range had a difficult time, and this was particularly true of the Trichardts who pioneered the trail. They were faced with a maze of steep-sided valleys, most of them ending in cul-de-sacs; fast flowing rivers which had to be crossed and recrossed; huge cliffs up which their dismantled wagons and unfortunate animals had to be hoisted; altitude sickness and sleeping sickness; malaria and the tsetse fly. For two months it seemed there was no way through.

We were all in great distress, *writes Trichardt*, and on the point of giving up, but I told my companions to put their trust in God . . . and suddenly there was nothing ahead. The mountainside dropped away in sheer walls and jagged krantze, and far below us lay gray-green plains fading into the horizon.

This was a great feat of exploration; and even today those who live in the shadow of the Drakensbergs speak with

Below: The structure of a typical ox-wagon as used by the *Voortrekkers*.

Left: A black slave in South Africa holds a copy of the announcement of the abolition of slavery in 1833, the event that inspired the Great Trek.

Right: The difficult terrain of the Drakensbergs, nonetheless crossed successfully by many of the *Voortrekkers*.

Above: The Battle of Blood River in December 1838 was a victory for the trekkers over the Zulus and is still remembered in Afrikaner history as securing, for a time at least, the survival of the trekkers in Natal.

Left: A contemporary engraving of the difficulties of crossing the Drakensberg.

awe of the first white people who suddenly appeared among them with their wagons and oxen, apparently out of the sky.

Few of the Trichardts survived the next six months; for the fever of the coastal plains proved more deadly than that of the veld, and by the end of 1838 every one of the family had either died or returned to Cape Town.

What happened to the Trichardts and the Van Rens-burgs underlines the fact that the *Voortrekkers* had a hard time. Eventually they defeated the Zulus, brought the tsetse flies and the mosquitos under control, and took possession of a land that was beautiful, fertile, and could boast the richest goldmines on Earth. But they had had to pay dearly for this land with their blood, sweat and tears, and often their lives. What is hard-won is not often easily given up.

The Search for the Sources of the Nile

Bruce and the Blue Nile (1768 – 1772)

As little as 150 years ago the Nile was an enigma. It came pouring out of an arid desert, seemingly without either rainfall or tributaries to augment its flow, and no-one had ever been able to follow it upstream to discover where it came from. 'Of the sources of the Nile,' wrote Herodotus in the 4th century BC, 'no-one can give any account. It enters Egypt from parts unknown.' And this was about the sum total of our knowledge about the river until late in the 18th century.

It used to be thought that the first European to explore the upper reaches of the Nile was 'Ethiopian Bruce', a gifted but irascible Scot who reached the source of the river's main feeder, the Blue Nile, in 1770. In fact the first European to reach the headwaters of the Blue Nile was a Jesuit priest, Father Lobo, who had established a mission on the shores of Lake Tana a century earlier. It was, how-ever, Bruce who provided the first description of this part of the world which was widely read.

He prepared for his journey with great thoroughness, learning Arabic, practising for several years as a doctor in Cairo, and arming himself with letters of introduction to just about every influential official in Ethiopia. His original plan was to push upriver from Aswan; he was, however, thwarted by hostile tribes, and was obliged to

Above & left: Two views of James Bruce discovering the source of the Nile which indicate the hold this quest had on the imaginations of his contemporaries and the Victorians. At left Bruce is depicted drinking the health of King George III in celebration of his discovery.

Eng^d by S.Freeman

cross to the Red Sea and head inland from Massawa. Late in 1770 he struggled through to the Ethiopian capital of Gondar. Here he had enough adventures to fill a volume of the *Arabian Nights*, curing the palace children of smallpox, getting drunk on honey-wine at endless banquets ('All the married women ate drank and smoaked like men; it is impossible to convey any idea of this bacchanalian scene in terms of common decency',) and being given command of a troop of Imperial horses. It was while campaigning with the latter that he visited the Tissiat Falls where the Blue Nile empties out of Lake Tana, and the swamp known as Ghish Abbai then regarded as the river's source.

The fall he describes as

the most magnificent sight I had ever seen . .. The river fell in one sheet of water, above half a mile in breadth, and with a force and noise truly terrible, which stunned me and made me dizzy. A thick fume or haze covered the falls and hung over the course of the steam, marking its track, though the water was not seen.

Bruce knew that Lobo had seen the falls before him and made no attempt to claim their discovery, though as a militant Presbyterian he felt obliged to try and discredit 'the fanatic priest' by disputing his description and measurement of the Falls. He went on to visit the swamp where the Little Abbai River seeps up from underground springs. Having made these discoveries, he was eager to return home. He was, however, delayed in Ethiopia for more than a year; for the country, then as now, was in the throes of famine and civil war. When, in 1772, he was at last allowed to leave, he followed the Blue Nile downriver to its junction with the White Nile at Halfaya. Here he took measurements which indicated that the latter river was deeper and had a stronger flow; nonetheless he continued to claim that he had discovered the source of the Nile.

Back in Britain, he published an account of his adventures which was hugely and deservedly popular. Its title says it all: *Travels to discover the Sources of the Nile in the Years 1768, 1769, 1770, 1771, 1772 and 1773 by James Bruce of Kinnaird Esq. F.R.S., Vols. I to V.* It was a long, opinionated, erudite, entertaining and boastful work; it was also almost entirely truthful – although this was often doubted at the time. For Bruce was his own worst enemy, and his tetchiness and vanity invited disbelief. It is only posthumously that he has been recognized as the first of the great European explorers who very definitely 'put Africa on the map.'

Top left: James Bruce, 1730-94 He reached the source of the Blue Nile in November 1770.

Above: Burton in disguise as Haji Abdullah during his journey to Mecca in 1853.

Left: Burton photographed in 1876.

Burton and Lake Tanganyika (1857 – 58)

In the 1840s three German missionaries traveling in Kenya unexpectedly sighted snow-capped mountains astride the equator. These, it was thought, might turn out to be the legendary Mountains of the Moon, where the ancient Greeks had sited their 'fountains' which fed the Nile. In 1856 the Royal Geographical Society sponsored an expedition to follow up the missionaries' sighting; the man they chose as its leader was Richard Burton.

Burton was formidable in appearance – he described his looks as 'Satanic'; formidable in intellect – he spoke 26 languages and was the world's leading authority on Islamic erotic literature; and formidable in achievement – for he had already traveled in disguise to the forbidden cities of Mecca and Harar. With his second-in-command, the quietly obstinate John Hanning Speke, he set out with 100 porters from Zanzibar in June, 1857.

They made slow progress, for the climate was humid and the terrain difficult; soon both Burton and Speke had succumbed to malaria. It took them nearly 5 months to struggle the 500 miles to Tabora, a center of the slave trade. Here they were told of 'a great inland sea' only a couple of hundred miles to the west; this, they felt, was a likely source of the Nile, and in the expectation of making a major discovery they headed into the unknown. It was a terrible journey. They suffered from just about every illness that white people in equatorial Africa are prone to: fever, dysentery, hallucinations, sleeping sickness and elephantiasis. Burton's legs became paralysed; Speke went both deaf and blind. But at last they came to 'the great inland sea'. Here they suffered what to say the least was a disappointment. For when they explored the lake they found that although several great rivers flowed into it, none flowed out of it. They had discovered Lake Tanganyika; but it was not the source of the Nile.

On their way back they heard rumors of another great lake 'which no white man has ever seen'. Burton, whose legs were still paralysed, stayed at Tabora; while Speke,

who had partially recovered his sight, followed up this new lead. After a trek of 25 days, he came suddenly to

a vast expanse of pale blue water, stretching into the distance as far as the eye could see . . . I had no doubt but that the lake at my feet gave birth to that river which has been the object of so many explorers.

He came back to Burton and said that he had found the source of the Nile.

Burton was happy to acknowledge that his companion had discovered a great lake which might be part of the Nile river-system. But as he rightly pointed out Speke had no evidence to support his claim that his lake was the sole source – or indeed any source – of the Nile for he had explored only a small section of its southern shore, and had not seen any river – let alone the Nile – flow out of it. They agreed to go back to London and report jointly to the Society.

After another harrowing trek, with Burton still having

Above: A scene on the shores of Lake Tanganyika, taken from a contemporary account of the travels of the Bakers.

Below: The desert camp of Richard Burton, after the painting by Charles Tyrwhitt Drake.

to be carried in a stretcher, and Speke now racked by convulsions which made him bark like a dog, they eventually reached Cairo. Here the flamboyant Burton dilly-dallied in a brothel, 'a precious scene of depravity, beating the Arabian Nights all to chalks!' while the dutiful Speke returned to England and made his report to the Society. The next step was obvious. Another expedition was needed to investigate Speke's Lake. The question was who should lead it? The Society decided on Speke rather than Burton: a choice which triggered off bitter controversy and a personal feud between the two explorers which developed into a *cause célèbre*.

Speke and Lake Victoria (1860 – 63)

Speke set out in the spring of 1860. With him were James Grant, a self-effacing Scot as his second-in-command, and a cumbersome entourage of Hottentot policemen, Indian soldiers, and Negro slaves; also large numbers of mules, donkeys and goats. The country they passed through was thickly populated, and as they approached Lake Victoria a succession of local rulers milked the expedition of its valuables. The most demanding – and the most dangerous – was Mutesa, the king of Buganda, a 19th century Idi Amin. As Alan Moorhead wrote in *The White Nile*,

Hardly a day went by without some victim being executed at Mutesa's command, and this was done wilfully, casually, as a kind of game. A girl would commit some breach of etiquette by talking too loudly, a page would neglect to close or open a door, and at a sign from Mutesa they would be taken away, screaming, to have their heads lopped off. Torture by burning alive, the mutilation of victims by cutting off their hands, ears and feet, the burial of living wives with their dead husbands – all were taken as a matter of course. Mutesa crushed out life as a child steps on an insect.

Speke had to be careful. It is, however, to his discredit that he seems never to have voiced the slightest protest at the king's reign of terror, and inexcusable that he gave him one of his rifles as a present – when he asked how the king had enjoyed using it, he might have anticipated the reply: 'His highness could not find any animals to shoot, but he managed to kill a large number of people.' It was six months before Mutesa let the explorers go,

having relieved them of virtually all their valuables, including Speke's gold watch.

In July 1862 the expedition was at last approaching the north shore of Lake Victoria where, they had been told, a river cascaded out of the lake over a waterfall known as 'The Stones'. They were almost within sight of The Stones when Speke ordered Grant to stay behind. He went on alone, not wanting, it seems, to share with anyone the *kudos* of his discovery. (Fifty years later Peary was to do the same to his companion, Bob Bartlett, only a few miles from another explorers' desideratum, the North Pole.)

28th July, *Speke wrote*, At last we arrived at the extreme end of our journey, the farthest point ever visited by the expedition. The "Stones" was by far the most interesting sight I had seen in Africa, and my sketch book was called into play. They were

Above: Sir Richard Burton in oriental dress. As well as describing his travels in west and east Africa, Burton wrote accounts of Sind in India, Brazil, Syria and Iceland.

Left: Speke and Grant meeting with an African leader.

Left: Speke watching a group of Uganda warriors. Like Burton, Speke had served with the British forces in India before coming to Africa.

about 12 feet high and 400 to 500 feet broad, and were broken by rocks . . . The expedition had now performed its function. I saw that old father Nile without doubt rises in (*Lake*) Victoria, and, as I had foretold, that lake is the source of the river.

Speke made no attempt to follow the river which cascaded over The Stones, but headed directly for the Nile at Gondokoro, some 300 miles to the north. When he got there he met two other explorers, Samuel and Florence Baker, who were on their way up the river to try and discover its source. Speke told them they were too late. However, in exchange for their boat and some provisions, he gave the Bakers copies of his maps, and suggested they went in search of another great lake, the Luta Nzigé, which was thought to lie to the west of Lake Victoria and might turn out to be a subsidiary feeder of the Nile. He then returned *post haste* to England, pausing only at Cairo to cable. 'All well. The Nile is settled.'

He arrived home to a hero's welcome; but the Nile was far from settled.

Speke had done it again. He had made a major discovery, but had failed to follow it up . . . It was now apparent there was a whole cluster of lakes in central Africa and a whole series of rivers running out of them. Speke had *assumed* that the river he had seen flowing out of Lake Victoria was the same river that flowed, 300 miles away, through Gondokoro; but he had not *proved* it; and this his critics – and in particular Burton and his supporters – were quick to point out. Speke now made life difficult for himself by quarreling with just about everyone. He quarreled with Burton, which was understandable; he quarreled with Livingstone, which was unwise because the old man was regarded as the *guru* of African exploration; and he quarreled with the Society, which was biting the hand that fed him. It seems that he made enemies more readily than friends; for as Burton put it, 'to a quiet and modest demeanour and an almost childlike simplicity of manner, he united an abnormal fund of self-esteem.' A meeting was arranged at which Burton

Below: The Ripon Falls where the White Nile emerges from Lake Victoria.

and Speke were to thrash out their differences in public debate. It would have been a confrontation to remember; but the evening before it was due to take place, Speke died in a shooting incident on his cousin's estate; it seems that he accidentally shot himself.

Another expedition was about to be launched when the Bakers – whom everyone had given up for dead – emerged with the final piece of information which enabled cartographers to delineate the sources of the Nile.

Samuel and Florence Baker and Lake Albert (1863 – 65)

In the spring of 1863 the Bakers attached themselves to a group of traders who were heading towards the Luta Nzigé. It was an uneasy liaison, and Samuel's account of their exploits during the next two years, *The Albert Nyanza*, has all the ingredients of the classic African adventure story. Here is Allan Quartermain setting out into the jungle with a lovely young girl at his side, and together they face every hazard with pluck and determination. A rogue elephant attacks them, and Samuel stops the charging animal dead in its tracks with his last bullet. Their porters mutiny, and he knocks out the ringleader and orders the rest to fall in. Their mules and horses die, and they are forced to ride oxen; their food runs out, and they are forced to eat grass. Fever renders them insensible, their guides mislead them, slave traders cheat them, hippopotamuses overturn their boats; they are attacked with poisoned arrows, and are seldom out of the hearing of war drums. Through it all the incredible Florence never flinches – 'She was not,' her husband tells us, 'a screamer.' And if one wonders where he had found such a companion, the answer is that he bought her, aged 17, at a slave auction in the Balkans, and fell in love with her.

The Bakers have a niche in history both as explorers and lovers.

Early in 1864 they were detained, midway between Lakes Victoria and Albert, by King Kamrasi.

I requested the king, *wrote Baker*, to allow us to leave. and in the coolest manner possible he replied, 'I will let you go to the lake, but you must leave you wife with me!' We were at this moment surrounded by a great number of natives; but if this were to be the end of us, I resolved it should also be the end of Kamrasi. Drawing my revolver I held it about two feet from his chest, and told him that if I touched the trigger not all his men could save him. I said that in my country his insolence would have entailed bloodshed . . . My wife meanwhile had risen from her seat, and, with a countenance about as amiable as Medusa, made him a little speech in Arabic (not a word of which he understood!) Whether this so impressed Kamrasi with British female independence that he wished to be quit of his bargain, I can't say; but with an air of astonishment he said, 'Don't be angry. It is my custom to give my visitors one of my pretty wives, and I thought you might like to exchange. But if you don't like the idea, there's an end to it.' This very practical apology I received sternly, merely insisting on starting our journey.

A couple of months later, after a terrible trek during which Florence succumbed to brain fever, and had to be carried in a makeshift stretcher, 'perfectly insensible as though dead,' they at last neared the Luta Nzigé (Lake Albert.)

14th March *wrote Samuel*, The day was beautifully clear, and having crossed a deep valley we toiled up the opposite slope. I hurried to the summit, and the glory of our prize burst suddenly upon me! There like a sea of quicksilver, far beneath us, lay a grand expanse of water – a boundless sea-horizon, glittering in the noon-day sun. It is impossible to describe the

Left: Sir Samuel and Lady Baker. After his exploring feats Baker led a British-sponsored expedition to help suppress slavery in the areas around the upper Nile.

triumph of that moment. The path to descend to the lake was so steep and dangerous we could only descend on foot. I led the way, grasping a stout bamboo. My wife, in extreme weakness, tottered down, supporting herself on my shoulder and stopping to rest every 20 paces . . . At last we gained level ground. Waves were rolling on to a white pebbly beach, as I ran into the lake, and thirsty with heat and fatigue but with a heart full of gratitude, drank deeply from the sources of the Nile.

The Bakers spent several weeks exploring the lake in a dugout canoe fitted with a mast and a sail of Highland plaid. They were overturned by hippopotamuses, almost eaten by crocodiles and nearly drowned in a storm; but they made important discoveries: that the Victoria Nile flowed into their lake, *via* the magnificent Murchison

Right: A Victorian engraving of Murchison Falls on the upper Nile.

Left: Sir Samuel Baker (bearded) during his campaign in upper Egypt.

Falls, and that the Albert Nile flowed out of it *en route* to Gondokoro. With this information, the last link in the chain delineating the Nile, they struggled back to England.

Their story had a fairy-tale ending. Samuel was given the Gold Medal of the Royal Geographical Society, and a prestigious appointment in Africa. In the autumn of 1865 he and Florence married, and his wife became the toast of London Society. Only Queen Victoria was not amused; outraged that the Bakers had not been legally married when they explored the headwaters of the Nile, she refused to let Florence be presented at court! Posterity has not been so bigoted. The Bakers are now recognized as among the élite of explorers.

Livingstone and the Slave Trade (1849 – 73)

On 1 May, 1873 David Livingstone died, kneeling in prayer beside the upper reaches of the Lualaba (Congo) River, which is about as close to the center of the continent as one can get. His African friends buried his heart at the foot of a mupundu tree, embalmed his body and carried it over 1000 miles to the coast – an eight months' journey of great difficulty and danger. His corpse was then shipped to England where it was buried in Westminster Abbey. Flags, throughout the British Isles, flew at half-mast; people wept in the streets. 'It was', wrote a newspaper, 'as though the whole nation had lost a friend.'

Why, one wonders, was this frail and obstinate man so deeply loved not only by his own people but by the people of Africa?

He was born near Glasgow in 1813, and 'brought up in virtuous poverty.' At the age of 10 he was working in the local cotton mill, and is alleged to have spent his first week's wages on a Latin grammar. He had an insatiable thirst for knowledge. By the time he was 25 he was a qualified doctor and an ordained missionary, and was sent to the London Missionary Society's station at Kuruman in Bechuanaland.

He quickly established a rapport with the local Africans, learning their language and getting to understand their customs. He also established a rapport with the senior missionary's daughter whom he married in 1844. The Livingstones set up their own mission at Mabosta, 250 miles north of Kuruman, and for several years dedicated themselves to converting the Africans to Christianity and improving their quality of life. This brought them into conflict with Boer farmers and Arab slave-traders. The Boers' attitude was 'the Blacks can work for us in consideration for letting them live on our land'; when Livingstone pointed out that the land was the black people's, his family were threatened and his mission burned to the ground. The slave traders were a greater evil. Each year thousands of Africans were torn from their families and herded into slave-caravans; it has

Bottom left: The plight of slaves was an inspiration to Livingstone.

Below: Title page illustration from a contemporary account of Livingstone's travels.

been estimated that two out of three died before they even reached the coastal slave-markets where they were auctioned. 'Almighty God', Livingstone prayed, 'Leave not your children to Satan.' It was because of his hatred of the slave trade that he became an explorer. For he reckoned that if Africa could be opened up to legitimate 'Christian' trade, then the slavers would be put out of business.

He set out on his first journey in 1849, teaming up with the big game hunters, Oswell and Murray. His route took him across the Kalahari Desert, and led to the discovery of the dried-up and salt-encrusted Lake Ngami. A couple of years later he and his family crossed the desert again, this time by a different route. Their oxen perished and they ran out of water and very nearly died of thirst before struggling through to a tributary of the Zambezi. These journeys brought Livingstone to the attention of the Royal Geographical Society, who were to sponsor his subsequent travels. They also convinced him that his family would be safer in England. In future he traveled alone.

He set out on his second and greatest journey in November 1853, attempting to cross the continent from east to west. His companions were 26 Makololo (a branch of the Zulus) who had been converted to Christianity. The Makololo were not porters in the conventional sense; they were free to come and go, work or not work, as they pleased; for Livingstone was one of the first white Europeans to treat the people of Africa not as servants but equals. They took with them half-a-dozen canoes and a minimum of baggage – 'the art of successful travel,' wrote Livingstone, 'is to take with you not impedimenta but your wits.' At first their journey was near idyllic, through the upper reaches of the rivers Zambezi and Chobe: 'green grassy meadows, all flooded with the bright African sunshine.' Livingstone plotted their track with meticulous accuracy and filled 800 pages of his notebooks with detailed observations of flora and fauna. It was when they came to the rain-forests at the junction of present-day Angola, Zaire and Zambia that their troubles started. Food became scarce, and they were reduced to eating vermin and fungi. It rained without respite. Livingstone suffered continuous bouts of fever and dysentery.

Have eaten nothing for 4 days, *he wrote*, yet my bowels are acting every 10 to 15 minutes, except when I am under the influence of opium. The agony drenches me in tears, saliva and perspiration. I am reduced to a skeleton.

He was a doctor, and must have realized his days were numbered; there is no cure for chronic malaria and colitis. By February 1854 they had reached Lake Dilolo. They

were now in the very heart of Africa: on a vast 1500-meter plateau, covered in dense and humid rain-forest. The tribal chiefs through whose land they passed did not known what to make of Livingstone and his humility and poverty. One, feeling sorry for him, offered him a ten-year-old girl. Another demanded one of the Makololo as a slave. 'I told the chief,' wrote Livingstone, 'that we would die for one another rather than deliver up one of our number as a slave . . . but if he insisted on taking one of us he had better take me.' At last they reached the coast, near the Portuguese port of Luanda, where Livingstone was nursed back to health, and his Makololo offered work at wages beyond their dreams.

Among the ships anchored off Luanda was the frigate *Polyphemus*, and Livingstone was offered a free passage back to his wife and children in England, where his exploits were becoming headline news. He turned the offer down, because, he said, he had to take his Makololo companions back to their homes on the Zambezi. It was a gesture which caught the imagination of the world: the frail fever-ridden white man, turning his back on home and fame and heading one again into the Dark Continent for the sake of his friends. He became a cult figure: the Good Shepherd, willing to lay down his life for his flock.

The return journey took nearly a year with the latter part of it, as the Makololo neared their homeland, turning into a triumphal procession. Livingstone, however, did not regard the expedition as a success; for it was obvious that the route he had pioneered was too long and difficult to be used for trade.

In 1856 he began his third series of journeys: exploring the rivers of east Africa – the Limpopo, Zambezi, Shire and Rovuma – in the hope that they could be used as trade-routes. It might be said that these expeditions also failed. For although Livingstone broke new ground and made major discoveries, including the Victoria Falls – 'the most wonderful sight I ever saw' – it was obvious that the rivers were too full of rapids and waterfalls to become trade routes.

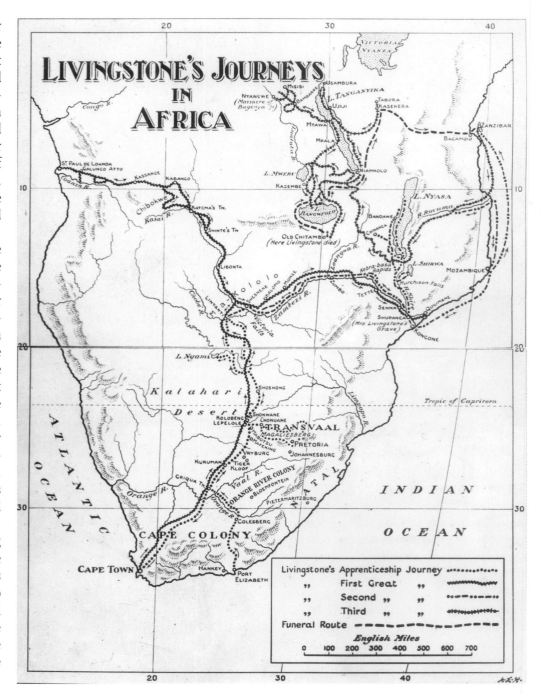

Above: A map from an atlas of the time details Livingstone's movements.

Left: The famous meeting of Livingstone and Stanley. Stanley commented, rather unconvincingly, on the composition, 'This Engraving, for which I supplied the materials, represents my meeting with Dr. Livingstone at Ujiji, Lake Tanganyika; and is as correct as if the scene had been photographed.'

In 1866, under the aegis of the Royal Geographical Society, he began the last of his great journeys, to settle once and for all the source of the Nile. Livingstone was not convinced that Lakes Victoria and Albert were the only feeders of the Nile: 'Poor Speke,' he wrote 'his river at the Ripon Falls ("The Stones") was not large enough for the Nile.' He knew that not far from Lake Tanganyika a number of rivers flowed strongly to the north, among them the huge and mysterious Lualaba; and in the hope of proving that the Lualaba was a major feeder of the Nile he disappeared into the heart of Africa. After three years of silence, there were fears for his safety. Several expeditions set out to search for him, and it was Stanley's in 1871, which found him. Stanley could see that the doctor was dying, and did his best to persuade him to come back to civilization. Livingstone, however, felt that his work in Africa was not yet done. A couple of years later he was found dead beside a river that had no connection with the Nile. It might be thought he had failed again.

Yet his achievements far outweigh his apparent failures. He woke the conscience of the world to the horrors of the slave trade, and by his love of Africa and the Africans helped to disseminate a new image of the continent.

Left: David Livingstone, 1813-73, began his career in Africa as a missionary. He severed his links with the Missionary Society after his first expedition, so that he could be free to undertake further explorations.

Stanley, the Lualaba, and the Mountains of the Moon (1870–89)

Stanley has seldom been given the recognition he deserves. He is remembered by most people for his ludicrous greeting, "Doctor Livingstone, I presume;" but in his own right he was a highly successful – if controversial – explorer.

An orphan originally named John Rowlands he was born in Wales in 1841, brought up in the local poorhouse and hired out at £0.20 a week. When he was 15 he ran away to sea, and eventually found himself in New Orleans where he was adopted by a wealthy industrialist. When his benefactor died, Rowlands assumed his name, and for the rest of his life was known as Henry Morton Stanley. He became a journalist, and in 1870 the *New York Herald* sent him to Africa to search for Livingstone. It was a tough assignment, but Stanley was a tough character: strong, brave, and determined no matter what the cost to succeed; while others gave up, he managed to

track the missionary down. Although they were very different in character, the two men became friends, and as they traveled together Livingstone's fascination with the rivers of Africa rubbed off on his young companion. When Stanley visited England in 1872 he was given a hero's reception by the public but a frosty reception by geographers, who felt he was a journalist in search of a scoop rather than an explorer in search of geographical truth. Stanley was determined to prove them wrong, and to answer the question which had puzzled Livingstone: were the great north-flowing rivers beside Lake Tanganyika feeders of the Congo or the Nile?

In 1874 he headed inland from Zanzibar in command of one of the largest expeditions ever to explore Africa: 356 men with eight tons of supplies and the prefabricated sections of a 40-foot steel boat. When they reached Lake Victoria their boat, the *Lady Alice*, was assembled,

Below: The Arab port of Zanzibar was a major slave trading center. The slave trade in this area was finally suppressed under British influence from 1890. Livingstone had done much to open the eyes of the world to the evils of slavery and the campaign for its suppression owed much to his efforts.

and they circumnavigated and mapped the lake, proving that the river cascading over The Stones was its only major outfall. Stanley then turned his attention to the Lualaba. His descent of this river is one of the epics of African exploration. He had no idea where it would take him – it might have been north into Egypt or south into the unexplored forests of Zambia – but he knew that once he set out there could be no turning back against the fast-flowing current. His expedition faced almost constant danger and met with frequent disaster. They had to negotiate huge waterfalls and fierce rapids, and were frequently attacked by 'riverside cannibals.' The *Lady Alice* was wrecked, and they lost all their food and most of their ammunition. Every one of Stanley's white companions was either drowned or killed by poisoned arrows. But at last, after a voyage of 999 days and nearly

Above & below left: Two scenes from Stanley's expedition to rescue Emin Pasha in 1886-89. After this Stanley completed a varied career by becoming naturalized as a British subject and was elected a Member of Parliament.

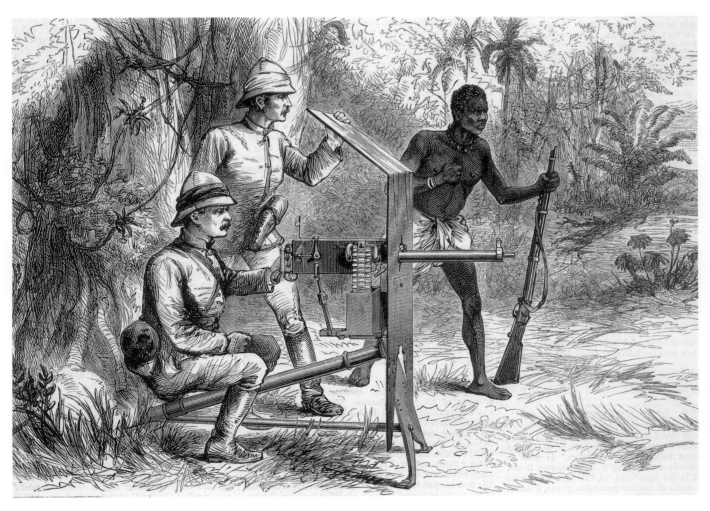

3000 miles, the survivors, 'emaciated as skeletons and pale as ghosts,' reached the mouth of the Lualaba (Congo) River. Stanley had certainly succeeded, but at a terrible price: over 240 of his men had suffered and died on the Lualaba, together with an unknown number of the 'riverside cannibals'.

Ten years later he was in Africa again, in command of an even larger expedition. This time his avowed objectives were to rescue the Governor of Equatoria who had been trapped by a Mahdist uprising and to locate the Mountains of the Moon; but there was more to his journey than this, for he had been sponsored by a number of organizations anxious to open up the Congo for commercial exploitation. He set out from the Atlantic coast in 1887 with five hundred men, and started hacking his way through the forests and swamps of the Congo basin. If ever a journey was hell, this was it. Dense and humid vegetation obscured the sun; myriads of insects infected the men's bloodstream with venom; jungle

tribesmen showered them with poisoned arrows and hid poisoned splinters of wood under the rotting leaves – those who trod on them died in agony of lockjaw. They ran out of food, and for weeks on end had nothing to eat but fungi, slugs and ants. Stanley's hair turned white but he struggled on, maintaining harsh discipline: a man who stole food was given 300 lashes, a man who stole a rifle was shot. And at last, after eight terrible months, they emerged from the rain forest and saw ahead the grassland of present-day Uganda. They rescued the Governor of Equatoria, and discovered the Ruwenzori, the Ancients' Mountains of the Moon. Stanley had succeeded again; but again at a terrible price; 350 of his expedition and an even greater number of tribesmen lay dead in the rain forest.

Stanley was a great explorer who put the last major river (the Congo) and the last major range of mountains (the Ruwenzori) on the map. But the trails that he carved through the heart of Africa ran red with blood.

Above: Henry Morton Stanley, 1841-1904.

'The Animals Shall Not Die': The Creation of Wildlife Reserves (1890 – 1990)

Africa has an abundance of mammals. In particular the plains of present-day Mozambique, Zimbabwe and Tanzania support vast herds of herbivores which are preyed on by large numbers of carnivores. These animals had a role – albeit a minor one – in the exploration of Africa; for their presence ensured that explorers with compasses were swiftly followed by hunters with guns. A typical big-game hunter was Frederick Courtney Selous.

He arrived in Cape Town in 1871, his only possessions a gun 'with a kick like two mules,' and a wirehaired terrier named Punch who developed a penchant for chasing elephants and rhinos. The two of them disappeared into the little known country north of the Zambezi and within a couple of years Selous had traveled thousands of miles and killed hundreds of elephants – and made his fortune. His technique was simple.

When his horse became exhausted, he would leap to the ground, and, wearing only a shirt and sandals, pursue his quarry on foot. Closing in on the elephant at full tilt and reloading his gun from a powder bag as he ran, he would slither to a halt and fire at point blank range . . . He and Punch had a thousand narrow escapes from savage buffalo, charging rhino, marauding lions and maddened elephants.

Selous and his fellow-hunters were a link between explorers and farmers; they helped to open up thousands of square kilometers of virgin territory to European settlement.

One of the first people to try to protect the animals was the wife of the Kaiser. In 1904 her husband gave her 6000 square kilometers of what was then German East Africa as a present, and, determined 'that the animals shall not die,' she insisted it was turned into a wildlife sanctuary – to this day people living on the border of what is now the Selous Reserve call it *Sham Ya Bibi*, 'The Woman's Field'. For some years the sanctuary was efficiently patrolled and guarded, and the animals mutiplied. However, when East Africa came under British jurisdiction, the colonial Game Preservation Department made a fundamental mistake. To please conservationists they trebled the size of the Reserve, and to please the local tribespeople they allowed inside it a limited amount of human settlement. The compromise did not work; for to quote a subsequent official report 'there was found to be a basic incom-

patability between a successful sanctuary for animals and human cultivation.'

In spite of the efforts, between the wars, of men like Constantine Ionides – 'the father of conservation in Africa' – the Reserve did not become viable until it became depopulated. This happened by chance. In the 1950s East Africa suffered an epidemic of sleeping sickness; the Selous Reserve happened to be in the middle of the infected area and was compulsorily evacuated; and once the people had left they were not allowed back. Today, thanks to the commitment of the Tanzanian government to conservation, the Selous provides protection to more wild animals than any other reserve in the world.

And the rangers who guard the Selous, have much in common with the botanists who research in the rain forest. They too are helping to protect and understand our planet. They too are explorers.

Left: F.C. Selous. Among his publications was *A Hunter's Wanderings in Africa* which graphically described his exploits.

Central and North America

The first people to explore North America were Mongoloid hunter-gatherers who about 30,000 years ago, crossed from Asia to Alaska by what was then 'the broad and dry highway of the Bering land-bridge.' In those days the northern part of the continent was an ice cap over which travel would have been difficult; but, about 11,000 BC an ice-free corridor began to open up to the east of the Rockies, and through this hunter-gatherers came streaming south into the plains.

Here they found a cornucopia of prey: bison with a horn-span of 6 feet, towering beaverlike creatures called casteroids, huge ground-sloths, lion-sized cats, mastodons and mammoths. For something like a millenium these enormous creatures provided our ancestors with an abundance of meat – a mastodon weighing over a ton would have kept a whole tribe happy for weeks – but in the end they were hunted to extinction. (We know it was man who was responsible for their disappearance because cave-paintings that show the huge creatures being driven over cliffs or trapped in swamps have been found all over America; while their skeletons confirm that they often met their death from flint-tipped arrows and spears.) It therefore seems likely that by about 9000 BC Stone Age hunter-gatherers, in search of a diminishing supply of meat, had explored virtually the whole continent.

The diminution of their meat-supply forced our ancestors to find other things to eat; they turned to cereal growing and the cultivation of root crops. This transition from hunting to farming led to a more static way of life; the tempo of exploration slowed, and different cultures began to put down roots in different parts of the continent. The most sophisticated of these cultures were in the south. In the Yucatan peninsula the Mayas established a civilization which could boast hieroglyphic-writing, enough mathematical know-how to calculate the orbit of Venus, and well-laid-out cities with over 100,000 inhabitants. In Mexico the Aztecs established a civilization which, like the Roman, was efficient, warlike and demanded constant propitiation by tribute. And in the mid-reaches of the Mississippi and Ohio Rivers Hopewell Indians built up a mini-empire characterized by intensive farming and impressive burial rituals. There seems to have been comparatively little trade between these civilizations – certainly nothing to compare with the Europeans' continual to-ing and fro-ing in search of incense, spices and gold – they evolved in isolation, each with its own language, customs and characteristics. And what was true of the major civilizations, was true also of the minor tribes; they tended to be self-sufficient, each with its own territory (which it kept to except in time of war), its own language and its own culture.

When Columbus arrived in the New World he called all the indigenous people *los Indios* (Indians.) Subsequent explorers perpetuated his error, thus saddling the inhabitants of North America not only with a bogus ancestry – they have of course not the slightest connection with the people of India – but also a bogus homogeneity – for there is as much difference between an Aleut, a Huron, an Apache and a Maya, as between a Japanese, a Tibetan, an Arab and a Scandinavian. This diversity was a problem to the European explorers. They kept coming into contact with different tribes with different languages and different customs who presented them with different problems.

Another problem facing explorers was the diversity and sheer size of the terrain. From north to south those who sought to penetrate the interior were faced with tundra, where one needed specialized knowledge to sur-

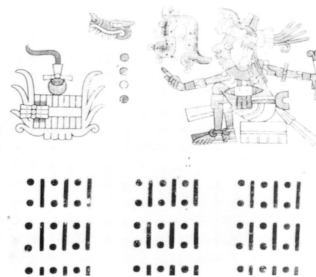

Previous page: Joliet and Marquette during their exploration of the Mississippi.

Left: An example of the bat and dot code used by Maya mathematicians. The Maya were an intellectually advanced civilization which mysteriously collapsed around 900 AD.

vive; a shield of granite overlaid with frozen lakes and coniferous forest, where food was scarce, conditions harsh and travel difficult; a belt of deciduous woodland whose inhabitants resented and opposed settlement; an area of savannah where the soil was poor and the inhabitants again hostile; an area of near-impenetrable swamps; an area of near desert; and finally a thickly populated area ruled by an efficient and warlike people. It

Below: A relief from a Maya temple showing a sacrificial victim overlooked by the war god Kukulkan, about to have his tongue ripped out with a rope entwined with thorns.

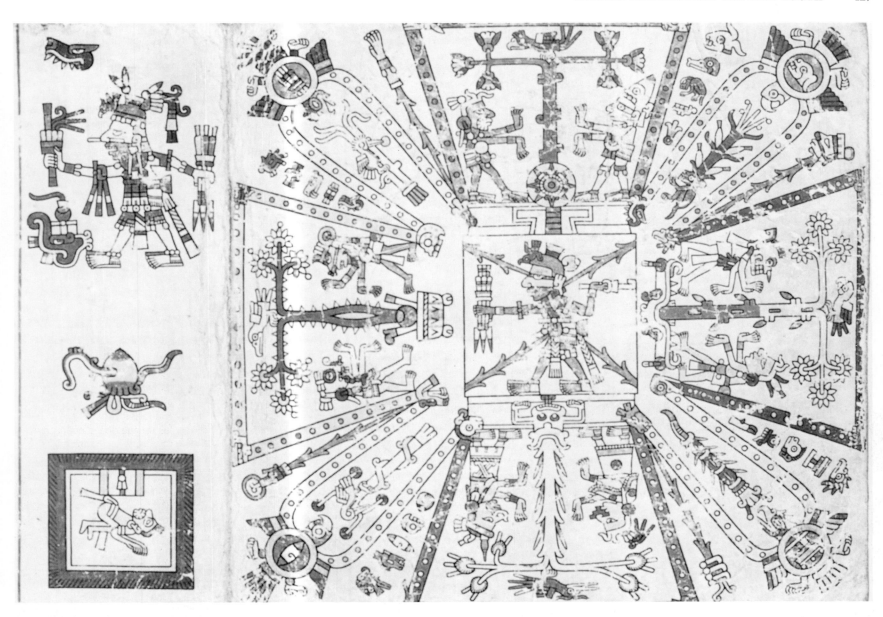

Above: A magical Aztec calendar. Early civilizations took a great interest in astronomy because accurate calculation of the time of year was essential to agriculture.

is difficult to generalize about the exploration of so large and diverse a land-mass. Indeed about the only generalization it *is* safe to make is that North America was opened up not by a small number of far-ranging expeditions, but by a large number of local probes. The true explorers of the continent were the trapper who waded upriver to one more beaver-dam, the backwoodsman who cleared one more acre of virgin forest, the cowboy who drove his herd over the crest of one more hill.

One other factor added complexity to an already complex scenario. The explorers of North America often found themselves locked in combat not only with the terrain and the Indians but with one another. For the feuds of the Old World spilled over into the New, and

Spaniards, French and British fought one another from the shores of Hudson Bay to the forests of Panama, and from Chesapeake Bay to the Golden Gate. It is one of the illogicalities (some would say injustices) of history that dreams conceived in the woods and plains of North America should so often have been either realized or dashed on the battlefields of Europe: that the Spaniards who explored the whole of Central America and the deep south should have ended up with nothing; that the French who explored most of present-day Canada should have ended up with what they consider to be a minor role in 'their' territory; and that the British who did least exploring of all should have ended up (albeit temporarily) with possession of virtually the whole continent.

Spanish Explorers in Central America and the Deep South

The first Europeans to explore the continent were the Spanish Conquistadors. Because of their background (*see* Chapter 2) the Conquistadors were not good emissaries. They regarded non-Christians as sub-human – 'what matter if they are consigned to the fires of hell today since they will be consigned to them in any case tomorrow' – and were interested in one thing only: 'we have a sickness of the heart for which there is only one cure: gold.' They came as looters, not caring how much suffering or damage they caused or how many Indians they killed.

Balboa Discovers the Pacific (1513)

Vasco Nunez de Balboa was a typical Conquistador. He arrived in the Caribbean in 1501, searched for pearls and gold near the mouth of the Magdalena River, was ship-

wrecked off Hispaniola, and went bankrupt trying to run a sugar-cane plantation. In 1510, together with his dog which he took with him everywhere, he escaped his creditors by stowing-away in a biscuit-barrel in a ship bound for Panama. Once on the isthmus, his fortunes improved. He allied himself to a native *cacique* (chief) named Comogre, whose son agreed to lead a group of Conquistadors 'to the shores of the fabled sea, where men ride camels and even the cooking pots are made of gold.'

There was much talk of this 'fabled sea' on the Spanish Main in the early 1500s, but no European had ever managed to cross the isthmus and set eyes on it; for the terrain is about as difficult as any on Earth: steep-sided hills, impenetrable rain forest, rivers that rise 40 feet in an hour and a network of swamps. Balboa's expedition was a large one: 190 Spaniards and 800 Indians. They left

Cortes and the Conquest of Mexico (1519-39)

Hernando Cortes was only 19 when he arrived in the Caribbean in 1504. He took part in the conquest of Cuba, proved himself able and ambitious, and was appointed King's Treasurer in Santiago. It was a position in which a lot of money passed through his hands; some of it stuck, and he managed to buy control of an expedition which was about to sail for the Yucatan Peninsula, where there had been reports of magnificent buildings and gold artefacts.

The expedition was a large one: 11 ships, about 650 men, 16 horses, 'a considerable number' of cannon, and the usual pack of dogs that had been trained to savage the Indians. They landed on the peninsula in May 1519, and at once came across evidence of the past splendor of Mayan cities. Advancing along the coast, they reached the small town of Tabasco, where they found a man and a woman who were to play key roles in the coming campaign. The man was Geronimo de Aguilar, a shipwrecked Spanish seaman who had spent 6 years with the Indians, had learned their language and could act as interpreter with the Maya. The woman, soon to be known as Dona Marina, was a beautiful Aztec girl, who had been captured and enslaved by the Maya and was soon to become Cortes' mistress. Her knowledge of Aztec language and customs was to prove invaluable to the Conquistadors. Cortes was impressed by the Mayas. 'Their country,' he wrote, 'is thickly populated, with many masonry houses. The people go about in garments of cotton. They cultivate

Left: A few days after first sighting the Pacific Balboa waded into the sea to claim it for the Spanish King.

Below : Balboa's first view of the Pacific Ocean. A typical Conquistador, Vasco Nunez de Balboa (1475-1517), was also one of the more successful. Unlike many of his compatriots, he actually returned from his expedition with some of the fabled treasure of the New World.

Darien on September 1st, 1513, plunged into the jungle, and soon found themselves harrassed by heat-stroke, malaria and the Indians of the interior. In one battle alone they killed 600 Indians in an hour, captured their chiefs, accused them of 'the most abominable sin' (homosexuality) and had them torn to pieces by the dogs. For 26 days they hacked their way forward, until at last they were climbing a hill from whose summit, their guides told them, they would be able to see the Great Ocean.

Then Balboa, accompanyied only by his dog, went forwarde alone to the toppe. And there, prostrate upon the ground, and lifting up his eyes to heaven, he poured forth his thanks to almightie God. And when he had made his prayers, he beckoned to his companions, pointing out to them the great maine sea, heretofore unknown to the inhabitants of Europe, Aphrika and Asia.

This was one of the great moments in the history of exploration, indicating that America was divided from Asia by a major ocean.

A couple of days later the Conquistadors were standing on the shore of this ocean, and Balboa waded into it, in his hand an image of the Virgin and Child, and 'took possession of these seas and lands and coasts and islands . . . for as long as the world shall endure.' They found no camels on the shore of the Pacific – the animals whose outline the Indians had drawn for them in the sand were llamas – but they did find vast quantities of gold. At the end of three months they returned laden with treasure to the Atlantic coast.

Balboa's success, however, was short-lived. Once the Spanish authorities realized that there was gold on the far side of the isthmus, they were eager to bring about Balboa's downfall and get their hands on the untapped wealth he had discovered. He was arrested, on trumped-up charges, on the orders of his father-in-law, and summarily executed: an ill-deserved end for one of history's more colorful adventurers.

maize, and possess small quantities of gold.' Far greater quantities of gold, Dona Marina told him, were possessed by the Aztecs, whose capital Tenochtitlan lay some 200 miles inland on the Mexican plateau. Cortes was well aware that the Aztecs were powerful, warlike and that their troops outnumbered his by something like 500 to 1. He burned and scuttled his boats as proof of his decision to conquer or die, and headed for Tenochtitlan.

It was a difficult march, first through the humid coastal plains, then over the 15,000-foot Sierra Madre Oriental, and finally across the Mexican plateau with its snow-capped volcanoes. Soon they were met by emissaries from the Aztec king Moctezuma. Moctezuma was not sure what to make of the Conquistadors. His scouts had brought back terrifying reports of them:

They are men of iron. In iron they clothe themselves. With iron they cover their heads. Iron are their swords . . . and those which carry them on their backs, their deer, are tall as roof-terraces.

Moctezuma had a sneaking suspicion they might be heralds from the god-king Quetzalcoatl who, according to Aztec legend, would one day destroy them because he had not been sufficiently propitiated. His emissaries brought gifts for the Spaniards – beautifully-crafted animals in solid gold, and food which had been soaked in human blood. It would be difficult to imagine gifts *less* likely to deter the Spaniards; the gold excited their cupidity, the blood-soaked food their disgust. Cortes continued his advance, defeating tribes who opposed him and allying himself to those who were prepared to join him to throw off the yoke of the Aztecs. As they neared Tenochtitlan the Conquistadors found evidence of the appalling human sacrifices that the Aztec theocracy demanded: priests tearing the hearts from literally thousands of victims and offering them still throbbing to their idols. In one town alone they counted more than 100,000 skulls arranged in symmetrical piles. Cortes ordered the sacrificial platforms to be cleansed with lime, and altars dedicated to the Virgin to be built on top of them.

Eventually, from the slopes of Popocatepetl, they stood looking down on the Aztec capital. 'It was like a vision,' wrote del Castillo, one of Cortes' troops, 'so beautiful we could hardly believe our eyes.' Tenochtitlan was sited on

a cluster of islands in the center of a huge lake. Each island was close-packed with buildings, and connected to its neighbors and to the shore by drawbridges and causeways 'so wide that 8 horsemen abreast could ride down them.' There were huge temples, magnificent palaces and beautiful flower-gardens (many of them on floating platoons.) 'We were but human,' wrote del Castillo, 'and feared death. We couldn't stop thinking about it, and commended ourselves to God and Our Lady.' However, having burned their boats, there was only one way they could go: forward into the city, to where Moctezuma was waiting for them.

If Moctezuma had ordered his troops to seize the Con-

Above: Balboa's success merely provoked jealousy among the Spanish authorities, and he was executed on the flimsiest of charges in 1517.

Below left: Hernando Cortes (1485-1547), and *below*, his fleet bound for Mexico in 1518.

quistadors they could hardly have survived; but still fearing they might be the harbingers of Quetzalcoatl, he invited them into his palace, offering them fine clothes and gourmet meals, loading them with gifts (including gold) and pledging obedience. The Conquistadors were able to hold him virtually a prisoner in his own palace. They demanded a huge quantity of gold, and when this had been given demanded more. 'Gold is all they care about,' an Aztec priest remarked contemptuously. 'They lust after it like pigs.' There followed a succession of torturings, murders, massacres, uprisings, attacks and counter-attacks, which ended with the virtual obliteration of the Aztec empire and the reduction of its capital to a charnel-house – though not from the causes one might have anticipated.

Cortes had been in the capital only a few months when he learned that Velasquez, the governor of Cuba, had sent a force of Spanish troops to take him prisoner on the grounds that he was furthering his own ambitions rather than those of his country. Cortes defeated the troops sent to capture him, and enlisted them as supporters. However, on returning to Tenochtitlan, he found that one of the Conquistadors had ordered his men to attack an Aztec procession; fighting had broken out, and it was clear an uprising was imminent. Cortes forced Moctezuma to appeal to his people not to attack the Conquistadors; but the luckless king was stoned to death, and on *la noche triste* (June 30th 1520) Cortes was forced to retreat from the capital, losing nearly one third of his men. A year later, supported by several of the local tribes (who were no friends of the Aztecs) he was laying siege to Tenochtitlan, cutting off its water-supply, and eventually attacking the city with 13 brigantines which had been built on the coast and manhandled in sections over the Sierra Madre. Fighting went on for 80 days, and when at last the Conquistadors forced their way into the city they found few people alive. 'A man could not put his foot

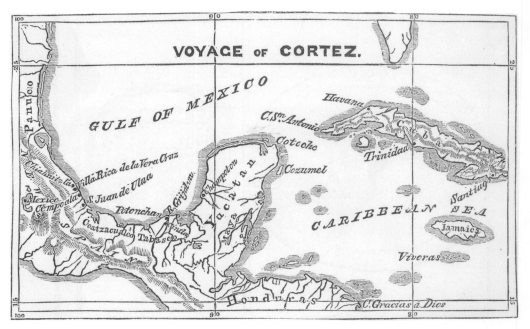

Above: Hernando Cortes spent 35 years exploring the Caribbean and Central America. Between 1519 and 1539 he conquered Mexico and its Aztec and Mayan peoples.

Left: The Aztec ruler Moctezuma at first welcomed the Conquistadors with gifts, believing them to be emissaries from their god-king Quetzalcoatl.

Below: Before setting off to conquer the Aztec capital of Tenochtitlan Cortes burned and scuttled all his boats to signify his intention to conquer or die.

Left and below: Although the initial contact between the Conquistadors and the Aztecs was cordial, they quickly developed a mutual distaste, the Aztecs for the Conquistadors' lust for gold, the Spanish for the Aztec custom of human sacrifice.

Below left: The Aztec capital of Tenochtitlan, built on an island in the middle of a lake, astonished the Spaniards by its beauty and spaciousness.

down,' wrote Cortes, 'unless on the decomposing body of an Indian.' It was not, however, the Spaniards' swords, lances and cannon-fire that had killed most of them . . .

Among the troops who had been sent by Velasquez to take Cortes prisoner was a West African Negro who was a carrier of *Variola*, the virus of smallpox. Smallpox was the most contagious and the most deadly of the diseases transmitted from the Old World to the New; the Maya and Aztec had no immunity to it, and it spread faster and with a more terrible effect than the Black Death which a couple of centuries earlier had devastated Europe. Within 6 months the population of Mexico had fallen from over

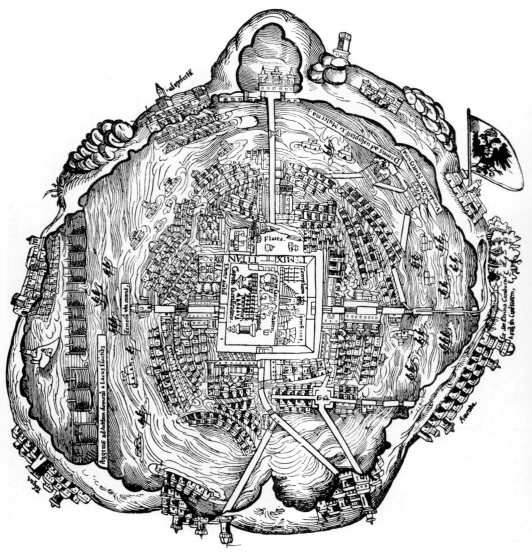

Above: Fighting broke out between Conquistadors and Aztecs after the Spanish attacked an Aztec procession. Cortes was forced to retreat but later returned to lay siege to the city. It fell after 80 days of fighting but the Spanish conquest of Mexico was due more to the scourge of smallpox on the defenseless Aztec and Maya, than to Spanish military skill.

Left: After the Spanish conquest Tenochtitlan became capital of New Spain and the site of modern-day Mexico City.

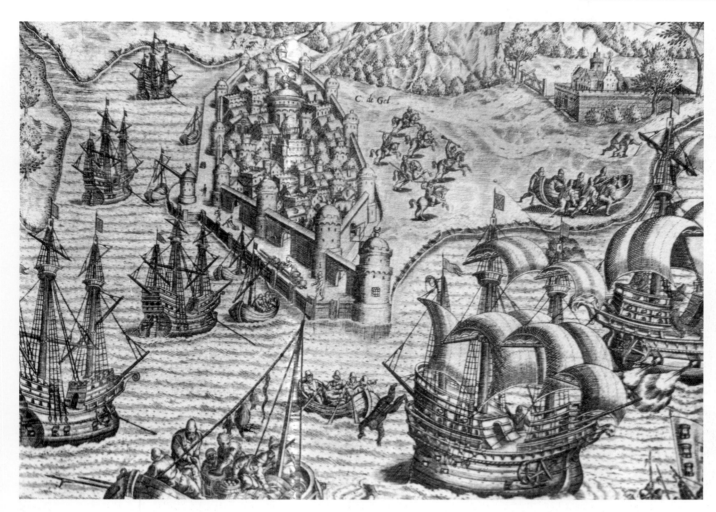

Left: In 1537 Hernando de Soto, who had taken part in the conquests of Peru and Nicaragua, was granted a license to explore Florida, then thought to be an island. His expedition of 15 ships landed at Tampa Bay on May 30th, 1539.

12,000,000 to under 3,000,000; and it continued to decline for the rest of the century, reducing the once prosperous kingdoms of Mesoamerica to a depressed and impoverished backwater.

After the capture of Tenochtitlan Cortes was given the grandiose title of Governor and Captain General of New Spain. He rebuilt the Aztec capital and renamed it Mexico City. Disappointed by the relatively small amount of gold, he rewarded his followers with land; he then initiated and took part in several major journeys of exploration.

In 1523-4 Pedro de Alvarado led an expedition which reached the Pacific at the Gulf of Tehuantepec, and advanced south along the coast into present-day Guatemala. In 1524-6 Cortes himself led a larger expedition which cut across the base of the Yucatan Peninsula into present-day Honduras. The terrain was appalling – steep mountains, dense rain forest and ubiquitous swamps – and the Spaniards failed to find the ancient Mayan cities which they had hoped to loot. In 1532 his cousin Diego de Mendoza, commanded a fleet which discovered Los Tres Marias Islands at the approaches to the Gulf of California. And in 1535 Cortes with 3 ships discovered the Baja California. He landed in La Paz Bay, near the foot of the Baja, where he attempted to found a colony. However, food was scarce and gold non-existent, and at the end of a year he returned to Mexico City. The last expedition he initiated was a voyage by Francisco de Ulloa, who explored and charted the Gulf of California; Ulloa also sailed north along the Pacific seaboard of the Baja (probably as far as San Diego), and was one of the first Europeans to realize it was not an island but a peninsula.

Cortes retired to Spain in 1540 and died in 1547. He was probably the ablest and certainly one of the more attractive of the Conquistadors. He inspired the loyalty of his men and of several women; he was intelligent, brave, no more ruthless than he needed to be, and made a genuine attempt to explore his domain and govern it fairly. However, two factors weighed against him. The Spanish authorities were probably right in regarding him as an adventurer, a man who was basically his own master rather than a servant of the crown; he was forever being restrained and rebuked, and the allegations and plots against him continued even after his retirement. It also told against him that the Aztec empire turned out to have less gold than had been anticipated, and his journeys of exploration failed to find more; Mexico therefore came to be regarded as the poor relation among Spain's New World dominions, and Cortes' achievement in adding it to the Spanish crown has not always received the recognition it deserves.

De Soto Penetrates the Deep South (1539-43)

No European explored a greater area of the New World than Hernando de Soto. In 1524 he took part in Cordoba's conquest of Nicaragua. In 1531 he took part in Pizarro's conquest of Peru – he was the first European to meet the Inca emperor Atahualpa, whose murder he subsequently opposed. In 1537 he was appointed Governor-General of Cuba, and granted a licence to explore the adjacent and vaguely-defined 'Island of Florida.'

He got together an impressive expedition: 15 ships, 622 men, 200 horses, the usual packs of dogs, and a herd of pigs to provide food on the march. They left Havana on May 18th, 1539, and 12 days later landed at Tampa Bay on the west coast of Florida.

The journey that followed has been called 'a cruel, courageous and sad undertaking,' and the adjectives are well chosen. It was cruel because it involved pointless and bloodthirsty skirmishes with the Indians – the Apalachee, Creek, Choctaws and Chickasaws – through whose territory they passed. What happened in the bayous of Louisiana was typical. The Creek Indians 'came out to greet (them), singing and playing on flutes'; presents were exchanged, and for a while relations were friendly. However a quarrel about the price of some food led to fighting, and the fighting led to a pitched battle in which 18 Spaniards and 2500 Indians were killed. It was courageous because for 4 years the Spaniards suffered discomfort, hunger, illness, hardship and danger without

Above: Hernando de Soto lands in Florida in 1539.

Left: Lake Charles, Louisiana where de Soto and his men spent the second winter of their four year expedition. It was four years that they regarded as wasted, because they did not find the one thing they were searching for – gold. They traveled through some of the most fertile areas of the southern states, but failed to realize their potential for colonization.

Above: An early Spanish settlement in Florida.

either reward or complaint; it might be argued that they had no choice except to follow where de Soto led, but the fact that they survived is a testimony to their toughness and courage. It was sad because the Conquistadors had one desideratum only: gold. Every wigwam they entered they asked where they could find it, often torturing their hosts in the mistaken belief they were withholding information. What made this doubly tragic is that gold was about the one thing the Southern States of America did not have to offer. The Conquistadors' travels took them through the rich pastures of Tennessee, the fertile floodplain of the Mississippi and the exotic bayous of Louisiana; but they were so blinkered by their lust for gold that they failed to realize the potential of these areas for colonization.

A reconstruction of their journey makes one realize the rich diversity of the terrain they passed through. On leaving Tampa Bay they headed north across the swamp-forests and water-plains of Florida. 'Here (were) no lofty peaks, no mighty glaciers or rushing streams . . . only a land tranquil in its quiet beauty.' As they trekked through the endless plains of sawgrass the going would have been more monotonous than difficult; but at least their dogs must have had a field-day chasing the ubiquitous water-fowl. By October they had reached present-day Tallahassee, and here they spent the winter, harrassed by the Apalachee Indians. The Apalachee, probably in an effort to get rid of them, told them of a great and wealthy queen who lived in the far north, and in the spring de Soto and his men set out in search of her. They found her on the Savannah River, a little below present-day Augusta; but the source of her wealth turned out to be not gold but freshwater pearls. Disappointed, the Conquistadors headed northwest toward a distant range of mountains. Passing from Georgia to Tennessee, they crossed the Appalachians, more than 200 years before what is often said to be the first crossing by a European, that of Daniel Boone. They were now in rich and beautiful country – Boone and his compatriots were subsequently to go into ecstasies over it – but because there was no gold the Conquistadors complained of the cold and the pine-needles and headed south into Louisiana where they spent their second winter. In the spring they headed northwest and began a series of journeys through Mississippi and Arkansas. They first sighted 'Ol' Man River' (which they called the Rio Grande) on May 8th, 1541, crossed it in barges built to the design of one of their number who happened to be an ex-shipwright, and headed west into Arkansas. Not all the Indians they met were hostile; nonetheless their numbers were steadily whittled away by accident, illness and skirmishing. By the fall they had only 40 horses left out of 200 and only 300 men out of over 600, the Chickasaw had made off with most of their pigs, and only their dogs flourished, having become a wild ravenous pack, breeding *en route* and savaging anything or anybody they could get their teeth into. De Soto's priority now was not finding gold but getting his depleted expedition home.

They spent the winter in Arkansas, not far from the Ovacita Mountains, and in the spring returned to the Mississippi, hoping to follow the river to its mouth. They had reached Natchez when de Soto, who had been growing progressively weaker, died of fever. His body, weighted with sand was lowered into the river, and command of the expedition devolved on Luis de Moscosco.

Moscosco is not a name many people have heard; yet he proved a resourceful and competent leader Failing to make satisfactory progress by land, he ordered the building of 7 small boats; and after a voyage down-river pursued by Indian canoes and across the Gulf of Mexico pur-

sued by tropical storms, the exhausted Spaniards struggled ashore north of Vera Cruz after a journey of five-and-
one-half years and 3000 miles, much of it through terrain
no European had before set eyes on.

Explorers tend to be judged not by the difficulty of
their journey but by its results, and the results of de
Soto's expedition were negative. Disappointed that there
was no gold in the 'worthless' Southern States, the
Spaniards turned their back on a potential empire. It was
200 years before Europeans were again climbing the
Appalachians and canoeing down the Mississippi; and
this second wave of explorers were not Spanish but
British and French.

Coronado's Search for 'The Golden City of Cibola' (1540-43)

At the same time as de Soto searched for gold to the
northeast of the new Spanish lands, Francisco Vasquez
de Coronado searched for it to the northwest.

Coronado arrived in the Caribbean in 1535, and the following year was appointed governor of Galicia, a department of New Spain on the Pacific seaboard. He initiated
an expedition into present-day Arizona led by the Franciscan friar Marcos de Niza. De Niza's expedition proved
more colorful than meritorious. Their chief scout was a
Moroccan ex-slave who was accompanied everywhere by
a mini-harem, while the friar himself brought back
highly fanciful reports of 'the fabulous Seven Cities of
Cibola, large and powerful villages, four or five stories
high, wherein is said to be much gold.'

History has branded the friar a romancer. Coronado,

Above: After nearly three years
traveling through what are now
the states of Florida, Tennessee,
Louisiana, Arkansas, and
Mississippi, in a fruitless search
for gold, de Soto died of a fever
and was buried in the
Mississippi.

Left: Coronado marking his
'discovery' of the Missouri.

however, saw no reason to disbelieve him, and in the hope of making a major discovery set out in 1540 with an ambitious follow-up expedition: 336 Conquistadors, 1000 Indian 'helpers' (an euphemism for porters), and more than 1500 horses and mules. They headed inland from the Gulf of California *via* the Sonora Valley, and were soon climbing the Sierra Madre Occidental. This western arm of the Sierra is a range not of towering peaks separated by valleys, but of massive plateaux split by canyons: a rocky-cum-sandy desert dotted with creosote bushes, cactus and genera of plants that have managed to make their peace with aridity. It was not the easiest terrain to trek through. Nonetheless Coronado made good progress, and at the end of four months was nearing the fabulous Cibola. Alas, for his dreams! The golden city turned out to be an uninspiring huddle of adobe huts. When captured from the local Indians (the Zuni) they were found to contain no trace of gold: only the Zunis' hard-won beans, maize and squash. De Niza was sent home in disgrace, and Coronado split his expedition into a number of reconnaissance parties which, during the next two years, carried out extensive journeys of exploration.

One party of 25 led by Garcia de Cardenas headed northwest to investigate rumors of a large red river. After 20 days they made a spectacular discovery. Cardenas' description of one of the wonders of the world, the Grand Canyon, is, to say the least, prosaic – although this is not altogether surprising since few people in those days had much appreciation of the wonders of the natural world. He simply tells us that as he and his men were crossing a high, dry and bitterly cold plateau they came to the bank of a river. Looking down, it seemed as though the river below was only a few feet wide, yet the Indians insisted it was almost one mile wide.

We spent 3 days on this bank, *wrote Cardenas*, looking for a way down to the river . . . but it proved impossible to descend, although our most agile men made an attempt, and clambered down until those above were no longer able to keep sight of them.

Only in the naming of their discovery did the Conquistadors do it justice. They called it the Colorado

Canyon: *colorado* being the Spanish for a coppery-red (which is the exact color of the rocks) and *canyon* the Spanish term for a narrow street hemmed in by tall buildings (a good description of the sheer-sided nearly one mile deep gorge.) It was to be more than 200 years before another European, the Jesuit Father Francisco Garcas, set eyes on the Grand Canyon.

The main party meanwhile headed southwest into present-day Texas. Here they made contact with an Apache whom they christened the Turk and who led them into the high plains of the Panhandle. This was home to an abundance of wildlife, including bison.

At first our horses were terrified of them . . . Their eyes bulge at the side, so that when they run they are able to see those who follow them. They are bearded, like huge she-goats.

Here were riches, but not the sort that the Spaniards hankered after, and being told by the Turk that there was

Above: Coronado set out on his expedition to find the 'fabulous Seven Cities of Cibola,' encouraged by fanciful tales of gold related by the Franciscan friar, Marcos de Niza.

Left: Although Coronado's expedition failed to find the fabled gold, either at Cibola or later at Quivera, they were the first white men to see many of the natural wonders of the West, including the Grand Canyon.

gold to the northeast in Quivera, Coronado and his men headed through present-day Arkansas and into Kansas – probably passing only a couple of hundred miles from where de Soto was camped in the Ovacita Mountains. Quivera, home of the Wichita Indians, turned out to be as big a disappointment as Cibola. There was no city, and no gold. Convinced that the Turk had deliberately misled them, the Conquistadors beheaded him, and began the long trek back to Mexico City, which they reached in the summer of 1543 after a journey of 3 years and 3500 miles.

Coronado's expedition has much in common with de Soto's. Both were considerable feats of exploration, cutting deep swathes into the unknown; and both had negative results. For in the northwest, as in the northeast, the Spaniards' failure to find gold made them reluctant to extend the frontier of their empire. For the next couple of hundred years about the only people to push north along the Pacific seaboard were Jesuit priests.

Jesuit Explorers of the Pacific Seaboard (1687-1767)

Lack of gold was not the only reason for Spain's reluctance to colonize the Pacific coast; an equal disincentive was the arid nature of the terrain. Mexico's Pacific provinces Sonora and Baja are not easy to cultivate; the Baja in particular – a narrow, 800-mile peninsula that is dry, precipitous and unbelievably stony – is ill-suited to human settlement. People needed a special incentive to venture into such unpromising terrain. The Jesuits had such an incentive, their vocation to proselytize.

The first Jesuit mission in Mexico was founded in 1572 by Pedro Sanchez, and within 100 years the Society could boast over 30 colleges and 100,000 converts, with its priests working as far south as Guatemala and as far north as California. The most important of these Jesuit-explorers was Father Kino.

In 1687 he founded a mission near the mouth of the Sonora River and, in his own words, 'over the next 21 years made more than 40 expeditions to the west, northwest and north, some of 50 leagues, some of 100 leagues and some of more than 200.' What made these journeys of special interest is that Kino was an excellent surveyor, and brought back from his travels the first accurate maps of Sonora, Baja California and Arizona. He delineated the major river-systems, the Gila and Colorado, and paved the way for an eventual Spanish advance into California. He also supervised the building of a number of Jesuit missions in the Baja. This was stony ground in more ways than one. However, in the late seventeenth and early eighteen centuries a number of dedicated priests – men like Fathers Ugarte, Salvatiera and Glandorf – managed to establish more than a dozen isolated but flourishing missions which cared for both the physical and spiritual needs of the local Indians. This work came to an abrupt end in 1767 when the Jesuits were expelled from Spain and their missions all over the world were closed down.

In the same way that the Jesuit missions collapsed because of events in Europe over which they had no control, so the Spanish North American empire collapsed because Spain herself suffered defeats in Europe and was obliged to concede or sell vast areas of her New World territory to France, Great Britain or the emerging United States of America. However, long after Spain's troops departed the legacy of her culture remained: her religion, her grid-pattern towns with their plaza and church, her social structure and her domestic animals and crops co-existing with and soon becoming part of the indigenous culture.

French Explorers in the Saint Lawrence and Mississippi Valleys

Below: John Cabot sighting the New Found Land in 1498.

The early Spanish explorers of America were looters, in particular looters of gold. The early French explorers were traders, initially in fish and subsequently in fur.

When, in 1498, John Cabot discovered off Newfoundland 'waters as thick with fish as the Sargasso is thick with weed', he may have been sponsored by an English king (Henry VII) and sailing from an English port (Bristol), but it was the Norman, Breton, Basque and Rochellais seamen of France who were first to exploit his discovery. These French fishermen put ashore in Newfoundland to split, dry and salt their catch, and were soon trading in fur (in particular the fur of the beaver) with the local Indians. The desire to expand this trade in fur was one motive for the French exploration of North America.

Another motive was the desire to find a seaway to the Pacific. It took Europeans a long time to realize the true extent of the Americas. Early explorers regarded the land they came into contact with as little more than an inconvenient barrier that had to be breached before they could make their way to the Pacific and the treasures of the East. For years the *coureurs de bois* and *voyageurs* who pushed west through the rivers and lakes of North America expected any moment to break through to the ocean beyond and make contact with China. It typifies this attitude that as late as 1640 one of the greatest of these French explorers, Jean Nicolet, carried with him 'a ceremonial robe, made of Chinese damask, all strewn with flowers and birds of many colors' to impress the Chinese dignatories whom he expected to meet. The first

of these French explorers who came to America in search of China was Cartier.

Cartier Discovers the Saint Lawrence (1534-42)

In April 1534 Jacques Cartier of Saint Malo left his home port with two ships and secret orders from King Francis I. After a voyage of only 20 days he made landfall off the coast of Newfoundland, and followed the shore north until he came to the Strait of Belle Isle (the narrow, ice-cluttered reach of water between Newfoundland and Labrador). He nosed through this strait and into the estuary of the Saint Lawrence, being impressed by the 'many deep and excellent harbors', but unimpressed by the land: 'it is composed of stones and jagged rocks; nowhere did I see as much as a cartload of earth.' Early in July he crossed to the south side of the estuary, where he made contact with 'les sauvages' – the French never made the mistake of calling the people of America Indians –

> more than 300 persons in 40 canoes . . . we gave them knives, glass beads, combs and other trinkets, at which they showed much joy, singing and dancing in their canoes.

It was an augury. Of all the European nations who in the 16th, 17th and 18th centuries fanned out across the world, the French have the best record in their relationship with indigenous peoples.

Landing near Gaspé Bay, in present-day New Brunswick, Cartier raised a wooden cross and took possession of the land he had discovered in the name of Francis I. He then tried to stand northwestward, 'in the hope of discovering a strait,' but was forced back by a combination of adverse currents and head-winds. He beat to and fro for several weeks, making little progress, but discovering Anticosti Island, and sighting 'great beasts, the size of oxen, which have two tusks and swim about in the water' (walrus). In August, afraid that the ice might be thickening in the Strait of Belle Isle, he very prudently headed for home, reaching Saint Malo on September 5th after a short but eventful and important voyage: important because the rivermouth he had discovered (that of the Saint Lawrence) was for two centuries to be the gateway

through which explorers penetrated into the heartland of Canada and the United States.

Next year Cartier was back again. His three ships (the *Grande Hermyne*, the *Petite Hermyne* and the *Ermillon*) were well-provisioned, with sufficient food for him to winter in the New World. His orders were 'to complete the discovery of the western lands already begun to be explored.'

He again passed through the Strait of Belle Isle, and worked his way into the estuary of the Saint Lawrence, keeping first to the north bank, then to the south. At the end of a month of slow sailing in difficult conditions the estuary was still 25 miles wide, but ever-narrowing, and Cartier became increasingly convinced that he was entering not a strait but a great river. His good relations with 'les sauvages' continued, and at Bic Harbor he took aboard two young Hurons to act as pilots. The Saint Lawrence is a difficult seaway, with frequent shoals and rapids, a current often flowing at 6 or 7 knots and rocky banks. It says much for French seamanship and Huron pilotage that Cartier's ships proceeded upriver un-

Above left: Jacques Cartier's 1534 expedition to Canada failed to find the hoped-for route to China.

Above: This 16th century woodcut shows early fishing settlements in Newfoundland. In the background the catch of cod is being dressed, at the right the livers are being pressed for oil, and in the foreground the cod is being dried.

Below: Cartier raising a cross at Gaspé Bay, New Brunswick, in 1534.

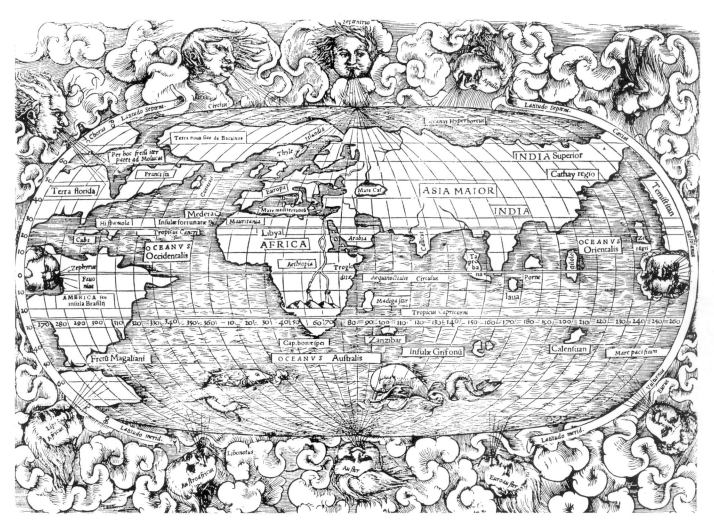

Left: This woodcut map of 1540 by Sebastian Münster appears to acknowledge, in the name 'Terra Francisca,' the voyages of Jacques Cartier in 1534-35. It shows, however, North America as being nearly bisected by the imaginary 'Sea of Verrazano' and Newfoundland arcing across the Atlantic to join with Scandinavia.

Below: Cartier's first meeting with the Indians at Hochelaga (the site of present-day Montreal) in 1535. Of all the European explorers of the 16th to 18th centuries the French have the most humane record regarding their treatment of the indigenous peoples.

damaged. In mid-September they came to a magnificent rock promontory 300 feet high, with the village of Stada-cona (the site of present-day Quebec) at the foot of it. Here Cartier left his ships, with orders to prepare winter quarters, while he took his longboats and 28 volunteers farther upriver. He made slow progress through a succession of narrow channels and rapids, before reaching the stockaded village of Hochelaga (the site of present-day Montreal) where the Huron chief Donnaconna and some 1000 of his warriors gave him an enthusiastic welcome.

This was the high-point of Cartier's success as an explorer. What followed was anti-climax His first disappointment came when Donnaconna took him to the top of a nearby hill, Mont Réal, from which he had a bird's eye view of the surrounding terrain. It was beautiful country, but there was obviously no seaway through it to China: for south-west of Montreal the Saint Lawrence narrows

to a succession of impassable rapids. Cartier retreated to his winter quarters. Here he suffered another disappointment: the winter turned out to be far more severe than anticipated. His ships became frozen into the ice, and his crew had a thoroughly miserable time, numb with cold and ravaged by scurvy. Several died. With the coming of spring Cartier returned thankfully to France, blotting his copybook by kidnapping and bringing back with him the chief Donnaconna and a young Huron boy and girl.

In spite of his unfavorable reports on the country, it was decided to try and establish a settlement; and in 1541 Cartier returned to the Saint Lawrence for the third time

Above left: Samuel de Champlain built on the discoveries of Cartier (above) to discover the Great Lakes.

Left: Champlain receiving his commission to explore into North America from King Henry IV of France in 1603.

with 5 ships and some one thousand colonists, including women and convicts. They built a camp at Cap Rouge, upriver from Quebec. However, the cold was daunting, the soil poor, and the Huron increasingly unfriendly. The following year the settlement was abandoned.

Cartier had discovered the entrance through which Europeans were to open up the northern United States and Canada; but because of the harshness of the terrain and the preoccupation of France with wars in Europe, it was 50 years before this entrance was put to use.

Champlain Discovers the Great Lakes (1603-1635)

In terrain where Cartier had failed to found a settlement, Champlain founded an empire.

Samuel de Champlain made several voyages to the Caribbean before arriving at the mouth of the Saint Lawrence in 1603. He was fortunate in his timing, in that Europe was at peace and there was a growing demand for furs. On his first voyage (1603-4) he revisited the Huron village of Hochelaga, but found it deserted. On his second voyage (1604-5) he explored the coast of Nova Scotia and founded a settlement at St. Croix only to see it almost at once wiped out by scurvy. On his third voyage (1608-9) he returned to the Saint Lawrence and built three large well-insulated cabins on the site where 60 years earlier Cartier had passed such a disastrous winter. This time the settlement took root and prospered, and within a couple of generations Quebec had become the fur-trading centre of an empire which stretched, albeit tenuously, from Hudson Bay to New York State, and from the coast of Nova Scotia to the banks of the Mississippi. It was Champlain who provided the impetus which brought this empire into being.

He had three objectives: to find a waterway to China, to expand the fur trade, and 'to bring the word of God to the people of New France' (Canada). It was the way he tried to achieve these objectives that made him such an important figure in the history of exploration.

The cornerstone of his policy was to form a working relationship with the local inhabitants, initially the Huron. He traveled with them, lived with them, fought with them, and concerned himself with their well-being, with the result that the French were able to establish a genuine rapport with the Indians. Some 100 years after

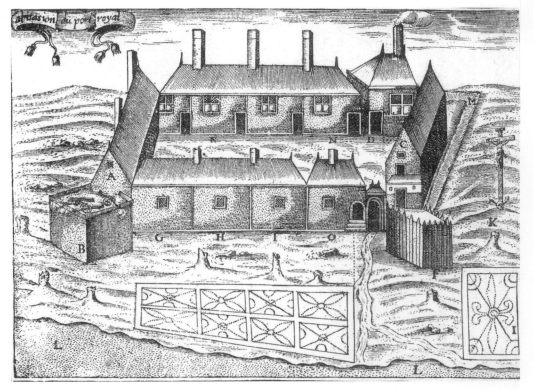

New France had been swallowed up by the British, an Indian chief said:

When the Frenchmen arrived at these falls they came and kissed us. They called us children, and we looked on them as fathers. We lived as one family in the same house. They never mocked our ceremonies, and never molested the places of our dead. Seven generations have passed, and we have not forgotten them. Just, very just they were towards us.

There was only one disadvantage to Champlain's policy. He so identified himself with the Huron that he became involved in their tribal wars; in particular he made enemies of the Iroquois, a powerful and warlike group of tribes who occupied roughly the area of New York State and who promptly allied themselves with the British.

Champlain's objectives called for expansion and hence exploration.

In 1609 he accompanied a group of Huron and Algonquin warriors on a raiding party. They traveled up the Saint Lawrence as far as Lake St. Pierre, then headed south *via* the Richelieu River until they came to the long, narrow and beautiful Lake Champlain. Here they

Above: The 17th-century French settlement of Port Royal.

Above right: Champlain so identified with the Huron Indians that he became embroiled in their struggles with the Iroquois. This attack of 1609 took place at the site of present-day Fort Ticonderoga.

Left: This convivial scene at Port Royal expresses the warmth of the French relationship with the Indians.

Right: Etienne Brule at the mouth of the River Humber (in present-day Toronto) in 1615.

attacked a stockaded Iroquois village, French muskets
enabling the Huron to achieve a rare victory over their
enemies.

In 1613, with two birch bark canoes, he set out from
the Lachine Rapids on the Saint Lawrence in search of the
'Great Salt Sea' which one of his *coureurs de bois* claimed
to have sighted. He struggled up the Ottawa River, 'partly
by portage (carrying) and partly by tracking (towing).' It
was beautiful but difficult country, and Champlain found
himself repeatedly thwarted by rapids, exhausted by portages, ensnared in woodland and plagued by mosquitoes.
When at last he struggled through to Lake Allumette, the
Indians thought '(he) must either have fallen from the
clouds, or be tired of life that (he) should make so difficult a journey.' He found no Great Salt Sea – although
there were plenty of rumors of a vast sheet of water to the
west – what he did find was a tangle of rivers, lakes and
beaver dams, a cornucopia for the fur trader.

In 1615, with a group of *coureurs de bois*, he again followed the Ottawa west, through 'an ill favored region full
of pines, birches and a few oaks, very rocky and rather
hilly,' before coming at last to Georgian Bay, the huge
island-strewn extension of Lake Huron. It was the end of
one of Champlain's dreams: the Great Salt Sea turned out
to be a great freshwater lake. However, his other dream,
of expanding the fur trade, was about to be realized. For
northwest of Lake Huron lay the empire of the beaver,
one-and-one-half-million square miles of unspoiled
woodland and stream, rock and lake. By aligning the
French with the Indians, Champlain ensured that his
coureurs de bois not only regarded the indigenous people
as allies but were regarded *by* them as allies.

His contribution to exploration is summed up in his
own words, 'only those willing to settle in the New World
and learn from its inhabitants, deserve to open up its unknown regions': a concept very different from that of the
Conquistadors, and about three centuries ahead of its
time.

Groseilliers and Radisson: Entrepreneurs of the Fur Trade

It is difficult to understand Canadian history without knowing something about the beaver. For in the same way that the quest for gold led explorers ever-deeper into South America, so the quest for the fur of the beaver led them ever-deeper into North America.

The beaver (*Castor canadensis*) has been described as a water rat with a bushy tail; it has also been described, more perspicaciously, as 'having the highest skills to be found in any animal apart from man.' Beavers are not much to look at: dumpy, squint-eyed, webbed-footed, long-toothed and scaly-tailed, they average about 50 pounds in weight, mate for life, care for their families and their injured, fell on average about 215 trees a year, and are best known for those marvels of animal architecture, their lodges. The basic requirement of a lodge is that the water in which it is built should be at a constant level. To ensure this the beavers dam back streams and lakes with huge structures that are anything up to a mile long and 40 feet wide, and dig-out complex canals complete with spillways and locks, so that the water-level can be controlled literally to the nearest inch. The lodges themselves, built of wood and plastered with mud, are like miniature castles, each with its moat, underwater entrances, winding passageways and well-ventilated eating and sleeping quarters, the latter furnished with beds of grass, regularly changed. An expert on the beaver, Frank Conibear, writes:

The Indians who were my companions along the traplines told me that the larger lodges usually contained three rooms, a room for sleeping, a room for eating and a smaller (underwater) room where the beaver passed their excrement, which was cleaned out at regular intervals. In addition the mother of the family, in the spring, hollowed out for herself an additional small room in which to have her young. What I have seen convinces me that the Indians were, as usual, right.

What made the beaver such a potent factor in exploration was partly its fur and partly its life-style. Its glossy, long-haired pelt was highly valued; and even more valuable

was its underhair, which could be shellacked into a wonderfully lustrous and durable felt. Beavers are non-migratory, relatively slow breeders and need large areas of woodland-cum-waterway in which to flourish; so once a river or lake had been 'beavered out', the trappers were obliged to move on, pushing ever-deeper into the vast lake-impregnated forests in search of their prey. As Eric Morse puts it: 'the beaver, by its defenselessness no less than by its value, was responsible for unrolling the map of Canada.'

It was the *coureurs de bois* who hunted the beaver: or, to be precise, who got the Indians to hunt them, and offered steel tools and weapons in exchange for their pelts. Typical of these tough, colorful adventurers were Medard Chouart Sieur de Groseilliers and Pierre-Esprit Radisson, known to generations of schoolchildren as Gooseberries and Radishes.

Above: Pierre-Esprit Radisson together with Medard de Groseilliers, explored deep into the heartland of North America in search of beaver pelts. They found a great unexplored area rich in beaver to the north of Lake Superior and when they failed to gain backing from the French government they switched allegiance to King Charles II of Great Britain. The company they founded, 'The Company of Adventurers of England trading into Hudson's Bay' (the Hudson's Bay Company), was to provide one third of Britain's earnings from foreign trade in its heyday.

Left: The fur-traders made their living not by trapping beaver but by trading with the Indians who had been skilled trappers for centuries.

Groseilliers was the elder, the more stable and cerebral and the better educated; Radisson was more flamboyant and mercurial and had had no education at all – as a child he had been captured by the Indians, and had had red-hot skewers driven through his feet, his fingernails torn out and his raw finger-tips dipped into canisters of burning coal – if ever a man was woodwise it was Radisson. They became known as 'the brothers', although in fact they were brothers-in-law, and in 1655 they disappeared into the rocky triangle of the Laurentian shield which extends south from the Great Lakes. It is difficult to piece together their exact comings and goings; but it is certain that wherever they went they encouraged the Indians to collect beaver-pelts and bring them westward for barter. In the latter stages of their journey there were operating almost 1000 miles from their base on the Saint Lawrence. It was no longer possible to carry the food they needed in their canoes; they therefore built a number of store-houses at strategic points, many of which developed into mini-trading-posts, and, a generation later, into fortified camps – fortified not against the Indians but the English.

In 1658 they made an even more important journey, venturing into the unknown territory to the north of Lake Superior. That winter, round the campfires of the Sioux and the Cree, they heard stories of the unending chains of beaver-ponds that lay close-packed between the shores of the Great Lakes and an ice-choked sea to the north (Hudson Bay). They were on the threshold now of the beaver heartland: more than one million square miles of sparsely-populated untapped wealth. That spring the Indians brought them an abundance of pelts, 'larger and more lustrous than any we had seen'; these Groseilliers and Radisson took back to Quebec, where they anticipated a heroes' welcome. Instead, they were thrown into prison for trading without a licence and their furs confiscated. Radisson felt that the man responsible, the Governor of Quebec, 'wished to grow rich on the labors and hazards of others.' Whatever the Governor's motive (and it may have been no more than a determination to uphold the letter of the law) his act was one of the major gaffes of history. For the outraged *coureurs de bois* went to France for redress, and failing to get it transferred their allegiance to England. They put to King Charles II a plan simple in concept but far-reaching in consequence: that they get the Indians to paddle their pelts down the many rivers that flow into Hudson Bay, where they would be met by ships from England with trade goods.

Charles II backed Groseilliers and Radisson unequivocally. In 1668 their ship the *Nonsuch* dropped anchor in Rupert Bay (the southernmost extremity of Hudson Bay); a fort was built; highly profitable terms-of-trade were initiated; and from the success of this voyage sprang that great trading conglomerate still known as 'The Company of Adventurers of England trading into Hudson's Bay.'

In its heyday the Hudson's Bay Company owned land ten times the extent of the Holy Roman Empire, and its profits accounted for more than one-third of England's earnings from foreign trade. It has been said that its employees not only tamed a wilderness but forged a nation. Soon Company posts were springing up from Greenland to Alaska and from the Great Lakes to the Arctic Circle; and the flags flown from these posts were not French but British.

Joliet and the Discovery of 'The Great Water' (1671)

Louis Joliet was the first major explorer of North America to be born in the New World (in Quebec *circa* 1645). It is

sometimes said he was the first white man to reach the Mississippi from the north. This, however, is doubtful; Jesuit priests and *coureurs de bois* almost certainly pushed through to the upper reaches of the river in the 1650s and 60s. What can be said is that Joliet was the first white man to follow the Mississippi for the greater part of its course and to bring back an accurate description.

He made two major journeys. In 1669, returning from an abortive search for a coppermine on the shores of Lake Superior, he pioneered a new water-route between the Saint Lawrence and the interior. His craft was a *canot du nord*, a 25-foot birchbark canoe which could hold up to two tons of supplies (or pelts) yet was light enough to be carried by two men. After a short portage across the isthmus between Lakes Superior and Huron, Joliet followed the shore of the latter until he came to the Saint Clair River; this he followed (with another brief portage) into the Detroit River which in turn brought him to Lake Erie.

Above: A fur-trader weighing pelts on a steel yard.

Left: Evangelizing zeal as well as desire for wealth turned men into explorers in North America. Here a missionary is negotiating the passage of his canoe across a waterfall.

He paddled along the north shore of Erie until he reached the Grand River which led him towards Lake Ontario; from here it was an easy passage through the Thousand Islands and down the Saint Lawrence to Quebec. This is a route which may look obvious with the benefit of a modern map, but which took some finding in near-virgin territory; it had many advantages over the route *via* the rapid-strewn Ottawa which it soon superseded.

His second journey was more far-reaching. As a young man Joliet had thought of entering the priesthood and had trained at the Jesuit College in Quebec; he regarded proselytizing as an essential adjunct of exploring. Listening to talk round the Indians' campfires, he had often heard rumors of a 'Great Water' far to the west, and in 1672 he teamed up with the Jesuit Père Marquette to search for it. They set out from Saint Ignace, on the north shore of Lake Michigan, and paddled their *canot du nord* through the great inlet of Green Bay and up the Fox River. Soon they were picking their way through a labyrinth of lakes and rivers into which few white men had ventured. With the help of Indian guides they crossed the watershed between the Great Lakes and the Mississippi Valley, and came to the upper reaches of the Wisconsin River. They were on the threshold now of a major discovery, and after a week of paddling-cum-drifting down the Wisconsin came to its junction with another and far larger river flowing strongly out of the north. This, they realized, was the Indians' *Missi* = great *Sippi* = water, and set out to follow it downstream. Soon they were passing through the vast featureless prairies of the midwest, marvelling at the herds of bison, 'as many of the ungainly creatures as there are stars in the sky.' They followed the river south for almost 700 miles, till they came to its junction with the Arkansas. Here they turned back, having convinced themselves that the Mississippi would discharge not into the Pacific but the Gulf of Mexico. They returned to New France via the Illinois River, reaching Lake Michigan in September 1673 after a journey (or to be more accurate a voyage) of over 3000 miles.

This was an important piece of exploration, laying the foundation for France's claim to the Mississippi Valley.

La Salle: Visionary and Coureur de Bois Par Excellence

La Salle is best remembered today as the explorer who completed what Joliet had begun by voyaging down the Mississippi to its mouth. This, however, was only one episode in his 20 year crusade to extend French influence in the New World.

René-Robert Cavelier, Sieur de La Salle was born in Rouen in 1643. Like many French explorers he trained as a Jesuit before coming to New France as a pioneer-fur-trader in 1666. He quickly proved himself a man of great vision but little patience, 'with an incurable way of trying to build superstructures before foundations were set.' In 1669 he took part in an expedition which explored the south shore of Lake Ontario; this was followed by a series of extensive journeys, mostly on foot, during which he conceived two grand designs: first, to stimulate the fur trade by using the Great Lakes as a waterway through which pelts could be carried by a succession of ocean-going vessels; and second, to contain British and Spanish expansion by building a line of French forts-cum-trading-posts along the shores of the Great Lakes and the length of the Mississippi Valley.

La Salle and his second-in-command Henri de Tonti built forts on Lakes Ontario, Erie and Huron; they also established a shipbuilding yard on the Niagara River, and

Above: The death of Father Jacques Marquette in 1673.

from here *Le Griffon* was launched in 1679, the first sailing ship to ply the Great Lakes. If *Le Griffon*'s maiden voyage had been successful, La Salle's career might have been a great deal happier; as it was the vessel disappeared – probably foundering in a storm – and La Salle's enterprise collapsed with more creditors than supporters, leaving him and Tonti to attempt hair-raising retreats on foot from their far-flung trading-posts. La Salle and a handful of men made what has been described as

the most difficult journey ever undertaken by Europeans in New France . . . through heavy rain, melting ice and woods so entangled that in 2 days the men's clothing had been cut to pieces and their faces became so scratched and bloody as to be unrecognisable.

De Tonti fared even worse. He was captured by the Iriquois:

They plunged a knife into my chest, breaking a rib near the heart . . . meanwhile a man behind me kept lifting my hair. They were undecided whether to scalp me and burn me or set me free.

Left: René-Robert Cavelier, Sieur de la Salle's vision was of a great French empire controlling the major rivers of North America.

der Gucht Scul:

Left: La Salle arrived in America in 1666 as a pioneer fur-trader. One of his grand designs was to stimulate the fur trade by using the Great Lakes as a waterway through which pelts could be carried by ocean-going vessels.

Below: La Salle took possession of Louisiana and the Mississippi in the name of the King of France on April 9th, 1682.

Both men survived; but it was the end of one of La Salle's dreams.

His program of fort-building, however, continued, with the support of Louis XIV; and in 1682 he set out with a flotilla of canoes intent on establishing French suzerainty throughout the Mississippi Valley. He reached 'The Great Water' via the Illinois, and descended it without too much difficulty, being greatly impressed (as had been Joliet) by the great size of the river, the fertility of the soil, the abundance of game, and the prosperity of the tribes through whose territory they passed. They landed at frequent intervals, entering into formal treaties with the Indians, and setting up stockades and flags as evidence of suzerainty. They saw little sign of the Spaniards – only a single sword and three old guns hanging unused from the wall of a cabin. On 9 April, 1682 they came to the open sea:

Advancing with all possible solemnity, we performed the ceremony of planting the cross and raising the arms of France. After we had chanted the Te Deum, the Sieur de la Salle, in the

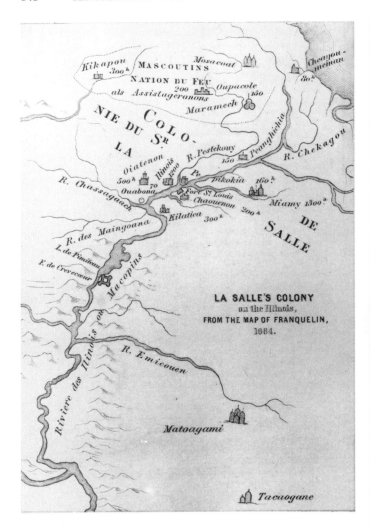

name of his majesty, took possession of that river, of all the rivers that enter into it and of all the country watered by them.

They named the vast territory to which they laid claim 'Louisiana', in honor of Louis XIV, then set out on the return journey. Heading upriver against the current they made slow progress, and it was more than a year before they were back in Quebec.

If La Salle's descent of the Mississippi had been followed up successfully it might have had far-reaching consequences. However, when he tried to return to the river-mouth by sea with the intention of founding a colony he met nothing but disaster. He failed even to find the delta of the Mississippi, and ended up 400 miles away among the brackish lagoons near present-day Houston. Calamity then followed calamity – the loss of their store-ship, quarrels, desertions, sickness, hunger and eventually mutiny, which ended with La Salle being lured into an ambush and shot by his own men: a sad end for an ex-

plorer who may have been tactless, demanding and impatient, but whose vision of a great French empire controlling the major rivers and lakes of North America was by no means impractical.

La Salle was the last of the great French explorers of the New World. In terms of the distances they covered, the discoveries they made, and their relationship with the Indians, the French were the most successful explorers of North America. It was, however, the British who were to reap where the French had sowed.

Above left: As he traveled along the Illinois river toward the Mississippi, La Salle entered into treaties with the Indians and set up stockades and flags as evidence of suzerainty.

Above: La Salle, like many explorers before and since, met a violent death. His final expedition by sea to find the mouth of the Mississippi went disastrously wrong and he was lured into a trap and shot by his own men.

British Explorers push Inland from the Atlantic Seaboard (1607-1783)

The British did less exploring in North America than the Spaniards or the French. Only in the far north, heading inland from Hudson Bay, did they make journeys comparable with those of de Soto and Coronado, Joliet and La Salle. Whereas the Spaniards explored in search of gold and the French in search of furs, the British put down roots and made the continent their home. The site of their first settlement was North Carolina.

The Roanoke Island and Jamestown Settlements (1584-1620)

In 1584 Richard Grenville and a party of some 100 men landed on Roanoke Island off the coast of North Carolina.

They were reinforced three years later by an expedition organised by Walter Raleigh but commanded by a Portuguese pilot; the latter, however, was so keen to turn pirate and plunder Spanish shipping that he ignored Raleigh's orders to move the colony to a better site in Chesapeake Bay (some 100 miles to the north), and dumped his men and supplies at the old site on Roanoke. Because of the attempted invasion of England by the Spanish Armada it was several years before a vessel could be spared to reprovision the settlers, and when a supply ship did get through to Roanoke there was no trace of the settlers; they had vanished as mysteriously as the crew of the *Marie Céleste*.

In 1607 a more permanent foothold was established in

Left: John Smith did much to save the ill-fated English Colony at Chesapeake Bay. Here his life is being saved by Pocahontas, daughter of an Indian chief. She returned with Smith to the colony and later married John Rolfe who introduced West Indian tobacco into Virginia.

Below: Sir Walter Raleigh commanded one of the earliest expeditions to colonize North America.

Chesapeake Bay – but at a terrible cost. Under the aegis of the London Company some 115 men arrived to establish a fort-cum-trading-post. They made a thorough reconnaissance of the Bay and chose about the worst possible place in which to build: the swampy banks of the James River, a site which could be easily defended but had little else to commend it. Their first impressions were favorable: broad rivers, lush meadows, strawberries three times the size of those in England, 'mussels and oysters thick as stones. I was almost ravished at the sight thereof' wrote one of the settlers. Their euphoria was short-lived. It was not long before they were dying of malaria, dysentery, Indian arrows and, incredibly, hunger. For the majority of them were 'gentlemen adventurers', happier fighting the Spaniards than dirtying their hands with agricultural labor. They failed to plant the crops on which their survival depended. Their food ran out, and during that first winter their numbers declined from 104 to 38, 'the most part of them dying of mere famine.'

The settlement owed its survival to two men: John Smith and John Rolfe.

Smith was chosen by the settlers to try and negotiate with the Indians for food. He came back not only with game and maize but with Pocahontas, the daughter of an Indian chief. On the strength of this success and a forceful character, Smith controlled the embryo colony for several years with a firm if not always popular hand, repeatedly asking the London Company to send out 'not gentlemen and women, but carpenters, gardeners, fishermen, blacksmiths and diggers-up-of-trees.' It was some time before the Company got the message; and in 1609 the arrival in Jamestown of 400 ill-assorted new settlers precipitated a crisis known as 'the starving time'. Cannibalism became an accepted way of life – one man is rumored to have killed, salted and eaten his wife – and by the spring of 1610 only 60 settlers remained alive. The Company was about to abandon the settlement when, almost overnight, it became metamorphosed to a gold mine.

Little is known about John Rolfe except that he married Pocahontas (the Indian girl who had befriended John Smith) and introduced West Indian tobacco to Virginia.

The native tobacco had, according to a contemporary, been 'poor, weak and of a bitter taste'; it was smoked by the Indians but had little appeal to Europeans. However, in 1612 Rolfe imported a number of the highly esteemed Caribbean tocacco plants. They flourished. And after a couple of years experimenting to decide the best method of planting and curing, a highly-profitable cash-crop was established: a crop which was for centuries to fulfil a worldwide demand. Soon tobacco was being planted in the streets of Jamestown and throughout the hinterland of Chesapeake Bay.

Many consequences stemmed from the cultivation of Rolfe's 'pernicious weed'. Because tobacco could be grown most economically on large estates worked by slave labor, this was how the social structure of the settlement evolved. Because tobacco growing needed no help from the Indians, this determined the settlers' attitude towards them: 'It is best,' wrote a Governor of Virginia, 'to have no heathens among us, who are at best but thorns in our sides.' And because all the land that was needed for tobacco growing could be found near the coast, this determined the settlers' attitude to exploration. It was something they had no need of. The story of British exploration from Virginia can be told in a few sentences.

In 1607 Christopher Newport worked his way up the James River as far as Richmond. A year later Smith ascended the Potomac as far as the Falls. In the 1640s the Governor of Virginia attempted to expand the fur trade, and a number of frontiersmen, the most active of whom was Abraham Wood, were encouraged to push west into the Blue Ridge Mountains. It was, however, 1670 before the mountains were climbed by Doctor John Lederer. Lederer had hoped, from the summit-ridge, to sight the

Pacific; but all he could see to westward was the main range of the Appalachians stretching away into the distance. This disappointment put paid to further large-scale exploration for almost a century.

The Spaniards, within a few years of founding Mexico City, had pushed some 1000 miles to the north into Colorado and Tennessee. The French, within a few years of founding Quebec, had pushed some 900 miles to the west into the beaver-country beyond Lake Superior. The British, within 150 years of founding Jamestown, still had not pushed over the Blue Ridge Mountains less than 100 miles from the coast. Yet in the fable of the tortoise and

Above: The first English settlement of North America was on Roanoke Island off the coast of North Carolina.

Below: The early years at Jamestown were extremely hard. The settlers were unused to working the land and starvation and even cannibalism plagued the colony.

the hare it is worth remembering who won the race. The British in Virginia may have been tardy explorers; but the land that they did clear and plant they had no intention of quitting; they were there to stay.

What was true in Virginia was true in New England.

The Newfoundland, Acadian and New England Settlements (1605-1670)

The first Europeans to settle in North America were not (as is sometimes claimed) the Pilgrim Fathers who in 1620 landed at New Plymouth, but un-named West Country fishermen who round about 1605 began over-wintering in the cod-salting stations of Newfoundland. It was quite usual for these fishermen to bring their wives with them; some wives overwintered too; children were born, and in sheltered coves around the Newfoundland coast a permanent population gradually accumulated – 'a kind of flotsam washed up on the beaches from the harvest of the sea.' Once a family had taken root it was joined by others, often friends from the same home port, which explains the close ties which have for centuries existed between a particular cluster of homes in Newfoundland and a particular port in Europe. The lives of these early settlers were orientated to the sea; they were slow to explore the hinterland, whose vast rock-bound forests had little to offer them.

To the southwest, in Acadia, a totally different type of settlement was taking place: French rather than British, and land-based rather than sea-based. Round the shores of the Bay of Fundy a wilderness of vast, fertile mud-flats and salt-meadows was dyked and ditched by French peasants under the direction of Dutch engineers. Once brought under cultivation the reclaimed land had much to commend it, yielding an excellent harvest of grain, vegetables and fruit. The Acadians built massive log cabins overlooking their dyked fields, enjoyed a good relationship with the local Indians (the Micmac), and soon evolved into a sequestered, close-knit settlement with little incentive to explore a hinterland which was a good deal less attractive than the littoral they had reclaimed.

Left: From a very early date English fishing fleets were working off the coast of Canada, sometimes overwintering in Newfoundland.

Still farther to the southwest another type of settlement was taking place. On 11 November 1620 the *Mayflower* dropped anchor in Cape Cod Bay, and 102 men women and children scrambled ashore 'at the place God chose for us' – they had been bound for Virginia, but were blown off-course by storms. These Pilgrim or Founding Fathers as they became known had come to the New World not to loot, to trade or to proselytize, but to find a place where they could worship God in the way they thought right: 'with simplicity, purity and without popish ritual.' They were homemakers rather than pathfinders, and for many years were too preoccupied with survival to think of exploration. For, like the settlers in Jamestown, they initially suffered heavy casualties. In their first

Below: The Pilgrim Fathers aboard the *Mayflower* dropped anchor in Cape Cod Bay on November 11th, 1620.

winter, decimated by sickness, hunger and sheer hard work, more than half of them died.

At times *wrote their leader William Bradford*, there were no more than 6 or 7 strong enough to hunt, cook and care for the entiry company . . . but they, with an abundance of toyle and hazard to their own health, fetched them wood, made them fires, washed their clothes, all willingly and cherfully.

Willingness and cheerfulness were about the only things that winter that the Pilgrim Fathers were *not* short of. It

was touch and go next spring if the settlement survived. What tipped the scales was that the local Indians taught them how to plant and fertilize maize, and with the benefit of a reliable crop, an improved water supply and reinforcements from England, the settlement at New Plymouth gradually took on an aura of permanence. By 1621 a self-sufficient community of some 200 people had taken root, living in a well-laid-out town with about 30 buildings, including fort, storehouse and meeting-house. Bearing in mind that the climate was harsh and the ter-

exploration would follow settlement. It did not. And this was for two reasons. The Puritans' desideratum was to create a new Zion, a society in which everyday life was conducted according to the teaching of the Bible: 'We shall be as a city upon a hill,' proclaimed the first Governor of Massachusetts; 'the eyes of all people are upon us.' This sort of society was best nurtured in a close-knit, patriarchal community (a bit like an ancient Greek city state), and this was the way that the various Puritan towns along the New England seaboard evolved; and having crossed from the Old World to the New to establish these utopian theocracies the Puritans were loath to leave them. When they did leave them it was not for the land but the sea.

One of the first explorers of the eastern seaboard summed up its characteristics in half-a-dozen words. 'The sea is rich,' wrote Jacques Cartier, 'the land poor.' This was confirmed by the early Puritan settlers who soon discovered that their fishermen could lower a basket off the Great Bank and haul it in half-full of cod, whereas a farmer would take 90 days to clear an acre of land of its glacial boulders only to find the following year another outcrop of boulders heaved up by the winter frost. There was of course a certain amount of agricultu-

Above: Unlike many previous settlers in the New World, the Pilgrim Fathers came not to loot, trade, or proselytize, but to find a place where they could worship 'with simplicity, purity and without popish ritual.'

Left: 'Virginia,' John Smith, 1612. Based on a description given by Smith and engraved in England by William Hole, this immensely influential regional map, oriented north to the right, is full of fascinating detail. Among the surviving place names are Jamestowne, Appamatuck, capes Henry and Charles, and Poynte Comfort. The different types of trees indicate the nature of the various forests. Note the inset of Chief Powhatan's council chamber.

rain difficult, and that the Founding Fathers had few technical skills, their survival was a triumph of hard work and team work; many better-equipped colonists in easier conditions have failed to establish a settlement at the first attempt.

What happened in New Plymouth was, in the next 10 years, repeated many times along the New England seaboard, as Puritan immigrants flooded into the New World – in the decade 1621-31 their numbers rose from under 100 to over 20,000. One might have thought that ral development (as in Martha's Vineyard) and a certain amount of pushing into the interior (as in the fertile Connecticut Valley); but by and large the Puritan settlements depended for their prosperity on their exploitation of the North Atlantic fisheries, and their cornering of the North Atlantic seaborne trade. A cod became the symbol of Massachusetts; and by the end of the seventeenth century vessels from Boston were carrying New England timber, fur and fish, Virginian tobacco and Caribbean sugar to Europe, and on their return voyage distributing European goods to the east coast settlements.

It was the start of a love affair with the sea: a love affair in which New England seamen were to penetrate every ocean, put into ports in every continent and traverse the world from Arctic to Antarctic as they harvested and distributed the riches of the oceans.

'Caesars of the North': The Hudson's Bay Company Rolls Back the Canadian Frontier (1670-1755)

Under the terms of its 1670 charter the Hudson's Bay Company was given control over about one-and-one-half-million square miles of Canada – the catchment area of the rivers that drained into the Bay. In effect this gave them control of most of present-day Canada except the Saint Lawrence Valley and the Great Lakes. All the crown got in exchange was '2 elks and 2 black beavers whensoever wee or our heirs and successors shall enter into the said Territorys.' This was one of the great bargains of history, on a par with the Alaska and Louisiana purchases, and one might have expected the Company to do more exploring than they did. Their policy, however, was largely restrictive: to allow only Company employees to trap, trade and explore in their territory, and not to go in search of beaver but persuade the Indians to bring pelts to their York Factory on the shores of the Bay. Nonetheless several Company men made major journeys: Hearne and Mackenzie in the Arctic (see Chapter 8) and Kelsey and Henday in the conglomoration of lakes, woodland and prairie that form present-day Manitoba and Saskatchewan.

Henry Kelsey spent almost his whole life in the service of the Company, ending up as one of its governors. In 1689, when not much more than a boy, he explored the Nelson, Severn and Churchill Rivers, 'delighting much to Indians' company, and being never better pleased than when traveling amongst them.' The following year he set out on a longer and more important journey, although its original objective was limited – 'to call, encourage and invite the remoter Indians to bring their furs to us on the Bay.' Heading southwest from York Factory he reached the Saskatchewan River, which he followed into the open country around present-day Saskatoon. No white man had ever penetrated this far west, and Kelsey was the first European to see the Canadian prairies and their great herds of bison: 'here is nothing but Beast and grass . . . a black Buffilo great, and an outgrown Bear which is good meat.' Unfortunately Kelsey didn't keep a Diary but recorded his travels in execrable verse:

Now Reader Read, for I am well assur'd
Thou dost not know the hardships I endur'd . . .
This wood is pople ridges with small ponds of water,
There is Beavour in abundance but no Otter

This has not endeared him to historians who have tended to dismiss his narrative as insubstantial; not did it help his reputation that the Company made no effort to follow his journey up, and no report on it was published until 1926. Nonetheless his travels were important, opening up a route into the previously unknown prairies.

Anthony Henday, an outlawed smuggler, who was apprenticed as a net-mender in the York Factory, set out in 1754 'to explore the countrie in the far west, to promote trade.' Like Kelsey before him and Hearne after, he traveled as a supernumerary with Indians who were heading back to their home territory. After four months canoeing through the rivers and lakes of Manitoba and Saskatchewan, where conditions were difficult and food scarce, they came to the plains of Alberta, where travel was easy and food plentiful – wild strawberries, saskatoon berries and great herds of bison which the Indians hunted on horseback. This was Blackfoot country, and

Above: The coat of arms of the Hudson's Bay Company. The company's full name was 'The Company of Adeventurers of England trading into Hudson's Bay.'

Left: Inside a Hudson's Bay Company trading store.

Henday was amazed and at times disconcerted by the Indians' prosperity and sophistication. He was ushered into a tented city: 200 neatly laid-out painted tepees, and a huge meeting hall, where he was greeted by 50 tribal elders. The hall was kept fragrant with sweetgrass smoke, and Henday was offered 'buffalow tongues and 2 comely young women.' However, when he tried to persuade the Blackfeet to bring their furs east to the Bay, he was put firmly in his place. The Blackfeet, he was told, had no wish to leave their horses and their bison, they did not know how to use canoes, and they had heard that food was scarce in the east and many Indians were starving. 'Such remarks', Henday admitted in his Diary, 'I thought exceeding true.'

He trekked west across the prairie until he was within sight of the Rocky Mountains – 51°50'N, 114°W was his most westerly position. Then, realizing he had no hope of reaching the Pacific, which was still a desideratum for every westbound traveler, he headed back for the Bay, accompanied on the latter stages of his journey by a flotilla of up to 60 canoes. He reached York Factory in June 1755 after a journey of 13 months and 1600 miles, for which he was given a £20 bonus, but no promotion.

Henday made several farther journeys to the west, and recommended his employers to send out traders 'with roving commissions to encourage the Indians to trade, and to root out the French.' His advice was ignored; for the Company was making handsome profits from playing a waiting game in the Bay, and saw no need to embark on adventures that might prove costly in the interior. Henday's journeys were therefore played down and discredited, his account of Indian horsemen in particular being ridiculed. The judgement of history has been fairer, and the net-mender who was little appreciated in his lifetime is now recognized as one of the more important 'Caesars of the North' who helped to roll back the Canadian frontier.

Above left: Samuel Hearne. As well as being an important official of the Hudson's Bay Company at Prince of Wales Fort, Hearne explored deep into the territory controled by the Company.

Above: Like Hearne Alexander Mackenzie explored the Arctic regions of Canada (*see* chapter 8); in 1792-93 he also crossed the Rockies to reach the Pacific.

Russian Explorers of Alaska (1741-1867)

Only just over 100 years ago Alaska was a department of Imperial Russia; its main port, Little Archangel, was one of the most prosperous in the Pacific; its hunter-trappers, the *promyshenniki*, were making vast fortunes out of the pelts of the northern fur seal, and the profits from this northern fur trade were the largest single item in the receipts of the Tsar's treasury.

Russian claims to the North Pacific seaboard stemmed from the 1741 voyages of Bering and Chirikov (see Chapter 2), and were reinforced by the flood of *promyshenniki* who, in the second half of the eighteenth century, crossed the Bering Sea to harvest the whales, walrus, sea otters, salmon and above all fur seals which thronged these rich but little-known waters. To quote Elliot's *Alaska and the Seal Islands*:

The success of the early fur traders was so great that soon every Siberian merchant who had a few thousand roubles was putting out craft to engage in this lucrative business. They all carried on their operation in the same manner. The owner of the vessel engaged a crew on shares. The cargo of furs brought back was divided into two equal divisions: half to the owner, and the other half divided between captain and his crew as

could be agreed. After this division, everyone gave one-tenth of his portion to the Government at Saint Petersburg, which, stimulated by this generous swelling of its treasury, never failed to keep an affectionate eye on its Pacific subjects!

The spate of individual voyages was brought under the aegis of a central authority by Aleksandr Baranov, who founded the Russian American Company, a trading conglomerate which in its heyday matched the Hudson's Bay Company for size and profitability. Baranov, a Siberian trader, was appointed by the Tsar to oversee his American interests. In 1791 he explored the chain of the Aleutian Islands in his galliot *Tri Svyatitelya* (*Three Saints*) until wrecked off Unalaska. In 1793 he transferred his attention to the mainland, exploring the magnificent Cook Inlet and Prince William Sound, and establishing a trading post on Baranov Island (Sitka). Within 20 years this trading post had become 'a glittering metropolis' officially called Little Archangel but often dubbed 'the Saint Petersburg of the Pacific.' It could boast ironfoundries, brick-yards, factories, shipbuilding yards that launched 60 vessels a year, Catholic and Greek Orthodox churches, and huge houses 'often 150 feet in length and 3

Left: For most of the 19th century the profits from the trade in the furs of the northern fur seal were the largest single item in the receipts of the Tsar's treasury.

stories high, beautifully constructed and exotically furnished,' all overlooked by Baranov's castle (a fortress which with its palisades and turrets might have been lifted out of the Middle Ages) and some of the most spectacular coastal scenery on Earth.

The territory controlled (in theory) by the Russian American Company was enormous, stretching from the Arctic Circle to California and for an unspecified distance inland. The Company initiated several expeditions to explore its vast kingdom. By sea, Golovnin in the *Diana* and Vasilyev in the *Blagonamerennyi* carried out extensive voyages between Bristol Bay and Norton Sound, discovering Nunivak Island in 1821. A few years later (1826-29) Litke in the *Senyavin* and Stanyukovich in the *Moller* produced the first accurate charts of the east coast of the Bering Sea. The results of these and other voyages were

Below: In 1793 Aleksandr Baranov established a trading post on Baranov Island in Sitka Sound (seen below). Within 20 years it had become 'the Saint Petersburg of the Pacific.'

co-ordinated by M.D. Tebenkov to produce in 1852 his classic pilots' guide, *An Atlas of the Northwest Coast of America*. By land, exploration was more difficult and less far-ranging. In 1817-18 Pyotr Korakorsyk crossed the main range of the Aleutian Mountains from Cook Inlet to Kvickak Bay, discovering en route Lake Iliamna. Between 1833 and 1838 Andrey Glazunov explored the complex and marshy delta of the Kwikpak (Yukon) River; and a few years later Lieutenant Zagoskin of the Imperial Navy, in a major feat of exploration, ascended the Yukon for some 500 miles (almost as far as present-day Tanara) thus opening up one of the major arteries of the inland fur trade.

In its heyday Russian America was protected by an Imperial *ukase* (arbitrary decree) which prohibited foreign shipping from entering a huge arc of the North Pacific from the Kurils in the west to Vancouver Island in the east. This monopoly was gradually whittled away, as Great Britain exerted territorial pressure through the Hudson's Bay Company, and the United States exerted diplomatic pressure through the Monroe doctrine. In the aftermath of the Crimean War Russia was vulnerable to pressure, and her New World empire was first leased to the Hudson's Bay Company, then sold to America in 1867 for the knockdown price of $7,200,000.

Once Alaska came under American control the tempo of exploration quickened, with a number of private concerns (like the Western Union Telegraph and the Signal Service) collecting data on the region's geology, meteorology and natural history. Further exploration was stimulated by the discovery of coal, gold and oil; and in recent years aerial surveying has completed the delineation of this vast, majestic and scenically beautiful territory.

Manifest Destiny: American Settlers Push West to the Pacific (1767-1850)

The first people in modern times to reach the New World from the Old saw a frontier ahead of them; a vast, unexplored wilderness disappearing into every sunset. It was, however, several centuries before this frontier was thought of as something that might be rolled back by a process of continuous settlement. Early explorers, it is true, headed west in search of the ocean which they always hoped might lie the other side of the farthermost hill but not until the eighteenth century was there a feeling among the settlers that it was their destiny to expand westward to forge one nation out of all the vast territory that lay between the Atlantic and the Pacific.

Some people think that this commitment to unrolling the frontier stemmed from the Peace of Paris (1783) when the United States won control of territory west of the Appalachians and threw off the yoke of British suzerainty. Others that it stemmed from the Louisiana Purchase (1803) when Spain gave up her claim to almost half a continent. Yet before any of these events took place there was one part of America where the frontier was already being rolled westward. The date was 1767. The place was the Iroquois 'great meadow' of *Ken-ta-ke*. And the instigator of the surge to the west was the folk hero and Indian fighter Daniel Boone.

Daniel Boone and 'The Paradise of Kentucke' (1767-1798)

Boone was born of Quaker parents in 1734. His father was a frontier-farmer in present day Pennsylvania, and this was where young Daniel developed those skills in shooting and woodcraft for which he was soon to be famous. In 1755 the family moved to North Carolina, where Boone married and tried to settle down, like his parents, as a frontier farmer. Conditions were difficult: constant skirmishes with the Cherokees, constant friction over land-speculation and tenure, and a surfeit of horse thieves and robbers. Boone found that he was happiest in the woodland beyond the frontier, hunting bear and buffalo, and pitting his wits against the Indians. In 1767 he decided to cross the Appalachians in search of the legendary great meadow, where according to hearsay the grass was blue and the buffalo multitudinous as the stars. However, on his first journey he picked an unlucky route, and had difficulty penetrating the tangle of laurel woods that cover the Cumberland uplands; he found plenty of salt-licks but little good farming country.

A couple of years later he tried again, backed by Richard Henderson, an ambitious land speculator; and this time he was more successful. He discovered a pass through the mountains that was soon to be known as the Wilderness Road: a narrow, tortuous and rocky trail that cut through the last great barrier of the Appalachians. It was the gateway to paradise. Once over the pass, Boone followed an Indian trail that skirted the laurel-woods and brought him to the bluegrass meadows that lie astride the Kentucky River as it flows north to the Ohio. It was beautiful country, and he fell in love with it.

He passed through the forest noting nothing but the beauty of its fruits, leaves and flowers, and the abundance of its game, especially the wild turkeys. Coming to the bluegrass, he was amazed by the vast droves of buffalo feeding in the meadows; and a frontierman's eye told him how good the soil was. He was happy, and spent the next couple of years exploring the region until he knew it intimately.

In these two years he had enough hair-raising escapes to fill an adventure novel. Twice he was captured by the Indians. The first time he escaped by throwing himself

Below: Daniel Boone's first view of Kentucky. Boone immediately fell in love with the rich pastures of the bluegrass country and spent two adventure-filled years exploring it on his own.

over a 60-foot cliff and landing, miraculously unhurt, in a maple tree. The second time he was about to be scalped when a Shawnee chief intervened and adopted him; for several months Boone lived as one of the tribe, his face painted, naked except for a loin-cloth, and his head shaved except for a scalp-lock; by the time he managed to escape there was little he did not know about the Indians and their way of life.

When he returned to North Carolina his stories of the rich land beyond the frontier sparked off an exodus that was small to start with but soon was to gather pace. In 1773 a party of 7 families including the Boones, together with all their possessions and livestock, set out down the Wilderness Road. These first settlers were given a hard time by the Indians; they came under frequent and savage attack; many, including Boone's eldest son, were killed; and in the place where they chose to settle (Boonesborough) the first building they constructed was a fort. However, the land was fruitful, game was abundant, and others quickly followed where Boone and his friends had led.

There seems to have been an air of infectious enthusiasm about this first great stride into the interior. In the words of one of the settlers: 'No Adventurers Since the days of donquicksotte ever felt so Cherful and Ilated, every heart abounded with excitement.' Statistics confirm the scale of the migration. In 1774 the white population of present-day Kentucky was no more than a few dozen solitary and nomadic hunters-cum-trappers; by 1784 it had risen to over 30,000, with settlers literally queuing up to cross the Mississippi some 1000 miles from the coast.

Among those eager to venture yet again into new territory was a disillusioned Daniel Boone. His disillusion was

Left: Daniel Boone alone in the wilderness.

Below: When Daniel Boone took his family along the Wilderness Road into Kentucky in 1773 they came under frequent attack from the Indians whose territory they were encroaching on. This illustration reflects Boone's status as a folk hero protecting his family against 'savages.'

Left: The Louisiana Purchase of 1803 transferred large tracts of land to United States' control and made possible the Lewis and Clark expedition of 1804.

due in part to the fact that he had been cheated out of his hard-won territory by crooked land speculators, who took advantage of loopholes in deeds and records to strip him of every acre he possessed and then claim he was still their debtor. But there was another and even deeper cause of his disillusion. To quote Hugh Brogan's *History of the United States of America*:

> He (*Boone*) was a divided soul. He wanted to be rich in land, chiefly for his wife and children's sake; he sought out good acreage on the frontier, and knew it could only be secured from the Indians by a mass movement of population; so he led his countrymen down the Wilderness Road. But at the same time he was in love with the untouched wild; happiest when, in deerskin shirt and moccasins he was stalking bear or buffalo, his rifle in his hand.

It was a classic case of someone killing the thing that he loved.

In 1798 Boone crossed the Mississippi with his family and friends, and was awarded the 'headright' to 9000 acres of virgin territory by the Spanish government; he was therefore one of the founders not only of Kentucky but also of Missouri. However, once again he lost everything; for in 1804 the territory west of the Mississippi passed from the suzerainty of Spain to that of the United States. The old man proved remarkably resilient. Cared for and loved by his family, and becoming even in his lifetime a folk hero, he lived to the age of 85, and in the last decade of his life was still exploring, being one of the first white men to reach the Yellowstone region of Wyoming.

Boone and his family were archetypal frontier-folk, ever seeking land in the new west, yet never wholly severing their ties with the old east. Such sporadic, relatively small-scale migrations – with women playing as important a role as men – were not usually *per se* important; but their cumulative effect was enormous. A folk song catches the spirit in which they were made:

> Oh, don't you remember sweet Betsy from Pike
> Who crossed the big mountains with her lover Ike,
> With two yoke of cattle, a large yellow dog,
> A tall Shanghai rooster, and one spotted hog;
> Saying, goodbye, Pike County, farewell for a while.
> We'll come back again when we've panned out our pile.

By tens-of-thousands of such journeys the frontier was rolled westward.

'To Explore even to the Western Ocean': Lewis and Clark Pioneer a Trade Route to the Pacific (1804-06)

A very different type of exploration was carried out under the aegis of the US Government by Lewis and Clark.

Almost as soon as President Jefferson took office he proposed to Congress that 'an intelligent officer, with 10 or 12 chosen men, might examine the Missouri River . . . and such other streams that may offer practicable water-

Left: Although he was personal secretary to President Jefferson, and a skilled diplomat and scientist, Meriwether Lewis was also an accomplished frontiersman.

communication across the continent, for the purposes of commerce.' The idea at first was little more than a pipe dream; but the Louisiana Purchase gave it feasibility, and Jefferson began to look for an expedition leader. He chose his personal secretary, Meriwether Lewis, who had been a keen supporter (and indeed initiator) of the project and was a skilled diplomat, scientist and frontiersman. Lewis invited his friend William Clark – a brilliant cartographer – to be co-leader; the personnel were mostly hunters, *voyageurs* and men with practical trades (like carpenters, metal-workers and gun-smiths); and it was a well-chosen and well-equipped expedition which set out from St Louis on May 14th 1804.

Their ostensible aims were to find a trade route – if possible by water – across the continent, to make treaties of friendship with the Indians through whose territory they passed, to collect scientific data and to make accurate maps of their journey. However, the expedition also had a more fundamental is less tangible objective. The Russians were building up a trading empire in Alaska, the British were showing interest in Oregon, Spanish influence still permeated California, and it seemed to Jefferson that if the emergent United States was to gain control of the whole continent, an official showing of the flag in the distant Pacific territories was called for. Important issues were therefore at stake that spring, as Lewis and Clark headed northwest.

The first part of their journey was unremarkable: 45 men in 8 canoes paddling up the 'Big Muddy'. The current in places was strong enough to disconcert the *voyageurs*, there were frequent sandbars, infrequent rapids, and 'a continuous plague of ticks, musquiters and knats'. To start with the country they passed through (South Dakota) was familiar to French and British traders; but by late summer they were coming to the unknown. At Omaha they smoked their first pipes of peace with the much-feared Sioux, who allowed them to cross, but not linger in, their hunting grounds; and by early October they were approaching the Mandan villages. The temperature now was dropping, a scum of ice was forming on the banks of the river, and Lewis began to look for a site for their winter quarters.

The most costly item on their manifest had been 'pre-

Above: Emigrants crossing the plains.

Below: Fur Traders Descending the Missouri by George Caleb Bingham, 1845.

sents for Indians – flags, feathers, coins, cocked-hats and frock-coats'; and by distributing these the expedition established good relations with the Mandan, and were given permission to build a cluster of well-stockaded cabins. Here they spent a trouble-free winter, frequently visited by Indian chiefs, one of whom at least was not impressed.

Had I these white men in the upper plains, boasted the chief of the Hidatsa, *my warriors would do to them as they would to so many wolves; for there are only two sensible men among them, the worker in iron and the mender of guns.*

After Christmas the expedition was joined by Toussaint Charbonneau, a Montreal fur-trader, his Indian wife Sacajawea and their newborn child. Sacajawea was a Shoshoni, a tribe living near the headwaters of the Missouri (terrain that the expedition would soon be passing through), and Lewis was quick to realize her potential value as an interpreter and peace-keeper.

In March the ice began to break up; the water-level rose, and soon the expedition was again heading upriver: 32 men, 1 woman and 1 child, their belongings crammed into a couple of pirogues and 6 canoes, 'these little vessels containing every article by which we were to subsist and defend ourselves.' At first the pirogues made good progress under sail; but as the river narrowed, sail gave way to oars, and oars to tow ropes, with the men often up to their armpits in the water. The bottom was rocky, and a pair of moccasins lasted only two days, one day new and one patched. Both Lewis and Clark had a healthy curiosity about the land they passed through, 'where the foot of civilised man has never trodden'. They recorded the seams of what looked like coal, the trees of cottonwood, and the huge 'gangs' of elk, deer, buffalo, prairie dogs and

wolves – 'the Game is gitting so pleanty and tame that Some club them out of their way.' One creature not susceptible to clubbing was the grizzly bear. A third of a ton in weight, 8 feet from nose to tail, and 'so hard to die,' wrote Lewis, 'I would as soon fight two Indians as one of these gentlemen.'

As they approached the Rockies, the river was joined by its major tributaries, the Little Missouri, Yellowstone and Marias. Uncertain which to follow the expedition split up. On 13 June Lewis came to the Great Falls, a succession of rapids where the river drops 400 feet in a few miles. The portage was difficult, and it was a fortnight before they had manhandled their canoes and belongings to a spot where the river was again navigable. From this point onward the terrain became increasingly barren – 'nothing but rattlesnakes and prickly pears' – and Lewis

Above: A contemporary illustration of Lewis and Clark holding a council with the Indians.

Below: Grinnell Point in the Glacier National Park remains much as it did when first seen in the distance by Meriwether Lewis in 1806.

was anxious to make contact with the Shoshoni and exchange his canoes for their horses. The expedition was
now on the watershed between the Atlantic and the
Pacific. This was familiar terrain to Sacajawea. One day
she recognised the spot where, years earlier, she had
been captured and carried off by a Hidatsa war party. And
a few days later, when they were approached by a group
of Shoshoni horsemen, she recognised her brother.

They did not linger among the Shoshoni; for summer
was giving way to fall, and fall in the Rockies was far
harsher than in their native Virginia. They 'made the
Indians sensible of their dependence on our government,' gave them medals, knives, looking-glasses and

beads, and purchased horses and guides. Then they were
heading over the bleak ranges of the Bitterroot, 'high
rugged mountains in every direction as far as I could see,'
wrote Clark. Each night their blankets were rimed with
frost, game was scarce and the forests difficult to penetrate. It took them more than 50 days to cover less than
300 miles; but in late September they struggled through
to a major west-flowing river, the Clearwater. The Clearwater led them to the Snake, and the Snake to the
Columbia. Here, with the help of Nez Perce Indians, they
built 5 dugout canoes, and embarked on the final stage of
their journey, tackling shoals, rapids and frequent portages on a diet of dried salmon and elk. Their first

Above: Arthur Jacob Miller,
*Shoshone Encampment at
Trappers' Rendezvous on Green
River* (detail), 1837. Meriwether
Lewis traded his canoes for
horses with the Shoshone
before crossing the Rockies.

Below: Map showing Lewis and
Clark's joint and separate
courses.

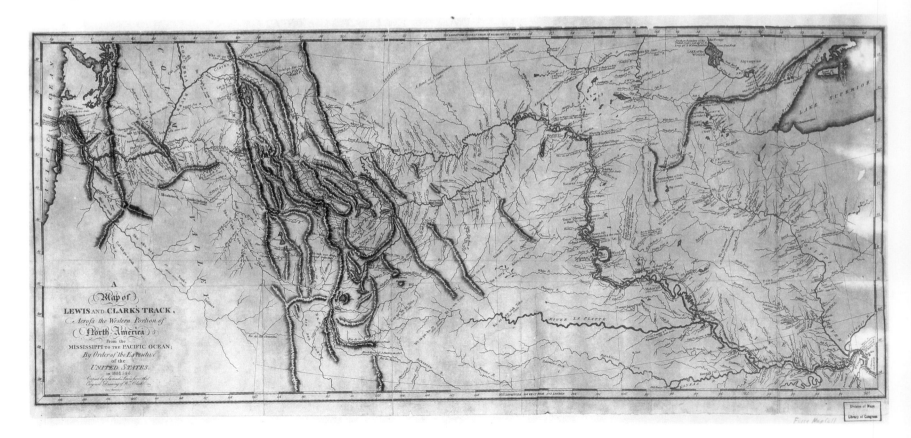

intimation that they were nearing the Pacific was the increasing number of white men's trinkets (brass teakettles, seamen's jackets and knives) seen in the Indian villages; their second intimation was the sight of seals somersaulting among the rocks. Soon they were feeling the ebb and surge of tides, a heavy swell was threatening to capsize their dugouts, and at last, on 15 November 1805, they saw ahead of them the mouth of the estuary.

'Ocian in view!', wrote Lewis. 'O! the joy!' On a promontory at the mouth of the Columbia they carved their names on tree trunks, 'the men much Satisfied with their trip.' There was, however, little time for celebration. For the men were sodden, flea-bitten and weak with dysentery, and winter was almost on them. They built a great stockaded cabin at a site they called Fort Clatsop (after the local Indians), not far from present day Astoria; and it was as well they had plenty of food and firewood, for the weather that winter was dispiriting; a raw wind and incessant rain-cum-sleet – in the 5 months that they spent at Fort Clatsop they had only 6 days of sunshine. The fact that they came through the winter in good health and good spirits is a testimony to Lewis's unobtrusive but eminently sensible leadership.

They began the return journey – thankfully – on 23 March. Once they had crossed the Rockies they again split up and completed their exploration of the Yellowstone and Marias. It was September 1806 before they returned to St Louis after a journey of 7690 miles and 860 days.

This was one of those expeditions which might be even better known if it had not been so successful – if, for example, Lewis had got lost or massacred by the Indians. As it was, there were no disasters and few highlights, only a steady accretion of meritorious exploration. To list only a few of Lewis and Clark's achievements: they met and made treaties with some 50 Indian tribes, they brought back details of 122 species of fauna and 200 species of flora, they discovered a practicable route through the Rockies, and most important of all they delineated and consolidated the claim of the United States to the whole vast area embraced by the river-systems of the upper Missouri and the Columbia.

They welded the prairies to the Pacific.

Left: Charles de Saint-Memin, *An Osage Warrior,* c. 1804. At President Jefferson's request Meriwether Lewis arranged for twelve Osage Indian Chiefs to visit Washington and other eastern cities in order to establish firm diplomatic relations with the Indian Nations within the boundaries of the Louisiana Purchase. Saint-Memin, a French émigré artist, was employed to make portraits of the Chiefs; these are the earliest known likenesses of Plains Indians.

'Knight of the Buckskin': Jedediah Smith Pioneers a Route to California (1823-30)

Most of the better known explorers of North America – even Daniel Boone – had precursors: unknown and usually unlettered hunters-cum-trappers, 'wanderers following their own star'. Eric Newby puts it well:

Such a man, with only his horse and perhaps a pack mule for company, was one to whom the lonely and dangerous life appealed – a man who, like the Indians with whom he came into contact, was always retreating before the advance of a civilization for which he cared little. Such men were the first to trace the tracks over which large sponsored expeditions traveled during the 19th century.

These Mountain Men, as they were called, were usually anonymous figures whose exploits were never recorded; an exception was Jedediah Smith.

Smith was born in New York in 1799 of a Puritan family, which explains his aversion to drinking and chewing tobacco, and why he took on his journeys not only a rifle but a Bible – although the latter never seems to have inhibited his use of the former. When he was in his teens his family moved to Pennsylvania, and Jedediah, like many adventurous young men of his day, became involved in the fur trade. He was only 24 when he set out on the first of his three great journeys.

He left Fort Kiowa on the Missouri in September 1823, together with 11 experienced trappers who worked for the American Fur Company. This company, controlled by the able and ambitious Henry Ashley, was determined to break the monopoly of the Company of Adventurers Trading into Hudson's Bay and trap the beaver-rich territory west of the Rockies. The aim of the expedition was therefore trade rather than exploration. They kept

initially to the south of the route pioneered by Lewis and Clark, heading through the Badlands and Black Hills of South Dakota and into the Bighorn Mountains of Wyoming where they exchanged their canoes for horses. Conditions were difficult. Water was scarce, and twice they came close to dying of thirst. The Indians were hostile. So were the bears; one was not killed until hit by 11 musket balls, and another had Smith's head literally in its jaws before it was killed – 'I got one of the men to sew my scalp together,' he wrote, 'and we resumed the march.' Attempting, with more valor than discretion to cross the Rockies in February, they were caught by a heavy snowfall in Union Pass and nearly frozen to death. A few

Above: Frederick Remington *The White Trapper*, 1890. Cheap, colored engravings such as this propagated the mythology and romance of the frontiersman for a new nation eager for a heritage.

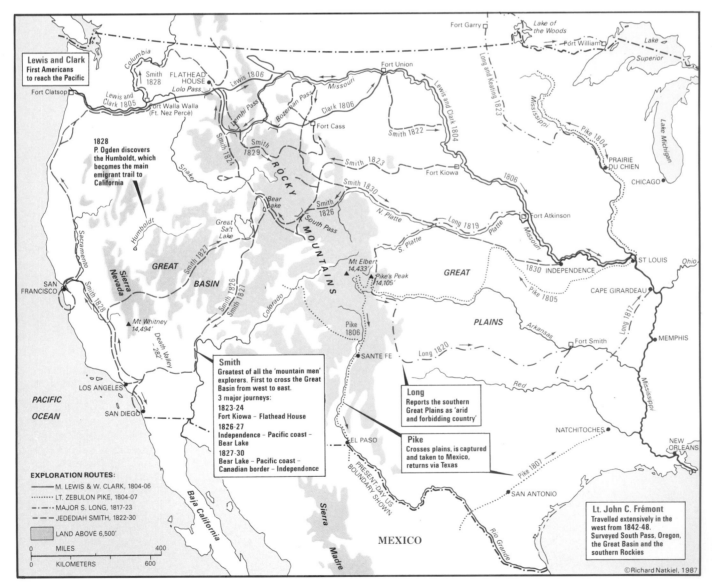

Right: The unwelcoming aspect of California's Death Valley shows the sort of conditions that Jedediah Smith survived before he was shot by the Comanche on his fourth journey.

Left: This map shows the routes of the four most important explorers of the west in the early 19th century.

months later they managed to cross the continental divide via South Pass. This was an important discovery. In the short term it led them to rich trapping grounds; in the long term it opened up a trail to Salt Lake City and beyond. Once the expedition had crossed the main range of the Rockies they headed northwest, making for the Hudson's Bay Company post on the Columbia, where they arrived, exhausted and short of food, in the autumn of 1824. The *camaraderie* of the beaver-dam proved stronger than the antagonism of the boardroom; although competitors, the trappers of the rival companies spent the winter together, before Smith and his men returned by a more northerly route to the Missouri.

A couple of years later he was again heading west, this time as a member of the Rocky Mountain Fur Company, a group of trappers and businessmen (again controlled by Ashley) dedicated to pioneering trade-routes across the mountains to the Pacific. In the spring of 1826 he explored the periphery of the Great Salt Lake in search of a river, the Buanaventura, said to link the lake to the Pacific. Finding the Buanaventura a myth, he headed southwest into the Great Basin, one of a cluster of deserts that cover some 500,000 square miles of southwestern America and northwestern Mexico. This is a bleak environment with an annual rainfall of under 3 inches, most of which is sucked up by the westerly winds: the home of cacti, creosote-bushes, yucca and crucifix thorn; of lizards, gilas, rattlesnakes and scorpions, and of 'Digger' Indians who, like the Aborigines of Australia, lead nomadic lives in an everlasting search for food. Smith and his party of 16 headed first down the Virgin and Colorado Rivers, then through the Mojave Desert, following the twists and turns of a river that Smith aptly called the Inconstant. The names that lie scattered across maps of the Mojave are evidence of the hardships they suffered: Eagle Crags, Granite Peaks, Red Mountain, Soda Lake, Dry Lake, Devil's Playground, Mirage and Death Valley. It took them three months to cross the Mojave, following roughly the line of the present day Santa Fe Railroad; and when, on 27 November 1826, they stumbled into the San Gabriel Mission to the north of San Diego they were the first white Americans to reach California by land from the east.

Their return journey was even more gruelling. San Diego, in those days, was Mexican territory. Nonetheless Smith was welcomed, hospitably treated and told he could return by the same route. This, however, did not suit him; and he violated the Mexican Governor's orders by sailing to present day Los Angeles, then heading up the San Joaquin Valley, still hoping to find the legendary Buanaventura. He found instead the spectacular snow-capped barrier of the Sierra Nevada. Attempting to cross the mountains he was twice forced back by driving snow and sub-zero temperatures; however, in May 1827 he at last forced his way through, a little to the north of the Yosemite National Park, only to find himself facing the equally daunting Nevada Desert. It took him two months of anxious and exhausting travel to reach the Great Salt Lake, where he arrived in July, having done what no white man (and probably no Indian) had done before: crossed one after the other North America's highest mountains and widest desert.

His third journey was less successful. While again crossing the Mojave, ten of his men were killed by the Indians; and when the survivors struggled through to San Diego they were thrown into jail – the Mexicans had not forgotten how Smith, a couple of years previously, had flouted their orders. He was only released after signing a $30,000 bond and agreeing to leave Mexican terri-

Left: Half Dome Mountain in the Yosemite National Park gives some idea of the sort of terrain Smith had to contend with.

tory within two months. Once again heading north, his depleted expedition was fiercely attacked by Indians, and only Smith and two of the others survived the subsequent fighting.

His fourth journey was his last. In the desiccated tableland between the Arkansas and Cimarron Rivers, he was ambushed and shot to death by the Comanche.

Smith's journeys were not only feats of great endurance, they were of great consequence; for they stimulated Americans' interest in the Pacific seaboard. Smith was the first man to pioneer practicable routes to California, and the first to bring back reports of its enormous agricultural potential. He was only 32 when he died; but in 8 years of almost continuous exploration he covered over 16,000 miles and opened the floodgates to a great surge of westward migration.

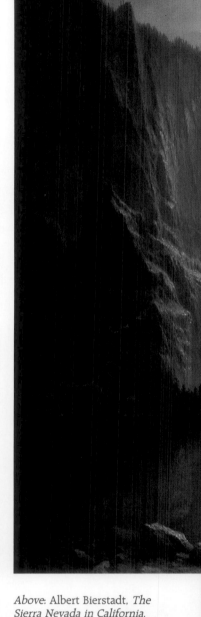

The Sante Fe, California, and Oregon Trails (1820-50)

It might be thought that after Smith's great journeys the whole of North America had been explored, and certainly by 1830 the major features of the continent had been delineated. However, the map was skeletal; the arteries connecting east to west were few and tenuous; 99 per cent of the population still lived east of the Rockies; and although Americans believed it was (in the words of the New York *Morning News*) 'our manifest destiny to overspread and to possess the whole of the continent,' this was still more dream than reality. What gave manifest destiny substance, what fleshed-out the skeletal map, were the mass migrations of the 1830s, 1840s and 1850s along the Santa Fe, California and Oregon trails.

Santa Fe, like many towns in the southwestern United States, began as a mission station. Ray Allen Billington describes what was the usual sequence of events.

A lone friar would set out from the frontier to found a new (mission) station. He chose an Indian village in some fertile valley, returned to his own mission and led back a party of 3 to 10 missionaries, as many families of Christianized Indians and a handful of soldiers. On the chosen spot they urged the Indians to help build crude habitations, then began the task of religious instruction. Within a year or two the faithful were set to work on a permanent church, often an elaborate structure of plastered adobe, richly ornamented to please the natives. Nearby were scattered a home for the missionaries, a blacksmith shop, flour mill, weaving rooms, carpentry shops and the homes of Indians who had been persuaded to abandon their nomadic lives for the ways of the white man . . . Here the friars labored mightily, their task not only to win souls but to teach the agri-

culture and industries which would convert Indians into useful citizens.

From such beginnings Santa Fe had grown by 1810 into a sleepy isolated little town, whose 2000 inhabitants produced furs, silver and mules, but found it almost impossible to market these commodities in Mexico City which was divided from them by 1500 miles of tortuous and little used trail. Common sense called for direct trade between Santa Fe and the Mississippi Valley; this, however, was prohibited by Spanish law. Not until the Mexican revolution of 1820 was Santa Fe able to throw off the shackles of Spanish restrictions. Then the floodgate opened.

William Becknell of Missouri is usually regarded as 'the Father of the Santa Fe trade', although in fact he had a host of precursors most of whom ended up in Spanish jails. In the fall of 1821 Becknell was following the Arkansas River westward to barter with the Comanche, when he met a party of Mexican soldiers who told him that 'the Mackeson province Had de Clared Independence of the mother Cuntry and is desirous of a traid With the people of the united States'. Altering course to the south, Becknell brought his pack-train to Santa Fe, and had no difficulty converting his merchandise into bagsful of silver and bundles of fur. Next year he was back again, with 3 heavily loaded wagons, and earned a return of 1500 per cent on his investment. Others followed where Becknell led. In 1824 as many as 25 wagons and 150 pack-horses

Above: Albert Bierstadt, *The Sierra Nevada in California*, 1868. Bierstadt was the most popular (and richest) of the painters of the west.

Left: Traders on their way to Texas on the Santa Fe Trail in 1855.

Right: Handcart emigrants following the Oregon Trail. Whereas the Santa Fe trail was basically a trade route the Oregon trail was used by countless thousands of families seeking a new life on the Pacific coast.

made the journey between Independence (on the Missouri) and Santa Fe, converting $30,000-worth of trade goods into $200,000-worth of silver and furs.

While Americans were forging a trade route to the east of Santa Fe, Mexicans were doing the same to the west. In 1829 Antonio Armijo, with 60 pack mules, made the difficult 800-mile journey from Santa Fe to Los Angeles via the Colorado Desert. This was always too arid, rocky and precipitous a route for wagons (and hence for migration), but it allowed a steady and valuable trickle of trade goods to pass between the Pacific coast and the central prairies. Within a decade Santa Fe had burgeoned from being a sleepy backwater to become the hub of a major trade artery.

Settlers were soon to follow where traders had led.

The Santa Fe was always basically a trade route. However, from 1840 onward the more northerly California and Oregon trails were used by countless thousands of families who sought that rainbow's end which had become suddenly attainable, the Pacific coast.

The California trail followed a route used by the early fur trappers. It too started from Independence, and the settlers who headed down it in their lumbering Conestoga wagons had an easy first 500 miles over the plains. Climbing the Rockies, they crossed the continental divide by South Pass before coming to the most difficult part of their journey, the deserts of Utah and Nevada. 'Over large stretches,' writes Eric Newby, 'the route was marked by the skeletons of stock animals that had died of thirst.' There were human skeletons too. In 1846 a party of 89 settlers led by George and Jacob Donner tried a short cut across the Great Salt Lake Desert; they fell behind schedule, began to cross the Sierra Nevada in winter and became frozen in on the shore of Lake Donner; 42 of them died. The more fortunate settlers headed west *via* the Humboldt, Sink and Walker Rivers, 'hemmed in by naked mountains whose summits still retained the snows of perhaps 1000 years', until they came at last to a river that flowed west, the Stanislaus. This they followed into the San Joaquin Valley, where, as they had been promised, they found 'paradise . . . a healthful climate, a good soil, and a happy mixture of level and elevated ground and vicinity to the sea.'

John Bidwell was the first man to lead a party of emigrants to the Pacific by this difficult route, a feat which earned him the title 'Prince of the California Pioneers'. In May 1841 he left Independence with 69 settlers and had an easy journey as far as South Pass. Here the party split up, half of them following the Oregon Trail to the northwest, the other half plunging with Bidwell into the little-known desert, with 'nothing to guide them save the admonition to keep heading west'. They abandoned their wagons in favor of pack animals, which enabled them to travel more quickly, and after an anxious and exhausting journey of 6 months struggled through to the promised land. Hearing of their success, others very naturally soon followed.

The California trail was the most direct and marginally the shortest of the routes to the Pacific; it was not, however, the most used. That notable distinction belongs to the Oregon.

The Oregon trail followed the same route at first as the California. However, beyond the continental divide it turned northwest rather than due west, and headed *via* the Snake River and the Grande Ronde into the Blue Mountains of Oregon. Here it picked up the Columbia River, the settlers converting their wagons to boats and floating down stream to Fort Vancouver. It was by this longer but easier trail that the Pacific seaboard was initially populated.

The first major wagon train to follow the Oregon trail set out from Independence in 1843, led by Peter Burnett. And what a train it was with more than 1000 men women and children, and more than 5000 oxen and cattle. 'Such a migration,' wrote Horace Greely of the New York *Tribune*, 'wears an aspect of insanity'; but events were to prove him wrong. The train was marshalled with military precision: first a 'light' column, containing those who had virtually no cattle, and second a 'cow' column, containing those with sizeable herds. Keeping such a motley assortment on the move together was in itself a major achievement; for

Left: The Wagon Boss – a mounted cowboy at the head of a wagon train.

Above: A view of Devil's Gate by the Sweetwater River on the Oregon Trail in central Wyoming.

Right: Brigham Young, the Mormon leader who brought his followers to the Great Salt Lake in Utah in 1847.

some had wagons drawn by oxen, and others wagons drawn by horses; some had hacks, some had mules and a few brought nothing but themselves.

Some families traveled in lightweight farm-carts, covered by a makeshift canvas; others traveled in heavy Conestoga wagons carrying up to 3 tons of supplies. Included in the latter was heavy and valuable furniture (soon jettisoned) and fashionable ladies' clothing (soon 'discarded, seized by the red men and worn without regard to age or sex'.) By day scouts rode ahead, while the wagons advanced where possible in 4 parallel columns, ready if attacked to form into a hollow square. By night a corral was established:

a circle 100 yards deep, formed by wagons connected to each other by chains, a strong barrier that no ox can break and forms no contemptible intrenchment in case of attack.

In spite of fears for their safety, the train completed the 2020-mile journey in 184 days with remarkably few losses. Within a few years the population of Oregon had mushroomed from under 500 to over 10,000.

Without wishing in any way to belittle the achievements of well known explorers like Mackenzie, La Salle and Lewis and Clark, it was largely through the efforts of anonymous trappers, mountain men and emigrants like those who braved the Oregon trail that the frontier of the United States was rolled back to the Pacific.

South America

After the break-up of the supercontinent Gondwana the landmass subsequently known as South America drifted in isolation through the Southern Ocean, its flora and fauna (like Australia's) evolving without contact with the rest of the world. It was only during the ice age, when sea levels were low, that South America became attached to North America by the land-bridge of Panama. About 18,000 years ago a multitude of creatures, among them man, began to cross this land-bridge, and South-America became subject to the influences of the outside world.

The first human beings are thought to have arrived in the content about 13,000 BC – in terms of evolution not so much yesterday as late this morning – and it was these Stone Age hunter-gatherers who were South America's first explorers. Within the span of not much more than a thousand years they penetrated to every part of the continent, from the snowline of the Andes to the heart of the Amazon rain forest, and from the mangrove swamps of the Caribbean to the ice-rimed beaches of Tierra del Fuego. This great burst of exploration was motivated by the fact that the continent offered them few places where they could put down roots and prosper. For most of the terrain of South America was, and still is, inimical to man.

Everything is on so vast a scale and subject to such violent extremes. The Andes, for example are by far the largest range of mountains on Earth (nearly three times the length of the Himalaya), and they include just about every conceivable variety of climate and terrain. Here are the world's driest desert, wettest rain forest and most precipitous valleys; glaciers at sea-level, snow fields on

the equator, cloud-woodland where the trees suck moisture not from the ground but the air, forests so thick it is impossible to set foot on the ground, vast saltpans and mineral-encrusted lakes, the highest inhabited plateau and the most active volcanoes in the world. In the high reaches of the southern Andes the air is so cold and dry that

a man leading his horse over the pass, paused but for a moment and he was frozen to death; and 6 years later others crossing the pass found him still leaning against an outcrop of rock, leading his horse, the reins in his outstretched hand, all perfectly preserved.

The Amazon Basin is equally daunting. The river itself is gargantuan, and of its 1100 tributaries more than a dozen are larger than any river in Europe. Its basin covers 2½ million square miles,

permanently awash with water and sprouting with luxuriant vegetation. Here are enormous trees crowned with thick foliage, decked with fantastic parasites and festooned with lianas, some slender threads some pythonlike coils. Everything is covered with tree ferns, mosses and lichens. Sunlight never reaches the ground, and the mud comes often up to one's knees.

This rain forest is a world of billions of insects: more termites than in all the rest of the world put together, blackflies by day, mosquitoes by night, and ticks and jiggers which burrow under the skin to lay their deadly eggs.

How, one wonders, was Stone Age man able to put down roots in such a hostile environment?

Previous page: Mist shrouds the eastern slopes of the Peruvian Andes as they begin their descent into the Amazon Basin.

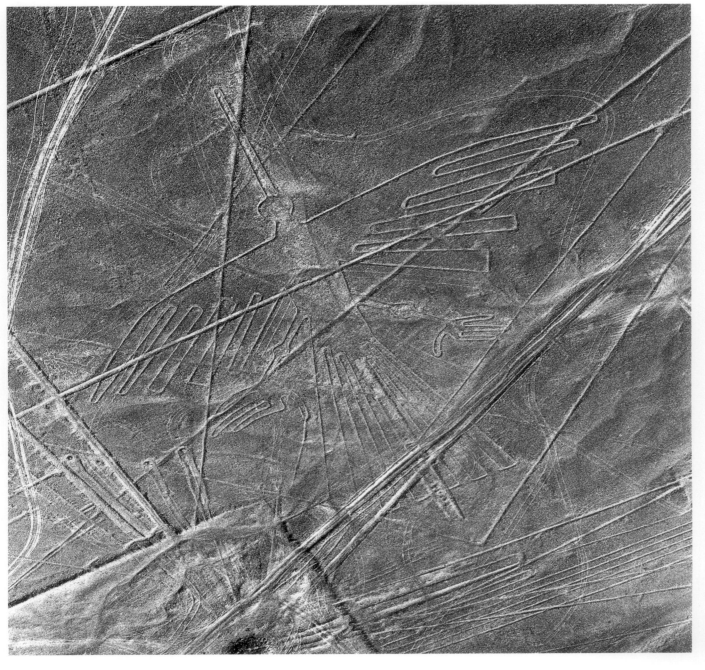

Left: The so-called 'Nazca Lines' cover an area of roughly 40 by 10 miles of the Andean plateau in Peru. The 'lines' are made up of paths cleared of stones and form bird and animal figures like the condor shown. Like much else relating to the Nazca civilization, their purpose remains a mystery.

Right: The remarkable terraces and stonework of Machu Picchu.

Stone Age Explorers of the Altiplano and Rain Forest

The first hunter-gatherers to reach South America must have had a field day; for their quarry would have been the lumbering and slow-witted *toxodon, macrauchenis* and *mylodon* which had survived in the altiplano and rain forest long after they had been exterminated in other parts of the world – there is evidence that only about 10,000 years ago *mylodon* (giant 15-foot sloths) were kept walled up in Chilean caves, like cattle in pens awaiting slaughter. However, when the exotic fauna had been hunted to extinction a shortage of food would have made it difficult for our Stone Age ancestors to put down roots. Indeed the first people to settle in static communities are thought to have relied not on hunting but fishing.

By about 4000 BC small villages had sprung up in the coastal oases and river estuaries of Peru. It is clear from the excavation of their middens that the inhabitants of these villages initially ate little but sea food, but over the millennia became increasingly dependent on root-crops and corn. It was their corn that turned them into explorers. Corn needs reasonable soil and a fair amount of fresh water, but in the coastal settlements both of these were in short supply. Irrigation was a short-term answer, and the lower reaches of the Peruvian rivers were the site of some of the earliest and most efficient irrigation systems in the world. However, the amount of water available for irrigation was limited; and eventually the people of the coast, in search of better land, began to explore the west-facing slopes of the Andes. This is unpromising terrain: a strip of desert from which enormous and barren mountains rise to over 20,000 feet: there was little scope here for corn-growing. However, in some places the Andes consist of two parallel ranges with a high plateau, the altiplano, between. Although this altiplano is high – much of it over 16,000 feet (higher than

the highest mountains in Europe) – it has pocket of fertile soil; and gradually this forbidding 'roof of the world' was not only explored but brought under cultivation by Stone Age agriculturalists. We do not know the details of this great achievement; but the net result was that the altiplano became the highest populated area on Earth, its inhabitants gradually developing special physical characteristics and special agricultural skills to cope with their demanding environment. They coped with the altitude by developing enormous hearts (20 percent larger than the average person's), a greater supply of blood (18 percent above average), many more red-blood corpuscles,

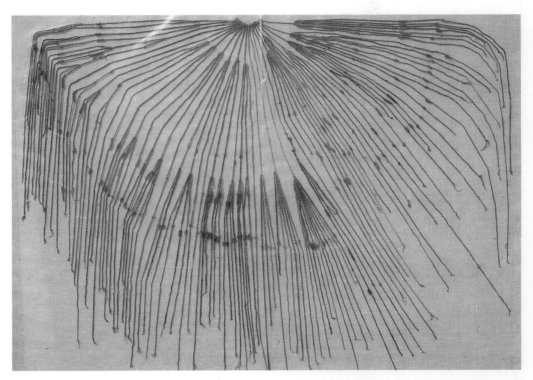

Below: Knotted and colored strings or *quipus* were used for record-keeping by the Incas.

Bottom: Part of the remains of the Inca fort at Sacsayhuaman, Peru, showing the highly sophisticated skills of the masons who built it.

cent above average), many more red-blood corpuscles, and huge lung sacs kept permanently dilated to help them get enough oxygen from the rarified air. And they coped with the difficult terrain by cultivating it by *allyus* An *allyu* is a cross between a village-community and a clan: a close knit group of families living in the same area and cultivating a specific patch of land by communal effort. This technique was called for because the agricultural potential of the altiplano could only be realized by large-scale terracing and irrigation; one family could not terrace a worthwhile area of hillside and irrigate it, but for a number of families working together the task was feasible. It would not be wrong to describe the transformation of the altiplano from a barren wilderness to a productive area as a major feat of exploration.

At the same time as Stone Age farmers were exploring the plateaux of the Andes, Stone Age hunter-gatherers were exploring the rain forest.

The rain forests of the Amazon, Orinoco, Parana and Magdalena basins cover roughly one third of South America: a primordial world difficult to move through and survive in. Indeed there is only one possible way to survive in it, and that is to become part of it. We do not know the details of how our ancestors did this, but the general picture is clear. Food is scarce in a rain forest. It can, however, be found in specific places at specific times – when a tree is in fruit it attracts birds; fish have set migratory patterns. Human beings survived in this complex environment by becoming part of the life-cycle of the forest, by moving – as the birds, fish and mammals move – from place to place. They became nomadic hunter gatherers, finding that once they got to know the rain forest it could provide all their needs. If they got headaches they cured them with the wax of pink bees; if they suffered burns they cured them with the wax of black bees; if they wanted to mulch their plants they used the detritus of termites, if they wanted to protect their plants they surrounded them with colonies of *aztecas* ants. By using but never abusing the resources of the rain forest, they made it their home. One of their sayings has particular relevance today: 'If you cut down a tree you should ask its forgiveness, or a star will fall out of the sky.'

The Campaigns of the Incas Pachacuti and Topa Yupanqui (c. 1450 – 1490)

In the same way that Alexander the Great extended Hellenic culture through the Middle East, so the Emperor Pachacuti and his son extended Inca culture through the Andes. In the 40 years 1450-90 these two great soldier-statesmen increased Inca territory by over 1000 percent, carving out an empire which extended from the volcanic peaks of Colombia, to the 'Vales of Paradise' in Chile, and from the Pacific seaboard to the Amazon rain forest.

Before the mid 1450s the Incas were a not-very-powerful mountain tribe who were hard put to it to defend their capital Cuzco against the attacks of their neighbors. The young emperor Pachacuti – 'one of those protean figures like Alexander or Napoleon' – soon altered this. He defeated his local rivals, reorganized his army and began a series of campaigns designed to bring all the people of the Andes under the aegis of the Inca sun-god. These campaigns took him and his son not only through terrain already populated, but over hitherto unclimbed ranges, across the most arid desert on Earth, and through near-impenetrable rain forests. Their empire building started in the 1460s when Pachacuti led his army – probably about 15,000 men – into the cordillera north of Cuzco. This was a land of steep valleys and fast streams, with slopes of barren scree alternating with swathes of dense forest: difficult country to fight in. Yet the very difficulty of the terrain made the Incas' task easier. For the people of the cordillera were isolated valley-dwellers, cut off from one another by barriers physical, political and cultural. The Incas conquered them one by one. And as they advanced through the Andes they built the world's most magnificent roads, and, at strategic points, the world's most magnificent temple fortresses. The farther north they advanced, the more fertile and prosperous the valleys became, and soon vast quantities of booty, including the exotic produce of the Amazon, were flowing back to Cuzco.

When Pachacuti had extended his embryo empire some 500 miles to the north he turned his attention to the south, conquering the people of the altiplano as convincingly as those of the cordillera. Heading south beyond Lake Titicaca he was soon in unknown territory, the plateau of Tapac-Ri (in present-day Bolivia).

Below: A group of Inca warriors.

There is not a scrap of good land here, *one of his troops reported.* Nothing but cliffs, rocks and stony wastes. The only things that grow are cactuses, with thorns as long as a man's finger. Hot springs emit clouds of steam and a stench of sulphur.

Probably feeling that such a bleak new world was hardly worth the conquering, Pachacuti returned to his capital. Here he spent the rest of his life, transforming Cuzco into one of the most beautiful cities in the world, and promulgating a code of laws which regulated almost every aspect of some 10,000,000 people's life. His army he handed over to his son.

In 1485 Topa Yupanqui, with an army now numbering close on 100,000, pushed through the cordillera which had been earlier pacified by his father, then followed the Maranon River as it flowed north into the unknown. This again was demanding terrain: vertiginous valleys trembling to the roar of fast flowing rivers, and rising above the clouds the great snow-capped peaks of the Cordillera Blanca. The Incas advanced on tribe after tribe, demanding allegiance. Those who consented to accept the ideology of the Sun God were absorbed peacefully into the empire; those who refused were crushed and absorbed by force. It is, of course, standard practice for victors to claim that they acted for the good of the vanquished; but in the case of the Incas this claim would seem to have substance. What happened to the Canari (a tribe on the coast of Ecuador) is typical.

They promised that instead of worshipping the Moon they would worship the Sun; and in return the Incas built storehouses for them, dug irrigation channels, and extended their cultivated fields. The Canari were delighted and became excellent subjects, many of them joining the Inca army.

With the altiplano and the cordillera under Inca suzerainty, Topa now turned his attention to the coastal plain. What followed was not so much a campaign as a triumphal procession. One by one the ancient civilizations collapsed and were integrated into the Inca empire.

Then, in one of the most amazing marches in history, Topa led his army south: his objective the distant 'Vales of Paradise' in central Chile.

They had to cross the Bolivian highlands, the main range of the Andes and the Atacama Desert: all formidable obstacles. The highlands are bleak: a mosaic of saline flats, lava-plateaux and glaciated massifs where the climate is harsh – searingly hot by day, numbingly cold by night, with little but violent rain. The Andes were an even greater barrier, a chain of 20,000-foot volcanic peaks where the air is dry and there are few passes. Those with first-hand knowledge of this frozen world rate Topa's crossing of the southern Andes as a greater achievement than Hannibal's crossing of the Alps. The last obstacle was the toughest: the Atacama the driest desert on Earth.

Above: An 18th-century etching of the 15th-century Inca emperors of Peru, who extended Inca culture throughout the Andes.

Left: A 16th-century drawing of an imprisoned Inca, from the manuscript of Poma de Ayala.

Scouts were sent ahead to find a route. They suffered terrible privations. Many died, but others managed to cross the desert, leaving markers every 5 miles. They came and went like ants, laying secret caches of food, until at last the Inca army was able to advance in two columns, each of 10,000 men, and each laden with supplies carried by llamas, which could also be used as rations.

Once he had crossed the Atacama Topa was operating over 1500 miles from his base; yet we are told,

he took particular care to keep his men supplied with reinforcements, arms, provisions, clothing and footwear. Soon he had a force of 50,000 in Chile, as well supplied with everything as if they had been within a few miles of Cuzco.

The Incas were an efficient, numerate people, who excelled at logistics.

At the end of a bitterly-fought campaign Topa established a line of fortified posts along the River Maule, which became the southern limit of the Inca empire; an empire now almost the size of the Roman and more densely populated. For a couple of generations, under the benevolent despotism of Pachacuti and his successors, the people of the Andes enjoyed peace and prosperity: peace being ensure by the Incas' large and well-organized army, and prosperity stemming from their agricultural expertise which they passed on to the subject tribes. We shall never know how long this state of euphoria would have lasted without outside interference; for early in 1531 Inca soothsayers began to predict disaster, and during a religious festival an eagle, symbol of the Sun-God, came plummeting out of the sky, pecked to death by buzzards. A couple of weeks later Pizarro and 180 tatterdemalion adventurers landed on the coast of Ecuador.

Left: A map of South America made for King Henry II of France in the 16th century.

The Conquistadors: Pizarro, Almagro and Orellana

The conquest of the Incas by the Conquistadors is an astonishing story. How, one wonders, could a well-organized empire defended by some 200,000 excellent soldiers have been defeated by 180 adventurers? The Conquistadors were helped by their steel swords and horses; but the basic reason for their success is that they arrived in the middle of a civil war, managed to capture one of the warring emperors and proceeded to play the rival factions one against the other. When they had gained control of the Inca empire they destroyed it – 'what can be burned is burned, the rest is broken' – stripped it of its gold and butchered anyone who stood in their way. It was, in the words of the Incas, 'as though night fell at noon.'

The Conquistadors' campaigning and looting involved a good deal of incidental exploration, three journeys in particular being ventures into the unknown: Pizarro's march through the Andes to Cuzco, Almagro 's ill-fated reconnaissance of Chile, and Orellana's involuntary voyage down the Amazon.

Pizarro was lucky not to have to penetrate the heart of the Inca empire to make contact with its ruler, for in the autumn of 1531 the emperor Atahualpa was making a triumphal tour of his domain, and he and his army were camped by the hot springs of Cajamarca, not far from where Pizarro landed; he invited the Spaniards to visit him. To reach Cajamarca Pizarro and his men had to climb the Andes, being the first Europeans to set foot on the main cordillera. It was a daunting experience, the great peaks twice as high and three times as bleak as any they had known in Europe and the 12,000 foot passes, even in midsummer, covered in snow; if they had not been able to follow one of the Incas' magnificent roads they would probably never have got there. And having reached Cajamarca, the sight of the Inca army was more daunting even than the Andes.

The Indian camp looked like the most beautiful city. There were so many tents that we were filled with apprehension. For we had never thought that Indians could maintain such a proud estate in such good order.

The 170 Spaniards spent the night in a small temple-fortress that had been set aside for them, surrounded by an estimated 75,000 Inca troops.

Few of us slept. We kept watch, and could see all around us the fires of the Indians. They were camped on a hillside, so close-packed, that it looked like a star-studded sky. We discussed what should be done.

The plan they hit on has few equals for audacity. They decided to capture the emperor and use him as a hostage.

Next afternoon Atahualpa, surrounded by 7000 troops entered the temple-fortress. His troops were unarmed; for it seems never to have occurred to him that the handful of strangers would dare even to think of harming him – for in the somber words of the historian Prescott, 'he did not know the character of the Spaniards.' At a given signal Pizarro's men flung themselves on the Incas and slashed and hacked them to death.

The Indians were thrown into confusion and panicked. They were so filled with terror that they climbed on top of one another, forming great mounds and suffocating. Our horsemen rode over the top of them, wounding and killing.

A group of Spaniards, led by Pizarro, fought their way through to Atahualpa's litter.

Many Indians had their hands and arms cut off, yet still they tried to support their ruler's litter on their shoulders. Not one of those escorting the Inca abandoned him; all died round him.

The eagle had fallen to the buzzards.

ATHABALIBA
ultimus Rex Peruanorum

Below left: Atahualpa, 1500-1533, the last Inca emperor of Peru.

Below: Atahualpa carried on his throne, much as he must have looked when he was attacked by Pizarro's Conquistadors.

Left: An extremely stylized painting depicting Pizarro's treacherous attack on the Incas. None of Atahualpa's troops was armed, so Pizarro's avaricious band faced little resistance.

Pizarro's plan worked better than he had dared to hope. Atahualpa agreed to fill a room 22 feet by 17 feet and 15 feet high with gold in exchange for his freedom. When the Inca had fulfilled his side of the bargain the Spaniards had him garrotted. Another claimant to the Inca throne was poisoned, and another joined the Spaniards who promised to install him as emperor.

Pizarro's march on Cuzco was another audacious feat. His force now numbered only 130, and between him and the Inca capital were 75,000 hostile troops and more than 500 miles of daunting terrain: 'a wild, magnificent, vertical land of steep mountains deeply cut by fierce rivers plunging towards the Amazon.' The Spaniards had to climb first the Cordillera Occidental then the Cordillera Vilcabamba, great snow-capped ranges of 17,000 feet. Beneath the cordillera lay the puna, a bleak treeless terrain where the Spaniards were seared by heat in the day and cold in the night; and beneath the puna the arid and airless beds of the canyons. It would have been impossible country to traverse if it had not been for the Inca roads, described by Pizarro's secretary.

Now we had to climb another stupendous mountain. Looking up at it, it seemed impossible for birds to scale it flying through the air, let alone men on horseback climbing by land. But the road was made less exhausting by ascending in zigzags rather than a straight line. It consisted of huge stone steps that greatly wearied the horses, and wore down their hooves, even though they were being led.

Easy terrain, one might have thought, to defend; and the Incas certainly tried. Pizarro had to fight four pitched battles and any number of skirmishes on his way to Cuzco. The Conquistadors, however were magnificent soldiers, and time and again, although outnumbered 100 to 1, they drove the Incas back with heavy loss of life. In November 1533 Pizarro and Manco Inca rode side by side into Cuzco.

The Conquistadors had pirated an empire. This empire they proceeded not to govern but to loot, stripping the temples and palaces of their gold, raping the women including the Inca's wife, and claiming for themselves huge tracts of territory. One of them, Diego de Almagro, was given a licence 'to discover, conquer and settle those

Having slaughtered the Inca king's bodyguard and many of his subjects, Pizarro promised Atahualpa his freedom in return for vast quantities of gold. The picture, *below left*, shows the Incas collecting the king's ransom. Once the treasure had been amassed, the Spanish killed Atahualpa, *below*, and made off with their newly acquired wealth. From engravings by de Bry, *c.* 1595.

lands which lie south of Cuzco and north of the Strait of Magellan.'

Almagro is described by contemporaries as 'a foundling of humble birth . . . a man of short stature and ugly features, who had great courage and powers of endurance.' Officially he was Pizarro's second-in-command; but he seems seldom to have got the recognition he deserved – probably because of his 'humble birth' – and now instead of gold ingots he was given a barren tract of *terra incognita*. In July 1535 he set out to explore his vast new domain with a force of 200 Spaniards and 15,000 Indians.

The 15,000 Indians had been given to him by Manco Inca as an escort in case they were attacked by local tribes. Almagro used them as load-carriers; and never before or since have the members of any expedition suffered such ill-treatment and hardship. To quote the priest who accompanied the expedition:

Those who would not come with us voluntarily were dragged along in ropes or chains. By night they were kept well-guarded; by day they were forced to carry heavy loads with no rest and no food except for a little maize and water. Those who fled were hunted down and dragged back in chains together with their wives and children and any attractive women the Spaniards could get their hands on for personal service . . . When the mares of the Spanish horsemen produced foals, these were carried in litters by the Indian women. And some Spaniards had themselves carried in litters, leading their horses by the hand so they could become strong and fat . . . A Spaniard who could boast that he had killed many Indians acquired the reputation of being an important person. One locked 12 Indians together in a chain without food until they all died, then boasted of his achievement. Another cut off the head of an Indian and left him in place in the chain to terrify the others and avoid having to undo the shackles.

Almagro's Indian guides advised him to head south via the coastal road and the Atacama. The Conquistador, however thought he knew better, and headed south via the inland road and the Andes. It was a mistake. For it was winter.

As they advanced, *Alonso de Ovalle tells us*, they met nothing but vast deserts and a wind so cold it pierced them through and through. It is not possible to imagine what they endured. Here a man would fall into the snow and be buried alive. Here

another would lean only for a second against a rock and be frozen on to it in death. If any stopped, they would die almost instantly, fixed as though cast in iron; and a Negro leading his horse by the hand did but pause and turn his head to see who called him, and he and his horse became frozen like two statues. The Indians, unprovided with clothes, died in their thousands. The greatest suffering was in the night time; for there was no food and no wood to light fires, and the Indians ate the bodies of their companions out of hunger. It is estimated that their died in these mountains 70 horses and more than 10,000 Indians.

The remnants struggled through to the plains of Chile, where they were given shelter and food. After a brief recuperation Almagro pushed south to the Maule River where, like the Incas before him, he met fierce resistance from the Araucanians. Disillusioned, he gave up and returned to Cuzco via the Atacama Desert. He had passed close to the richest deposits of silver in the world (round Potosi), and through some of the richest farm-land in the

Far left: Francisco Pizarro (*c*. 1470-1541) was created a marquis by the Emperor Charles V in recognition of his monumental achievement in claiming Peru for Spain.

Left: Diego de Almagro (*c*. 1475-1538) was nominally Pizarro's deputy. His expedition across the southern part of the continent in 1535 was fraught with difficulties and resulted in the deaths of 14,000 Indians.

Below: The Conquistadors did not find the fabled Eldorado but in 1545 they did discover huge deposits of silver at Potosi in Bolivia. This page from a book of 1585 shows how tales of this wealth had spread.

world (the Vales of Paradise of central Chile); but because the Conquistadors were seeking short-term loot rather than long-term prosperity they described the country as sterile; and their expedition as a disaster. It was certainly a disaster for the Indians; 15,000 set out, less than 1000 returned.

An equally disastrous expedition, although it led to a major feat of exploration, was the search for El Dorado by Pizarro and Orellana.

Gold was the desideratum of every Conquistador – 'We have a sickness of the heart,' admitted Cortes, 'for which there is only one cure, gold.' Even when Pizarro and his followers had stripped the Inca empire of its wealth, they still hankered after El Dorado, a mythical crock of gold which they were ever hoping to find at some rainbow's end. In February, 1541 Gonzalo Pizarro and Francisco de Orellana set out to search for this crock of gold in the headwaters of the Amazon. Their expedition consisted of 220 Conquistadors, 200 horses, great numbers of pigs and llamas, 4000 press-ganged porters, and a pack of hunting-dogs specially trained to savage recalcitrant Indians. Within a fortnight of leaving Quito 500 Indians had died of cold and exposure as they crossed a spur of the Andes. Then they were heading into the humid and precipitous rain forest. Here, we are told, 'both the Spaniards and their horses became exhausted from the great hardships they had to endure, climbing and descending the mountains, and building bridges over the many rivers.' Pizarro called a halt and asked the local Indians how much farther it was to El Dorado. The Indians told him they did not know of such a place, but Pizarro refused to believe them. Some he tortured to death, some he burned to death, and some, including women, he threw to the dogs who tore them limb from limb and ate them. The expedition, with increasing frustration, then continued to hack its way through the jungle, leaving in its wake a trail of charred and mutilated bodies. Eventually they found themselves out of food, hopelessly lost on the bank of a river they could not cross,

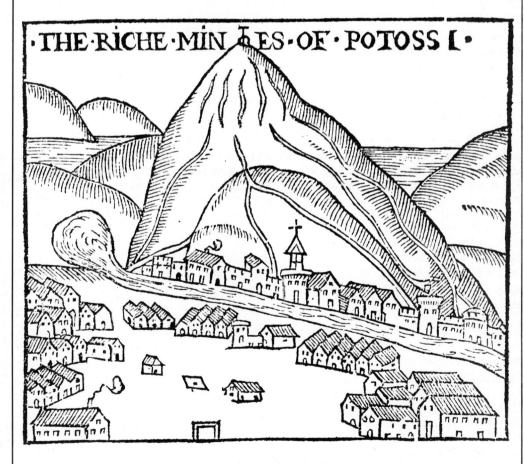

THE
DISCOVERIE AND CONQVEST
of the Prouinces of *PERV*, and
the Nauigation in the South
Sea, along that Coaſt.
And alſo of the ritche Mines
of *POTOSI*.

·THE·RICHE·MINES·OF·POTOSSI·

¶ *Imprinted at London by* Richard Ihones. *Febru.6.1581.*

and with every one of their 4000 porters either dead or fled. They built a boat, and Pizarro's second-in-command Orellana, and 60 men, set off on a reconnaissance.

There are two versions of what happened next. Orellana claimed that he was swept down-river by so strong a current his crew were unable to get back. Pizarro claimed he was deserted. Whatever the truth, Orellana made his way first down the Napo, then the Solimoes and finally the Amazon, and kept going until he reached the river-mouth: a 2000-mile odyssey through a world no white man had before set eyes on. On his way down-river he met tribes whose first contact with men from another race must have been a terrifying experience. Some fled and allowed the Spaniards to ransack their villages at will; some greeted them with dignity and offered them food, and only turned against them when they began to pillage and loot; others met them with war drums and arrows. One tribe who resisted particularly fiercely was said by the Dominican friar Gaspar de Carvajal to have been led by women:

Ten or twelve of these Amazons were seen fighting in front of the men as female captains. They were tall, white and went naked with only their private parts covered, and each did as much fighting as ten Indian men.

These female warriors were never seen by any of Orellana's expedition, but were the invention of subsequent chroniclers who knew the legend of the Amazons of Greek mythology. Nonetheless the river is still named after them. Having been swirled out of the mouth of the Amazon, Orellana headed northwest along the coast, until in September 1542 he half-drifted half-sailed on to the islands of Margarita off Venezuela. In the 18 months since he left Quito he had traveled 400 miles by land and 4000 miles by river and sea; a leap into the unknown that was not so much a *tour de force* as a miracle.

Pizarro meanwhile was in trouble. Realizing he could expect no help from Orellana, he turned back. By now men were dying every day of fever, exhaustion and starvation. They ate the last of their dogs; then they ate the last of their horses; then they ate the last of their saddles and stirrups. It rained without respite, and the jungle became a swamp through which they had to wade waist deep in water. 'They became so sick, sore, wan, wretched and afflicted it was pitiable to look upon them.' But at last the survivors – less than 100 out of 4220 – staggered back to Quito, 'without a single horse and with nothing left them but the swords in their hands . . . having failed altogether to reach the land they had gone to seek.'

The Conquistadors were men of great courage, great powers of endurance and considerable military expertise. They were also greedy, arrogant, brutal and devoid of humanity. As they suffered and died in search of their mythical El Dorado, they got what they deserved.

Above: A Spanish missionary at work to convert his South American charges.

The Scientists: Godin, Ruiz, Malaspina, Humboldt Darwin, Wallace, and Bates.

Comparatively little exploration took place in South America during the two centuries that followed the conquest of the Incas by the Conquistadors. For Spain was too busy trying to retain what she already had to feel the need to search for more. South America was turned into a no go area for foreigners – even shipwrecked seamen faced imprisonment and the death penalty; trade was permitted only with Spain, and the wealth from *haciendas* and mines was channeled back to the mother country. Throughout the 16th and 17th centuries much of the Andes and most of the Amazon rain forest remained cocooned in mystery. However rumors seeped back to Europe of the New World's exotica: its gold and emeralds, its carnivorous fish which hunted in packs and devoured men (piranha), its magic leaves which staved off pain (coca), and its gargantuan mountains (Chimborazo the Incas' 'Watchtower of the Universe', was thought to be the highest mountain in the world.) And in the 18th century a new breed of scientific explorers – geodesists, botanists, surveyors and naturalists – sought permission to come to South America to study these phenomena.

First in the field were the geodesists.

Godin and the Earth-Measurers (1735 – 1743)

In the early 18th century scientists were uncertain of the shape of the Earth. The French believed it was a prolate spheroid (slightly elongated at the Poles), the British believed it was an oblate spheroid (slightly flattened at the Poles.) The question was of more than esoteric interest – it was important in map-making and navigation – and it was agreed to settle the issue by measuring a degree of latitude both on the Arctic Circle and the Equator. In May, 1735 a French expedition left La Rochelle for the Andes.

The expedition was led by the self-effacing but highly competent Louis Godin, with the flamboyant Charles-Marie de La Condamine as second-in-command, and two Spanish naval officers, Jorge Juan y Santacilia and Antonio de Ulloa as supernumaries. It is an indication of the difficulties of 18th century travel that it was a year before they even sighted the Andes, and eighteen months before they reached the base of their operations, Quito. 'The city,' wrote La Condamine, 'has a spectacular setting; its white buildings cling to the slopes of a valley which nestles among a veritable tribe of volcanoes.' It did not look easy terrain to triangulate.

They set up a base line on the plains of Yarqui, a little to the north of Quito. From this they made a series of triangulations which eventually extended over 3 degrees of latitude (i.e. for over 200 miles.) This involved climbing the peaks laden with surveying apparatus, and taking accurate bearings on other peaks which would in turn be bases for further triangulation. Their instruments were primitive. Conditions were difficult: 'In mid afternoon our mercury soars to over 100 degrees, during the night it plummets to under zero'; on the peaks they were plastered with snow, battered by hail, lashed by violent winds and terrified by volcanic eruptions. Their equipment was stolen. Their Indian helpers deserted. One of their scientists died of malaria; another went out of his mind; their doctor was battered to death by an enraged mob who believed that the scientists' measuring-poles were divining-rods for locating gold. And at the end of it

all they found that a degree of latitude on the equator was less than on the Arctic Circle. As Voltaire succinctly put it: 'both the Earth and the French have been flattened.'

This was a bitter disappointment to Godin. However, he completed his work, and at the end of eight years of painstaking triangulation produced a survey of the Quitan Andes which was a model of accuracy, and set a standard of excellence unsurpassed for more than a century.

Left: Charles Marie de La Condamine (1701-74). As well as his geodesic work, he also investigated the properties of curare and rubber.

Below: Godin is remembered in Quito at least, where this statue stands outside the astronomical observatory.

Ruiz and the Plant Collectors (1778 – 1788)

The next major expedition was also a Franco-Spanish venture, with the French hoping to stimulate their economy by introducing new plants from South America, and the Spanish hoping, in the words of King Charles III, 'to examine and identify the natural products of my American dominions in order to promote science, foster commerce and form herbaria and collections.' What made such an expedition possible was that the Swede Carl von Linné (Linnaeus) had just perfected a universally-accepted system by which plants could be categorised; botany was at last breaking free from the mumbo-jumbo of the Middle Ages and becoming a science which called for the detailed study of specific plants. Ruiz and his botanists were therefore told not only to collect different species but to make detailed drawings of them and bring back samples of their bark, leaves, flowers, fruit, sap and seeds; also their local name, their history and the uses to which they were put. They arrived in Lima in April 1778, expecting their work to take 'about 4 years.' At the end of 10 years they had amassed a fine collection, but realized that far from being finished their work had barely begun.

The expedition leader was the young Spaniard Hipólito Ruiz, who had under him two botanists including the distinguished Frenchman Joseph Dombey, and two first-class botanical artists. In their first year they confined their activities to the coastal plain around Lima; then they headed for the wilder but more rewarding *montana*. Pushing through the snow-capped peaks they reached the little town of Tarma which lies close to one of the Inca highways; here they spent the next two years collecting the exotic flora of the Andes.

Most explorers have a goal to aim for: a summit to attain, a river to trace or a desert to cross. Naturalists, however, simply move from place to place collecting more and more plants; their work has no climax and is never finished. There are therefore few highlights to Ruiz and Dombey's nine years of plant-collecting, first in the Peruvian Andes then the Chilean. There was, however, a great deal of hard work and privation. Cloud and rain forests are not a healthy environment for outsiders, who lack immunity to the poisonous thorns, stings and bites and the parasites that enter the bloodstream undetected. As well as facing natural hazards – forest fires, flash floods and violent extremes of heat and cold – the botanists succumbed to scurvy and *mayco* (an agonizing skin disease); Dombey became parblind and had to give up. One of their artists died. And to cap it all the ship into which they had loaded the better part of their collection was wrecked on the voyage back to Spain.

Nonetheless Ruiz succeeded in bringing back 2980 dried plants, 2264 illustrations of these plants, 12,000 pages of botanical descriptions and between 250 and 300 living specimens. His expedition was important both for the data it brought back and the precedent it set: the precedent of a team of scientists studying the Earth's phenomena in pursuit of scientific knowledge.

Malaspina and the lost survey of America (1789 – 1794)

Malaspina's fame is not commensurate with his achievements. Today probably not one person in a million has heard of this efficient and liberal-minded Lombard nobleman who, in the service of Spain, charted the coastline of most of North and South America with unprecedented accuracy.

Alessandro Malaspina did for the Spanish navy what Cook did for the British. By his insistence on high standards in diet and hygiene he virtually eradicated the threat of scurvy. After his successful voyage round the world in the *Astrea* he was appointed commandant of Marines in Cadiz, an influential post which enabled him to promote a project particularly dear to his heart 'to make hydrographic charts of the whole of America, including its remotest regions.' His preparations were thorough. He was given two specially built ships, the *Descubierta* and the *Atrevida*, and a free hand in choosing his crew, provisions and equipment, with the result that the expedition which left Cadiz in July 1789 was particularly well-found. However, a chance remark of Malaspina's reveals his Achilles heel; he told a friend that 'on a scientific voyage (he) preferred the rule of reason to military discipline.' Malaspina was an idealist.

There are few highlights in his five-year voyage – one of the longest in the history of seafaring – but the distances he covered and the accuracy of his surveying were remarkable. He arrived off the Rio de la Plata in September 1789, and after a thorough charting of the estuary his two ships headed south, delineating a difficult coastline in difficult weather. They produced the first accurate map of the Malvinas (Falkland Islands), corrected Cook's placing of Cape Horn by 21 minutes, measured the 'Patagonian giants' and found several were 6 feet 10 inches tall, then proceeded along the Chilean coast to Callao. From here

Below: Alexander von Humboldt, the great German scientist, on his first trip to South America. This picture shows him collecting samples of the continent's flora.

they worked their way up the Pacific seaboard and into the Bering Sea, where, like many explorers both before and after them, they searched in vain for a North-West Passage. Malaspina then headed west for the Philippines, before returning via the Marianas to Callao in July, 1793. What made his voyage such a *tour de force* was that for most of the time he kept close inshore – a dangerous tactic for sailing ships – and charted the far-flung coastlines that he followed with meticulous accuracy.

On his return to Spain he was arrested and flung into prison . . . It would seem that his expedition had had not only the overt objective of surveying the coast of the Americas, but also the covert objective of making an economical and political evaluation of Spain's South American empire. The latter proved Malaspina's undoing. Most of what he did or said was right; but walking on the side of the angels won him few friends in high places. In the Malvinas, for example, he rebuked New England fishermen for 'hunting the seals with such energy they were in danger of destroying the species;' he ordered them off the islands, almost precipitating an international incident. And for South America he proposed an autonomous system of government based on 'what was

good and beneficial for the Americans.' For this very sensible advice he was branded a revolutionary. His charts were locked away. Parts of his diary were diplomatically 'lost'. And it was only after the South American Wars of Independence that his work was resurrected and its importance appreciated; by then the great cartographer was dead.

Von Humboldt's travels in the Amazon, Andes and Atacama (1799 – 1803)

Alexander von Humboldt has been described as 'the greatest scientific traveler who ever lived.' He was indeed a traveler rather than an explorer, since most (though not all) of the places he visited had already been mapped. However by bringing to his travels an inquiring mind and a passion for collecting and integrating data in subjects as diverse as botany, geology, seismology, oceanography, meterology and geomagnetism, he originated the concept of a new science – geography, the study of the Earth. This concept triggered off a spate of scientific exploration which has been gathering momentum ever since.

In 1798 the young von Humboldt submitted a memoir

caballitos (little horses.) The *caballitos* turned out to be mountain Indians, who were obliged to carry white men up the most arduous part of the ascent. 'It makes ones blood boil,' wrote Humboldt ' to hear human beings described as though they were horses or mules.' A remark which underlines his dilemma in South America: he saw a lot going on of which he disapproved, but as a guest of the king of Spain he was reluctant to be too outspoken. He spent a year in the Andes in the vicinity of Quito, where more than a dozen great volcanoes were intermittently active. His research work was dangerous, and rather than risk the lives of Indians to carry his scientific equipment, Humboldt carried it himself, often doing tests on the lip of craters liable at any moment to erupt. At the time his best-known feat was his attempt to climb Chimborazo, where he struggled to 19,170 feet, suffering from nausea and bleeding from both nose and mouth, only to find his way to the summit blocked by a huge crevasse. However, of more lasting significance was his research into the magnetic nature of volcanism, and his concept that volcanoes are distributed along lines of weakness in the Earth's crust.

Humboldt next made a study of the Peruvian Current. He found that along the 2000 mile coastal strip of the Atacama the water-temperature was a constant 60 degrees, and the land-temperature an almost constant 73 degrees, a reversal of the normal ratio. From this he deduced that when air from the Pacific moved inland its

Far left: Alexander von Humboldt camped beside the Orinoco River on his first journey through South America in 1799.

Left: Humboldt was accompanied by the French botanist Aimé Bonpland. They collected information on a cornucopia of subjects.

Below: One of von Humboldt's amazingly detailed and exquisitely executed paintings of the wildlife of South America.

to Charles IV of Spain, pointing out the benefits that might accrue from a scientific study of his South American empire. Rather to his surprise he was given a free hand, with no strings and no restriction, to go wherever he wished. 'It was a dream come true,' he wrote. 'Never before had so comprehensive a brief been given to any traveler, and never before had a foreigner been honored with such confidence.' He made three great journeys through South America first through the Amazon basin, then the Andes, then the Atacama.

In fall of 1799, together with the French botanist Aimé Bonpland, he headed inland from Caracas: his objective to find out if there was a connection between the Rivers Orinoco and Amazon – contemporary maps suggested that a huge lake was a source of both rivers. The explorers first crossed the vast and featureless *llanos*, then ascended the upper reaches of the Orinoco. This was an important journey *per se*. What made it more important was that both men were forever collecting data in a variety of fields. One day they would be studying the symbiosis of ants and fungus, next day dissecting electric eels, and the next making notes on the infanticide rituals of the Orinoco Indians. No phenomenon escaped them; their curiosity encompassed every facet of nature At the end of 9 months they returned to the coast, having proved that 'the great lake does not exist, and must be reduced to an area of swampland only 2 or 3 miles in circumference.' They brought back an accurate map of the area, also a cornucopia of specimens, both living and dead including 16,000 pressed plants.

In April 1801 they were off again, traveling this time from Cartagena to Lima, their objective to study the vulcanology of the Andes. The first part of their journey took them up the slow-moving Magdalena, where for 45 days Humboldt kept a meticulous record of the river's direction, width, temperature and velocity. Then came a hair-raising ascent of the Andes. In some places the path consisted of steps less than 20 inches wide cut in a vertical rockface. In other places, where it was too steep for mules, the travelers were offered a ride on the backs of

temperature would be raised and its moisture-carrying capacity increased; so the clouds instead of voiding moisture *onto* the land suck moisture *out of* it – so succinct and logical an explanation of the Atacama that one can only wonder no one had thought of it before.

After leaving South America Humboldt settled in Paris to write his *Kosmos*, a gargantuan work setting out his theory of the harmony of nature: i.e. the interlocking relationship between the various disciplines of geography. It was 40 years before the appearance of the first volume, and he died at the age of 90 before the appearance of the last. Of the many accolades that he received that of Simon Bolivar might well have pleased him most: 'Baron von Humboldt did more for South America than all the conquistadors put together.'

Darwin and *The Origin of Species* (1831 – 1835)

The Andes and the Galapagos provided Charles Darwin with many of the scientific facts on which he based his revolutionary theory of evolution. In 1831 he was appointed naturalist to HMS *Beagle*, a 240-ton brig which had been ordered to carry out a survey of South America and the Pacific islands; and during the next 4 years, as *Beagle* worked her way round the coasts of Brazil, Argentina, Chile and Peru and through the archipelagos of the Pacific, Darwin had ample opportunity to study phenomena ashore.

In April 1832 he was off the mouth of the Amazon. 'The noise of the insects is amazing,' he wrote: 'so loud it may be heard in a vessel anchored several hundred yards offshore.' Even more amazing than their noise was their diversity; almost every other specimen that Darwin collected seemed to be of a different species; and it was here in the Amazon rain forest that he first began to wonder how on earth Noah could have had room for so many

species in his ark. A year later, on the coast of Tierra del Fuego, he found the near-perfect skeletons of

numerous gigantic and extinct Quadrupeds . . . the giant sloth Megatherium, the Scelidotherium, as large as a rhinoceros, an extinct kind of horse, and the Toxodon, perhaps the strangest animal ever discovered, equal to an elephant in size, but with a tooth structure related to the Gnawers (an order which now includes only the smallest quadrupeds) and almost certainly aquatic.

Why, he asked himself, had these species become extinct while others had survived?

Throughout 1834 and 1835, as *Beagle* worked her way along the Pacific seaboard, Darwin found himself in almost daily contact with the greatest range on Earth. 'What forces,' he asked himself, 'could have created such

Above: In 1831 HMS *Beagle* embarked on a scientific survey of South American waters. The *Beagle* is shown here in the Straits of Magellan, with Mount Sarmiento in the distance.

Below: The *Beagle* ashore at Santa Cruz. The ship had been damaged by rocks and had to be repaired.

a fine chaos of mountains?' He spent long spells ashore, journeying high into the cordillera to collect samples of rocks and plants: behavior which the locals reckoned at best eccentric and at worst sacrilegious. 'I don't like it,' wrote a Valparaiso lawyer, 'Why should a country send out someone to pick up such rubbish? Something fishy is going on!' Two discoveries gave Darwin an inkling of how the Andes might have been formed. At 7000 feet in the cordillera east of Valparaiso he found a cluster of petrified pine trees embedded in rocks which were of marine origin; and a few weeks later at 12,000 feet he found a stratum of fossilized seashells. It looked as though the mountains had been raised from the sea. In February 1835 he witnessed how this had happened.

He and his assistant were resting in an orchard when a sudden wind swept through the trees and the ground began to tremble. They staggered to their feet, sick and giddy, as 'the world, the very emblem of all that is solid, moved beneath our feet like crust over a fluid.' They were on the periphery of an earthquake. During the next few days, as *Beagle* headed north towards the epicenter, Darwin saw and heard what had happened. A chain of volcanoes had erupted. In the early hours of February 20th formations of sea-birds had been seen flying inland, and the dogs in the coastal settlement had fled to the hills. The shock waves started at mid-day and built up to a terrifying crescendo. The ground heaved and split open. Fissures reeking with the stench of sulphur zigzagged inland. The sea drained out of Talcahuano harbor, then, with an appalling roar, swept back in a succession of tidal waves. Ships were tossed ashore like flotsam. Whole houses were picked up, carried inland, then sucked out to sea to disappear in sulphurous whirlpools. The city of Concepción was demolished in 6 seconds. When a few days later, Darwin rode through it, instead of streets there were lines of rubble; not one building was standing. And when *Beagle* continued her survey, it was found that, along the shore, vast reaches of rock had been

heaved out of the sea, sometimes by as much as 20 feet. The Andes, Darwin realized, had not been created in the Biblical 6 days, but had been prised up from the seabed by volcanic pressure over countless millennia.

Later that year in the Galapagos, some 600 miles off the coast of Ecuador, Darwin found evidence that the creatures of the Earth (like the Earth itself) were not immutable but in the throes of evolution, ever changing to adapt to their environment. For he found that in this Shangri-La of naturalists the animals, birds and reptiles had developed in isolation from the rest of the world and were subtly different from their continental cousins on the American mainland. And, what was even more significant, he found that the creatures of one island were different from those on another. On one the lizards were black, to blend in with the black rocks, on another they were red-brown to blend in with the red-brown rocks. On one island the finches had beaks adapted to pecking; on another they had beaks adapted to grubbing. Even the giant tortoises differed in size and shape from island to island. 'I felt myself close' he wrote, 'both in space and time, to that mystery of mysteries: the appearance of new forms of life on Earth.'

Although the terrain that Darwin set foot on had been trodden before, few explorers have broken so much fresh ground.

Above: The *Beagle* made a lengthy journey around the coast of South America. While her captain charted the coastline, Darwin observed the flora and fauna, as well as the natives. He was particularly interested by the Fuegians of Tierra del Fuego.

Left: Charles Darwin (1809-82). The discoveries he made on the *Beagle*'s five-year voyage formed the basis of his knowledge for his great work, *The Origin of Species*.

Wallace and Bates in the Rain Forest of the Amazon (1848 – 1852)

Little is known about the exploration of the Amazon during the 200 years that followed Orellana's involuntary drift down the river; for both Spain and Portugal adopted a restrictive trading policy,and information about the area was suppressed rather than disseminated. One thing, however, is clear. This was the age of the missionaries, with Capuchins, Carmelites, Franciscans and above all Jesuits setting up stations along the mainstream and its tributaries. The desirability of converting the heathen may be open to question; but without doubt the Catholic friars and priests who opened up the Amazon were often men of heroic stature. To quote Goodman's *The Explorers of South America :*

They had intellectual curiosity and amazing and varied skills. Products of the finest tradition of European humanism, they were well trained in science and noted down everything of interest. They were the first naturalists, the first anthropologists, the first geographers and the first cartographers of the interior of the continent.

They were also almost invariably the Indians' friends, championing their cause against those who sought to exploit them: a tradition still very much alive today, when Catholic priests in South America are continually speaking out against injustice, and being tortured to death in Chilean prisons and flung to their death from Contra helicopters for their pains.

In the wake of the missionaries came the naturalists, among the first being La Condamine. When he had completed his survey of the Andes around Quito, La Condamine returned to Europe via the Amazon: following the Maranon to the Solimoes, and the Solimoes to its junction with the Negro at Manaus. This was a long and hazardous journey, with his canoe being sucked into whirlpools, and his Indian crew succumbing to smallpox; and perhaps more important than the journey itself was its aftermath. For La Condamine spent the rest of his life experimenting with and promoting a wide variety of South America products such as rubber, curare and qui-

nine; he also (before Jenner) pioneered vaccination against smallpox – a technique he had seen used in Amazonia by a Carmelite friar. Few men have done more to make the wonders of South America known to the outside world.

The next major traveler was the eccentric Charles Waterton, who believed that the poison used by Chamilon Indians on their arrows might be a cure for rabies. He collected a whole menagerie of birds, snakes and vampire bats; also a live 7-foot cayman which he wrestled with and held pinned to the ground while his helpers tied its jaws together. A more serious traveler was Auguste de Saint-Hilaire who made five forays into the Amazon rain forest, and collected specimens of 6000 insects and 7000 plants. While a more ubiquitous one was Comte François de Castelnau who spent nearly a decade in the Mato Grosso, Amazon-basin and Andes, discovering the source of the Paraguay and studying the area's magnetic field and climate. However, the explorers who probably did most to open the eyes of the world to the wonders of the Amazon were an unlikely pair of apprentices from the dark satanic mills of industrial England.

Alfred Russel Wallace was tall, gangling and myopic: a shy self-effacing man with a mind of his own – he was an agnostic, a pacifist and one of the few 19th century explorers totally devoid of racial prejudice. Henry Walter

Above: The dramatic site of Machu Picchu.

Left: The French zoologist Auguste de Saint-Hilaire did much work on the classification of South American flora and fauna.

Bates was short, birdlike and had an almost childish love of nature in general and living creatures in particular – he was forever crawling after giant anacondas, handling poisonous spiders and wasps without gloves, and swimming with alligators. They were brought together by a mutual interest in beetles, and in 1848 pooled their resources – under £100 – and set off on what Bates called their 'rash adventure': a journey to the Amazon to collect insect specimens and ship them back at threepence a head to museums and research establishments in England. The museums and research establishments got more than they bargained for! Over a period of 11 years Bates collected 14,712 different species of insect, of which 8000 were previously unknown. We do not know how many Wallace collected, because most of his specimens were lost when the ship on which he was returning to England caught fire and sank.

To start with they confined their research work to the neighborhood of Para. Then they moved upriver, into territory where few white men had ventured. Bates concentrated his research in the upper reaches of the Tocantins, and Wallace in the upper reaches of the Negro. It was during these years in Amazonia that Bates' study of butterfly mimicry provided practical evidence of how natural selection works – 'On these expanded membranes nature writes, as on a tablet, the story of the modification of species.' While Wallace collected evidence which enabled him to realize (at the same time as Darwin) that 'creatures change in order to improve the species, so that the inferior are killed off and the superior remain – that is to say THE FITTEST SURVIVE.'

The Amazon was the crucible in which Wallace and Bates, at the same time as Darwin, forged the theory of evolution.

Above left: Alfred Russel Wallace (1823-1913). As well as his travels and collecting in the Amazon basin, Wallace also worked extensively in Malaysia.

Above: The valley of the Urubamba River near Pisac in Peru. This area is often described as the Sacred Valley of the Incas. Machu Picchu is nearby.

The Mountaineers: The Incas, Fitzgerald, Bingham, and De Agostini

About a third of South America consists of the longest range of mountains on Earth: the Andes: a continuous chain of volcanic peaks which stretch from the tropical isthmus of Panama to the ice-bound approaches to Antarctica. No other continent is so dominated by mountains, and in no other continent have mountaineers played such a major role in exploration.

The first people to explore the Andes were South American Indians.

The Incas' 'Watchtower of the Universe'

The people of the Himalaya regard their mountains as wholly beneficial; they give them names like Annapurna, which means Bringer of Life; they adorn them with prayer-flags; they worship them as gods. The people of

the Andes have a more ambivalent attitude. For they see their mountains as both bringers of life – in that their snow provides the water on which their lives depend – and bringers of death – in that they include a high percentage of active volcanoes. They propitiate them with *apachita*, little mounds of presents which they leave at strategic intervals; and it used to be thought that they were too afraid of them to climb them. This last assumption, however, has recently been disproved.

One of the most spectacular peaks in the Southern Andes is Licancabur, a dormant 19,000-foot volcano which for a long time was thought unclimbable, since its final 5000 feet consists of steep slopes of highly unstable shale. Eventually, in November 1953, a team led by Henning Kristensen struggled to the summit, only to find to their amazement that someone had been there before

them. 'A little below the rim of the crater,' wrote Kristensen, 'were the remains of three stone shelters, the largest about 15 feet by 6 feet, their walls being of the *pirca* type, the unworked stones fitting snugly together without mortar. Beside the buildings was a pile of wood, much weathered and fragmented.' It was evident that the Atacama Indians had used the summit of Licancabur as a watchtower, lighting beacons on it to give warning of an approaching enemy – much as Atacama shepherds today light bonfires to give notice that they are driving their flocks from one pasture to another.

This was no isolated incident. Time and again in the early 20th century, Europeans making what they hoped was a first ascent found that South American Indians had been on the summit before them. The first European to climb Liullaiaio (22,057 feet) found on the summit the remains of Nazca (i.e. pre-Inca) stonework. The first Europeans to climb Chuculai (17,782 feet) found on the summit an Indian copper knife at least 400 years old. On the summit of Pular (20,423 feet) was found the remains of an Inca altar; on Cerro de Toro (20,951 feet) the mummified body of a young Inca; on Cerro El Potro (19,127 feet) the stick of an Inca courier. More than fifty major peaks (12 of them over 20,000 feet) are known to have been climbed before Europeans ever set foot in South America. Indeed it is possible that the greatest peak of all, Aconcagua (22,835 feet) may have been climbed long before its usually accepted first ascent in 1897. For in the 1940s two climbers (Kopp and Heroldd) who were making a traverse of the summit ridge came across the perfectly preserved carcass of a guanaco. There is no way a guanaco could have got there of its own volition, and it seems probable it was carried there by Indians, either for food or sacrifice. It might well be argued that the cradle of mountaineering was not the Alps but the Andes.

One peak which the Indians never tried to climb was Chimborazo (20,700 feet), whose vast glaciated massif dominates the Andes of Ecuador. This was the Incas' 'watchtower of the universe'; they believed it was the highest mountain in the world, and therefore sacred. When the summit of Everest was triangulated at over 29,000 feet, the Incas' belief appeared invalidated. Yet in a way they were right. For, because the Earth is an oblate spheroid and Chimborazo lies astride the equator, the summit of the Incas' 'watchtower of the universe' is indeed the spot that is farthest from the center of the Earth.

FitzGerald and the ascent of Aconcagua (1897)

One of the most difficult mountains in the world to climb is Aconcagua in the southern Andes. It does not *look* difficult: the route to its summit presents few technical problems, and many peaks in the Himalaya and Karakoram are several thousand feet higher. Yet Aconcagua has a more daunting casualty-rate than almost any other mountain; for the surrounding terrain is desolate, the distances vast and deceptive, the cold crippling, the wind debilitating, and, above all, the air is so dry that breathing, even at comparatively low levels, is difficult. The problem when climbing Aconcagua is altitude sickness.

In 1897 a team of five mountaineers arrived in Buenos Aires determined to conquer this highest peak in the New World; they were led by Edward FitzGerald, and included the experienced Alpine guide, Mattias Zurbriggen. Traveling to what was then the terminus of the embryo Transandine Railway, they found what looked like a suitable site for their base camp and settled down for the night. Next morning they had a rude awakening. A fierce wind swept down from the mountains, enveloping them in clouds of dust-cum-sand; their tents

Left: The magnificent ruins of the Inca city of Machu Picchu, which was discovered in 1911 by Hiram Bingham.

Below: The daunting prospect of the Andes, seen from Mendoza in western Argentina.

collapsed, and, together with their bales of food and equipment, were picked up bodily and deposited several hundred yards down valley. Their search for a better site was unavailing; for everywhere the soil was barren and devoid of grazing for their horses and mules, the water was black as ink and impregnated with sulphur, and the wind ubiquitous. Eventually they headed up the Vacas Valley in search of a possible route to the summit. The Vacas Valley was about as inviting as the face of the moon: 'the most desolate spot imaginable; nothing but endless vistas of sand, with here and there a stunted bush or a few blades of withered grass peering through crevices in the rock.' And when they at last caught sight of the summit of Aconcagua rising over the terminal moraine at the head of the valley, both FitzGerald and Zurbriggen agreed, with a notable degree of understatement, that 'it did not look very accessible from this side.' They accordingly retraced their steps, and headed up another valley, the Horcones.

It was Zurbriggen who pioneered a possible route to the summit; and in mid-December an assault-team was heading up-valley. They were soon in difficulty.

That first night one of our Swiss porters, a powerfully-built man named Lochmatter, fell ill. He suffered from nausea and faintness, and we thought he was going to die . . . Next night it was my turn. I couldn't breathe. Sometimes I was obliged to cough; this stopped my breathing altogether, and ended in a most unpleasant fit of choking. (*At 18,000 feet their fire was too starved of oxygen to heat their food*): All we could do was melt the frozen lumps of Irish stew in our mouths, then try to swallow them; the result, yet more violent spasms of nausea. (*Next day they tried to climb higher*) but found we were all so weak at the knees we had to pause every half-dozen steps to get our breath back; frequently we had to rest as much as ten minutes before we were able to move on . . . it was impossible to sleep that night for more than a few minutes before being awakened by a violent spasm of choking.

They retreated to the Horcones Valley.

Over the next few weeks they made four more attempts to reach the summit, only to be thwarted by altitude sickness and the physical impossibility of putting one foot in front of another. Zurbriggen succumbed to frostbite. One of their porters 'turned sickly green, all color left his lips and he was unable to stand let alone walk unsupported.' Again and again FitzGerald collapsed in pain and nausea. They suffered snow blindness, dehydration, hypothermia and were 'afraid to sleep for fear we might choke to death in the night through lack of oxygen.' Eventually, on January 14th, Zurbriggen alone managed to struggle on to the summit.

FitzGerald was typical of the mountaineers who, in the last decades of the 19th century, climbed many of the world's major peaks without oxygen. It is easy to criticize these early climbers. Their treatment of animals was callous; they regarded the people whose mountains they were climbing as little more than tiresome beasts of burden, and this attitude extended to their own porters. (During the ascent of Aconcagua, Lanti and the brothers Pollinger carried heavy loads to over 21,000 feet; they saved FitzGerald's life and reached a higher point on the mountain than their expedition leader; without their efforts Zurbriggen would never have got near the summit. Yet in his book *The Highest Andes*, FitzGerald does not even mention his porters in the index.) However, if the shortcomings of these early mountaineers are obvious, so too are their virtues and achievements. They were pioneers: men of great courage who risked their lives to test, at high altitude, the limit of human endurance, and to collect scientific data.

Bingham and the discovery of Machu Picchu (1911)

Machu Picchu has been described as the most dramatic man-made structure ever created. Its discovery in 1911 by Hiram Bingham focussed the attention of the world on the lost splendors of the Inca empire.

Bingham first came to South America to climb Coropuna, a peak in the Peruvian Andes then thought to be higher than Aconcagua. He succeeded, but found to his chagrin that the mountain was only 21,160 feet. While traveling to and from Coropuna, Bingham had been impressed by the magnificent Inca ruins so often found in the most inaccessible places; in particular he had been intrigued by rumors of 'the lost city of Vilcabamba' from which Manco Inca was said to have defied the Conquistadors. His search for this city was a fine piece of deductive exploration which led him to the valley of the Urubamba at a propitious moment, just as it was being opened up for the first time in centuries by a road. No-one has described what happened next better than Bingham himself.

In July 1911 we first entered the marvelous canyon of the Urubamba, where the river escapes from the cold regions near Cuzco by tearing its way through gigantic mountains. This is a land of matchless charm. Not only has it great snow-peaks looming above the clouds two miles overhead, and huge precipices of many-colored rock rising sheer above the rapids; it also has orchids and tree ferns, the delectable beauty of luxuriant vegetation and the mysterious witchery of the jungle.

On the morning of July 24th Bingham left the road, crawled over a ramshackle bridge and began to clamber

Above: Hiram Bingham who led the Yale expedition of 1911. He discovered the site of Machu Picchu by a combination of deduction and good fortune.

up a little-used path through the rain forest. It was a hard climb. At mid-day he came to a grass-covered hut where two Indians gave him a welcome drink. The Indians told him that there were ruins 'a little farther on.' Bingham, who had heard that story before, was sceptical; but eventually, with a ten year old Indian boy as his guide, he resumed his climb, and almost at once, rounding a hillside, made what would in itself have been a major discovery: a flight of huge stone agricultural terraces, each 10 feet high and roughly 100 yards long, climbing for some thousand feet up a steep hill. More was to come.

Crossing the terraces, I entered the forest beyond, and suddenly found myself in a maze of the most beautiful granite houses. Covered with trees, moss and the growth of centuries, could be seen walls of white granite ashlars carefully cut and exquisitely fitted together . . . The walls of the buildings followed the natural curve of the rock, and were keyed to it by the finest examples of masonry I have ever seen. These beautiful walls were clearly the work of a master craftsman; the flowing lines, the symmetrical arrangement and the careful graduation of the courses, combined to produce an effect softer and more pleasing than the marble temples of the Old World, and with none of the harshness of mechanical accuracy . . . Surprise followed surprise in bewildering succession; and further examination showed that I had found a huge, remote and beautiful fastness, protected by natural bulwarks of which man had taken advantage to create the most impregnable stronghold in the Andes. It did not take an expert to realize that these were the most extraordinary ruins.

Bingham had discovered Machu Picchu, the most spectacular of the Inca temple-fortresses.

It was many years later before the complex was cleared and researched – as late as the 1980s a team from the Royal Geographical Society was still uncovering and restoring its irrigation channels. Research has dispelled many of the myths that used to surround Machu Picchu. We now know it was *not* Manco's last stronghold, and it was *not* a refuge for the Virgins of the Sun; it was almost certainly built by Pachacuti *circa* 1450, and it seems likely that within 100 years of its foundation stones being laid it was abandoned. Nevertheless it ranks as the *pièce de resistance* of Inca architecture and the most evocative tangible manifestation of their way of life.

The Incas were a people both spiritual and earthbound, and this is reflected in their masonry-work. Tied by their religion and the practicalities of everyday life to their land, they created the most magnificent monuments in stone which mirrored the landscape in which they were set. It was as though they wanted by labor and artistry to emphasize that the god they worshipped was the same god who had created the spectacular and enduring contours of the Andes; they made their shrines in imitation of his. To quote *Monuments of the Incas:*

The aspiration for the union of heaven and earth is most strongly felt at Machu Picchu. At this unique sanctuary the buildings are fused with granite outcrops in a way that is more sculptural than architectural. Steep stairways lead one up and into small plazas with views precisely orientated to surrounding peaks. The altar on the highest pinnacle is open to the heavens, yet it also looks directly down to the Urubamba 2000 feet below. The shapes of other altars echo the shape of the landscape, while others, like the awesome sacrificial condor stone, express the dark and terrifying forces of nature which demand continual propitiation.

Hiram Bingham's discovery of Machu Picchu may not seem on the face of it to have been a major feat of exploration; yet in the long term it has added enormously to our knowledge and understanding of the people of South America.

De Agostini and the exploration of Patagonia (1910 – 1956)

Patagonia is the name, meaning 'Land of the big feet', given by Magellan to the region round Saint Julian where he wintered during his circumnavigation of the world; today, by popular usage, it is applied to the tip of South America south of the 42nd parallel. Its Atlantic (Argentine) coast consists of arid undulating prairie. Its Pacific (Chilean) coast consists of a maze of islands and fjords where the spine of the Andes disappears into the waters of the sub-Antarctic; this is a region of spectacular peaks, magnificent glaciers, dense forests, violent winds and torrential rain: a vast wilderness-area described by an early missionary as 'the uttermost part of the Earth.'

Below left: The ruins of Machu Picchu show that Inca architecture was extremely sophisticated. The site was untouched by the Spanish conquerors of the 16th century, and has therefore provided archeologists with excellent first hand knowledge of life in pre-Columbian America.

Below: Machu Picchu was built on steep slopes between twin peaks, and this necessitated the construction of a complex terrace system, still clearly visible today.

In 1910 a young Salesian priest, Alberto de Agostini, arrived in Patagonia as a missionary. It was a daunting first parish, with the trees outnumbering the people by something like a million to one. To find, let alone get to know his parishioners, De Agostini had to be both mountaineer and explorer.

For 46 years he dedicated his life to seeking out and caring for the people of Patagonia. Within a few weeks of his arrival he was exploring the Martial Mountains of Tierra del Fuego: a heavily-glaciated range rising sheer from the sea where no European before had set foot. In 1913 he attempted to climb Mount Sarmiento (7165 feet) whose massive bulk is a well-known landmark to seamen rounding Cape Horn; he got to within 1000 feet of the summit, only to be defeated by a near-continuous avalanche of snow-blocks. In the 1920s and 30s he turned his attention to the cordillera of the mainland, spectacular pinnacles of granite soaring to 11,000 feet out of the Earth's largest icecap outside the polar circles, a hazardous world of near perpetual blizzard.

His achievements were outstanding in two fields. As a priest he won the respect of the Chilean and Argentine settlers, and the love of the Indians whose rights he never failed to champion. As an explorer, he amassed a wealth of information about Patagonia's geomorphology, geology, glaciology and climate; he made the first scientific map of the area, took the first (and some of the finest) photographs, and made the first ascent of most of its major peaks. A summary of the mountains he was first to set foot on reads like a Baedeker of Patagonia.

Seldom has one man done so much to unveil such difficult terrain.

Above: Members of the Kaipo tribe from the rainforest of Brazil protest against plans to dam the Xingu River. The plight of the Amazonian Indians has attracted increasing world-wide attention.

The Conservationists

Our concept of exploration is continually being modified. Five hundred years ago its motif was the discovery of new lands; one hundred years ago it was the amassing of scientific facts; today an accepted facet of exploration is the safeguarding of our planet, the efforts being made to preserve threatened species – be they plants, animals or human beings.

One of the first South Americans this century to advocate a policy of protecting the people of Amazonia was Candido Rondon. In 1907 he was put in charge of building a telegraph line through the Mato Grosso. He proved a competent surveyor and engineer, and (which was unusual at the time) a staunch advocate of Indian rights. Initially, the Indians opposed the telegraph line; they kept burning it down. Rondon, however, went alone and unarmed into their lands, and eventually won them over. To quote his citation:

He penetrated this vast and little-known area, and by his fear-lessness, resolution and personality succeeded in making friends with the Indians . . . Eventually he persuaded them not to destroy the telegraph posts but guard them.

It was during these negotiations that he coined the phrase which epitomised his dealings with the people of the Mato Grosso: 'Die if need be, but kill never.' Subsequently he accompanied Theodore Roosevelt on his exploration of the Rio Pilcomaya, and founded Brazil's first Agency for the Protection of Indians.

Between the 1940s and 1970s the policies advocated by Rondon in the Mato Grosso were put into practice by the Villas Boas brothers in the rain forest of the Amazon. Claudio, Leonardo and Orlando Villas Boas devoted their lives to seeking out and making contact with the remote and often warlike tribes of the Amazon basin, many of whom had never seen a *civilazado.* This was delicate and dangerous work: the leaving of gifts, the patient waiting, arrows scything unexpectedly through the trees, more gifts and more waiting, the momentary glimpse of a half-seen figure, and at last the first wary encounter, the first touch and the first halting attempts at communication. Few men have done more than these gifted and dedicated brothers to bridge the gulf between people of divergent culture. On the foundations they laid teams on anthropologists are today living with and studying tribes such as the Kayopo in the headwaters of the Xingu.

A different approach to conservation is that of the large fact-finding expedition, whose scientists collect data in specialized fields. Such ventures are invaluable in providing a foundation of informed facts on which conservation can be based. One such expedition, led by Iain Bishop, went to Brazil in 1967 under the aegis of the British Royal Geographical Society. Over a period of 3 years they made a detailed study of an area of forest between the Rio Xingu and Rio das Mortes. The botanists classified 8000 species of plants, in each case pressing, drying and tabulating ten specimens. The zoologists collected 100 species of fish, 263 species of birds and over 4000 varieties of termite 'the most numerous and influential creatures of the rain forest.' The doctors sought ways of making the Indians immune to infection and pioneered research into leishmaniasis. Of even greater significance in the longterm was the work of the geomorphologists, who compiled a report on what was likely to happen if the rain forest was burned down and the land used for farming.

The low fertility of the dystrophic soil will be a limiting factor to agricultural development. The reserve of nutrients is low and is concentrated in the organic fraction of the soil . . . Agricultural use requires the felling and burning of the vegetation, and this will allow a brief period in which crops can be sustained by the released nutrients. However, the rapid mineralization of soil humus following clearing will result in a sharp fall in the capacity of the soil to retain nutrient ions, and the leaching released by mineralization will result in extremely low nutrient levels within one or two years of the burn. Continual crop production or grass growing will then be impossible.

If this warning had been heeded successive Brazilian governments would have been more cautious in their efforts to exploit the rain forest: a policy from which only land-speculators have benefited.

Above: The dense forests and precipitious slopes of an Andean valley.

Left: The indigenous inhabitants of Tierra del Fuego were regarded as so unusual that they were on occasion exhibited in Europe and North America like this group shown in the late 19th century.

Australasia

Australia is the most isolated and hence the most distinctive of the habitable continents.

About 90 million years ago our planet consisted of two landmasses, Laurasia in the northern hemisphere and Gondwana in the southern, divided by a single ocean, the Sea of Tethys. In the north Laurasia has remained relatively static; the continents have stayed close together,

and birds animals and human beings have been able to move freely from one to another. In the south, in contrast, Gondwana broke up; India moved from one hemisphere to another and collided with Asia; Africa moved north and collided with Europe; South America attached itself to North America, and Australia and Antarctica were left, cut off from other landmasses, circling the

Previous page: Robert Burke and William Wills were the first white men to succeed in crossing Australia from south to north.

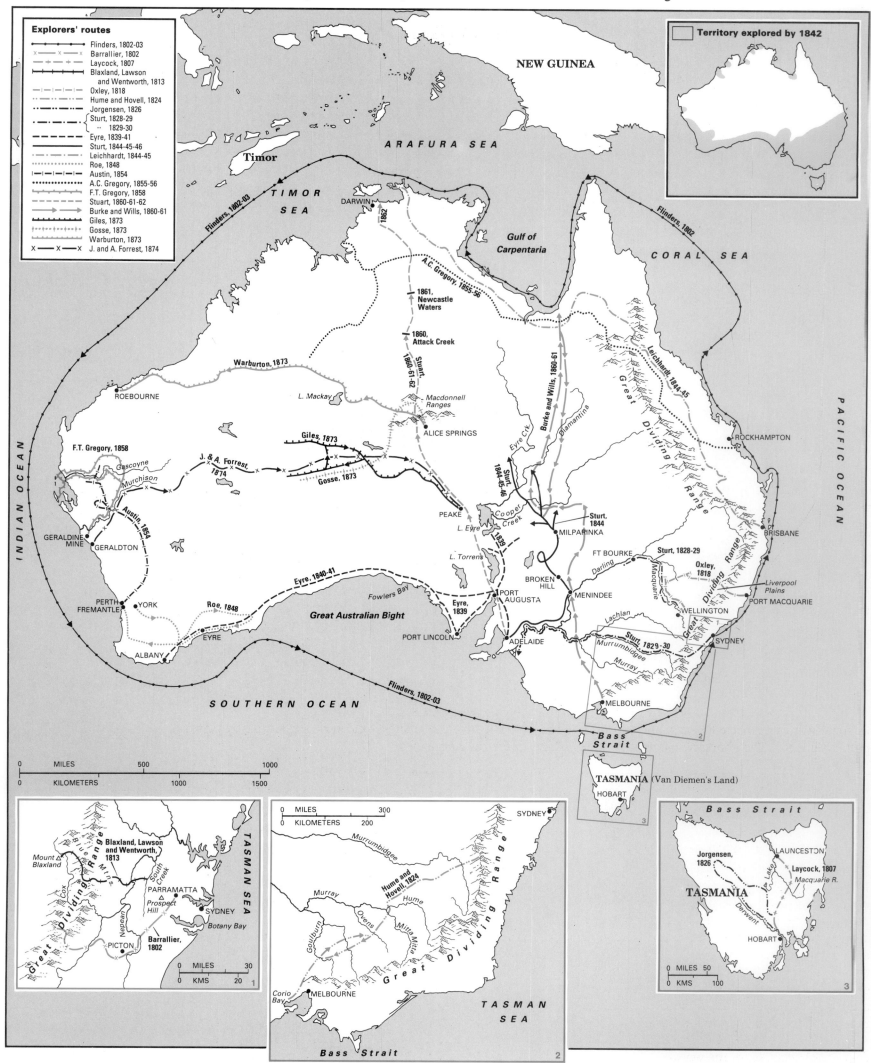

Explorers' routes

Flinders, 1802-03
Barrallier, 1802
Laycock, 1807
Blaxland, Lawson and Wentworth, 1813
Oxley, 1818
Hume and Hovell, 1824
Jorgensen, 1826
Sturt, 1828-29
1829-30
Eyre, 1839-41
Sturt, 1844-45-46
Leichhardt, 1844-45
Roe, 1848
Austin, 1854
A.C. Gregory, 1855-56
F.T. Gregory, 1858
Stuart, 1860-61-62
Burke and Wills, 1860-61
Giles, 1873
Gosse, 1873
Warburton, 1873
J. and A. Forrest, 1874

Territory explored by 1842

Above: Ancient Aboriginal paintings in the Kakadu National Park, Northern Territory. Paintings in this area are probably around 18,000 years old.

South Pole. Eventually, some 60 million years ago, Australia became detached from Antarctica and began to drift towards its present position. It was isolated then; it has remained isolated ever since.

So the *flora, fauna* and people of Australia were left to evolve, free from outside interference, in their own distinctive way. On the trees the leaves developed so that they 'hung upsidedown, not so much evergreen as evergrey'; the outback became the home of huge birds which never flew and strange animals which hopped rather than walked and kept their young in pouches; while the Aborigines developed a nomadic earthbound culture unlike any other in the world.

The exploration of this idiosyncratic continent proved in some ways unexpectedly easy, and in others unexpectedly difficult. The Aborigines were no problem. 'They are,' wrote Cook, who was one of the first Europeans to make contact with them, 'a gentle inoffensive people, in no way inclined to cruelty . . . or to war;' they lacked the wherewithal to oppose the European newcomers who swiftly dispossessed them of their lands. The terrain was another matter. Australia is vast; it is farther from Sydney to Perth than from New Orleans to San Francisco, and a single cattle station in the Northern Territory covers an area greater than the whole of Texas. It is also the driest of the populated continents becoming increasingly arid as one approaches its center, which consists of huge sandy-cum-stony deserts devoid of river or lake. No wonder the early white explorers described this desolate region as 'a ghastly blank on the map.'

The first and greatest explorers of this 'ghastly blank' were the Aborigines.

'A Walk Through the Dreamtime': The Aborigines as Explorers

It is thought that the first people to reach Australia were Negritos who about 40,000 years ago made their way to the continent *via* a land-bridge which during the Ice Age joined Australia to New Guinea. The Negritos were a short, stocky and dark-skinned people, who settled mainly around the coast, and in particular the east coast, where, during the forming of the Great Barrier Reef, fish and shellfish would have been plentiful. It seems likely that the Negritos were followed first by people who came originally from the Philippines, and then by people who came originally from India. At about the time that these races were amalgamating to form the Aborigines, the Ice Age ended, the sea-level rose, and Australia again became cut off from the rest of the world.

We do not know exactly why or when the Aborigines began to venture into the outback; but undoubtedly their journeys were piecemeal, dictated by local needs and motivated at least partly by an expanding population anxious to find new sources of food. By 10,000 BC the Aborigines had fragmented into something like 500 tribal units, each leading a peripatetic existence within its clearly defined territory. On the coast and in fertile inland areas such as the Murray Basin a tribe might spend a certain amount of time in one place; but in the outback the Aborigines were constantly on the move, trekking from one waterhole to the next, exhausting one meager supply of food before moving on to another. Their lives were uncomplicated and devoted to a single purpose:

staying alive. They had no homes, no crops, no clothes and no possessions. The few things that they did have they shared – food and wives, children and laughter, tears and danger and thirst. They seldom fought one another; their children hardly ever cried, and they cared for their old and their sick.

To some people, *wrote Cook*, they may appear wretched, but in reality (*they*) are happier than we Europeans. They live in Tranquillity. The Earth and the Sea furnish them with all things necessary.

Long before Tut-ankh-amen was laid to rest in his pyramid, the Aborigines had explored the outback, had found every waterhole, crossed ever saltplan and climbed ever desiccated peak.

Because the members of each tribe lived all their lives in one particular area of land, ever traveling through it and drawing sustenance from it, it was inevitable that they should become bound to their land by ties both physical and spiritual. Aborigines don't merely believe that their gods live *in* the land, they believe they *are* the land. Colin Simpson in *Adam in Ochre* puts it well:

The Australian Aboriginal does not transplant. His altars are waterholes, hills and rocks. He is, by the nature of his beliefs, identified with and bound to a particular patch of earth, his tribal land. That land, and no other, is identified with his "dreaming".

If you take away a Christian's land you don't take away his faith. But an Aborigine dispossessed of his land is dispossessed also of his god – which explains why these once 'gentle and inoffensive people' so often take to petty crime and the bottle when forced to live on the periphery of cities.

Above: Abel Tasman (1603-59), the skilled Dutch navigator who discovered Van Diemen's Land in 1642. The island was renamed Tasmania in 1825.

The First Landings: The Dutch (1629)

Australia remained isolated from the rest of the world until the 17th century. Stone Age fisherfolk from New Guinea may have sighted land in the south and one or two may have been swept on to the coast of Australia by storm, and a ship from Cheng Ho's expedition may have circumnavigated the continent in 1410; but the first fully authenticated sighting of the continent by Europeans took place in 1606 when two Spanish vessels, *San Pedrico* and *Los Tres Reyes* passed through the Torres Strait and saw Banks Island off the tip of the Cape York Peninsula.

A few years later there were a spate of sightings and the occasional landing by the Dutch.

Dutch vessels on a direct route from Cape Town to Batavia often found themselves becalmed in the doldrums of the central Indian Ocean. A sea-captain named Hendrik Brouwer discovered that by keeping farther to the south he could avoid the doldrums, pick up the Roaring Forties, and make a far quicker passage; he stayed in the storm-belt until he reached Australia, then turned north and followed the coastline to Indonesia. In 1613 all vessels belonging to the Dutch East India Company were ordered to follow this route; and in the next couple of decades Company *jachts* and *fluyts* frequently sighted the coast of Western Australia. In 1616 the *Harmony* anchored off Shark Bay; in 1618 the *Mauritius* anchored off Exmouth Gulf; in 1619 the *Amsterdam* made a landfall near Perth – 'we could find no place to put ashore,' wrote her captain, 'because of the heavy surf.' A few years later the *Lioness* and the *Golden Seahorse* rounded the southwest tip of the continent and entered the Great Australian Bight.

It soon became apparent to the Dutch that they had

Below: Canton in the 17th century, one of the main bases of the ubiquitous Dutch East India Company whose officers made important navigational discoveries that opened the south Pacific to European shipping.

KANTON.

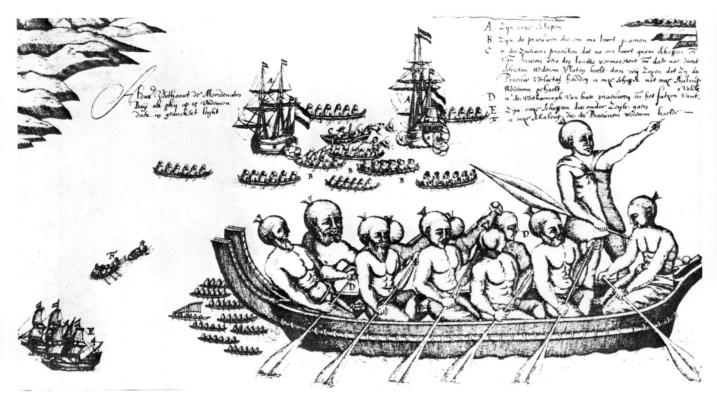

Above: William Dampier (1652-1715), a former pirate, who made two voyages around the northwest and west coasts of Australia. His discoveries complemented those of Tasman.

Above left: A page from Tasman's journal, showing some of the natives he encountered on his voyage.

discovered a great new continent. Yet they made no attempt to land on it and establish colonies. This was due partly to the nature of the terrain and partly to the nature of the Dutch. The west cost of Australia is a lee shore and a barren shore; the wind blows straight on to it from the sea, making it a graveyard for sailing ships, and the hinterland is featureless and arid; there were no easy pickings here for traders. And it was trade that the 17th century Dutch were interested in. They wanted commodities not colonies; and because Australia seemed to have none of the gold, timber and spices so dear to their hearts, they described it as worthless; the only use they had for it was as a turning point on their frequent voyages to Batavia.

Throughout the early 17th century there is no record of a Dutch ship's company trying voluntarily to settle on Australian soil. There was, however, one brief and terrible involuntary settlement.

In June 1629 the *Batavia*, flagship of the East India fleet, ran aground on the Abrolhos a chain of low islands and reefs to the north of Perth. The *Batavia* was carrying over 200 passengers, and a valuable cargo including gold, and even before she ran ground the thoughts of some of her crew had been turning to mutiny and loot. The shipwreck gave them their chance. Within hours of running aground the *Batavia* had broken up. Her ship's company salvaged what they could and found temporary safety on the tiny offshore islands. Their best hope of survival, they

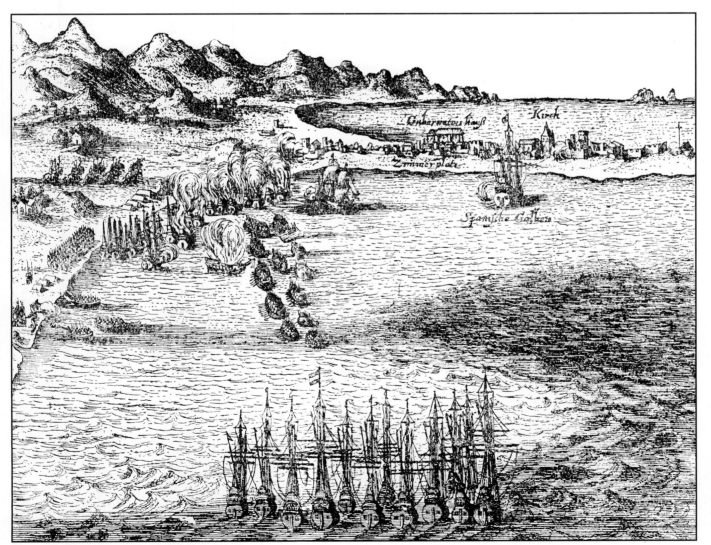

Left: An engagement between Dutch and Spanish ships at Callao de Lima, Peru. From Gottfried's *Neieue Welt*, 1655. An indication of the rivalry between the two nations for influence in the Pacific.

decided, would be for some of the crew to take their ship's boat, try to reach Java, and from there mount a rescue operation. This they did. However, the voyage to and from Java took several months, and it was a terrible scene to which the rescuers returned. The crew who had stayed behind had seized the *Batavia*'s cargo, and, with appalling brutality, had murdered 120 of the passengers. It seems that men-passengers were given the option of joining in the killing or being killed, and women-passengers the option of submitting to the crew's sexual demands or being murdered. At the subsequent trial in Batavia some of the testimony was almost beyond belief.

Jonas was told to go with Zeevanck and others to Seals' Island, and kill the 4 women and 15 boys who had avoided death in the previous massacre . . . Jonas went up to Mayken Soers who was pregnant and took her hand and said, "Now Mayken, my dear, you must die"; and he flung her to the ground and cut her

throat. Having done this, he saw that another man was having difficulty killing Janneken Gist, so he went to his help and stabbed Janneken to death with his knife. The two remaining women and the young boys were then killed by the others.

This gruesome story has a little-known sequel. The mutineers were rounded up; some were hanged on the spot; some were taken to Java where 'they were tied to a wheel in public and their bodies broken from under upwards'; and two, Wouter Looes and Jan Pelgrom, were marooned. We are told that Looes and Pelgrom were given a well-provisioned ship's boat, and set adrift near the mouth of the Murchison River. Undoubtedly they would have struggled ashore, and undoubtedly they would have survived for weeks if not months or even years. They were the first white settlers of Australia. One wonders what the gentle Aborigines thought of them?

Captain Cook and the British

The 17th century Dutch discovered but took no interest in west Australia. The 18th century British discovered and immediately colonized east Australia. This very different approach was due partly to the fact that the east cost is more immediately inviting than the west, and partly to the fact that the British were in search not of trade but of strategic bases, and these the east coast could offer.

When Cook left England in August 1768 the ostensible purpose of his voyage was scientific – 'to observe the passage of the Planet Venus over the disk of the sun'; but he

also had secret orders – 'to observe with accuracy such lands as you may discover and take possession of them.' Having fulfilled the first part of his mission in Tahiti, Cook stood southwest, and after two months sighted New Zealand. He surveyed the islands, with meticulous accuracy, then decided 'to steer to the westward until we fall in with the East Coast of the land discover'd by the Dutch.' On April 9th, 1770 Cook's ship the *Endeavour* was close-reefed in high winds and a heavy sea when the officer on watch, Lieutenant Hicks, sighted land: 'an agreeable countrie: of low hills covered in part with trees

Right: A secluded stretch of shoreline on the north coast of New South Wales, which has probably changed little over the past 200 years.

Below: A plaque at Botany Bay, NSW, commemorates the landing of Captain James Cook in 1770.

and bushes, and interspersed with tracts of sand.' Their landfall was Point Hicks Hill, roughly midway between Sydney and Melbourne. This was a major discovery. It was not, however, as is often claimed, the first sighting by a European of the east coast of Australia, because the French explorer Bougainville had almost certainly sighted Cape Flattery on the coast of northeast Queensland a couple of years earlier.

Cook followed the coastline north, until he came to Botany Bay, where he landed. Here he made a rare mistake, describing the anchorage as 'tollerably well sheltered' when in fact it is exposed to the easterlies, and the soil as 'promising' when in fact it is poor and sandy. A more perspicacious description of the bay was that of his naturalist, Joseph Banks, who called it 'a veritable treasure trove of strange plants and insects.' During their stay of less than one week Banks collected over 200 plants and insects unknown in Europe – the outside world's first intimation of the continent's unique flora and fauna.

Cook's passage north along the coasts of New South Wales and Queensland was a fine piece of seamanship (see Chapter II). But in the long term the hazards that he faced and overcame were less important than his assessment of the suitability of the new-found land for settlement. He was optimistic – perhaps in view of the colonists' subsequent difficulties over-optimistic.

The Countrie is well diversified, *he wrote*, with Hills and Plains. The soil of the hills is dry and stoney, yet it produceth thin grass and a little wood. The soil of the Plains is sandy and friable, and produceth long grasses and Shrubs etc. It is indifferently well watered with many small Brooks but no great Rivers. The Climate is warm and fine, and the air wholesom.

He makes it sound near-idyllic. No wonder that within a few months of Cook's return to England the British government had decided to 'establish permanent bases in this new land, which should prove most convenient for crops and livestock.'

Above: Sydney harbor at the end of the 19th century. The First Fleet arrived in Botany Bay in 1788 to discover it was entirely unsuitable for settlement. Only 12 miles north was 'what is surely the finest harbor in the world': Sydney.

Below: Sydney Parkinson's sketch of a kangaroo made at the Endeavour River during Cook's first voyage.

Convicts and Whalers

Above: Cook's *Endeavour* is careened after striking the Great Barrier Reef during his first voyage.

The convicts were an afterthought. The original idea was to colonize Australia with American farmers who had lost their land as a result of the War of Independence. It was only when the American farmers proved reluctant to be shipped to the opposite side of the world that one of Cook's officers, James Matra, suggested convicts were sent instead. In March 1787 the first convict fleet set sail from England, and their voyage was one of genuine exploration, for they were embarking on a long and dangerous (if involuntary) journey into the unknown.

It was a large fleet: 2 warships, 3 supply ships and 6 transports. The crew and escort numbered 233, the convicts 759. In command was Captain Arthur Phillip, and it was due largely to his ability and humanity that the voyage was accomplished with few casualties. It could easily have been otherwise; for the ships were old, the provisions inadequate and the distance covered and the time taken enormous. On a similar voyage 5 years earlier Admiral Anson had lost 60 percent of his ship's company from scurvy. Phillip lost 2 percent. And when, after a voyage of 15,000 miles and 247 days he dropped anchor in Botany Bay, he must have hoped his troubles were over. In fact they were about to begin.

Botany Bay was not a good place for a settlement, for the harbor was shallow and exposed to the easterlies, and the hinterland swampy and unhealthy. Phillip searched for a better site and, only 12 miles to the north, found Sydney.

I have the honour to inform your Lordship, *he wrote in dispatches to England,* that we have had the satisfaction of finding what is surely the finest harbour in the world, in which 1,000 ships of the line might ride in safety . . . It has springs of sweet Water, and numerous sheltered Coves, formed by narrow necks of land covered in Timber.

Sydney was an excellent site, but the settlement did not take root easily; indeed for at least a decade its survival was in the balance. Within weeks of their arrival 'sickness and scurvy were raging in a manner most extraordinary' – the first building to be built at Sydney Cove was a hospital. The soil turned out to be basically poor; their sheep and cattle died; their seeds were eaten by ants; their crops were destroyed by insects, fungi and bacteria to which they had no immunity; and among the convicts was a hard core of malcontents who responded neither to discipline nor kindness. However, the British government were loath to see the settlement go under, and kept sending in more ships with more supplies and more convict-settlers; a handful of dedicated men – Phillip himself, his doctor Wentworth and the convict-architect Greenway – refused to admit defeat; and by the end of the century a small reasonably self-sufficient agricultural community had taken root.

There was, however, a big difference between surviving and prospering. Prosperity for the settlers seemed a far-distant dream, until they found that they had on their doorstep a commodity for which the world was clamoring. It was not, initially, the pastures of New South Wales which brought wealth to Australia, it was the richer pastures of the sea.

As the crew of the first fleet approached Australia they saw 'great numbers of black whales which kept pace with our ship for many hours.' The crew of the second and subsequent fleets came equipped with harpoons, and it

A View of Sydney Cove – Port Jackson   *March 7th*

was soon noticed that when one of the black whales was killed, unlike most species, it remained afloat. These whales, *Eubalaena australis*, became known as the Southern Rights, because they were the 'right' whales to kill; and it wasn't long before British and New England whale-ships were following in the wake of the convict-transports.

They found a whalers' El Dorado. The southeast corner of Australia lies on the migratory route of the Southern Rights; and twice a year vast herds of these 60-foot, 60-ton creatures flocked into the coastal waters of Victoria, South Australia and Tasmania, often so close-packed that they disrupted shipping and kept the Governor of Tasmania awake with their 'snoring'. Each whale yielded two tons of oil and a ton of baleen (or whalebone), the latter valued at £2,500 – sufficient in those days to finance a complete whaling voyage to Australia. With the incentive of such profits no wonder whaleships from Great Britain and New England descended on their pray like vultures on to a carcass. Initially they operated from Sydney; but it was not long before they discovered other

harbors – Melbourne, Adelaide and Hobart all came into being as bases for the whaling industry . Whalers were the first Europeans to sight much of the southeast coast of the continent, and in the early years of the 19th century literally hundreds of bay-whaling stations sprang up along a shoreline previously known only to the Aborigines. It was for these gentle people the sounding of their death-knell. What happened in Tasmania was typical. The Aborigines' wells were poisoned with arsenic, and they were hunted to death with packs of dogs. Within 50 years of the whalers' arrival in Tasmania not a single Aborigine remained alive.

The gentle people and the playful animals died; but the settlements lived, nurtured, it would be no exaggeration to say, on their victims' land and blood. It would be hard to over-estimate the influence that the whaling fleets had on the settlement and exploration of Australia. At the turn of the 19th century statistics show that the number of whalers in the continent was greater than the number of convicts, guards and free-settlers combined.

Date	Naval/ Military Personnel	Convicts	Settlers	Whalers
1780	233	759	-	-
1800	625	1,977	311	3,584

As Herman Melville succinctly put it in *Moby Dick*: 'the whaleship is the true mother of that mighty (Australian) colony.'

Left: A View of Sydney Cove and Port Jackson, c. 1792-4. This shows the wilderness bordering on the new settlement.

Above: Having survived a fairly unpleasant voyage, convicts arriving in Australia found an inhospitable land peopled by natives who were not always friendly.

Below left: The crews of the first fleet noticed vast numbers of whales in Australian waters, and by the early years of the 19th century whalers were operating from scores of stations along the south coast of the continent.

Below: The chain gang in Hobart, 1831. Tasmania was not settled until 1803, and until 1856 was a convict settlement with an unenviable reputation for brutality.

'One Land to which I give the name Australia': Flinders Circumnavigates the Continent (1801 – 03)

In 1800 the outline of Australia was still a matter of conjecture. In the west the Dutch had discovered a coast and named it New Holland. In the east the British had discovered a coast and named it New South Wales. In the north and south sightings had been few and indeterminate; large sections of the coast were unknown, an many people thought that New Holland and New South Wales would turn out to be separate island divided by a strait. It was not known what rivers drained the continent, and many people thought they must flow inland into a central lake. To settle these questions Matthew Flinders, a 28-year-old lieutenant in the Royal Navy, left England in June 1801 in command of HMS *Investigator*.

Flinders was no stranger to Australia. Together with George Bass he had already circumnavigated Tasmania and proved it an island, and had then set himself the task of 'exploring these (Australian) waters so thoroughly that no man after me shall find it necessary to explore them again.' He succeeded: although a series of misfortunes – none of them of his making – transformed his exploratory triumph into a personal tragedy.

His first misfortune was that a few days before *Investigator* was due to leave England a Sea Lord visiting his ship discovered Mrs Annette Flinders 'seated in the captain's cabin not wearing a bonnet . . . an indication that she regarded the ship too much as her home.' The Admiralty, outraged at such lack of decorum, gave Flinders the choice of leaving his wife behind in England or giving up the command of his ship. It was a cruel decision, for Matthew and Annette had only recently been

Below: The southernmost point of the Australian continent: Wilson's Promontory, Victoria, a dramatic area, with steeply forested slopes and rocky outcrops rising out of the sea.

Right: Cape York was first mapped in detail by Matthew Flinders in 1801. It is the most northerly point of the Australian mainland.

married and were deeply in love. But Flinders had a strong sense of vocation. 'Whatever my disappointment,' he wrote with more pith than gallantry, 'I will give up the wife for the voyage of discovery.' A week later, as *Investigator* stood south into the Atlantic, it became apparent that Flinders' second misfortune was his ship. The *Investigator's* hull had been weakened by having gunports cut into it, and her new copper sheathing disguised but did not alter the fact that her timbers were rotten; she made water at the rate of 5 inches an hour. And if one wonders why the Admiralty should have sent so unseaworthy a vessel on so important a voyage, it was because, during the Napoleonic Wars, she was all that could be spared. And this was Flinders' third and most injurious misfortune: that his voyage coincided with a great European war, when, for the British, a minor victory in Europe was of more significance than a major discovery on the opposite side of the world. His achievements were appreciated only in retrospect.

Flinders describes their passage to Australia as uneventful, and neither health nor navigation seem to have been a problem. In matters of health he imitated Cook: frequent fumigation of the lower-deck, much airing of bedding, no restriction in the use of drinking water, and regular issues of limejuice to combat scurvy; 'as a result my entire crew remained in excellent health.' In navigation he was both a perfectionist and an innovator, inventing the 'Flinders Bar' – iron stanchions still used today for evening out the effect of a ship's magnetic field on its magnetic compasses – as a result the *Investigator* made an accurate landfall off the southwest tip of Australia, and in December 1801 entered the magnificent anchorage of King George's Sound. Ahead lay several thousand kilometers of shoreline which was not only unknown but which few human beings had ever set foot on.

The circumnavigation which followed was more painstaking than exciting. Initially there were no disasters or dramatic discoveries: simply a meticulous survey of very foot of coast. His Diary says it all.

January, 1802. In running along the South Coast I endeavoured to keep as close-in with the land as I could so that waves breaking along the shore were ever visible from the deck. In this way no river or opening could escape being seen. Such close proximity involved much danger and loss of time, and I was constantly at the masthead. All bearings were laid down immediately they were taken; and when we haul'd off from the coast at night, every precaution was taken to come in at exactly the same place next morning.

This meticulous work continued month after month, with occasional forays ashore by the ship's naturalists – the gifted botanical painter Ferdinand Bauer and the more than competent botanist Robert Brown. The result was twofold: from Flinders himself a map of the Australian coast so accurate that it was still being used by shipping after the Second World War, and from his naturalists the first detailed evidence of Australia's unique flora and fauna – in the Great Australian Bight alone Bauer made sketches of 450 previously unknown plants and creatures, while Brown collected and classified 750 previously unknown plants and grasses.

When, in May 1802, *Investigator* stood into Sydney her crew were in good health and 3000 kilometers of unknown coastline had been delineated. Things had gone well. As soon as he had reprovisioned, Flinders continued his circumnavigation, charting the east coast as accurately as he had charted the south. It was when he came to the north coast that his troubles started.

The climate off the north coast of Australia is humid and unhealthy, and it was not long before the crew of the *Investigator* succumbed to tropical fevers. Even more serious was that *Investigator* herself began literally to fall apart at the seams. As they neared the foot of the Gulf of Carpentaria water was pouring into her at the rate of 14 inches an hour; her pumps could barely keep pace with the influx; and, in real danger of foundering, Flinders was forced to run his vessel aground. He hoped to recaulk her; but as his carpenters assessed the damage their reports became increasingly gloomy.

Out of ten top timbers one is partly rotten and five entirely rotten . . . on the larboard quarter all timbers are completely rotten . . . the stemson is decayed, the tree-nails rotten, and with any sea running the ship would founder.

The chief carpenter summer up his report with the words: 'In 12 months, I doubt she will be afloat, for there will scarce be a sound timber in her.' Flinders was in a quandary. If he turned back he would have to face head winds and heavy seas, and it seemed likely his ship would founder. If he continued his circumnavigation he would have easier conditions but a greater distance to cover, and it seemed likely his ship would disintegrate before he got back. He decided to continue his circumnavigation, his task now not surveying but surviving. With his crew growing weaker and his ship settling ever lower

Above: Matthew Flinders (1774-1814). His circumnavigation of Australia was fraught with difficulty, but he produced maps that were still used 150 years after his death.

Below: The official artist with Flinders' expedition was Ferdinand Bauer, a gifted botanical painter. Together with the ship's botanist Robert Brown, he provided the first detailed evidence of Australia's amazing array of flora and fauna.

in the water, his voyage became a race with death. At the end of six nightmare months he managed to struggle back to Sydney. But by this time nearly half his crew had died or were so weak they could not stand; while the shipwrights who came to examine *Investigator* declared her 'totally decayed and nor worth repairing;' most of her timbers were so rotten a piece of bamboo could be pushed through them.

What happened next makes tragic reading. When he tried to return to England, Flinders' ship was wrecked and his charts and diaries damaged. Setting out again, he was captured by the French and held prisoner for 7 years in Mauritius. By the time he was released he was a sick, indeed a dying, man. Reunited at last with Annette, he was retired on half-pay and devoted the last years of his life to writing his magnificent epitaph, *A Voyage to Terra Australis*. The book was finished in 1814; but Flinders never saw it; he died the day it was published.

Above: Koalas drawn by Bauer. Bauer sketched 450 previously unknown plants and creatures from the area of the Great Australian Bight alone.

Breakthrough: Crossing the Blue Mountains (1798 – 1814)

The soil around Sydney is more sandy than fertile, and the settlers were soon seeking better pastureland for their cattle and sheep. Barring their path were the Blue Mountains, a range which lies some 40 miles from the coast, and has no well-defined summit-ridge but consists of a mosaic of steep-sided ravines choked with scrub: a difficult barrier to breach.

In January 1798 a party of 4 convicts and 2 Aborigines led by John Wilson – himself a time-expired convict – set out to explore the mountains. At the end of a year they returned, saying they had crossed the range and seen on the far side a huge level plain 'across which there flowed a sluggish river big as the Hawkesbury.' In 1802 there was another crossing; this was led by Ensign Barrallier who came back with an accurate map and reports of 'a plain as vast as the eye could reach.' Both these expeditions had used the traditional technique for crossing mountains, by tackling them *via* their valleys. The next expedition, led by Gregory Blaxland, tried something different.

1813 was a year of drought in east Australia; the rivers and wells dried up, the sheep and cattle died. Three farmers Blaxland, Lawson and Wentworth, decided that rather than sit and watch their livestock die, they would try and drive them over the mountains to the plains beyond. Because they had animals with them they avoided the scrub-filled valleys and kept to the barren more open ridges; and these provided an easier way across. On May 28th the three explorers stood on Mount York, looking down on 'wooded pastureland sufficient to support the entire stock of the colony for the next 30 years.' A couple of days later the explorers were feasting on kangaroo and cod, and their animals on the lush grass on the Nepean Valley. The barrier had been breached. Within a year a road had been built – by convict labor – along the route which Blaxland had pioneered, and soon flocks and herds were streaming over the mountains into one of the great pasturelands of the world.

It would, however, be wrong to imagine that as soon as the settlers crossed the mountains they found themselves in a land of milk and honey. The Murray-Darling basin covers an area far larger than the British Isles. Although parts of it are fertile grassland, other parts are swamp, scrubland and tracts of poor red sand; it is subject to long spells of drought punctuated by short spasms of violent flood; and its river-system is complex – some streams meandering north to peter out in the desert, others flowing first north then west then south, but at the end of it all having no apparent outlet to the sea. These rivers, it was realized, were the key to settlement. In 1817 Cunningham set out to follow the Lachlan, but soon found himself in 'a desiccated country choked with scrub . . . it seems that for all practical purposes the interior west of a certain meridian is uninhabitable.' In 1818 Oxley followed the Macquarie, and came across pockets of fertile land alternating with waterlogged plains. In 1824 Hovell and Hume sent back conflicting reports of the Murrumbidgee, the former saying he 'had seen no country better adapted for feeding sheep', the latter (more accurately) dwelling on the thick scrub, leeches and razorsharp grass; they could find neither the source of the river nor its mouth. It was Charles Sturt who finally solved the mystery of where the rivers went to. In 1828 he

and Hume floated down the Macquarie as far as its junction with the Darling; and the following year he and Macleary floated down the Murrumbidgee as far as its junction with the Murray. They were following the latter when, unexpectedly, they again came across the Darling. All the great rivers of the basin, Sturt realized, converged into the Murray/Darling which he now followed to the coast to where it flowed into a vast tidal lagoon, Lake Alexandrina; its egress to the sea blocked by a line of sandbanks.

This was an important piece of exploration. Not only did it delineate Australia's major river-system, it helped to open up vast new areas of territory with very great potential for farming.

Across the Continent: Burke and Wills (1860 – 61) and John McDouall Stuart (1863)

By the late 1850s the periphery of the continent had been explored, but the central deserts remained an enigma, 'a ghastly blank of the map.' Two goals in particular were not yet attained: no European had ever reached the geographical center of Australia, and no-one had ever crossed the continent. In 1860 two expeditions set out to attempt a crossing: Burke and Wills from Melbourne, John McDouall Stuart from Adelaide. The crossing developed into a race. And in this lay the seeds of tragedy.

On August 20th, 1860 Burke's expedition left Melbourne: 27 camels, 23 horses, 15 men and a cornucopia of supplies. The chairman of the Victorian Exploring Committee made it clear to Burke what was expected of him: 'Stuart has already left Adelaide, so it will be a race between you and he;' Burke was urged to be first across the continent 'for the honour of Victoria.' To start with all went well. It took them less than 3 months to reach Cooper's Creek (a little to the east of Lake Eyre) where they set up a supply depot close to one of the waterholes. From here four men – Burke, Wills, King and Gray – taking with them 6 camels, a horse and supplies for 4 months, made a dash for the north coast. They made it. And so much attention has been focussed on what happened next that they are not always given the credit they deserve for this fine piece of exploration.

Their troubles started as they began the return journey. They had arrived on the north coast at a bad time of year: in the wet. The terrain was difficult, and for weeks on end they had had to squelch through cloying mud with water up to their knees. The climate was unhealthy, and before long they were suffering from dysentery. They began to fall behind schedule, and Burke ordered a precautionary cut in their rations. The trouble was that their rations were already minimal; cutting them further, damaged their health. Gray became 'very unwell': so unwell that one night, he quietly died in his sleep. The others struggled on, killing first their camels then their horse, concentrating all their efforts on reaching the depot. Once there they reckoned their troubles would be over.

On April 23rd, 1861 they were nearing Cooper's Creek. 'I think I can see their tents,' Burke kept saying 'I *think* I see them.'

He was wrong. When they stumbled into the depot they found it deserted. No tents: no animals: no men. Yet the ashes of the fire were still warm, and the camel droppings not yet hardened. The depot-party, who should have been there to succor them, had pulled out to return to Melbourne that very morning.

The rest of the story is well known. Their despair. Their efforts to struggle on. The loss of the last of their camels in quicksands. Their hunger, thirst and physical deterioration. Their return to Cooper's Creek – at least there was water here. The efforts of the Aborigines to save them – 'the blacks brought us fish and nardoo seeds', wrote Wills. 'They are very hospitable and attentive.' But

Above: One of Charles Sturt's own sketches made during his journeys of 1828-31. This watercolor drawing depicts a section of the Murray River.

Above right: By the mid-19th century, curiosity was growing about the middle of the vast continent and the settlers were now secure enough to devote more time to exploration of their adopted country. In 1860 Burke and Wills left Melbourne in an attempt to cross the continent from south to north.

Right: An aerial view of the creeks and rivers near Karumba on the Gulf of Carpentaria, a marshy area of intense tropical heat, which severely weakened members of Burke and Wills' expedition.

the Aborigines were nomads, and the white men were by now too weak to travel. Wills died of starvation and exhaustion on about July 1st, and Burke a few days later. The only survivor was King, whom a relief party found three months later, 'in an appalling state, burnt black by the sun and half mad with starvation and loneliness.'

Burke and Wills had crossed the continent and died. Stuart crossed it and lived – but only just.

John McDouall Stuart was arguably the greatest of the explorers of central Australia. In 1860 he crossed the Macdonnell Ranges, and was first to set foot in the geographical center of the continent – 'Planted the flag,' he wrote, 'on a hill which I named Central Mount Sturt, after the father of Australian exploration.' In 1861, at the same time as Burke and Wills, he attempted to cross the continent with 12 companions and 40 horses. They reached Newcastle Waters in the Northern Territory, some 200 miles from the coast, and made 11 attempts to push through to the Gulf of Carpentaria. All failed: a setback which puts the achievements of Burke and Wills in perspective. In 1862 he tried again, and this time he suc-

ceeded; six months after leaving Adelaide he was 'washing (his) face and hands in the water of the Indian Ocean, as I had promised I would do if I reached it.' His journey back was harrowing. The horses were weak, provisions were low, water was scare, and Stuart was suffering from scurvy and incipient blindness. He had a succession of strokes, which left him so crippled that his men feared for his life – 'I asked King and Nash,' he wrote, 'to sit with me in case of my dying during the night, for it would be lonely for one man to be there by himself.' In constant pain and unable to stand, let alone walk, he had to be carried on a stretcher tied between two horses. At last, against all the odds he struggled back to Adelaide. But he never recovered; half blind and totally crippled, he retired to England.

Stuart's achievements went virtually unrecognized and unrewarded at the time. Yet not only was he the first man to reach the center of the continent, and the first man to cross it and survive, on all his expeditions he never lost a man; he was popular, and generous to a fault – even naming the center of the continent not after him-

self but after a friend. The telegraph-line from Adelaide to Darwin, the railroad through Alice Springs and the Stuart Highway all follow the route he pioneered. Few men have done more to help open up a continent.

Above: The return journey from Cooper's Creek to Melbourne proved too much for all but one member of the 1860-61 expedition. Burke died in early July and was buried by a relief party some time later.

The Exploration of the Outback

About two-thirds of Australia is outback (almost all the Northern Territory, most of Western Australia and much of South Australia): a wilderness of sand, stone and rock that is very dry (average rainfall under 10 inches a year), very hot (average mid-day temperature over 100 degrees F) and vast (apart from the Sahara it is the largest area of desert-cum-semi-desert on Earth.) In 1840 the whole outback was, to the European settlers, *terra incognita*; yet by 1875 it had been crisscrossed by explorers from almost every point of the compass, and even its most formidable deserts had been traversed. The motive for this remarkable burst of exploration was land hunger.

Early in the 19th century John Macarthur brought a handful of Merino sheep to Sydney. Merinos originated in Spain, and adapted well to the arid conditions on the periphery of the outback. Within two decades the number of sheep in the continent had trebled, and Australia had superseded Spain as the world's leading producer of wool. It became imperative to find new pastureland for the ever-increasing flocks.

The men who are usually given credit for opening up the outback are explorers like Eyre, Sturt, Stuart, Leichhardt, Warburton and the brothers Gregory and Forrest. This is the truth, but not the whole truth. The outback was opened up not only by famous explorers leading big expeditions; it was opened up also by a multitude of unknown farmers, ever driving their flocks and herds a few miles deeper into the unknown. In this respect Australia was like North America; the men who explored it were not outsiders (like Livingstone in Africa, Marco Polo in Asia or Scott in the Antarctic), but local frontiersmen who equated discovery with settlement. One of the first and greatest of these indigenous explorers was Eyre.

John Eyre and the Nullarbor Plain (1841)

Edward John Eyre was an overlander, whose experience in driving vast herds of cattle over vast distances had made him an expert bushman. And bushcraft, in exploring the outback, was vital. Not just success but life itself depended on it.

Water, water, water . . . the words runs like a refrain through the explorers' journals. The flight of birds, a darker line of bush, the trend of a dried-up creek, even the settling of a single

bird on a featureless plain – these were clues which meant water, and it took keen eyes to detect them and a bushman's experience to evaluate them.

The best bushmen were, of course, the Aborigines. And in February 1841 Eyre and the Aborigine Wylie set out from Fowlers Bay in South Australia to try and find a coastal stock-route to Albany in West Australia. Within a fortnight they were close to dying of thirst, for they were traversing one of the bleakest littorals on Earth, the Nullarbor Plain.

March 10, *Eyre wrote.* It was clear unless we discovered water that morning our horses must perish, while it was doubtful if we ourselves could save our lives.

Left: Edward John Eyre was the first white man to cross the waterless Nullarbor Plain, a journey of over 1000 miles from Adelaide in South Australia to Albany in Western Australia.

Prompted by Wylie, he dug for water in about the most unlikely place imaginable: on the crest of the great white sand-dunes that lined the shore – and found a life-saving well. They struggled on, plagued by flies, and tortured by heat and thirst. In April they survived by collecting dew. In May they survived by sucking the roots of the Plain's only vegetation, the occasional eucalyptus. In June they survived because of a chance meeting with a French whaler. Twice they went for a week without food or water. But at last they struggled through to Albany. They found no stock-route. But their 132-day trek through near-waterless desert delineated the southern perimeter of the outback.

Charles Sturt and the Great Inland Sea (1844-46)

Sturt was fascinated by Australia's rivers. In the late 1820s he pieced together the complex network of the Murray-Darling. And in the early 1840s he led an expedition into the outback in search of 'that great inland sea into which it is believed a number of rivers must drain.' He took with him 4 wagons, 11 horses, 15 men, 60 bullocks and 300 sheep; also, optimistically, a boat. This was the first major expedition to aim for the heart of the outback, and Sturt's Diary paints a vivid picture of the difficulties it ran into.

October 9th (*1844*) we have now arrived at the borders of that desert which has so far foiled the most enterprising explorers. The natives are not encouraging. They say "if you go farther, your bullocks will hang out their tongues, your waggons will tip over and you will die. For there is no great sea in the heart of the desert; nor water nor grass nor a stick to light fire with" . . . The ranges have now ceased, and we have all around us a level

boundless expanse, without a landmark to guide us. The temperature stands at 118° (*46°C*) in the shade. So great is the heat that every screw in our boxes has been loosened, the handles of our instruments have split, our hair has ceased to grow, our nails have become brittle as glass. Scurvy afflicts us all. We have violent headaches, pains in our limbs and swollen and ulcerated gums . . . Mr. Poole (*the expedition surveyor*) grew worse and worse; the skin over his muscles became black, and he lost the use of his lower extremities. On 14th July he died . . . Nothing could exceed the sterile character of this terrible desert, or the hopelessness of the prospect before us. But the moon being full we continued our journey, at times across the dry white bed of salt lagoons, at other times along the top of sandy ridges. The sky is cloudy, but no rain ever falls. We are struggling against difficulties that can not be overcome by human perseverance.

Sturt pushed on to within 150 miles of the center of the continent, then he very wisely turned back. For his prudence the Royal Geographical Society gave him their gold medal, remarking succinctly that the difference between a good explorer and a dead one was that the former knew when to give up.

Friedrich Leichhardt and the cornucopia of Queensland (1844-46)

Leichhardt was a German-born botanist who arrived in Sydney in 1841. Within three years he was setting out in command of an expedition to pioneer a stockroute from Sydney to Port Essington (near Darwin); and if one wonders how so inexperienced a traveler took on so problematical a mission, the answer lies partly in Leichhardt's enthusiasm, and partly in the fact that Sydney's farmers and businessmen were anxious to find new grazing land

Above: Charles Sturt (1795-1869), led important expeditions to trace the Murray-Darling river system, and to search for a great inland sea in the heart of the continent.

Below: The unforgiving, but beautiful sands of the Simpson Desert, which prompted Sturt to turn back.

and plied him with funds and equipment. He set out in October 1844: an unlikely figure wearing a coolie hat and brandishing a Prussian officer's sword, inviting disaster yet meeting with nothing but success. His route took him not into the outback but along its periphery, over the gently-rolling hills of the Great Dividing Range. Thanks to his Aborigine trackers, he never strayed more than 10 miles from water, and the terrain he traversed was benign. His Diary is a panegyric:

This (*the Mackenzie tableland*) is fine country, covered with rich grass and well watered. Here are open forests, and plains well-stocked with game; the honey is sweet as that of Hymettus, and the air fragrant with wild thyme and marjoram. No country could be better adapted for pastoral purposes . . . As night advances, the Black fellows' songs die away. The neighing of the tethered horse, the distant tinkling of the bell, or the occasional cry of night birds is all that interrupts the silence of our camp. The fire gets gradually dull, and smoulders slowly under the large pot in which our meat is simmering, while bright stars pass unheeded over the heads of the dreaming wanderers.

Leichhardt enjoyed being an explorer; and after a journey of 16 months and 1800 miles, he arrived in triumph at Port Essington. This was a fine achievement which paved the way for the settlement of Queensland.

He made two further journeys, first attempting to cross the continent from east to west, then trying to follow the course of the Barcoo River. The first ended in disaster, the second in tragedy, when in 1848 he headed into the outback and was never heard of again. At the end of some unknown chain of billabongs, where the Barcoo finally peters out in the desert, the country which Leichhardt loved so dearly extracted a terrible price for his ingenuous enthusiasm.

Augustus Gregory and the North Australian Expedition (1855-56)

Augustus Charles Gregory was the oldest of four brothers all of whom explored the outback. In 1846, together with his younger brother Frank, he surveyed the area north of Perth. This was unpromising terrain – 'extremely dry, with frequent whirlwinds of red dust, immense salt marshes and sandstone cliffs.' They found none of the hoped for grazing land. They did, however, find something else, which in the long term was to bring even greater prosperity to Western Australia.

The existence of garnets, iron pyrites and plumbago which were found in the geiss indicate a metalliferous formation, and I have little doubt that a further search would reveal sources of mineral wealth.

Failing to find grazing land in the west, Gregory turned his attention to the north; and in 1855 set out in command of a major expedition (2 ships, 18 men, 50 horses and 200 sheep) intent on surveying the little-known coastal regions of what are now the Northern Territory and Queensland. His expedition got off to a bad start. One ship grounded near the mouth of the Victoria River, and the other capsized among the sandbars. Many of their horses and sheep were lost, and over half their provisions ruined. At the end of a month the men were suffering from diarrhoea, vomiting and partial blindness; they were attacked by Aborigines, and to add to their troubles started bickering among themselves.

Gregory divided his contentious team into two: a sea-expedition which set out to chart the coast of Arnhem Land and the Gulf of Carpentaria, and a land-expedition which explored the Victoria, Daly and Roper Rivers, then followed the Barkly Tableland eastward into the part of Queensland which had been pioneered by Leichhardt. Neither expedition made any dramatic discoveries; but they did make an extremely accurate survey of almost the whole North Australian coast. From this it became increasingly evident that the terrain was unsuitable for settlement. The entries in Gregory's *Journal* have a depressing similarity.

October 1855. Entered a wide plain, thinly grassed, destitute of trees and bounded by rocky sandstone hills of a barren aspect . . . February, 1856. Came to a shallow valley, beyond it a vast plain with scarcely a rise to relieve the monotony of the surface; the country covered with triodia (spinifex), small acacia and gum bushes . . . July, 1856. Passed a ridge of barren sandstone hills. This country is of a worthless character; there is little grass and the soil is poor and stony. Eucalypti and triodia are abundant.

The British government who had helped finance Gregory's expedition, pointed to his frequent references to 'grassy plains', and did their best to encourage settlement. The Australian farmers, who had also put up money, pointed to his frequent references to 'triodia', and gave the area a wide berth. It was the Australians who were realists. Even today this northern fringe of the outback is one of the most sparsely populated areas on Earth.

Warburton and the Central Deserts (1873-74)

Peter Egerton Warburton found the heart of the outback even more daunting than Gregory had found its periphery. In 1873 he set out from Alice Springs with a cosmopolitan entourage – four white Australians, two Afghan camel-drivers and an Aborigine tracker; they had

Left: The remote southwestern quarter of Queensland, bisected by thousands of ephemeral water courses. This is the area where the German explorer Friedrich Leichhardt disappeared in 1848 while following the course of the Barcoo River.

Below: Sturt's Overland Expedition leaving Adelaide, 10 August 1844, by S T Gill: a painting which conveys the excitement provoked by the departure of Sturt's expedition.

Above: Egerton Warburton, who crossed the outback from east to west, traveling by camel through some of the most arid deserts in the world, in 1873.

Above left: Arnhem Land, bordered by the Victoria, Daly and Roper Rivers in the Northern Territory. This area was accurately surveyed for the first time by Augustus Gregory's expedition in 1856.

no horses, but 17 camels, and their objective was to cross the outback from east to west, via the Macdonnell Ranges and the Gibson and Great Sandy Deserts. Within a week of leaving Alice Springs they had 'to settle down for the night without water', an entry repeated again and again in Warburton's Diary during the next 8 months. For their route lay over some of the most arid terrain on Earth. First a desiccated plateau covered with 'the dreaded triodia'. (dreaded because, to quote the naturalist H W Bates who edited Warburton's Diaries, 'it is one of the most cheerless objects an explorer can meet. For the country it loves to dwell in is utterly useless for pasto-ral purposes.') Then a featureless and apparently endless expanse of stones – 'as if McAadam had thrown down here every cart-load of stones he had ever filled.' And finally a sea of sand-dunes – 'great petrified waves of sand, sixty or more feet in height, running across our line of advance.' Their camels died and were eaten. Again and again they ran out of water, and were saved at the last moment by finding Aborigine wells. By the time they came to the sea of sand-dunes they were covering on average no more than 50 miles a month. However, they had passed the point of no return, and had no option but to struggle on.

Below: Camels on the trans-continental road from Alice Springs. Camels were imported into Australia in the early 19th century, and used by Warburton in 1873.

Our position is critical, wrote Warburton; but should it please God to give us once more water I am determined to make a final push for the River Oakover. Some of us might make it, if not all.

Ten days later, their water-bottles having been empty for the last 36 hours, they half staggered half fell into the Oakover in the final stages of dehydration and exhaustion. Another dozen hours or dozen miles farther before reaching water and every one of them would almost certainly have been dead. 'We were all very thankful,' wrote the laconic Warburton, 'to have escaped with our lives out of this most horrid desert.'

The delineation of the 'ghastly void'?

In the 1870s a series of journeys through the outback filled in the last blank spaces on the map. In 1872 the humorous and romantic Ernest Giles discovered the Olgas – 'an extraordinary collection of rounded minarets, giant cupolas and monstrous domes.' In 1873 the young surveyor William Gosse discovered Ayres Rock – 'an immense sandstone monolith, its walls over 1,000 feet high, which looms over the surrounding plain like a tidal wave about to break.' And in 1879 John Forrest crossed the continent from Shark Bay in the northwest to Adelaide in the southeast. His route took him through some of the most arid regions of the outback, and he suffered agonies from heat, exhaustion, hunger and above all thirst. 'Our throats were so dry,' he wrote, 'that we were unable to speak. We shot a hawk and cut its throat in order to drink the blood, but it didn't do us much good.' Time and again his expedition was saved by their Aborigine trackers who, when all seemed lost, guided them to a waterhole where they could gulp a few pints of brackish water before pushing on. No wonder when, after seven months, they at last reached the telegraph line to Adelaide they 'broke into hoarse discordant cheers.'

Forrest's journey marks the end of an era. Within the span of forty years (1840 – 80) the center of the continent had been explored. Whereas maps of Australia in 1840 showed little more than a coastline, maps in 1880 showed an interior frequently criss-crossed and accurately surveyed: there was no longer the possibility of finding some major range or river, no hope of stumbling across some inland sea or belt of pasture. In view of the difficulty of the terrain this was a monumental achievement, and one which would have been the wonder and envy of explorers only forty years earlier.

In the wake of the explorers came surveyors, farmers and prospectors. Yet the outback has usually proved too difficult an environment for man to prosper in. Farmers have nibbled away at its periphery, driving their cattle or sheep to one still more distant waterhole; miners have settled in isolated pockets to extract iron or tin, uranium or gold; yet the heart of the continent still remains basically empty: more than 70 percent of Australia's enormous territory is occupied by less than one percent of her people. The unknown ghastly void has been delineated rather than filled.

Below: The Olgas, giant dome-shaped boulders 30 km from Ayer's Rock, discovered by Ernest Giles in 1872.

The Exploration of New Guinea

New Guinea has only recently become known to the outside world: 130 years ago no European had ever penetrated more than a few miles from the coast. Originally the island was populated by a Negrito people who arrived about 40,000 years ago from south east Asia. The Negritos remained comparatively isolated, and developed a lifestyle which was static, agricultural, tribal and addicted to ancestor worship and, occasionally, to cannibalism.

The first European to sight the island was probably the Portuguese Antonio d'Abrue in 1511, and the first to land on it Jorge de Meneses, who is believed to have sought refuge on the north coast from a storm in 1526. A couple of decades later another Portuguese, Ortiz de Retez, landed in much the same place and, thinking the natives looked like the people of the Guinea Coast in Africa, named it Nova Guinea. During the next 250 years many seamen – Jansz, Le Maire, Tasman, Dampier, Bougainville and Cook – skirted the island. Some put ashore; but they all decided that New Guinea had little to offer them. The huge sprawling coastline (from its west tip to its east tip is farther than from London to Istanbul) was thickly forested, the climate was unhealthy, the people unfriendly, and there were none of the spices so dear to the Dutch. The island was ignored.

It was the naturalists who put it on the map. From the 16th century onward the plumage of the most exotic birds had been shipped from New Guinea to Europe. It was the plumage only that Europeans saw, the uninteresting feet and legs having been removed to save storage space; this gave rise to the legend that the birds never alighted, and must have come from some celestial paradise. It was in search of these birds of paradise that naturalists first came to New Guinea. It was 1824 before a European sighted a living bird of paradise on the island, and 1872 before a major expedition penetrated the interior. Then the Italian Luigi D'Albertis ascended the Fly River in a 9-ton launch so loaded with arms and ammunition that its deck was almost awash. During the next five years there was hardly a dull moment. D'Albertis collected a large number of specimens – including 15 different species of the birds of paradise, and for these he paid the people of the river fairly. However, when thwarted, he lobbed 'skyrockets of dynamite' into their villages. In between times he 'charmed the women with kisses,' impressed the men by biting off the head of a poisonous snake, and entertained whole villages with extracts from Italian opera – 'although I would not venture to sing in any other country than New Guinea!' For all his faults and flamboyancy D'Albertis loved New

Below: New Guinea was visited by many explorers, but it lacked the resources to make it interesting to European explorers and merchants. Instead, naturalists and anthropologists began to study the immense variety of flora and fauna. Pictured here are tribesmen sporting headdresses with bird of paradise tail feathers.

Guinea; when he retired to the outskirts of Rome he built himself the replica of a Papuan house to remind him of 'that land of enchantment.'

It was the end of the 19th century before William Mac-Gregor traced the Fly River to its source among the great chain of 13,000-foot peaks which rise, snow-capped, only a few degrees south of the equator. And well into the present century before explorers broke through these peaks to find, unexpectedly, in the heart of the island 'broad well-grassed valleys, terraced gardens, fortified villages and the densest array of tribal communities in the world: over a million people, speaking some 400 different languages:' a Shangri-la of the tropics. These idiosyncratic communities had for millennia been evolving in virtual isolation from the rest of the world; and even in the mid-20th-century there was only one practical way of making contact with them: by air. Throughout the 1920s and 30s floatplanes brought explorers, missionaries, agriculturalists, naturalists and doctors to this mountain fastness; and the New Guinea highlands can claim to be one of the few places in the habitable world which has been explored mainly by air.

Left: Sydney Parkinson's sketch of a Maori chief, from the account of Cook's first voyage.

The Exploration of New Zealand

Because of its isolation New Zealand was one of the last habitable places on Earth to see the coming of human beings. The first people to set foot on the islands were almost certainly survivors from a Polynesian pahi blown ashore on the North Island by storm and by chance some time in the 10th century. Other landings by Polynesians followed – whether by accident or design is a matter of opinion – and settlements became established around the Bay of Islands and Bay of Plenty in the North Island and Banks Peninsula in the South Island. From these stemmed the Maoris, intelligent and warlike cultivators of the soil who, by the time Europeans arrived in the Pacific, had settled throughout most of the North Island and round much of the coast of the South.

The first European to sight New Zealand was Tasman who, on 13 December 1642 saw the snow-capped peaks of the Southern Alps rise unexpectedly over the horizon; he would have liked to land, but was frightened away by the Maoris – 'enormously tall men with rough voices and huge clubs,' who attacked and killed 4 of his crew. Next to arrive was Cook, who was not put off so easily. During his three great Pacific voyages (between 1769 and 1777) Cook visited New Zealand 5 times, accurately surveying about 95 percent of the coastline, noting the idiosyncratic flora and fauna, and establishing good relations with the Maoris, whom he described as 'strong, rawboned, well-proportioned and of a very dark brown colour . . . alert, vigorous and in all that they did most dextrous.' Cook was followed by a number of French explorers – Surville, Du Fresne, D'Entrecasteaux and D'Urville – who reconnoitered the islands but made little effort to establish a foothold ashore. The first Europeans to settle ashore were sealers in the South Island and whalers in the North.

Towards the end of the 18th century British and New England sealers paid increasingly frequent visits to the fjordlike channels of the southwest coast of Otago. One of the most successful was Captain Raven, who in 1792 landed in Dusky Sound, slaughtered 4500 seals, set up a shore-station and was one of the first people to realize the potential of the local flax. By the turn of the century sealers and flax-collectors had between them explored much of the rugged southern extremity of New Zealand, discovering Foveaux Strait and Stewart Island; but the hinterland – precipitous and thickly wooded – offered little reward to would-be exploiters, and for several decades the South Island remained sparsely populated and largely unknown. Exploration was stimulated by the journeys of Thomas Brunner in the 1840s, and the gold rushes of the 1850s and 60s. Thomas Brunner, a young surveyor, set out in 1846 to explore the west coast, taking with him Maori guides but little in the way of provisions – provisions were a luxury he could ill afford, since his expedition funds totalled only £36-18-4d (£36.92), out of which he had to pay his guides! His route lay across country that was scenically beautiful but difficult to travel through. 'Rain continuing,' he wrote, 'food scarce, strength decreasing, spirits failing, prospects fearful.' However, he struggled on, plagued by sandflies but sustained with seaweed by friendly Maoris. It took him 550 days to cover the 300-odd miles between Cape Farewell and Tititira Point and return. This was a fine achievement; but of greater significance to the opening-up of New Zealand was the discovery in 1861 of gold near the Clutha River in Otago. Soon prospectors were pouring into Otago at the rate of 2500 a week, and these prospectors and the local farmers between them opened up the Canterbury Plains and the foothills of the Southern Alps.

Below: An early etching of Maoris. New Zealand was one of the last places on Earth to be populated, the first inhabitants being Polynesians around the 11th century.

The prospectors triggered off temporary prosperity with their finds of gold, but it was the farmers who had the last word by turning the Canterbury Plains into one of the great sheep-pasturelands of the world.

At the same time as sealers were landing in the south of the South Island, whalers were landing in the north of the North Island. What the whalers wanted was fresh water and the Maoris' potatoes and fresh meat; what they offered in return was muskets. The introduction of firearms to a warlike people was a recipe for disaster. For several decades there was violence and bloodshed, with the Maoris fighting both the whalers and one another. One incident says it all. The crew of a whaling vessel burned down a Maori village and raped the women; the Maoris in retaliation seized another vessel (the *Boyd*) and not only killed the crew but ate them. The arrival of missionaries did something to improve relations, and it was members of the Church Missionary Society who were first to venture inland. In 1814 the Rev. Samuel Marsden established a station in the Bay of Islands, and during the next six years made three journeys round the Northland Peninsula. This was magnificent country: 'The views,' he wrote, 'are grand and nobly pleasing, the soil good and the timber fine.' It was also thickly populated: 'Everywhere the little naked children run about like rabbits in a warren.' Other missionaries subsequently made greater journeys – in 1831 the Williams brothers reached Rotorua and the younger went on to walk right across the Island, and between 1838 and 1847 William Colenso traveled extensively around Hawke Bay and Lake Taupo – but to Marsden goes the distinction of being the first European to venture among a warlike and often hostile people.

In the wake of missionaries came farmers. Sponsored

by the New Zealand Company, the first settlers arrived in 1839 and established a base near Wellington. Soon they were fanning out in search of agricultural land, traveling sometimes with Maori guides and nearly always by Maori trails. This, basically, is how New Zealand was explored: not by one or two epic journeys, but by cumulative small-scale forays with settlement synonymous with discovery. This exploration was neither particularly difficult nor dangerous, but in one way it was unique: it was carried out entirely by the settlers themselves. New Zealand was explored by New Zealanders.

The Arctic

The Polar Regions

The Arctic and Antarctic appear to have much in common – both are bitterly cold, covered in ice, and have total darkness in winter and unending daylight in summer – yet their differences outweigh their similarities. For the Antarctic is a high continent surrounded by sea, while the Arctic is a shallow ocean surrounded by land. Another difference is that the South Polar regions are far harsher and more inimical to life than the North Polar regions. South of the Antarctic Circle the only plants to eke out existence are a handful of lichens, the only in-

digenous wildlife are one-celled protozoa and wingless flies, and no human being can call the continent home. North of the Arctic Circle, in contrast, plants flourish (there are over 1000 species of wild flowers alone); there are also thousands of species of advanced wildlife, and hundreds of thousands of people live in comfort all the year round. Finally the two regions have a totally different history. Before 1821 it is doubtful if a human being had ever set foot in Antarctica, whereas people have been living in the Arctic for something like 40,000 years.

Pioneers of the Tundra: The Reindeer Herders

We do not know exactly where or when human beings first came to the Arctic. However, since Neanderthal man had the ability to make warm clothing, build shelters and control fire, it was probably about 50,000 years ago that hunters first came pushing through the forests of Eurasia in pursuit of game, and in particular reindeer. Reindeer-herding is one of the oldest human activities – even today it provides more people with a livelihood than any other form of hunting. As the last Ice Age was drawing to its close, vast herds of these migratory animals were roaming Eurasia as far south as the Baltic, and America as far south as the Great Lakes. Our ancestors who followed these herds through the tundra, often for many hundred miles, were the first explorers of the Arctic.

In several parts of the tundra the reindeer-herders discovered a secondary source of sustenance – fish; and over the millenia they evolved a way of life that depended on the migratory behavior not only of reindeer but of creatures such as salmon, whales, seals, narwhal and cod. The most successful colonizers of the north have been

Previous page: HMS *Intrepid* in the middle ice of Baffin Bay. This scene illustrates the difficulty of exploring the North Polar seas using conventional ships. The ice cap is in constant flux and ships can be trapped and crushed with little warning.

Left: Reindeer-herders were the first explorers of the Arctic, preceding European and Russian 'pioneers' of Polar exploration by about 40,000 years.

Below: The distinguished explorers of 'The Arctic Council,' convened to discuss the best means for locating the missing Franklin. Among those shown are Parry (seated 2nd left), James Clark Ross and Francis Beaufort (4th and 5th left). A portrait of Franklin appears in the background.

people like the Aleuts of the Aleutian Islands, the Inuit of Alaska, the Eskimos of Labrador, the Lapps of Lapland and the Chukchi of the Bering Strait, who have combined hunting and fishing. When we talk of seamen from Europe 'discovering' a North East or a North West Passage, it is worth remembering that many thousands of semi-nomadic hunters-cum-fishers had been living along the shores of these polar passages for millenia.

The Search for a North East Passage

The words North East or North West Passage conjure up for most of us pictures of sailing ships hemmed in by ice struggling unsuccessfully to force their way along the Arctic coastline of Eurasia or America; in fact these coastlines were delineated as much by land-expeditions as by voyages.

Exploration by Land: the Cossacks, Dezhnev, and Chelyuskin.

The first modern explorers to penetrate to the shores of the Eurasian Arctic were Cossacks. The name Cossack is a corruption of Kazakhs, a nomadic people whose wagon fleets still roll today, as they have been rolling for millenia, over the steppe of central Asia; and from about 1550 onward (as the Tartar grip on northern Europe slackened) those Cossacks helped push the Russian frontier northeastward very much as, two centuries later, backwoodsmen and fur traders helped push the American frontier northwestward. The Cossacks' first major foray was made by Yermak Timofeiev, who in 1579 crossed the Urals with a group of mercenaries-cum-traders and reached the River Ob; a few years later the river was followed to its mouth in the Obskaya Estuary. By 1600 Cossack fur traders had pushed east as far as the River Yenisey; by 1610 they had discovered the River Lena, and by 1638 had crossed the continent and reached the sea of Okhotsk in the Pacific. There followed a number of hazardous journeys as explorers like Dezhnev, Prontchishchev and Chelyuskin followed the rivers of Siberia to their outlets in the Arctic Ocean.

In 1648 Semeon Dezhnev traveled from the mouth of the Kolyma in the Arctic to the mouth of the Anadyr in the Pacific. There used to be doubt as to whether he traveled overland (a relatively short distance) or by sea (a distance of over 1500 miles). Recent research indicates the latter, that his ship was a shallow-draught *koch* with a single sail, and that he passed through the strait between Russia and America nearly a century before its usually-accredited discoverer, Bering.

In 1735 the Prontchishchevs and Chelyuskin sailed down the Lena, wintered close to its mouth, then pushed west along the desolate coastline towards Cape Chelyuskin, the most northerly point of Eurasia. They reached 77°25′N, on the cost of the barren Taymyr Peninsula, where they were halted by impenetrable ice. In one

Below: The prospect of new and valuable types of animals as prey tempted hunters farther and farther north. This comical late 17th century engraving shows walrus hunting.

of the more harrowing disasters to overtake an expedition, Prontchishchev and his wife died of exposure and starvation; Chelyuskin, however, managed to double the Cape and continue his journey to the Atlantic.

By the middle of the 18th century the Arctic coastline of the Old World was known in general outline; small settlements had sprung up near the mouths of some of the rivers, and fur-trappers and reindeer-herders were working the less barren parts of the hinterland. No ship, however, had been able to follow the coast from Atlantic to Pacific (or *vice versa*) because of the ice. This was not for want of trying.

Exploration by Sea: Willoughby and Chancellor, Barents, and Nordenskiold.

The search for a North East and North West Passage was carried out mainly by the British, French and Dutch who found to their chagrin that the southern routes to India and the Spice Islands were controlled by Portugal or Spain. Their search had a dual objective: first to find out if the northern sealanes had exploitable resources such as gold, whales, fish or fur; and second to see if a way could be found to the riches of the East *via* the Arctic coastline of either Eurasia or North America. It was the second of these objectives that inspired the expedition of Willoughby and Chancellor.

In 1553 three ships – the *Bona Esperanze*, *Bona Confidentia*, and *Edward Bonaventure* left England under the command of Sur Hugh Willoughby, with Richard Chancellor as 'pilot major'; they were bound for 'Cathay and regions unknown', and seem to have had little premonition of the perils ahead. Off Norway they became separated in a storm. Chancellor in the *Edward Bonaventure* rounded North Cape, and, hugging the shore, reached the White Sea and eventually the embryo port of Archangel. Learning from local fishermen that he was in the domain

Above: Members of Barents' expedition fighting the 'great white bear' on Bear Island.

of Ivan the Terrible of Muscovy, Chancellor, with great enterprise, set off by sledge for Moscow, where he met the Tsar and concluded a treaty with him; this led to the forming of the Muscovy Company, and the beginning of Anglo-Russian trade.

Willoughby was not so lucky. Rounding North Cape, he left the shore and headed boldly across what is now the Barents Sea on about latitude 72°N. On August 14th he sighted an unknown coast, lying at right angles across his path. He had discovered Novaya Zemlya. Not realizing that the new-found land was an island, he tried to follow the coastline north; but his ships were soon blocked by

Left: Barents' crew attempting to cut a pathway through the ice after their ship had been frozen in.

Left: Barents and his expedition were the first crew to survive an Arctic winter. They built themselves a *behouden-huis* or survival shelter, from their wrecked ships and driftwood, and kept a fire constantly alight in the middle of it.

ice and driven back by fierce winds. Willoughby began to look for winter quarters. Finding nothing in Novaya Zemlya, he headed back for Norway, and, as the ice was thickening, struggled into the bleak little anchorage of Kola Bay, not far from present-day Murmansk. He and his 80-odd crew must have thought they were safe; but they had no concept of the bleakness of the terrain or the severity of the Arctic winter. They sent out parties in search of food, but found no trace of anything edible. One by one they died of cold and starvation. There were no survivors. Russian fishermen putting into Kola Bay the following spring found their bodies frozen solid to the deck of their ships.

An explorer who faced even worse conditions but managed to save his ship's company was Barents.

Willem Barents was born on an island off the Dutch coast, and his whole life was played out within sound of the sea. He progressed steadily up the nautical hierarchy from cabin boy to pilot to mate, and in 1594 and 1595 was the driving force behind two Dutch expeditions sponsored by the States General to search for a North East Passage. These expeditions made minor discoveries, and, in a year when the ice was unusually late in forming, managed to reach the Kara Sea (to the east of Novaya Zemlya); here they were again blocked by ice. The States General decided that even if a passage existed it would be too long, too dangerous and open for too short a time each year to be of use for trade; they withdrew their support. Barents, however, was determined to continue his search; he found backers among the merchants of Amsterdam, and in May 1596 set out with two ships to renew his battle with the ice. Barents was a magnificent practical seaman; if anyone could have succeeded it would have been he. The tragedy was that 16th-century sailing ships were not built sufficiently strongly to survive in the far north; in particular they could not withstand being frozen into the ice during an Arctic winter.

Their voyage got off to a promising start. They landed on Bear Island, so named because they found there a 'great white bear', which they killed after a horrifying two-hour fight, also on Spitsbergen where they were impressed by the mild climate (due to the Gulf Stream) and the abundance of flora and fauna. One ship then returned to Holland, while Barents pushed on into the unknown waters north of Novaya Zemlya. He managed to round the northeast tip of the island, and spent a month trying to force his way through the inviting but deceptive leads in the ice, which seemed always to promise open water ahead but invariably turned out to be dead ends. When he tried to withdraw, he found he had left it too late; and on August 28th his ship was trapped in a seething mass of ice floes and driven ashore. The ice worked its way under their hull, so they were first frozen solid to it, then squeezed to destruction. As the pressure increased their rudder was wrenched off, and their timbers splintered with a sound like rifle-shot: 'It was most fearful both to see and hear, and made all the hair of our heads to rise upright with fear.'

Their ship would never sail again. Help and the nearest human beings were 1000 miles away. The Arctic winter was approaching; and no ship's company had ever before been frozen in for an Arctic winter and survived. Yet the prospect was not entirely hopeless. They had their ship's stores (which were considerable); they had their ship's boats in which they might eventually be able to make an escape; and close-by on the shore they discovered a pile of driftwood: 'certain great trees, roots and all, as if God had purposely sent them unto us to help us build a house and to burn all winter.'

They used the driftwood and the remains of their ship to build a *behouden-huis* (survival shelter): a well-designed single room, 32-feet by 20-feet and 11-feet high. Its walls were caulked and tarred; it had a central chimney, a bath made out of wine-casks, and bunks heated

with fire-warmed stones and bear skins. It took six weeks to build the *behouden-huis*; and a few days after they moved into it, the sun disappeared at mid-day below the horizon and they knew they would not see it again for three months. The Arctic winter closed in on them, and with the darkness came that requiem of polar explorers: cold.

The diary kept by the ship's doctor, Gerrit de Veer, gives us some idea of what Barents and his crew had to endure that winter:

November 21. Today we washed our shirts, but it was so cold they froze stiff, and although we laid them out by a great fire yet only the side that lay next to the fire thawed, the other remaining frozen hard as a board . . . December 12. Extreme cold so that the walls inside our house and the wood of our bunks were frozen a finger thick with ice; yea, and the very clothes upon our backs were white all over with frost and icicles. *Their clock stopped; their wine froze solid.* January 4. To discover which way the wind was blowing we tied up a piece of cloth to a pike and thrust it up the chimney; but the moment it was exposed to the air it froze solid as a board and the wind could not stir it.

All of them, that winter, suffered from hypothermia, exhaustion and scurvy; Barents, who was nearing fifty and by far the oldest, became so weak he was unable to stand; two men died; but the others, by courage, ingenuity and determination, survived; and with the coming of spring they were able to venture outside and start to prepare their ship's boats for a dash to safety.

It was early June before the floes broke up. Ahead lay 1000 miles of ice-strewn sea; their boats were small, open and vulnerable; only 14 men had survived the winter, and some were so weak they could hardly stand; it must have seemed that their only hope of getting home was a miracle. They set out on June 13th, and almost at once a storm blew up and they were trapped in a kaleidoscope of disintegrating floes: 'The ice drove upon us fearfully . . . We were borne away and so crushed between the floes that we thought our boats would burst into a hundred pieces. Every minute of every hour we saw death before our eyes.' Eventually they managed to scramble ashore,

jumping with ropes from floe to floe and hauling their boats after them. When the weather cleared they set out again. As they rounded the north tip of Novaya Zemlya Barents asked two of his crew to lift him up so he could take a last look at 'that cursed land'; a few hours later he died. His crew, however, lived. For in one of the most astonishing voyages ever made by open boat, the quiet and unassuming Van Heemskerck, who had for long played second fiddle to Barents, led his crew through the packice fringing the Arctic shore until they came at last to safety among Russian fishermen at the approaches to the White Sea.

Van Heemskerck's homecoming from the north coincided with the arrival in Holland of the first Dutch fleet from the south. The former limped back with no ship and no riches, thankful to be alive; the latter returned in triumph with the exotic produce of the Spice Islands. The lesson was plain. The Dutch in future set their sights on Indonesia, and the seaways of northern Europe became a backwater. Dutch whaling stations on Jan Mayen and Spitzbergen fell into decay; at the mouth of the Hudson River the little trading post of New Amsterdam was handed over to the British, and it was widely accepted that as a trade route a North East Passage did not exist.

For 250 years no further attempt to find a Passage was made; and when, in the late nineteenth century, the search was renewed its *motif* was more scientific than commercial.

Baron Nils Nordenskiold was the earliest of a group of great Scandinavian polar-travelers of the late nineteenth and early twentieth century who were part-scientist part-explorer. He was born in Helsinki in 1832, and qualified as a chemist and geologist. In the 1860s he traveled extensively in Spitzbergen, and tried to reach the Pole with sledges drawn by reindeer. In the 1870s he set himself a more attainable objective. Ships, he pointed out, were now much stronger than they had been in the 1590s; they were powered by engines as well as sail, and might well succeed in forcing a way through the ice where their predecessors had failed. He made two reconnaissances of Novaya Zemlya, planned his expedition with meticulous care, and in July 1878 set sail from Tromso in north Norway determined to succeed where Willoughby and Barents had failed.

His ships were the 300-ton *Vega*, an ex-whaling vessel built of oak, specially strengthened by an ice-skin of greenheart, and powered by both steam and sail, and a smaller steel-built tender, the *Lena*. His crew were two-thirds experienced whalers and walrus-hunters, and one-third scientists. And his voyage was so successful and so devoid of either accident or incident that it seldom gets the attention it deserves. Within a fortnight of leaving Tromso, Nordenskiold had forced his way past Novaya Zemlya; within a month he was rounding Cape Chelyuskin, the fog lifting to reveal a huge polar bear – 'a sentinel patrolling the northernmost tip of the Old World' – and within six weeks he was anchored off the mouth of the Lena. Such spectacular progress was too good to last, and towards the end of August the *Vega* was

beset by ice and fog. When the fog did lift, it revealed a landscape of drab anonymity: 'no glaciers, no cliffs, no high mountains to give the scene natural beauty; the coast was the most monotonous I have ever seen.' Soon they were nosing through coastal waters uncharted, shallow and made particularly hazardous by fog. Nordenskiold was obliged to send a launch ahead to take soundings; their rate of progress dropped from over 50 miles a day to under 5, and as summer gave way to autumn it became clear they were not going to reach the Bering Strait before the ice thickened and hemmed them in. They were eventually brought up short in the Gulf of Kolyuchin, only 130 miles from the Pacific. Here they spent the winter, moored to a massive floe which provided them with shelter, their specially strengthened hull enabling them to withstand the pressure of the seasonal ice. Their scientists had a field day, their research work disturbed only by an occasional visit from the nomadic Chukchi,

Below: In the late 19th century maneuvering a sailing ship through the Arctic was still a dangerous and laborious business.

whose down to earth approach to eating, sex and hygiene caused raised eyebrows among the more fastidious Europeans. It was 9 months before the ice cleared, and the *Vega* was able to complete the last stage of her journey. On 20 July, 1879, decked with flags and triumphantly firing her single cannon, she emerged into the Pacific. It had taken 326 years for Willoughby's dream to be realized.

Today, with the help of nuclear-powered ice-breakers the North East Passage has become a regular route for Soviet shipping, and plays an important role in helping to harness the resources of the Eurasian Arctic.

The Search for a North West Passage

The words North West Passage – even more than North East Passage – have a nautical ring. One thinks of Frobisher loading his vessel gunwale-under with fools' gold, Hudson and his young son cast adrift to die, and Franklin's men reduced to murder and cannibalism on the shores of Coronation Gulf. Yet the Arctic coastline of North America was delineated as much by indigenous landsmen as by European seamen. Its great explorers were not only Frobisher, Hudson, Parry and Franklin; but also Hearne, Mackenzie, Simpson and Rae – and of course those earliest explorers of all, the Aleuts and Eskimos.

Exploration by land: Aleuts and Eskimos, Hearne, Mackenzie, Simpson and Rae.

The Arctic coast of the New World was explored initially from the west. About 40,000 years ago Mongoloid hunter-gatherers came streaming across the Bering land-bridge, which in those days formed a dry highway for the migration of people and animals from the Old World to the New. Some of these hunter-gatherers worked their way south into the rich pasture-land of the American plains; others worked their way east along the shores of the Arctic. In broad terms the former became Indians: a semi-nomadic people of prairie and woodland who traveled on foot or by birch-bark canoe. While the latter became Aleuts and Eskimos; semi-nomadic people of the tundra, who traveled by snowshoe, dog-hauled sledge or skin-built kayak. We do not know how or when the Aleuts and Eskimos explored the tundra; but their artefacts (mainly weapons and ivory carvings, some of them 10,000 years old) have been found all over the Arctic, from the Bering Strait to Greenland, and as far north as the Parry Islands. The North West Passage may subsequently have become a graveyard for European hopes, ships and seamen; but long before its so-called discovery in the nineteenth century, thousands of Eskimos had been living for thousands of years along almost every mile of its shoreline.

Much of the modern exploration of North America has been by river, with some explorers following the waterways west to the Rockies and finally the Pacific, and others following them north to the tundra and finally the Arctic. The first white man to reach the Canadian Arctic Ocean *via* one of these north-flowing rivers (and hence the first modern explorer-by-land of the North West Passage) was Hearne.

Samuel Hearne, an employee of the Hudson's Bay Company, made three journeys into the Barren Grounds, that bleakly beautiful and permanently frozen desert which 'lies sprawled across the tip of North America like a discarded purgatory'. The Barrens have less rainfall than many parts of the Sahara, although what little rain that does fall is much in evidence, since, unable to penetrate the permafrost, it lies on the surface in huge patches of muskeg and endless chains of shallow lakes. Not much grows or lives in the Barrens; although in sheltered hollows one finds a few gale-blasted evergreens and scatter-ings of dwarf spruce which have taken three centuries to grow as high as a man. In 1769 Hearne headed into this forbidding wilderness with a group of Chipewyan Indians. His first expedition was a disaster, with the Chipewyans plundering his stock of food, and 'making the woods ring with their laughter as they mockingly told me to find my own way home.' It was, however, Hearne who had the last laugh. Against all the odds he *did* make his way home, subsisting on snared rabbits and porcupine, and when this meager diet dried up, gnawing the boiled hide of his jacket. He was a great survivor.

Next year he was again heading north, again in the company of Chipewyans. This time he made significant discoveries round the shores of the Great Slave Lake only to be robbed and deserted a second time by the Indians who left him to die with no food, tent, snowshoes or warm clothing. He was saved by a chance-in-a-million meeting with the Chipewyan chief Matonabbee, who materialised, as by a miracle, out of the Barrens. The two men formed an unlikely friendship, and later that year set out together to try and follow the River Coppermine to its mouth. During their journey north Hearne became a member of Matonabbee's extended family, a motly rabble of wives and ex-wives, warriors and hunters, captives and children.

No Canadian explorer, *writes the historian Maurice Hodgson*, ever depended so much on one Indian for the success of his venture. It is impossible to conceive of the success of Hearne's last expedition without appreciating the degree to which he allowed himself to be physically and psychologically captured by the Indians, and specifically by his attachment to and affection for Matonabbee.

During the 19 months it took him to reach the mouth of the Coppermine and return, Hearne so melded into the life of the Indians that he virtually became one of them.

Below: In 1576 Sir Martin Frobisher set off in search of a North-West passage to China. On Baffin Island five of his crew, trading with Eskimos, vanished. Frobisher took one Eskimo prisoner in return. On his second voyage in 1577 one English sailor was wounded and six Eskimos killed in the encounter depicted here, as the English searched for their missing comrades and dug up what they believed was gold.

Left: As more and more
explorers ventured into the
Arctic, they were increasingly
able to cope with the extreme
cold with appropriate clothing
and equipment.

And devotees of the cult of the Noble Savage should read
his *Journey from Hudson's Bay to the Arctic Ocean* as a
corrective; for a more depressing account of filth squalor
and inhumanity it would be difficult to imagine. The Chipewyans ate the lice that they picked from one another's
hair, feasted on raw buffalo foetuses, gang-raped the
women of defeated tribes 'in a manner so barbarous as to
endanger their lives', and cold-bloodedly massacred the
Eskimos. The night before they reached the mouth of the
Coppermine, Hearne tells us, the Indians crawled up to
the tents of the sleeping Eskimos and attacking without
warning. More than 20 men, women and children, 'their
faces still warm with sleep,' were killed in a couple of
minutes. A young Eskimo woman ran desperately
towards Hearne, the one man not engaged in the killing.
A Chipewyan plunged his spear into her back.

She fell at my feet, *wrote Hearne*, and twisted round my legs, so
I could hardly disengage myself from her dying grasp. Two
Indians were pursuing her. I pleaded for her life; but they both
stuck their spears through her body, transfixing her to the
ground. Then they began to ridicule me, asking me if I desired
an Eskimo wife, and not paying the slightest heed to the
shrieks and agony of the poor wretch who was still twining
round their spears like an eel . . . an old man was speared until
his whole body was like a cullender, and an elderly half blind
Eskimo woman who had been captured while fishing was
stabbed slowly in her non-vital parts so that she took a long
time to die.

Worse was to follow: events so bestial that even the matter of fact Hearne could only write: 'the brutish manner in
which these savages used the bodies was so shocking it
would be indecent to describe it.'

The day after the massacre Hearne stood at the mouth
of the Coppermine. To say he was disappointed would be
an understatement. He had hoped the river would turn
out to be a waterway through which Company ships
could trade, but he could tell at a glance there was no
hope of this; for the Coppermine ended in a succession of

rapids debouching into a shallow estuary whose outlet to
the sea was blocked by shoals: 'a rocky suburb of Hell.'
Even the copper turned out to be a chimera. After an all-
day search they found just one small lump. Hearne did
the only possible thing: 'erected a mark, took possession
of the coast in the name of the H.B.C.', and headed for
home, which he reached after a round journey of 574
days and 3520 miles – the equivalent of from Gibraltar to
Moscow.

He had proved that there was no viable trade route to
the Arctic by the rivers of north east Canada; he had also
pioneered a new technique of exploration based on the
ability to go native.

The rivers of north west Canada were delineated by a
more conventional explorer.

Alexander Mackenzie worked for the North West
Company, whose trading posts were centred around
Lake Athabaska. In 1789 he set out to try and realize a
centuries-old dream: that of finding a route across the
continent by water. The east half of such a route was
known to exist: *via* the Saint Lawrence, the Great Lakes,
Lake Winnipeg and the Churchill River. The west half
was *aqua incognita*; there were many Indian stories of
rivers that emptied into a tidal ocean, but no evidence
that these were based on fact. On June 3rd Mackenzie set
out from Fort Chipewyan (on the south shore of Lake
Athabaska) with 10 men and 2 birch-bark canoes. They
made swift progress, paddling downstream with the
occasional portage, and reached the Great Slave Lake on
June 9th, only to find it still covered in ice except near the
shore. However, the day after their arrival high winds and
rain began to break the ice up, and they embarked on a
hazardous 300-mile crossing of the lake, working their
way from floe to floe and island to island through a kaleidoscope of disintegrating ice. It was, to quote Mackenzie's biographer, 'a searching test of courage and leadership.' It took them three weeks to cross the lake and
discover the outlet of the river that now bears Macken-

zie's name; then they were swirled into the unknown, down a 'fair-sized river flowing strongly between banks of yellow clay.' For a while the Mackenzie ran west, or even occasionally southwest, and their hopes that it would lead to the Pacific were high. However, on July 2nd they sighted ahead 'a very high range of snowclad mountains (the Rockies) their tops lost in cloud, running north and south as far as our view could reach;' and, to their disappointment, the Mackenzie swung north, not penetrating the mountains but running parallel to them.

For a week they were swept downriver by a current so strong 'that it seemed in ebullition, and produced a hissing noise like a kettle coming to the boil.' The surrounding terrain became increasingly flat, rocky and barren, until they emerged into the huge delta of the Mackenzie, where the river split into sluggish channels meandering through a maze of low treeless islands. Mackenzie fixed his latitude – 67°47' – and was surprised and disappointed to find he was so far north. He spent a week exploring the delta and its estuary, his canoes at constant risk in the jostling ice; and the more he saw of the estuary the more obvious it became that the great river he had followed from source to mouth had brought him not to the Pacific but the Arctic. It would be of little use for trade. His journey back, against the current, was an arduous race against winter, a race he won with only hours to spare, reaching Fort Chipewyan on September 10th just as the first snow was falling.

In one short summer Mackenzie had traveled over 3000 miles and had traced the course of the second-longest river in North America. He had failed to find the hoped-for trade route, but had delineated the basic river system of north west Canada.

A few years later he set out again, determined this time to reach not the Arctic Ocean but the Pacific. He took with him Alexander Mackay as his second-in-command, 6 French *voyageurs*, 2 Indian hunters, and 3000 pounds of food and equipment, all sandwiched into a single 25-foot canoe which was light enough to be easily carried. They left Fort Chipewyan in June 1792, and arrived at the most westerly of the Company's posts – at the junction of the Peace and Smoky Rivers – in September. Here they allowed themselves to be snowed-in for the winter: a risky gambit, but one which enabled them to make an early start next spring in finding a way through the Rockies. By May 1793 they were again heading up the Peace, only to be brought up short almost at once by a formidable canyon, where for 20 miles the river comes cascading down from the mountains in a succession of rapids and falls. It took them a week to carry their canoe through thick woods and up sheer rockfaces to a point where the river was again navigable. This was the first of many such portages; for Mackenzie's second journey was to prove more arduous than his first. For 2 months they struggled through a maze of fast-flowing rivers, thick forests and precipitous ranges which seemed to run first in one direction then another. The Indians through whose land they passed were apprehensive and at times hostile; the mosquitoes were ubiquitous and distracting. Eventually they abandoned their canoe, put themselves in the hands of Indian guides, and trekked for 15 days through huge sepulchral forests, until they came at last to the longed-for shore of the Pacific. On a rockface in Dean Channel (roughly mid-way between Vancouver and the Alaskan border) they mixed vermilion with melted grease and inscribed 'Alexander Mackenzie, from Canada, by land, 22 July, 1793.'

A passage across the Canadian Arctic had been achieved.

Where Mackenzie led, Simpson and Dease followed. In 1836 Thomas Simpson and Peter Warren Dease, experienced members of the H.B.C., were given somewhat vague orders by the Company to 'examine the unexplored sections of the North American coastline.' They canoed down the Mackenzie, then made their way westward, initially by boat and subsequently by snowshoe and sledge, as far as Cape Barrow, the most northerly tip of Alaska. This journey delineated some 500 miles of previously unknown shore. Returning to the Mackenzie, they spent two winters frozen-in near the Great Bear Lake, then embarked on a journey as remarkable as it is little-known. They hauled their boats over the ice to the Coppermine, floated downriver, then followed the shore of Coronation Gulf, Queen Maud Gulf and King William and Victoria Islands (names subsequently to feature in the Franklin fiasco.) They failed to spot the small but vital Rae Strait – the key to a North West Passage by sea – but succeeded nevertheless in delineating another 500 miles of little-known shore. In 1839 Simpson, alone, pushed even farther east, to the mouth of the Great Fish (or Back) River.

It is one of the anomalies of history that Franklin, who was a hugely unsuccessful explorer and discovered virtually nothing, is now a household name; whereas Simpson, who was an excellent explorer and mapped some 1000 miles of coastline, is little-known.

Another explorer to whom history has seldom done justice is Rae.

Above: Dr John Rae was the first western explorer of the Arctic to adopt the living and hunting practices of the Eskimo in order to survive. In 1854 he discovered gruesome evidence that Franklin's party had perished.

Doctor John Rae was also an employee of the H.B.C. A tough, talented and unpretentious Scot, he was so far ahead of his times in his attitude to the Arctic and the people of the Arctic that his exploits earned him as many enemies as friends. Between 1841 and 1855 he led four major expeditions to the far north, in the course of which he traveled an incredible 23,000 miles, mostly on foot, and mapped 1700 miles of coastline. From the Company's point of view, he moved their trading frontier out of the woods of the beaver and into the tundra of the caribou. From the geographer's point of view, he discovered by land that North West Passage which the ships of the Royal Navy so repeatedly failed to discover by sea. While from the traveler's point of view, he pioneered revolutionary new techniques – Hearne had joined the Indians and traveled with them almost as a supernumerary; Rae, in contrast, adapted Indian and Eskimo techniques of survival and used them for solo journeying. Instead of erecting a tent at the end of a day's travel he built an igloo; instead of hauling a sled, he carried a back-pack; instead of going snowblind, he made himself whalebone goggles; and instead of carrying food he used his knowledge of indigenous flora and fauna to live off the land. Like a lone Arctic fox he swiftly covered vast distances in terrain that other white men died in.

Left: Sir Martin Frobisher was hailed as 'Lord High Admiral of all the Seas that lead to Cathay' when he returned to England from his Arctic expedition, but his achievements were slight.

He is best remembered today as the man who discovered the grisly remains of the Franklin expedition. While traveling in 1854 near the Gulf of Boothia he was told by an Eskimo that (to quote Rae's official report):

In the spring (of 1850) whilst some Eskimo families were killing seal near King William Land, forty white men were seen traveling southward over the ice, dragging a boat and sledges with them . . . The Eskimo were led to believe that the men's ship or ships had been crushed by the ice, and they were going to where they expected to find deer to shoot . . . At a later date the same season, the corpses of some thirty persons and graves were discovered about a day's journey to the northwest of the mouth of the Great Fish River . . . Some of the bodies were in tents, others under the boat which had been turned over to form a shelter . . . From the mutilated state of many of the bodies and the contents of the kettles, it was evident that our wretched countrymen had been driven to cannibalism as a means of sustaining life.

Rae collected articles, including a plate engraved 'Sir John Franklin, K.C.B', as evidence and took them back to England. Here he ran into a storm of abuse. This was partly because he voiced the opinion that future expeditions in search of a North West Passage should 'adopt as best they can the Eskimos' method of travel, lifestyle and clothing'; and partly because he refused to withdraw his allegation of cannibalism. On both counts Rae was unequivocally right; but this did not save him from the wrath of the establishment, the press and the British public. He was told that 'the objective of polar explorations is to explore properly, and not evade the hazards of the game through the vulgar subterfuge of going native', and that 'English gentlemen do not devour one another.' Because he refused to accept this sort of blinkered hypocrisy Rae made enemies in high places and has never been given the recognition he deserves.

Exploration by sea: Cabot, Frobisher, Davis, Hudson, Baffin, Parry, Franklin, Amundsen

The first man deliberately to seek a North West Passage was John Cabot, a skilled Venetian seaman in the pay of Henry VII of England. In May 1479 Cabot left Bristol in the diminutive Matthew with a crew of 18, and later that summer sighted either Nova Scotia or Newfoundland. He noted the abundance of cod in the sea and timber on the land, and returned to England claiming he had 'discovered off the coast of Asia an island lying close to Cipango' (the Spice Island of popular mythology). Henry was impressed; he gave Cabot command of 5 ships and sent him back the following year to explore more thoroughly. However, of the 5 ships only one, nearfoundering, returned; the others vanished.

The next step forward in the search was Cartier's discovery of the Saint Lawrence. The Saint Lawrence, however, turned out to be an artery into the heart of a continent (see Chapter 5), not a sea-route round its periphery; and it began to be appreciated that if a North West Passage did indeed exist it would be in the far north.

In 1576 Martin Frobisher sailed up the west coast of Greenland and landed on the desolate coast of Baffin Island. He found 'a great gulf seeming to divide two continents asunder,' and sailed into it for 150 miles without realizing he was in an inlet not a strait. He landed on the

Below: A contemporary woodcut illustration of Frobisher's Arctic expedition.

shore of what is now Frobisher Bay, captured an un-fortunate Eskimo, dug up some iron pyrites which he thought was gold, and returned to England, where he was hailed as 'Lord High Admiral of all the Seas that lead to Cathay.' His achievements were not commensurate with either his claims or his reputation.

He was followed in 1585 by a more attractive explorer, John Davis, who instead of kidnapping the Eskimo played them the lute. Davis sailed farther north than Frobisher, and discovered the strait between Baffin Island and Greenland which bears his name and which became the gateway through which most Arctic explorers were to approach the Pole and the North West Passage. He reached 72°N, and brought back surprisingly scientific reports on the wildlife, the geology and the people – 'gentle and loving savages.'

The exploits of the next great explorer led to a *cul-de-sac*. In 1610 Henry Hudson sailed from England in the *Discovery*, convinced that he would 'sight the Land of Spice before Candlemas'. It was, however, not palm-covered islands that he discovered, only the ice-choked graveyard of explorers' dreams now known as Hudson Bay. His voyage was a compound of treachery and tragedy. 22 men set out, only 8 returned, and they were certainly guilty of mutiny and arguably of murder, having turned Hudson and his young son adrift in the ice. And the aftermath of his expedition was also tragic. For the entrance to his bay lies to the south of the Davis strait, and seemed more likely to lead to a North West Passage, with the result that in years to come explorers were to try again and again to force their way through what in fact was a land-locked estuary. Men like Foxe and James suffered unbelievable hardships in the Bay, their ships foundering and their crew dying of cold, starvation and exposure; and at the end of it all they were not nearer to their goal but farther from it.

It was William Baffin who discovered the key to the passage, although because his maps and his tables of latitude and longitude proved 'troublesome and too costly to publish', it was some time before the significance of his discoveries was realized. Baffin made 7 voyages to the Arctic, of which the last (1616-17) was the most important. He stood into Davis Strait, managed to force his way through the ice which clings to the tip of Baffin Island, and 'stood to the westward in an open sea and a fair gale. On the 12th day (of July) we came to the opening of a great Sound in latitude 70°20'. This we called Sir James Lancaster Sound.' Baffin was not impressed with his discovery. Indeed almost as soon as he entered it he wrote in his Diary: 'here our hopes of finding a passage began to be less every day.' Later explorers, however, were to realize that Lancaster Sound was the gateway through which a passage might eventually be achieved – for as Davis Strait points the way north, so Lancaster Sound points the way west.

By the mid seventeenth century it was recognized that even if a North West Passage did exist, it would not be commercially viable. This was confirmed by Cook, who investigated the Pacific end of the passage and found it blocked (in an unusually severe summer) by an unbroken barrier of ice ten feet high. For more than a century the search languished.

It was revived after the Napoleonic Wars. This was partly because the large number of ships and men in the post-war Royal Navy needed to be kept occupied; partly because sea-travel throughout the world became the norm rather than a novelty (air-travel was to enjoy a similar boom after the Second World War); and partly because it was realized that scientific benefits – like fixing

Above: Dr Frederick Cook claimed in 1909 to have been the first person to reach the North Pole, but his claim is usually discounted in favor of Robert Peary's. He is shown here lecturing to the Danish Royal Geographical Society in support of his claim.

Left: Captain Edward Parry penetrated two thirds of the way to the Pacific in one of the most successful of all Arctic expeditions.

the position of the Magnetic Pole – would accrue if the search was continued.

In 1818 John Ross led an expedition to Lancaster Sound, which he entered in late August. Ross noted the heavy swell from the west, and thought this might indicate a link with the Pacific. However, on 1 September he believed he saw 'a range of mountains' (the mythical Crokers) 'forming a chain round the bottom of the bay'; and, faced with this seemingly impenetrable barrier, he turned back. Ross' second-in-command, the young Edward Parry, reckoned the mountains were a mirage, and that Ross had been at fault in not investigating them more thoroughly. The Admiralty agreed. And in May 1819 Parry left England in command of the bombship *Hecla* and the brig *Griper* with orders to try again.

It has been said that Parry, like Scott a couple of generations after him, was 'the blue-eyed boy of the naval establishment'. This is true; he was possessed of the traditional virtues of leadership, keenness, conformity and devotion to duty. However, there was more to him than that; he was unstuffy, a genuine innovator, and a born survivor who in moments of difficulty came up with the right answers. His expedition was such a success it is easy to overlook how daring it was in concept and how dangerous in execution. For Parry planned to push as far north and west as he could, then allow his ships to be frozen in for the winter, so that they could resume exploration the following season as soon as the ice loosened its grip.

He had a hard time forcing his way through the ice off the tip of Baffin Island, *Hecla* and *Griper* having to be either towed by their boats or warped ahead on their anchors; but by mid August the two vessels were fairly speeding down Lancaster Sound, through waters 'ice-

free, and without the slightest appearance of land to the westward.' The Croker Mountains had melted to oblivion. In the next 10 days Parry made remarkable progress, cutting a 600 mile swathe through the unknown, before being brought up short in Melville Sound, a shallow basin whose northern and western exits were choked permanently with ice. They cast round for several weeks, exploring the maze of channels and islands, sometimes battered by blizzards, sometimes becalmed in banks of fog. On September 24th they reached their farthest west (112°29'), and, after cutting a 2-mile channel through ice already 7 inches thick, ran their ships into a sheltered bay.

The winter that followed might have been purgatory (or even tragedy); but Parry, by his common sense and leadership, turned their incarceration into an almost cozy idyll. He had come well prepared, and as soon as *Hecla* and *Griper* had been dismasted they were roofed-in under a canopy of waterproof cloth. Galley-fires were kept burning day and night, and their heat channelled by piping throughout the ships. When snow fell, Parry had it banked-up against the hulls for insulation. Every day his crew baked fresh bread and brewed fresh beer; hunting parties brought in a regular supply of meat; lemon-juice and ship-grown watercress precluded scurvy. Outside the temperature fell to minus 50°; the sea in the bay froze to a depth of more than 7 feet; bears and wolves padded over the ships. But below-decks the crew were kept busy ever-improving their environment, publishing *The Winter Chronicle* and producing a play a fortnight. 'I verily believe,' wrote Parry, 'there never was a more merry and cheerful set of men than ours.' They not only survived the winter, they survived it in good health and enjoyed it, and the following summer were able to make an

Above: Parry's crew cutting a passage through the ice in the fall of 1819.

Left: John Ross's hazardous final Arctic expedition of 1829 at Cape Garry. He discovered the site of the North Magnetic Pole and brought back much useful information.

early start to their reconnaissance of Melville Sound, before returning to England in October 1820.

This has been described as 'one of the greatest of all Arctic voyages'. Parry penetrated two-thirds of the way to the Pacific: he charted over 1000 miles of unknown coastline; and perhaps most important of all, he proved that a ship's company could survive the Arctic winter in good health while frozen into the ice.

His success rekindled interest in the North West Passage. Expeditions to find it proliferated, the most important being those of Ross by sea, Back by land, and Franklin first by land and then by sea.

In 1829 the able, but contentious and unlucky John Ross was again heading into Lancaster Sound. He intended to search for a passage in exactly the right place: by standing west down Lancaster Sound, turning into one of the channels which led to the mainland, then following the coastline close inshore to the Pacific. Unfortunately he chose the wrong channel to turn into, and ended up in the icy *cul-de-sac* of the Gulf of Boothia.

In 1833 George Back led a land expedition to search for him. By the time Back's expedition arrived in Canada, the object of their search had emerged safely from a three-year incarceration in the ice; Back decided nonetheless to head for the Arctic coastline, 'our motive now not humanity but science.' He had trouble with the cold. 'The temperature is 60° minus. Ink and paint are frozen solid. While washing my face within 3 feet of our fire, my hair became clotted with ice before I had time to dry it.' He could also have had trouble with the Eskimos, who had the reputation of killing strangers on sight: but when his men were ambushed by a group of Eskimo hunters, Back went to meet them alone and unarmed crying *'tima'* = peace (he was the only naval officer of his generation to teach himself Eskimo). His gesture of friendship was reciprocated, and he went on to

reach the mouth of the Thelew-ee-choh, which, after a violent and tortuous course of 530 miles, running through an iron-ribbed country without a single tree on its banks, pours its water into the Polar Sea in latitude 67°11'N, longitude 94°30'W.

The mouth of the 'Thelew-ee-choh' lies at the junction of Rae Strait and Victoria Strait, a strip of ice-free coast that is the key to the North West Passage.

Sir John Franklin explored the Arctic both by land and by sea.

In the 1820s he commanded two expeditions which descended the Mackenzie and Coppermine Rivers and mapped the little-known coastline in between. It is hard to know what to make of these expeditions. On the credit

Below: Sir John Franklin, one of the best-known though least successful of Arctic explorers.

side, Franklin did succeed in charting parts of this little-known shore with commendable accuracy; he was assid-uous in collecting scientific data – on one journey alone he collected 663 different plants – and his relations with the Eskimos were usually good – 'their humanity towards us,' he wrote 'would have done honour to the most civil-ized people.' On the debit side, he never learned how to live off the land, never learned the best way to travel, and seems to have had a penchant for getting himself into dif-ficulties – more than one of his treks ending in death, cannibalism and murder.

In 1845 another major expedition set out for the Arctic: its ships those veterans of polar voyaging the *Erebus* and *Terror*, its commander the equally ancient Franklin. Franklin left England with high hopes, but without either of the prerequisites of success: the ability to live off the land, or the knowledge of exactly where to search for the passage. He made good progress as far as Melville Sound which he found blocked by ice-floes. In com-pliance with his not very inspired orders he stood north into Wellington Channel; here he was trapped by thickening ice and frozen in for the winter. The following season he tried to force his way out of Melville Sound, but found all exits blocked by ice except Peel Strait to the south. So south he went, but only as far as King William Island where he was frozen in for a second winter. It was now his troubles started. In theory he had food for 3 years. However, 700 tins of bully-beef are known to have gone bad, and recent research suggests that all their meat was badly canned, and that the crew were afflicted by lead poisoning. Scurvy broke out. Several men, including Franklin, died. Eventually the remainder (some 105 of them) abandoned their ships and tried to trek south to safety. They did not make it. Not far from the mouth of Back's Great Fish River the last survivors succumbed to cold, exposure and starvation. Recent research has con-firmed Rae's allegations . . .

Above: Franklin's ships, *Erebus* and *Terror*, ready to leave for the Arctic in 1845.

It is evident that they resorted to hacking half-frozen limbs off their companions and cooking them in boots over an open fire. Skulls and arm and leg bones show evidence of saw marks and were found long distances from corresponding pelvic girdles and rib cages.

From this dark face of exploration Victorian England found it more comfortable to avert its eyes.

There was a long and far-ranging search for Franklin, involving the British and American governments, the Royal Navy, the Hudson's Bay Company and a number of private sponsors. The search lasted 10 years, during which a plethora of ships and sledges crossed and re-crossed the Canadian Arctic. There were fine feats of sea-manship, some vessels being frozen-in for 4 consecutive winters; impressive feats of endurance, Rae sledging 5380 miles in 8 months; amazing coincidences, the

Below: The last terrible days of the Franklin expedition. When Dr John Rae's 1854 expedition found their remains, there were clear signs that they had resorted to cannibalism in an effort to survive.

Resolution and the *Investigator* arriving from opposite sides of the world at the same ice-locked bay; and much ingenuity, Ross catching and tagging Arctic foxes with his ship's position. By the end of it, Canada's north coast and its offshore archipelagos had been delineated with accuracy, and a tortuous route from ocean-to-ocean had been discovered – although such were its limitations that it was 50 years before a ship sailed through it.

Then in a well-planned 3-year voyage (1903-06) the Norwegian Roald Amundsen succeeded where everyone else had failed.

Amundsen's ship the *Gjoa* was a converted herring-boat, less than one quarter the size of *Erebus* or *Terror*; and Amundsen himself was so short of funds for his expedition that he was obliged to sail from Norway secretly by night to escape his creditors. And if one wonders why an impoverished Norwegian with a herring-boat should have succeeded where a British admiral with the largest navy in the world behind him failed, the answer is that one was an amateur, the other a professional. Franklin had many attributes; he was brave, determined, popular with his crew and fair with the Eskimos; but – like Scott a couple of generations later – he was a naval officer, not an explorer. Amundsen had his shortcomings; he was calculating, ruthless and could be self-opinionated; but he was a knowledgeable perfectionist for whom polar travel was not a game but a profession. When he set out to sail through the North West Passage he knew exactly what he was going to do and exactly how he was going to do it. His voyage – like his subsequent journey to the South Pole – was meticulously planned and went like clockwork; and in August 1906 the *Gjoa* emerged in triumph through the Bering Strait.

It had taken 427 years for John Cabot's dream to be realized.

Above: Roald Amundsen's ship *Gjoa* in which he successfully negotiated the North West Passage.

Left: Some of the pathetic relics recovered by Rae from the remains of the Franklin expedition.

Below: Amundsen was a lifelong explorer and in 1923 was still investigating new ways of exploring the Poles.

The Conquest of the North Pole: Kane, Hall, Greeley and Peary

The search for Franklin forms a watershed in Arctic exploration. Before it most expeditions had been British. After it the initiative passed to the Americans and Scandinavians.

One of the first Americans to explore the Arctic was Elisha Kent Kane, who managed to cram into his 37 years enough adventures to fill a dozen ordinary lives. After serving as doctor to an expedition looking for Franklin, Kane decided in 1852 to pioneer a route to the Pole. Like most subsequent American explorers the route he chose was *via* Smith Sound, the channel which leads north from Baffin Bay between Greenland and Ellesmere Island. He managed, with skill and perseverance to force his way almost as far north as the 80th parallel, discovering one of the world's greatest glaciers which he named the Humboldt. However, his dogs died; his ship the *Advance* became frozen in and had to be abandoned, and if it had not been for the Eskimos who provided his expedition with food, he and his men would almost certainly have perished.

A few years later Charles Francis Hall embarked on the first of his three forays into the Arctic. Hall was an unlikely explorer: a highly-strung Cincinatti printer who fell in love with the far north: 'Everything about the Arctic,' he wrote, 'is deeply interesting to me. I am on a mission of love'. His first expedition (1860-61) took him to Frobisher Bay, where he found relics of the Elizabethans' landing. His second (1865-70) took him to King William Island on 'a caretaking mission for (Franklin's) unfound dead.' His third and most important (1871-73) took him through Smith Sound, past the Humboldt Glacier, and as far north as 82°11' – no-one at the time had penetrated as close to the Pole. However, his expedition's acme was swiftly followed by its nadir. That autumn Hall died in mysterious circumstances; at the time there was talk of murder, and when his body was subsequently exhumed in 1968 it was found to contain lethal quantities of arsenic. After Hall's death, his ship the *Polaris* was damaged. Her crew (which included Eskimo supernumeraries) began to unload their stores on to the ice, only to see, to their horror, the *Polaris* swirled away by an unexpected blizzard, leaving them stranded on a floe some 4 miles in diameter. There followed one of the great survival stories of polar history, with the castaways drifting slowly south on their disintegrating floe, and the Eskimos time and again finding and killing a seal just as starvation seemed inevitable. With the ice melting, they were reduced to jumping from floe to floe, before, after a drift of 6 months and 1500 miles, they were fortuitously rescued by a whaler.

Another expedition to end in disaster was that of Major Greeley, who in 1882 led a 26-man team of US Army volunteers to Ellesmere Island, with the dual objective of collecting scientific data and setting a new record for 'farthest north'. Both objectives were achieved, but at a terrible cost. In the winter of 1883 the relief-ship which they had been promised failed to arrive to pick them up. Greeley did the only possible thing; he headed south until conditions became so bad that travel was no longer possible. At Cape Sabine, they built a cabin and waited, their provisions and their expectation of life dwindling. Scurvy broke out. One man was shot for stealing another's food. Most of the others died one by one 'in an atmosphere of hatred and cannibalism.' To quote *Man and the Conquest of the Pole*:

Left: Captain Robert Edwin Peary, dressed in his characteristic furs after his return from the North Pole in 1909.

When the men of the sealing ship *Thetis* put ashore at Cape Sabine in June 1884 they found a terrible scene. Greeley's cabin had collapsed. None of those underneath could move; but incredibly six men were still alive. One had his jaw hanging free and was blind; another was without hands or feet and had a spoon attached to the stump of his arm; Greeley on hands and knees, resembled a skeleton, his joints bulbous and swollen. All the food that remained was two repulsive-looking jars of 'jelly'.

The next major figure to cross swords with the Arctic was Robert Edwin Peary. British writers have not always given this great explorer the credit he deserves, Scott's gallant failure in the south often being more highly thought of than Peary's gallant success in the north. It is true that Peary was a difficult character; intolerant, selfish and inordinately proud of his macho image; but it should be pointed out that his obsession with manliness, virility and physical fitness was no pose; he was every bit as tough as he made out to be.

He made 11 expeditions to the far north on at least 7 of which he made major contributions to the exploration of the Arctic.

In 1886 he sledged for more than 100 miles into the interior of Greenland – farther than anyone had penetrated before. Together with his single Danish companion he climbed to over 7000 feet, before being nearly killed when he fell into a crevasse.

In 1891, taking with him his wife, Josephine, his black manservant Matthew Henson (who accompanied him everywhere) and 4 other companions he explored the northwest coast of Greenland. On this expedition he learned from the Eskimos how to make loose fur-clothing, and how to drive dog-teams. He perfected what he called 'the Peary technique of polar travel': the men on skis, the supplies on dog-drawn sledges, numbers and weight kept to the minimum, and everyone living as far as possible off the land. He also broke his leg, and only avoided death through starvation by eating the raw flesh of a musk-ox.

In 1893, backed by Theodore Roosevelt, he was again heading up the northwest coast of Greenland, this time with a larger team, including Josephine who was pregnant. Faced by exceptionally bad weather, they were overtaken by a series of disasters, which culminated in the calving of an iceberg that swamped their supplies. This wrung from Peary the classic cry of defiance: 'The fates and all hell are against me, but I'll triumph yet.' After a trek of unbelievable hardship and hazard, he struggled back to safety with his companions snowblind and half dead from exposure and one dog left alive out of 30.

In 1898 he tried to reach the Pole *via* Ellesmere Island, and managed to force his way to Fort Conger which had not been visited since *Thetis* evacuated the Greeley survivors. However the effort cost him dear. With the temperature down to minus 70 degrees his feet became frozen solid; seven of his toes had to be amputated, and Peary was dragged back to his vessel on a sledge. The doctors told him he would never walk without crutches. Peary thought differently. Although further operations were needed, and eventually every one of his toes was amputated, Peary was walking within 6 months and back in the Arctic within 12.

In 1900 he made three major journeys parallel to the north coast of Greenland. He could not yet stand upright; his feet were still tender, and each step over the uneven ice must have been agony. Yet he achieved another 'farthest north', and proved beyond doubt that Greenland was an island. However, the difficulty of these North Greenland journeys – with the ice moving fast and con-

Above: Peary and his men at 87° 16'N on April 21st, 1906, the farthest north then reached by any explorer. Out of his 120 dogs only 2 survived the expedition.

Left: Peary's own photograph of the snow mound he built at the North Pole, April 6th, 1909.

sisting of great crumbling pressure-ridges – convinced Peary that Ellesmere Island would be a better starting point for future assaults on the Pole.

In 1902 he set out from Fort Conger with his largest team to-date: 24 sledges and more than 100 dogs. The dog-teams were used to cache supplies along the line of advance, then one by one returned to base, eventually leaving Peary with a couple of companions to make a final dash for the Pole. However, the going was bad – huge pressure-ridges, and deep, soft snow through which the dogs could hardly haul themselves. In 3 exhausting weeks they covered no more than 100 miles. Then, in latitude 84°16′N, they were hit by a blizzard of such ferocity that it opened up leads in the ice. Peary dragged himself back to Ellesmere Island: 'My dream of 16 years', he wrote, 'is ended.'

However, the attainment of the Pole was now becoming for Americans a matter of national honor; and in 1905 Peary was again heading north, this time in the *Roosevelt*, a tough wooden-hulled vessel designed by Peary himself and paid for by the president. The *Roosevelt*, to quote her designer, 'was built of American timber in an American shipyard by an American firm with American metal. Even the most trivial items of supply were of American manufacture.' She proved an efficient ice-breaker, forcing her way round the northwest tip of Ellesmere Island, farther north than a vessel under way had ever penetrated. Here she was frozen in, while Peary with 27 drivers and 120 dogs set out for the Pole. However, a methodical advance proved impossible. On the moving ice their supply dumps drifted away, the dog teams found themselves bunching together at open leads, and although Peary reached a new farthest north (87°16′) he was again forced to turn back, his men snow-blind and his dogs dying of exhaustion. Their retreat, over drifting and disintegrating ice, was even slower than their advance had been. By the time they reached the *Roosevelt* 118 out of their 120 dogs had died; they were completely out of food, and owed their lives to a wandering herd of musk-ox, three of whom were shot and 'their flesh gobbled warm and raw.'

In 1908 Peary, now aged 52, was back for 'one last try'; and this time the gods were kind to him. The ice was in good condition; the weather was favorable; the 'Peary technique of polar travel' enabled his dog-teams to make steady progress, and within a month of leaving Ellesmere Island they were only 100 miles from the Pole. Peary, Henson and 4 Eskimos set off on a final assault and on April 6th, 1909 they achieved their goal. 'The Pole at last!!!!' wrote Peary. 'The prize of three centuries, my dream and ambition for 23 years. Mine at last.' He spent 24 hours taking soundings and observations, built a snow cairn, and raised the American flag which he had been carrying with him for 15 years, while the Eskimos did a ritual dance, chanting *'Ting neigh timah ketisher!'* ('We're there at last!') Then they headed back for the *Roosevelt*, which they reached on April 27th after a surprisingly easy journey.

If Peary thought that his battle with the Pole was over, he was mistaken. For that summer as *Roosevelt* stood south down the coast of Greenland, her crew spotted three men hauling a sledge. They turned out to be a white man and two Eskimos, all of them in the last stages of exhaustion. They were taken aboard and fed; and when asked who they were and where they had come from, the white man said matter-of-factly: 'I am Doctor Frederick Cook. And I have come from the North Pole.'

Frederick Cook is an enigma. He was a good doctor, a likeable man and an explorer of repute, accompanying

Peary on seven of his early expeditions and being one of the first men to winter in the Antarctic – where aboard de Gerlache's vessel the *Belgica* he did sterling work and was well thought of. There seems, however, to have been an element of instability about him; in particular his writing often contains flights of fancy more suited to a novel than an explorer's diary. What he claimed was plausible, and obviously had elements of truth. He said that starting from Axel Heiberg Land (to the west of Ellesmere Island) he and two Eskimos had reached the Pole on April 21st, 1908 – almost a year before Peary – but had run into difficulties on their return journey, and had been forced to winter on Devon Island before working their way to Greenland where they had been rescued by the *Roosevelt*. On their return to civilization both men claimed to have been first at the Pole. This sparked off a bitter controversy, during which Cook behaved with more dignity than Peary, and public opinion to start with was overwhelmingly on the side of the doctor – a newspaper poll in Pittsburgh indicated that 73,238 people believed Cook

Above: Dr Frederick Cook being fêted on his arrival in New York after he claimed to have reached the North Pole first. Although Robert Peary's claim is now generally accepted, doubt still remains about who was there first and some modern authorities believe that neither one could have reached the Pole in the time taken for their journeys.

Below: Cook during his Arctic expedition.

and only 2814 Peary. This verdict time has reversed, Peary's observations carrying more weight than Cook's plausibility; although it is worth pointing out that both then and now many explorers of the Arctic (Greeley, Amundsen, Nansen and Wally Herbert) have championed Cook.

There may always be a residue of doubt about the conquest of the North Pole. It is almost certain that Peary was first to reach it, on April 6th, 1909; there is, however, a faint possibility that Cook got there a year earlier. No such doubts exist about the first crossing of the Arctic Ocean.

Across the Arctic Ocean: De Long (1879-81), Nansen (1893-96)

In June, 1879 the *Jeanette* stood west out of the Golden Gate. She was a fine ship, recently strengthened, refitted and (in defiance of seafaring tradition) re-named; her crew had been hand-picked from 3000 volunteers, and her commander, George Washington De Long, was young, able and had a reputation for overcoming obstacles. It was hoped that the *Jeanette*, entering the Arctic Ocean via the Bering Strait, would work her way northwestward until she came to the land which in those days was thought to surround the North Pole; her crew then intended to leave their ship and sledge overland, *via* the Pole, to Greenland.

De Long passed through the Bering Strait in August, and inched his way northwest towards Wrangel Island, 'very much bothered by loose ice, which became ever heavier.' His Diary gives a vivid picture of how they were first frustrated by the ice, then trapped by it, and finally destroyed by it.

6 September. This is glorious country to learn patience in. As far as the eye can see is ice. Yesterday I hoped that today would make an opening for us; today I hope that tomorrow will . . . 15 September. We are held fast, and seem to be drifting, ice and all to the N.W. My disappointment is great for it now looks as though it would take an earthquake to get us out of our besetment . . . 11 November. A day of great anxiety. The ice is in motion, grinding and crashing and causing great upheavals. Our vessel groans and creaks at every squeeze, until I thought

the next would break her apart. Her decks bulge; the pitch is squeezed out of her seams. Great masses of ice, large as churches, come churning down on us, like a marble yard adrift.

A year later, still entombed in the ice like a fly in amber, they had been carried some 250 miles northwestward.

Pump, pump, pump. As soon as we pump out, the water comes in. The ship is wretchedly wet and uncomfortable, with everything covered in ice or sludge . . . How long, O lord, how long? People beset in the pack have usually been carried to land; but we are drifting about like a modern Flying Dutchman, ever on the move, but never getting anywhere. Coals are burning up, stocks of food are dwindling, and 33 of us are eating our hearts out like men doomed to imprisonment for life.

It says much for De Long's caliber as a commander that the morale of his crew remained high, even when they had to abandon ship.

For 21 months the *Jeanette* was battered, squeezed, tugged this way and that and subjected to unbearable pressure; at last in June 1881 she began to break up. She was abandoned in good order, with everything of value transferred to sledges or boats.

12 June. "Turn out if you want to see the last of her," the man on watch cried. Amid a rattling and banging of timber, the ship stood for a moment almost upright. Then she began to sink, with slightly accelerated velocity, her yardarms stripped and

Below: The wreck of the *Hansa* during an unsuccessful German expedition to the North Pole in 1869-70.

Right: George Washington De Long's expedition aboard the *Jeannette* ended, like so many before, in failure when the ship became ice-bound and sank.

parallel to the masts. So, like a great gaunt skeleton clapping its hands above its head, she plunged out of sight. We were now utterly isolated and beyond any rational hope of aid.

The events of the next 4 months have a tragic inevitability. The *Jeanette* had gone down 500 miles from the coast of Siberia, and in ice drifting northwestward away from the shore. In appalling weather the 3 ship's boats and 5 sledges headed south, their path over uneven ice covered in slush and crisscrossed now by sealanes over which the sledges had to be floated, and now by solid floes over which the boats had to be hauled. They were enveloped in mist and lashed by near-perpetual sleet. The ice tore the men's boots to ribbons – within 10 days of setting out they were barefoot. They were making for the mouth of the Lena River where, according to their maps, there were villages. What they did not know was that the villages were only inhabited in summer, so that even as the dying men struggled towards them the Russians were pulling back to the hinterland. After 10 weeks of terrible privation, the boats were scattered by a blizzard. One foundered, and her crew were never heard of again. One was cast up on the east side of the Lena delta, providentially close to the one village still inhabited. De Long was not so fortunate. His boat was driven on to the west side of the delta; there were no villages here, no food, no shelter; and between the first day of October and the last De Long and his men perished of cold and starvation. The men died. Their ship was resurrected.

On June 18th, 1884 a group of Eskimos fishing near Julianehaab in southwest Greenland, spotted flotsam embedded in the ice. They called Carl Lytzen, the Danish *Kolonibestryrer*, who identified the flotsam as from the *Jeanette*. Lytzen, who was an authority on polar currents, pointed out that there was only one way the wreckage could have got to Julianehaab:

It must have been borne for a great circle distance of over 3000 miles (almost as far as from North Cape [*of Norway*] to the Cape of Good Hope) by a powerful current flowing westward over the Pole . . . So although Polar explorers are bound to become embedded in the ice, yet this same ice will eventually carry them to safety.

What Lytzen suggested as possible in theory, Nansen proved in practice.

Fridtjof Nansen was born at Froen, near Oslo, in October 1861. He was one of those gifted men on whom the gods seem to have lavished every possible blessing. Handsome and of magnificent physique, he combined a gentle character with a keen scientific brain, and was successful in several fields – as explorer, scientist, artist, writer, politician, Nobel prize winner and humanitarian. As an explorer his greatest feats were the first crossing of the Greenland ice-cap, and the first crossing of the Arctic Ocean.

Before Nansen's crossing of Greenland it was thought that the center of the island consisted of alternate mountain-ranges and valleys. Nansen put forward the theory that it consisted of a relatively flat ice-cap, which it would be possible to cross on skis. The experts laughed at such an idea; but it was Nansen who had the last laugh; for in the summer of 1888 together with 5 companions he skied across the 500 miles of the Greenland plateau in less than three weeks.

Returning to Norway, he prepared for a more ambitious venture: that of putting Lytzen's theory to the test by deliberately allowing a specially strengthened ship to be frozen into the ice and carried across what we now know is the Arctic Ocean but which in those days many people thought was predominantly land (*vide* Allen Young in 1890: 'all previous navigators have reported mountains to the north, and I think that as he nears the Pole Dr. Nansen will find land in every direction.') The experts were sceptical if not hostile; the Norwegian government, however, had the vision to back Nansen, and for three years he prepared for his expedition with meticulous thoroughness. His ship the *Fram*, designed by the Scot Colin Archer, was 'a masterpiece of craftsmanship, ingenuity and attention to detail . . . designed with a smooth U-shaped hull so she could slip like an eel out of the embraces of the ice.' His supplies were sufficient for 5 years, and to quote Nansen himself, 'every single item was scientifically analysed and properly

Above: The *Jeannette* sinking into the ice.

Below: Fridtjof Nansen, 1861-1930. Nansen's ship the *Fram* has been preserved in a museum in Oslo.

packed – even bread and dried vegetables being soldered down in tins as a protection against damp.' His scientific instruments were the best available, his crew were hand-picked, and it would be difficult to imagine a better-found expedition than that which sailed in the *Fram* from Oslo in June 1893.

By early October they were nearing the New Siberian Islands.

Previous explorers of the Arctic, Nansen wrote, have always tried to keep close to land. But this is just what I want to avoid. It is the open, drifting ice I wish to get into. It therefore seemed to me that we could do worse than give ourselves up to the ice right away. A couple of days later: The ice is thickening round us. We are freezing-in faster and faster . . . winter is coming. The experiment has begun.

The events of the next 3 years proved Lytzen's theory and Nansen's patience. For after drifting embedded in the ice, without making a move of her own volition, for 2500 miles and 977 days, the *Fram*, relatively un-damaged, was spewed out of the pack-ice to the north of Spitzbergen.

Nansen, in fact, had been carried close to the Pole rather than directly over it. Nonetheless his voyage was an important piece of exploration. On the practical level, it delineated the Arctic, proving it to be a deep, steep-sided ocean, remarkably free of islands and with no land-mass at its center. During their three years in the ice the scientists in the *fram* kept meticulous records, and these established the basic facts about the ocean's structure and climate. On the ideational level, Nansen discovered not only cold, suffering and hardship in the Arctic, but beauty, delight and peace. No-one had ever evoked more powerfully the wonders of the natural world.

Late that evening I wandered on to the pack-ice. There is nothing more beautiful than the Arctic night. It is dreamland, painted in the most delicate tints; it is color etherealized. One shade melts into the next, so you can not tell where one ends

Above: A lively meeting with Nansen in the Arctic.

and one begins; yet every color in the spectrum is there . . . The sky is an enormous cupola, blue at the zenith, shading into green, and at its edges lilac. The icefields are patterned with cold blue shadows, with here and there a tint of pink as a ridge catches the last reflection of the vanishing day. Soon the aurora borealis patterns the sky with its veil of silver, which changes now to yellow, now to green and now to red. It spreads, contracts and spreads again, now forming bands of silver, now shooting out brilliant violet rays. The glory fades, melting away in the moonlight, until all that is left are a few wavering streamers – the dust flung from the aurora's glittering cloak . . . But now the brilliance is growing again, shooting out great shafts of light, and the endless game has begun anew. And all the while the absolute silence and the peace that passes under-standing.

Few explorers have done more to make people aware of the wonder of the natural world, and the spiritual fulfil-ment that stems from affinity with it.

Below: The Arctic has continued to interest and challenge explorers, even in our own time. In 1969 a four-man British Trans-Arctic expedition completed the first successful surface crossing of the Arctic Ocean, the 3000-mile trek taking 464 days.

The Antarctic

The Antarctic

Antarctica has been the most difficult of the continents to explore.

It lies far from the main centers of population, and its earliest explorers had to travel some 10,000 miles before they even approached it. And when they did approach it, they found that, like a medieval fortress, it had concentric lines of defense. Its first defense was the Southern Ocean, the most tempestuous seaway on Earth where winds average 40mph and waves 20 feet; in times of storm these figures are trebled; not easy conditions for sailing ships to survive in. Antarctica's second line of defense was pack-ice. The continent is ringed by a girdle of sea-ice which is anything up to 15 feet thick and (in winter) covers an area greater than the United States and Canada combined. This ice is never still; it drifts this way and that under the influence of winds and currents, expanding and contracting according to temperature and season. Most of the time it is impenetrable. And when explorers do at last reach the continent, they find that its weather – in particular the cold and the wind – make it difficult to survive let alone to explore. Antarctica is by far the coldest place on Earth; its weather stations frequently report minus 80 degrees Centigrade (more than 20 degrees lower than anywhere else.)

In this sort of cold, *writes the explorer John Berchervaise*, if you drop a steel bar it shatters like glass, tin disintegrates into loose granules, and if you haul up a fish through a hole in the ice, within 5 seconds it is frozen so solid it has to be cut with a saw.

Another explorer, Douglas Mawson describes the wind as 'Antarctica's most malevolent characteristic.' When he wintered in Adélie Land gusts of over 120mph were frequently recorded, and the average windspeed for June was over 60mph. 'In these conditions,' he wrote, 'it was possible to stand for no more than a few seconds, and then only by leaning forward at an angle of 45 degrees!'

Two hundred years ago no human being had ever set eyes on this desolate but beautiful continent. The first person to do was probably the Russian explorer Thaddeus von Bellingshausen.

The First Sighting: Bransfield, Palmer and Von Bellingshausen (1820)

It used to be thought that the first person to sight the mainland of Antarctica was either the British naval officer Edward Bransfield in the *Williams*, or the American sealer Nathaniel Palmer in the *Hero*.

In December 1819, in command of an ex-trading brig, the *Williams*, Lieutenant Bransfield sailed from Valparaiso with orders to 'survey whatever coasts you may encounter, and ascertain whether there is indeed an uncommon abundance of whales, otters and seals in these waters.' On January 16th, 1820 Bransfield arrived in the South Shetlands, and spent several days surveying and sounding, much hampered by fog. On January 28th he passed the volcanic crater of Deception Island, and tried to work his way south through waters shrouded in fog and strewn with icebergs and reefs. On January 30th, while heading south from Deception Island he 'unexpectedly saw land to the S.W. in latitude 64° . . . A round island we named Tower Island and the land we named Trinity Land.' Bad weather and fog then closed in; but on February 1st they sighted 'two high mountains covered with snow in position 63°40'S, 50°50'W.' These have been identified as the peaks Jacquinot (1600 feet) and Bransfield (2500 feet) near the tip of the Antarctic Peninsula. Two factors have limited the impact of this discovery. Firstly, Bransfield failed to follow up his sighting by making the sort of detailed survey of his new-found coast that a great explorer would have attempted. Secondly, the report he submitted to the Admiralty was unaccountably lost, and has never seen the light of day. Bransfield therefore remains a shadowy, and vaguely unheroic figure.

A more colorful explorer was the New England sealer Nathaniel Palmer, who in his 40-ton sloop, the *Hero*, also explored the South Shetland Islands in 1820. If too little was published about Bransfield, too much has been published about Palmer. For American historians (in particular Fanning), anxious to depict him as a folk-hero who discovered an unknown continent, gave his exploits an interpretation that Palmer himself never claimed for them. Fanning wrote:

During a very clear day Captain Pendleton sighted mountains (one a volcano in operation) in the South. To examine this newly discovered land Captain N.B. Palmer in the sloop *Hero* was despatched. (*He goes on to quote Palmer's log*): "Thick snowstorm . . . At 5 made the Land, stood along and examined it but were disappointed. Stood southward, saw an opening, stood in and found it to be a spacious harbour, with deep Water 50 to 60 fathoms . . . Got under way, found the sea filled with immense Ice Bergs. At 4 am Discovered a strait, literally filled with ice. Bore away to the Northward and saw 2 small islands."

It used to be thought that this described a voyage from Deception Island to the mainland; Palmer was therefore credited with the discovery of the continent, and part of the Antarctic Peninsula was named after him. However, since the only volcano in the vicinity is on Deception Island itself, and since Palmer's description exactly fits this island, it is now generally agreed that his voyage must have been between the islands of Livingstone and Deception, and that he never sighted the mainland.

However, later that summer he did meet the man to whom this distinction almost certainly belongs . . . On the night of November 19/20 *Hero* lay becalmed, enveloped in thick fog. At midnight her officer of the watch rang the ship's bell as usual, and was startled to hear what sounded like an echo. Each time that night as *Hero* sounded her bell, an answer tolled out of the darkness; and at dawn, as the fog lifted, Palmer and his crew could make out on either side of them tall masts and strange castellated hulls. They were lying between two warships. Uncertain of their nationality, Palmer hoisted the American flag; and the ships in reply ran up about the last colors that he expected: the eagle of Imperial Russia.

The Russians were latecomers as maritime explorers; by the time their ships emerged into the oceans almost every coastline in the world had been delineated and claimed, except in the Arctic and Antarctic so it was here that the Russians explored. In the north their seamen discovered the Bering Strait, the Aleutian Islands and Alaska. In the south they launched the first major expedition to try to discover Antarctica.

On July 16th, 1819 the *Vostok* and *Mirnyi* (*Peace*) left Kronshtadt, commanded by the 39-year-old Thaddeus von Bellingshausen. Their orders were to search for new lands, harbors and fisheries; also to bring back scientific information on magnetic variation, ice-conditions, the *aurora australis* and the weather. The expedition was well-found and well-led, Bellingshausen proving a caring and efficient commander in the mold of Cook – indeed the two men had much in common both in character and achievement. In late December (1819) the Russians sighted and surveyed South Georgia. And in early January (1820) they arrived at the virtually unknown South Sandwich Islands. The South Sandwich Islands are about the most unattractive archipelago on Earth: a scattering of black, volcanic cones, sheathed in ice and spewing out great clouds of sulphurous vapour. Bellingshausen charted them with accuracy, then continued south. On January 26th he crossed the Antarctic Circle, and almost at once was brought up short by ice. What happened next is recorded in his Diary.

Thick fog, and the snow so heavy we had to keep turning the ships sharply into wind to shake it out of our sails. Icicles fell from the rigging, and the ropes froze solid . . . 27 Jan. At mid-day in Latitude 60°21′28″S, Longitude 2°14′50″W we met a line of icebergs, which loomed up through the falling snow like white clouds. Had just hauled away from these, when we saw in front of us a solid stretch of ice running from east to west and covered with small hillocks. Again hauled away . . . 1 Feb. It seemed to grow lighter hour by hour, and at 1 am we again saw ice ahead, and soon were virtually encompassed by it. In the south were some 50 mounds or hummocks, frozen into this land of ice (*Materik l'da*) to which we could see no limit.

Historians have often pointed out that the Russians that summer must have been within a few miles (15 at the most) of the coast of Princess Martha Land in Antarctica; and the general view has been that they were unlucky not to have sighted the continent. Recent research, however, suggests that they *did* sight it. For Bellingshausen's description of an ice-sheet covered with 'small hillocks', 'mounds' and 'hummocks' exactly fits this part of the Antarctic coast; while his use of the phrase *materik l'da* suggests he may have realized he had come into contact with an ice-capped continent. And it is perhaps worth pointing out that if he did indeed sight Antarctica *circa* February 1st, this would predate Bransfield's sighting of January 30th because the Russians were still using the Julian calendar which was 12 days behind the Gregorian calendar used by the rest of the world.

First sightings or landings are not regarded as all that important today. What *is* important is that during the course of the next year Bellingshausen circumnavigated Antarctica on a track far to the south of Cook's, thereby further limiting the possible size of a Great Southern Continent; that he sighted land (Alexander Island off the Antarctic Peninsula); that he brought back a mass of scientific data, and that he was the first person to give an accurate assessment of the sort of place Antarctica was: in his own words, 'a great immovable sheet of ice extending over the Pole, passing in some places over shallow seas, in other places over land.'

This was a considerable feat of exploration; and if one wonders why Bellingshausen is not better known, it is because on his return to Russia his report was first kept secret then published in a heavily expurgated version. It is only in recent years that research by Soviet historians has revealed the true extent of his discoveries.

The First Major Landings: D'Urville (1840), Wilkes (1840) and Ross (1841)

The first person to set foot on Antarctica may have been the New England sealer John Davis (*see* Chapter 2.) His landing, however, is not fully documented, and the first landings that we can reconstruct in detail are those of the big national expeditions led by D'Urville, Wilkes and Ross.

D'Urville and the discovery of Adélie Land

In the autumn of 1837 a pair of unstrengthened French corvettes, the *Astrolabe* and *Zelée*, sailed from Toulon commanded by Jules Sébastien César Dumont D'Urville. '*Ah! ce bonhomme-la ne nous menera pas loin!*' (roughly translated, 'This old chap won't be taking us too far afield.') a seaman muttered as the ageing admiral, who was afflicted by gout, hobbled aboard; but in this he was wrong.

Arriving in the Antarctic early in 1838, D'Urville tried to penetrate the Weddell Sea; but the ice was unusually thick, and he was restricted to collecting scientific data among the South Orkneys and South Shetlands. He spent most of 1839 among the Pacific islands, then headed south from Tasmania. On January 19th, 1840 his ships crossed the Antarctic Circle, and late that evening several of his crew thought they could make out in the south 'a distant appearance of mountains.'

Next morning the weather for once was perfect: no wind, no cloud, and the sea a dark Mediterranean blue. And as the ships stood south, land became clearly visible: an unbroken coastline running west-north-west and east-south-east as far as the eye could see. Soon details of the shore were clearly visible. It consisted of sheer 200-foot cliffs of ice, with the snow above and beyond sweeping back in huge symmetrical drifts which disappeared into the distance like the dunes of a desert; and it came to D'Urville in a moment of amazed delight that the Great Southern Continent, which for centuries had adorned maps of the southern hemisphere in all the wrong places, had materialised at last. At mid-day he fixed his position

Below: D'Urville's ships *Astrolabe* and *Zelée* moored on their voyage to the 'great southern continent', 1838. In the foreground, some of the crew appear to be killing seals.

Left: The crew of the *Astrolabe* attempt to cut a path through the ice. When the going got really tough, D'Urville wisely returned home rather than fight an unequal battle against the ferocious elements.

Below: Captain Charles Wilkes whose dogged determination enabled him to map 2000 miles of Antarctic coastline.

– 66°30′S, 138°21′E – no more than a couple of miles from the mainland; then *Astrolabe* and *Zelée* began from close inshore to follow a coastline of awesome beauty, its cliffs sometimes fringed by sea-ice delicate as the petals of a flower, more often fringed by towering flat-topped bergs anything up to a mile in length.

It was, *wrote D'Urville*, as though our ships were threading their way through narrow streets between tall buildings. Our officers' orders echoed and re-echoed from the vertical walls of ice. The sea, rushing in and out of the channels, created sea-caves and dangerous currents and whirlpools, and so great was the heat of the sun that great waterfalls cascaded non-stop down the sides of the bergs.

On January 22nd their longboat managed to force its way on to a rocky promontory, where the French flag was unfurled, a bottle of Bordeaux was ceremonially drunk, and their discovery was christened Adélie Land, in honor of D'Urville's wife. Then bad weather put an end to exploration. The ships, struck by a succession of violent blizzards, became separated and stripped of their canvas; soon they were close to foundering, and their crews, suffering from frostbite, scurvy and exhaustion, close to the end of their tether. D'Urville very sensibly returned to France.

He at once retired and devoted the rest of his life to writing his magnificent *Voyage au pôle Sud dans l'Océanie sur les corvettes l'Astrolabe et la Zelée*: 23 volumes and 7 atlases graced by outstanding illustrations, meticulous charts and writing of considerable literary distinction: an erudite commemoration of one of the great discoveries in the history of exploration.

Wilkes and the Discovery of Wilkes Land

In the autumn of 1838 a mini-armada stood south out of Hampton Roads. Its commander, Charles Wilkes, knew that his six vessels – the *Vincennes*, *Porpoise*, *Peacock*, *Sea Gull*, *Flying Fish* and *Relief* – were unseaworthy and ill-provisioned, and his 345 crew disgruntled and ill equipped; but he knew also that his United States Exploring Expedition (which was basically a Navy project)

had influential civilian enemies who had been delaying it for more than a decade, and he felt that if he did not sail at once he would never sail at all. He arrived off Tierra del Fuego in January 1839, and his ships spent the summer trying individually to force their way south through the ice-choked Bellingshausen Sea. Wilkes' forebodings were now realized. The captains of both *Porpoise* and *Peacock* reported their superstructures were rotten, their gun-ports leaking and their vessels almost constantly awash. The captain of the *Sea Gull* reported even worse conditions: 'water freezing all over the deck, icicles enveloping everything, shipping huge seas, and it is next to impossible to make sail.' He was not exaggerating. His ship was soon to founder with the loss of all hands. Of these initial individual forays, only one came close to success. In a truly heroic voyage the diminutive *Flying Fish* forced her way through the ice to 71°S, where her captain, William Walker reported 'the water much discolored . . . and the icebergs stained by dark streaks with the appearance of soil.' Walker suspected he was close to land. He was right; and if the weather that March had been fine, he would almost certainly have sighted the continent.

By May Wilkes' depleted squadron had reassembled in Valparaiso, the *Sea Gull* having been lost and the *Relief* sent home as 'unfit for service'. The next 18 months were spent in the Pacific; and Wilkes' *Narrative of the U.S. Exploring Expedition* evokes very clearly the dilemma of the Polynesians who had lost their primordial innocence and were witnessing the collapse of their culture – the local girls were no longer offering themselves but selling themselves, and the American seamen were 'required to pay one shilling for the privilege of walking on the beach.' In November 1839 they put into Sydney to refit and re-provision, before again heading for Antarctica.

There are two interpretations of what happened next. Wilkes' admirers say he was a brave man who overcame the poor state of his ships, was first to sight Antarctica and went on to map 2000 miles of previously unknown

coastline. His detractors say he was a braggart who, in the words of his subsequent court martial, 'needlessly hazarded his ships . . . and made a false entry as to the date on which he sighted Antarctic Land.' The truth seems to be that on January 16th, 1840 (a few days before D'Urville) Wilkes claimed to have seen land: 'appearances believed to be land visible from all three vessels.' From his position, it is clear he was mistaken. There is, however, no evidence to suggest his mistake was intentional. Wilkes may have been ambitious, obstinate and headstrong, but he was a man of integrity; besides which he

could hardly have coerced the lookouts of three ships to make three simultaneous false sightings. It therefore seems reasonable to assume that on January 16th, Wilkes and his lookouts were neither the first men or the last to mistake icebergs for ice-mountains. What is beyond doubt is that a few days later, he *did* sight land, and that on February 14th he managed to work the *Vincennes* through a kaleidoscope of icebergs into a shallow bay; here his longboat landed on an offshore island, and his crew spent several hours ashore, tobogganing and collecting specimens.

A lesser man would have been satisfied and headed home. Wilkes, however, wrote in his Diary: 'I considered it my duty to proceed, and not give up the cruise until the ship is totally disabled.' So for week after week, like a demonic Flying Dutchman, he followed the coastline west, his ships near-foundering, his men dying of cold, scurvy, exposure and exhaustion – one was found frozen solid on to the sails he was trying to furl.

This was one of the most hazardous and demanding voyages ever made, charting 2000 miles of previously unknown coastline. Only Magellan and Cook have made a greater contribution to the map of the world.

Ross and the Discovery of the Ross Ice Shelf and the Transantarctic Mountains

James Clark Ross was born with a silver spoon in his mouth. He had everything: wealth, ability, good looks and good luck; he also had that backing from the establishment which the unfortunate Wilkes was denied. Between the ages of 12 and 32 he was almost continually at sea, searching for the elusive North West Passage; he became skilled in icemanship and an authority on magnetism. In 1839 he was given command of *Erebus* and *Terror* (bombships specially strengthened for work in the ice) with orders to search for the South Magnetic Pole. Arriving in Australia, he listened to the advice of sealers, who told him that round about longitude 180° a lagoon-like stretch of open water had been sighted beyond the pack-ice; this, he decided, might be a possible route to the Pole.

As *Erebus* and *Terror* headed into what is now known as the Ross Sea, the feeling of the crews was summed up by their doctor, Robert McCormick: 'Our future promises to be full of interest, for we may soon make discoveries in a region of our globe fresh as at creation's dawn.' However, on January 2nd the ships were brought up short by pack-ice. It stretched in front of them as far as the eye could see: a field of white, solid at the edge but with occasional leads of open water inside. Ross took a chance. He ran full-tilt at the ice. Ordinary vessels would have been stove-in; but after 'a couple of hours hard thumping' the specially-strengthened *Erebus* and *Terror* managed to force their way into a lead of open water; by nightfall they had penetrated about a mile into the ice. Here they became frozen in. Next day the weather worsened. The wind increased to a full hurricane; the swell steepened; the pack split-up, and soon great waves thick with blocks of ice were sweeping down on them.

Our ships, wrote Ross, rolled and groaned amidst the blocks of ice over which the ocean rolled its mountainous waves, throwing huge masses one upon another then burying them deep beneath its foaming waters, the while dashing and grinding them together with fearful violence.

Erebus' rudder was split and the sheathing ripped from her hull; *Terror* lost her rudder entirely and came close to foundering. But eventually the storm eased; the damaged

ships were repaired, then they again headed south through the broken ice. On January 9th they sighted open water ahead. On January 10th they forced their way through to it, and almost at once sighted land.

January 11th, *wrote McCormick*. At 2.30 am land was reported from the crow's nest. It appeared at first indistinctly through haze and light cloud. It extended from S.E. to S.W., very high and enveloped in snow . . . and it soon became clear that we had discovered a land so extensive and attaining such altitude as to justify the appellation of a Great New Southern Continent.

Next day (January 12th) they put ashore, and went through the usual ritual of raising the flag and taking possession of the land they had discovered. Then, through ice-free water and from close inshore, they followed the coastline south. Soon they were running parallel to a great chain of mountains, many over 9000 feet high.

Above: Ships passing between ice islands. Ross learned how to deal with the dangers of sailing through ice on his previous expeditions in the Arctic.

Below: Ross goes ashore on Victoria Land, before following the coastline through waters that were, miraculously, ice-free.

January 28th, *wrote McCormick.* We were startled to see a stupendous volcano in eruption. On going on deck, my attention was arrested by what appeared to be a snowdrift driving from the summit of a lofty crater-shaped peak. As we approached, this resolved itself into a dense column of smoke, intermingled with flashes of red flame, emerging from a magnificent vent in the centre of this mountain range encased in eternal ice and snow. This peak, which rises to 12,400 feet, was named Mount Erebus after our ship.

There followed another spectacular discovery. Southeast of Mount Erebus, Ross found his way blocked by a sheer wall of solid ice.

It presented an extraordinary appearance, *wrote Ross,* seeming to increase in height as we got nearer, and proving to be a perpendicular ice-cliff, about 200 feet high, perfectly flat at the top and without the slightest fissure on its seaward face. What lay beyond it we could not imagine . . . but it was clear we might as well try to sail through the cliffs of Dover as penetrate such a mass.

He had discovered one of the wonders of the natural world: the ice-barrier which now bears his name.

For the rest of that season and most of the next Ross tried to find a way round the barrier. He failed. He also failed to reach the South Magnetic Pole, although he calculated its position with accuracy. On the credit side, he established a 'farthest south' which was to stand for 60 years; his crew enjoyed good health and no fatalities; he

collected a wealth of scientific information, and his crew were the first human beings to sight – and to sight from close inshore – one of the most spectacular coastlines on Earth. He returned to England after a commission of 4 years and five months.

Above: The native inhabitants of Possession Island – 'myriads of penguins' as Ross noted – greet Ross and his crew.

The First Winter: The Ordeal of de Gerlache and the *Belgica* (1897-99)

The difficulties faced by D'Urville, Wilkes and Ross indicated that Antarctica would be almost impossible to colonize; so in the years immediately after these expeditions there was little incentive for anyone to go there. However towards the end of the nineteenth century the rationale of exploration began to change, the quest for knowledge superseding the old-fashioned quest for land. In 1895 the International Geographical Congress declared that 'the unveiling of Antarctica is the most important piece of exploration still to be undertaken, for the continent may prove a vast refrigerated storehouse of knowledge.'

First to march to the beat of this new drum were the Belgians.

On August 24th, 1897 a team of scientists sailed from Ostend. They were a cosmopolitan ship's company. Their captain, Adrien de Gerlache, and 5 seamen were Belgian; the mate and 4 seamen were Norwegian; the geologist and meterologist were Polish, the naturalist Rumanian and the doctor American. Among them were men soon to become famous: Henryk Arctowski who pioneered the study of polar climate, Frederick Cook who claimed to be first at the North Pole, and Roald Amundsen who was undoubtedly first at the South Pole. Their ship, the *Belgica* was a tough little battering-ram of a vessel. lacking beauty or comfort but ideally suited for work in the ice – she was sheathed in both greenheart wood and iron, her stern was five feet thick, and her bows were angled-up like the runners on a sledge to help her ride over the ice.

By January 1898 De Gerlache and his team were standing south down the Antarctic Peninsula, forcing their way through the ice, and making frequent landings – 19 in all – to collect scientific data. On January 31st they made history by being the first human beings to sleep on the mainland.

It was, *wrote Dr Frederick Cook,* a night of stormy discomfort. A wind came out of the glacier above us against which we could hardly stand. It took two men to hold up the tent and the combined efforts of all hands to prevent it being blown over the cliffs. On 1 February we struggled a few yards into the interior, but fog, wind and crevasses made frequent halts necessary. The sledges were almost impossible to move . . . After this first camping experience in the history of south polar exploration, we gladly betook ourselves back to the *Belgica.*

This was an incident which convinced at least one of them, Amundsen, of the foolishness of trying to traverse such country by man-hauled sledge.

Throughout February, at a time when most vessels in the Antarctic were heading for home, *Belgica* continued to force her way through the ice. She went a floe too far, and found herself frozen in for the winter about 310 miles inside the Antarctic Circle. De Gerlache was not at first unduly worried, for his ship was well-built and well-stocked with food and fuel. The Antarctic winter, however, was an ordeal not all of them would survive.

Their first problem was the ice.

March 16, *wrote Cook.* The ice suddenly cracked all about us, being forced together by the most terrible pressure. Huge hummocks rose up on every side as the floes were pressed together and against the vessel. Wood was gouged out of our hull, and we were flung on to our side, enduring the battering of the ice with cracks and groans.

It was fortunate that as winter set in, the ice became more stable. Their second problem was the weather. It was not unbearably cold that winter – most of the time the temperature was only a little below zero – but the wind was a near-continuous gale, the fog was omnipresent and the snow near-everlasting. Nothing aboard the *Belgica* was ever dry.

If only, *lamented De Gerlache*, we could be quit of this infernal humidity; our clothes, our equipment, our bunks, even our bodies are all the time beaded with moisture and veneered with ice.

Their third problem was the darkness. With the disappearance of the sun, the crew began to suffer mental and physical deterioration. To quote the *Belgica's* log:

The members of the expedition became affected with a terrible langor. In some the pulse rate rose to 150 per minute, in others it sank to 47. By mid-winter de Gerlache, Maaerts and Michotte were showing symptoms of scurvy. One man had bouts of hysteria; another went mad; Lieutenant Dance died of heart failure . . . The root cause of all this was the lack of sun.

Cook found an answer.

The best substitute for the sun is direct heat from an open fire. I have stripped and placed men whose pulse was almost imperceptible in this sort of heat, and within an hour their heart action has returned to normal.

No-one could have done more than Cook did that winter to maintain the health of his crew, and it was due largely to his efforts that when at last the sun reappeared like a small withered orange above the horizon all but one of De Gerlache's ship's company were still alive after their winter ordeal.

They were alive but their troubles were not over. For their ship remained embedded in the ice throughout the following spring and summer and well into the autumn. They tried to blast her free with explosives; they tried to winch her out by her anchors; but she would not move. In the end they had to cut a two mile 'canal' in the ice and haul her out with ropes. It was March 28th, 1899 before De Gerlache and his crew at length reached Punta Arenas in Chile, having endured a total of eleven out of the previous thirteen months frozen solid into pack-ice inside the Antarctic circle.

They were pathfinders: the first men to explore Antarctica solely in pursuit of knowledge, and the first to survive an Antarctic winter.

The First Foothold: Nordenskiold and the Swedish Scientific Expedition: (1901-03)

The year 1900 was a turning point in the exploration of Antarctica. Before it, exploration had been by sea, after it, it was by land. In 1901 three scientific expeditions put down roots on the mainland.

A German expedition in the *Gauss*, led by Erich von Drygalski, discovered Kaiser Wilhelm II Land (to the west of Wilkes Land.) They set up their base-camp on an offshore floe, and over a period of two years carried out extensive sledge journeys along the coast, collecting scientific data. They also experimented with surveying from a balloon.

A British expedition in the *Discovery*, led by Robert Falcon Scott, set up their base in McMurdo Sound (at the west end of the Ross Ice Shelf). In three years they collected a vast amount of scientific information, their only failure being that they never mastered what was undoubtedly the best method of travelling in Antarctica: by dog-drawn sledge.

Below: McMurdo Station, Antarctica, possibly the loneliest habitation on earth. This picture clearly shows the imposing bleak terrain tackled by explorers of the region.

A team of Swedish scientists, led by Otto Norden-skiold, landed on the east coast of the Antarctic Penin-sula. Few expeditions have been beset by so many hazards and survived. Their vessel, the *Antarctic*, put them ashore on Snow Hill Island, then stood north, in-tending to return and pick them up in a year's time. Nor-denskiold and his team erected their prefabricated house and settled down for the winter. It was as well the house was a strong one; for the temperature that winter dropped to minus 30 degrees Centigrade, snow fell almost non-stop, and the wind was a steady 50mph, gusting to over 100. Their house was never still, never quiet – 'it reminds us of a ramshackle railway carriage, hurtling at top speed over ill-built track.' With the com-ing of spring they set out to explore the Peninsula. They found that whereas 3 men could hardly move a 200-pound sledge, 5 dogs could pull a 480-pound sledge quite easily – 'in fact the dogs found it difficult to go as slowly as we did.' They sledged that summer for more than 400 miles around the Peninsula, collecting valuable scientific information – but at a cost. Several times they almost overreached themselves, and were forced to lie-up in their tents 'listening to the nerve-racking howl of the wind, knowing that our provisions are being used up, and that our dogs and ourselves are growing weaker day by day.' By the time they got back, their feet, hands and lips were swollen and raw, their hair had turned white, they were suffering from snow-blindness, frost-bite and insomnia, and they had all lost more than 15 pounds in weight. And to add to their troubles, as summer gave way to autumn and the sea-ice started to thicken, it became increasingly apparent that the *Antarctic* was not going to be able to force her way through to pick them up. They would have to face another winter on the Peninsula. They were short of food, but managed to kill a number of seals and penguins.

The killing of animals, *wrote Nordenskiold*, is always a re-pulsive business, and especially in Antarctica where the creatures have no fear of man and we had come to think of them as our friends; but without their fresh meat we would not have survived.

Next spring they continued their research work, know-ing that if the *Antarctic* failed them again they would be hard pressed to survive another winter. There followed a succession of remarkable rendezvous . . . Nordenskiold and a companion were sledging over the ice, not ex-pecting anyone to be within 500 miles of them when they saw two figures approaching them.

Men black as soot from head to foot: black clothes, black faces, black caps, their eyes hidden behind black wooden frames. I am asking myself to what primitive sub-species they can belong, when one of them holds out his hand: "You don't recognise us, do you! I'm Duse. From the *Antarctic*."

The story of Duse, Andersson and Grunden is an epic of survival.

The *Antarctic* had been unable in the summer of 1902 to reach the east coast of the Peninsula; she did, however, force her way through to the west coast, where she landed 3 men in the hope they could sledge the 200-odd miles across the Peninsula and let Nordenskiold know what was happening. The 3 men – Duse, Andersson and Grunden – soon discovered that they had been landed on an offshore island; there was no way they could reach Nordenskiold; they therefore went back (as agreed) to where they had been put ashore to await the return of the *Antarctic*. She never came. And it gradually dawned on them that they had been left with little food, no shelter

and no hope of rescue to face the Antarctic winter. Less resourceful and less well-adjusted men would have given up; but the three Swedes accepted their predicament with disarming nonchalance.

When it became clear, *wrote Andersson*, that the ship would not return, we built ourselves a stone hut. Since our food was inadequate, we killed about 100 penguins to supply us with fresh meat. Since we had little fuel, we burned seal blubber. And the winter passed uneventfully.

A masterpiece of understatement, which disguises the fact that the 3 men, their toilet and their penguin meat were incarcerated for the winter in an unlit hovel 7 feet by 7 feet, where the average temperature was -20°C. For 100 days they never saw the light of day, were never dry, and were so short of fuel and food they dared not heat even an extra mug of coffee to warm themselves. Their survival has been called a miracle. It might also be called an affirmation of the indomitable spirit of man.

Dramatic events now followed one another in quick succession. In November (1903) Nordenskiold and his men spotted the masts of a vessel approaching Snow Hill Island through the pack-ice. It was not, however, the *Antarctic*; it was the *Uruguay* of the Argentine Navy, commanded by Captain Irizar who had mounted a rescue operation. They were about to embark in the *Uruguay*,

Above: Otto Nordenskiold (1869-1928), led a hazardous scientific expedition to Antarctica in 1901. He was stranded with his colleagues for two years on the mainland when his ship was crushed by the ice.

THE RACE FOR THE POLE 265

therefore decided to fall back on the traditional naval method of polar travel: by man-hauled sledge.

No journey made with dogs, he wrote, *can approach the sublimity of a party of men who succeed by their own unaided efforts. Surely in this case the conquest is more nobly and splendidly won.*

These worthy but mistaken sentiments were his epitaph.

The British carried out a full program of scientific research that winter – three of them almost froze to death studying the hatching of emperor penguins – and on October 23rd they set out for the Pole, just 4 days later than Amundsen. Their motley assortment of tractors, ponies, dogs and men was soon in difficulty; the men could hardly move their sledges through the heavy snow.

We are wet through, wrote Scott's companion, Bowers. *Our tents are wet, our bags are wet, our food is wet; everything around us is wet . . . It is all we can do to keep the sledges moving forward for short spells of perhaps 100 yards. The starting is worst; it requires from ten to fifteen desperate jerks on the harness to move at all.*

What a contrast to the Norwegians' easy 25 miles-a-day with their sledges hauled by dogs! Eventually the support parties turned back, leaving Scott and 4 companions (Bowers, Evans, Oates and Wilson) to make the final assault. Their progress was slow and exhausting, and they fell behind schedule. 'I've never known such pulling', Scott wrote in his Diary. 'We covered 6 miles today, but at fearful cost to ourselves.' They struggled through to the Pole on January 16th, only to find flags and snow cairns. 'The Norwegians have beaten us to it,' wrote Scott. 'It is a terrible disappointment . . . it will be a wearisome return.'

Scott and his companions could not afford to rest; and with their supplies running low they could not afford to eat the big meals that their physical labor called for. They could only struggle on, growing progressively hungrier and weaker, until they died one by one of hunger, scurvy, exposure and exhaustion. Scott recorded their ordeal in his Diary . . . Evans died almost literally in harness; one afternoon he collapsed while man-hauling the sledge; by nightfall he was in a coma; by midnight he was dead. Oates' feet became frostbitten; they turned black with

Top: Amundsen's ship, the *Fram.*

Above & left: Amundsen spent the winter of 1911 laying food dumps along the proposed route to the South Pole, carefully marking them with black flags. Unlike Scott's team who died of hunger and exposure, Amundsen's men were well-fed and protected from the bitter temperatures.

gangrene, and he knew he was holding the others up. 'I'm just going outside,' he said one night, and limped away into the storm and was never seen again. 'It was,' wrote Scott, 'the act of a brave man.' Scott, Bowers and Wilson pitched their tent for the last time on March 21st. They must have recognized death in every moan of the wind; yet there is no hint in Scott's Diary of complaint or self-pity: 'We are very near the end, but have not and will not lose our good cheer.' The three men died on about 31st March, 1912, their deaths helping to perpetuate the peculiarly British myth that it is better to be a gallant loser than a dedicated winner.

Scott's failure may tug at the heartstrings more poignantly than Amundsen's success; but there is no doubt who was the better explorer.

These pages: All the pictures were taken by H.G. Ponting, the official photographer to Scott's ill-fated expedition.

Above: Sea spray formed into ridges of ice after a blizzard.

Left: Scott's ship the *Terra Nova* moored at Cape Evans, 1910.

Above right: The rigging of the *Terra Nova* silhouetted against the icy Antarctic landscape, the crew possibly peering into the unknown in the hope of seeing Scott and his colleagues emerge from the frozen wastes.

Below right: Scott and his men found it difficult to control dogs, and their motor-sledges broke down, so the only alternative was for them to haul their supplies themselves.

Across the Continent: Shackleton (1914-16), and Fuchs and Hillary (1956-58)

In 1914 a British expedition attempted to cross Antarctica. Their plan was simple. The *Aurora* (commanded by Mackintosh) was to land near the Ross Ice Shelf and lay food-caches towards the Pole; simultaneously the *Endurance* (commanded by Shackleton) was to land on the opposite side of the continent, in the Weddell Sea, and send sledge-teams overland *via* the Pole; it was hoped that these teams would pick up the *Aurora*'s food-caches on the final stage of their crossing. Nothing, however, went according to plan.

The *Aurora* managed to establish food depots as far south as the Beardmore Glacier. Then a blizzard tore her free of her moorings, and for over a year she drifted ice-bound in the Ross Sea, with half her ship's company stranded ashore. Eventually she managed to limp to New Zealand, and from there a rescue expedition was mounted – although by the time a ship got through to the Ice Shelf several of the stranded crew members had died.

The *Endurance* meanwhile was having an even more traumatic ordeal. She became trapped by the ice before she could reach the mainland and was frozen-in in the Weddell Sea. For months she drifted this way and that, at the mercy of wind and current, until she was caught between two converging pressure-ridges, flung on to her beam and squeezed to destruction. Shackleton was the last to leave her.

It was a sickening sensation, *he wrote*, to feel the deck breaking up under our feet, the great beams bending then snapping with a noise like gunfire . . . You could hear the ship being crushed, and as the ice ground into her, you felt as though your own ribs were cracking. Suddenly, inside her, a light went on for a moment, then went out. It seemed like the end of the world.

Shackleton and his crew of 27 found themselves stranded on an ice-floe, hundreds of miles from land, with no hope of outside help. They tried to head for the coast; but the going was not so much difficult as impossible: 30-foot ridges of jagged ice alternating with patches of slush through which men and dogs fell into the water. At the end of a week they had covered less than 10 miles, and Shackleton could see that his men would die of exhaustion before they reached land. He searched for a solid floe, established a camp (Camp Patience) and settled down for the ice to melt. Conditions were terrible. The wind seldom dropped below a gale; the temperature never rose above zero; it snowed on 19 days out of 20; they were short of food and short of fuel: 'We had,' wrote Shackleton, 'to resort to melting the ice for drinking-water by holding it in tins against our bodies.' They ate the last of their seal-meat then the last of their dogs. Only Shackleton's leadership kept them going. No explorer was ever more popular with his men or more

Below: Shackleton's ship *Endurance* being crushed by the ice floes. This was the first of several disasters to befall Shackleton and his crew.

Right: The camp on Cape Patience. Shackleton (extreme left) and his crew salvaged most of their supplies from the ship, but this camp disintegrated when the ice began to melt.

Below right: A crewman feeding Shackleton's dogs. In the background is the *Endurance*, and the lifeboats attached to the sides are similar to the *James Caird* in which Shackleton sailed the 800 miles from Elephant Island to South Georgia to launch a search party for his stricken crew.

admired by them. 'If he had half a pipe of tobacco,' one of his crew wrote, 'he'd share it. We all felt that so long as the Boss was in charge everything was going to be all right. He was undefeatable.'

As the ice melted, Cape Patience became increasingly untenable. Cracks opened up in their floe, so that one moment the men would be asleep in their tents and next moment fighting for their lives in the water. Three times Shackleton saved one of his crew from drowning. Eventually they took to their boats and headed for the nearest of the South Shetland Islands, some 100 miles to the west. It was a voyage of extreme hazard through heavy ice-choked seas. As one of the survivors, Frank Worsley recalled:

A howling gale was blowing, and a terrific sea running. One moment we were on the crest of a tremendous swell – you could see right away to the horizon, nothing but sea and ice and sky – then you'd drop into the hollow and see a great roller coming towards you, filled with blocks of ice . . . It was so cold that ice and frost fell off us as we rowed.

During every moment of a nightmare 3-day voyage their boats were in danger of being capsized or staved-in; but at last they struggled into a bleak but sheltered cove on Elephant Island.

By now, wrote Worsley, many of us were light-headed. Some reeled about, laughing uproariously. Others sat on the shingle, and let it run through their hands like harmless lunatics. It was the first land we had set foot on for 485 days.

They found and killed an elephant seal, and the great creature's flesh gave them the most nourishing meal they had had for months, and its blubber the most warming fire. For the moment they were out of danger. Their long-term prospects, however, were not good; for Elephant Island was bleak, uninhabited and seldom if ever visited; they could survive on it for a limited period only. Shackleton decided that their one hope was to get help, and the one place they could get help from was the whaling station on South Georgia. However, to reach the island they would have to navigate with pinpoint accuracy in an open boat through some of the heaviest seas on Earth for a distance of 800 miles. It sounded impossible; but Shackleton and 5 companions set out on what is generally regarded as the greatest voyage ever made by an open boat in the history of seafaring.

Twice, while still within sight of Elephant Island, their boat the James Caird almost capsized, and two of the crew were swept overboard and only saved by their lifelines. Once clear of the island, the greatest danger was ice, 'grotesque and wondrous shapes, all heaving, curtseying and jostling together in the swell, and coming together with a thud that would have smashed the James Caird like a gasmantle.' As they picked their way northeast the ice first thinned out, then disappeared; but they still had the heavy seas to contend with; great waves, one third of a mile from crest to crest and 50 feet from summit to trough, sweeping endlessly out of the west, each threatening to engulf and overturn them. To stay afloat was an achievement, to stay on course a miracle. Shackleton describes their 16-day ordeal.

The sub-Antarctic Ocean lived up to its evil reputation . . . So small was our boat that its sail would flap idly in the calm between the crests of the waves. Then we would climb the next slope and catch the full fury of the gale, as the whiteness of breaking water surged about us. Always there were gales . . . We put out a sea anchor to keep our head up; but even then the

Above: Sir Edmund Hillary plans the route of the British Trans Antarctic Expedition, 1958.

Left: Hillary (left) arrives at the South Pole with colleagues Derek Wright and Murray Ellis. Tractors with caterpillar tracks made the journey very much easier than anything faced by explorers in the early years of the century. Hillary and his companions laid a trail of food depots which were used by Fuchs on the second half of his trans-polar journey.

crests of the waves would curl right over us. A thousand times it seemed as though the boat must be engulfed; but somehow she lived . . . By now the *James Caird* had lost her resilience; with the weight of ice in her and on her she was becoming more like a log than a boat.

They threw away their spare oars and sleeping bags, and chipped away the ice with an axe, and the *James Caird* 'lifted to the waves as though she lived again.' Soon they were suffering from thirst – their water-barrel had been staved in – and the salt spray continually lashing their faces turned thirst into pain. Two of them became weak and close to insanity . . .

Things were bad for us those last few days, but the end was coming. At about 12.30 pm on May 8th we caught sight, through a rift in the clouds, of the black cliffs of South Georgia.

A full hurricane was blowing, and they did not have much choice as to where they landed; they were flung ashore on the southwest coast. The whaling station, however, was on the northeast coast: only 50 miles away, but separated from them by a range of precipitous 7000 foot mountains encased in ice. No-one had ever managed to climb these mountains before; but Shackleton set out to find a way over them with his two fittest companions, their only equipment 50 feet of rope and an adze. Their crossing of South Georgia was almost as great a feat of physical endurance as their voyage – having no tent and nowhere to shelter they knew they had to keep going or freeze to death – but at last they staggered through to the whaling station at Husvik: their first contact with the outside world for 21 months.

The two men left on the far side of South Georgia were soon picked up by a whalecatcher. The rescue of the men on Elephant Island was not so easy; but at last Shackleton

Left: Vivian Fuchs arrives in London after his successful polar crossing. Incredibly, it took them only 99 days to traverse 2158 frozen miles.

Below: Fuchs' vehicles at the South Pole, where his expedition rested before heading for the Ross Sea.

forced his way through to them in a tug on loan from the Chilean Navy. They were cold, hungry and debilitated by scurvy, but alive. Many times in the last couple of years it had seemed to Shackleton that not one of his crew would survive; in the end not one was lost.

It was 40 years before Shackleton's dream of crossing Antarctica was realized.

The British Trans Antarctic Expedition of 1958 was an updated version of the 1914 expedition: with Edmund Hillary and a New Zealand contingent in the role of the *Aurora*, and Vivian Fuchs and a British contingent in the role of the *Endurance*.

Hillary set up his base on Ross Island, greatly helped by the Americans who as part of a program for the International Geophysical Year were building an air-station in McMurdo Sound. He laid a succession of well-sited and well-stocked food-depots up the Skeleton Glacier and on to the polar plateau, then settled down for the winter. Improvements in technology (in the insulation of buildings, the packaging of food and communication by radio) were now making life a great deal easier for polar explorers. Fifty years ago the average temperature in Andersson's winter hovel had been minus 20 degrees Centigrade and his only food half-cooked penguin-meat. In Hillary's winter quarters the average temperature was well above zero, and they had 3 hot meals a day and wine on Sundays and birthdays. This is not to imply that the New Zealanders had an easy time. They were hit by blizzards and whiteouts, fell into crevasses, and found the

work of relaying ton after ton of supplies from sea level to the polar plateau both dangerous and exhausting.

To at last see our battered vehicles and laden sledges at the Plateau Depot. *wrote Hillary*, seemed the fulfilment of an impossible dream. I don't think that ever before, even on the summit of Everest. have I felt a greater sense of achievement.

Having laid his food-depots, Hillary advanced on the Pole, which he reached on January 4th, 1958.

Meanwhile Fuchs, from the opposite side of the continent, was also advancing on the Pole. His expedition had got off to an inauspicious start when his ship the *Theron* had to discharge the explorers in a blizzard on to an ice-floe some way from land. They had a difficult time getting their equipment ashore, and faced a difficult winter. As Fuchs wrote,

Wind, was the greatest enemy: relentless, unremitting wind driving before it a torrent of snow like a horizontal waterfall . . . with the temperature at -45 degrees F sleeping bags became heavy with frozen condensation, cracking and creaking as the men crept into them.

With the coming of spring his column of Sno-cats and Weasels set out for the Pole. Progress, however, was slow. This was partly because they were breaking new ground, partly because the terrain proved unexpectedly difficult, and partly because they carried out meticulous seismic recordings along their line of advance. November 3rd (1957) was a typical day:

Above: Richard Byrd is congratulated by Amundsen after flying over the North Pole. He was the first man to achieve this, and immediately turned his sights to the South Pole. Despite navigational problems, he succeeded three years later in 1929.

The ridge, with its mass of ice hummocks like a ploughed field, was now replaced by an elongated basin about 2½ miles long. Its smooth surface looked easy, but we were dismayed to find that tadpole-shaped depressions (a sure indication of crevasses beneath) occurred over the whole area. We covered a bare ½ mile that day. The Weasel broke through twice in 100 yards, and the second time we nearly lost it altogether, for it hung precariously over a crevasse. Had the crevasse been six inches wider it would have fallen headlong down. By midnight, when the "cat" had pulled it out backwards, there was a whiteout, and as we were very tired we camped where we were, surrounded by gaping holes.

It seemed that the Weddell Sea Party was so far behind schedule that the crossing might have to be abandoned. Then the terrain improved, and suddenly instead of one half a mile a day they were covering 30. They reached the Pole on January 19th, and after a few days rest in the luxury of the U.S. laboratory were heading for the Ross Sea. They were now traversing ground that was known, well marked and well stocked with depots of food and fuel. Progress was rapid, and on March 2nd, 1958 Fuchs' column of Sno-cats and Weasels reached the coast.

'Antarctica in its Symbolic Robe of White': Byrd (1929), Operation Deepfreeze (1956)

The American aviator Richard Byrd added a new dimension to polar exploration. 'At the time I was learning to fly,' he wrote, 'the airplane was becoming a tool which mankind could fit to its hand. It was my ambition to test this tool to the utmost through a series of long-range flights.' Byrd made the first aerial survey of Greenland, and was the first man to fly over the North Pole; in the 1920s he turned his attention to the South Pole.

Flying conditions in the Antarctic are the most hazardous on Earth. Planes on the ground are often destroyed by blizzards, engines are difficult to start, and once in the air, compasses are unreliable and distances difficult to judge. Byrd was to need patience, technical expertise and courage. His first step was to build an air base. The site he chose was near the Bay of Whales; and soon a mini-village, 'Little America', its hangars and fuel dumps hollowed out of the snow, was springing up on the edge of the Ice Shelf.

It is a beautiful and eerie location, *he wrote*. Out beyond the shacks the wireless masts and the spectral shapes of the planes, it is as quiet as a tomb. Nothing stirs. The silence is so deep one feels one can reach out and take hold of it.

On January 15th, 1929 the first aircraft (a Fairchild monoplane) took off from Little America, its flight encapsulating both the hazards and rewards of polar flying. Before take-off the Fairchild's engine had to be heated with an acetylene torch, icicles had to be chipped from its ailerons, and as it taxied out eight men had to hang on to

Left: Richard Byrd's achievement in flying over the poles is all the more remarkable when one realizes that aviation was still in its infancy.

Below: Byrd's monoplane *Floyd Bennett* which covered the 1600 miles from the Bay of Whales to the Pole in a mere 16 hours.

its wing to prevent it being blown over. Once in the air, however, its crew were able to 'peer down on an area never before seen by man'; on his first flight Byrd managed to photograph and survey 1000 square miles of virgin ice – almost as much as had been surveyed in 30 years by land.

It had been difficult simply to get a plane off the ground, to get one to the Pole seemed impossible; for it was 1600 miles from Little America to the Pole and back, and Byrd's aircraft could not carry sufficient fuel for so long a journey; also the Queen Maud Mountains barred his way with peaks of 12,000 feet, and his aircraft could climb only to 11,000 feet. Byrd, however, planned to use dog teams to establish a landing-strip-cum-fuel-dump at the foot of the mountains; to land there to refuel, then cut through the Queen Maud range by flying up one of the glacial passes. After 9 months of planning, reconnaissance and meticulous preparations the attempt was made on November 28th. All went well until they were nearing the top of the glacier, then their aircraft began to labor.

The stream of air pouring down the glacier tossed us about like a cork. The roughness became so violent we were forced to the right-hand side. Here the glacier rose in a series of icefalls and terraces, well above the altitude of the plane. These glacial waterfalls were the most beautiful I have ever seen. Beautiful, but with what finality they would deal with us if we crashed!

And it seemed all too likely they *would* crash. For the controls of their plane became increasingly sluggish, and they found they could not gain height. Byrd jettisoned everything possible – their reserve fuel, their emergency food and clothes, even their spare camera – and the lightened plane resumed its climb. They scraped over the

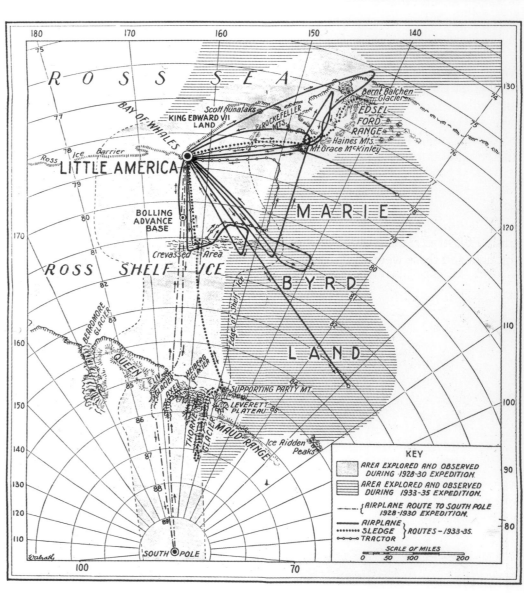

head of the pass with only a few feet to spare, and saw ahead of them the vast and featureless expanse of the polar plateau. The rest was anti-climax. They crossed the plateau without incident, and at 11.14 all calculations agreed they were over the Pole. They circled it briefly, taking photographs and dropping American, British and Norwegian flags, then headed back. 'The Pole,' wrote Byrd, 'lies in the center of a limitless plain, and that's all there is to say about it. It is the getting there that counts.' They arrived back in Little America on the morning of November 29th, having accomplished in 16 hours a journey that had taken Amundsen 4 months.

Byrd returned several times to Antarctica, on one ex-pedition voluntarily spending the winter alone in a hut frozen into the ice, and on another discovering Marie Byrd Land and the Rockefeller Mountains. His import-ance as an explorer was twofold: he pioneered the use in Antarctica of aerial surveying, and he had a concept of the continent as a world-heritage area that was far ahead of his times. In 1957, as a result of the International Geo-physical Year, Byrd's concept became reality.

The objective of the IGY was to promote the collection and exchange of scientific data. This had often been talked about; now it was put into practice. In Antarctica it was planned to set up 56 research-stations, manned by scientists of 12 nationalities. The Russians undertook to set up four posts, including one at the Pole of Inaccessi-bility. The Americans undertook to set up 6, including one at the Geographical Pole; the building of the latter was codenamed 'Operation Deepfreeze.'

'Deepfreeze' was entrusted to the U.S. Navy. After the icebreaker *Atka* had made a preliminary reconnaissance of the Ross Sea, it was decided to re-open the old air base at Little America, and build a new one at McMurdo Sound; this involved major construction work in con-ditions of extreme difficulty. The main fleet, commanded by Admiral Dufek, arrived in 1955: 9 ships, 19 aircraft, 3000 men, 10,000 tonnes of supplies and 4,000,000 litres of fuel; never before and seldom since has the solitude of Antarctica been disturbed by so huge a work-force. The airstrip in McMurdo Sound proved difficult to construct: tractors plunged through the ice, ships were damaged, men were killed; but by 1956 both landing areas were ready to take aircraft. There was, however, a problem. The range of the American Neptunes and Skytrains was 1690 miles, and the distance from McMurdo Sound to the nearest airfield (in New Zealand) from which the planes could operate was 1750 miles; so unless the planes had a following wind they would run out of fuel and crash. At last, after many abortive attempts, 4 planes got through, and these were used to reconnoiter and map a route to the Pole. A key moment came on October 31st, 1956 when one of the Skytrains made the first-ever land-ing and take-off at the Pole. It was a hair-raising perform-ance. The plane had to land down-sun and down-wind so that its shadow gave the pilot something on which to focus; touching-down it 'seemed to leapfrog for ever over the hard-packed snow,' and when the crew emerged 'the cold struck (them) in the face as though they had walked into a door.' They needed 15 jet-assisted take-off rockets to blast them off the ice and into the air.

Once the feasibility of landing had been established, the Pole became, in Dufek's words, 'an animated anthill,' with prefabricated buildings, food, fuel and scientific apparatus being airlifted in. Soon a huge rabbit warren of a laboratory had been built, more than a dozen com-partments connected by a web of tunnels – the com-partment for the washing and toilet facilities alone was larger than the whole of Scott's winter-quarters. In 1957

seventeen scientists were flown in to embark on a pro-gram of research for the IGY. This was the new face of ex-ploration: naval officers man-hauling their sledges being superseded by specialized scientists researching in fields as diverse as meteorology, geomagnetism, glaciology, botany, and geomorphology, and the results of their work being fed back to International Data Centers and disseminated throughout the world.

The spirit of international co-operation engendered by the IGY helped to bring about the signing in 1961 of the Antarctic Treaty. This treaty ensures the international status of Antarctica; it set aside national claims to terri-tory, and laid down guidelines to make sure the con-tinent was conserved not exploited, and the research work carried out in it made available to all.

This was Byrd's dream: a dream shared by most explorers today, that, in the words of his memorial plaque in McMurdo Sound

Antarctica, in its symbolic robe of white, will shine forth as a continent of peace, as nations working together there in the cause of science set an example of international co-operation.

From time immemorial the pursuit of knowledge has been the essential *leitmotiv* of exploration. In the past explorers used often to keep their discoveries secret. Today the knowledge gleaned from exploration is dis-seminated world-wide. Explorers, in many ways, have always been in the vanguard of human progress.

Above left: Gerlache Strait on the Antarctic Peninsula. The Strait is named after de Gerlache, an early French explorer of the region.

Below left: A map showing Byrd's flights over Antarctica, from his base at Little America.

Above: HMS *Endurance*, named after Shackleton's ship, has played an important support role to modern scientific and geological expeditions in the region.

Below: An Antarctic iceberg, sculpted by the action of the wind and the tides.

Underwater Exploration
by Gerald O'Brien

For most of the history of humankind, the surface of the sea has been a virtually impenetrable barrier to exploration. To look below it, people must either be provided with air and protection from the pressures of the depths or machines must look for them. Until these problems were solved, the depths of the seas remained a mystery cloaked in myth and legend. But the truth about what lies beneath the oceans is more significant, more magnificent, and vastly more complicated than anything the myth makers imagined.

There is wealth. From the earliest times the sea has been a source of commodities such as sponges, pearls and coral, but the true scale of the wealth waiting on the ocean floor has only recently begun to be fully appreciated.

One third of the world's oil reserves lie beneath the ocean floor; sand and gravel are mined extensively in coastal waters; suphur is taken from the Gulf of Mexico; rich phospher deposits lie off the coasts of California and Mexico, but the deep oceans hold the greatest wealth of all. Scattered in various locations across the floors of all the oceans are small, brownish lumps known as manganese nodules. Originally discovered by the *Challenger* expedition, the nodules are rich in copper, cobalt and nickel and are now an economically viable source for these metals. Other resources include basins on the floor of the Red Sea where there are metal-rich, gel-like sludges containing copper, zinc, silver and gold that may prove to be one of the greatest metal-deposit discoveries of all time.

As well as wealth there is knowledge. Studying the oceans has long been an important scientific activity but, again, it is only quite recently that their vital role in supporting the thin web of life around our planet has begun to be properly understood.

There is even some mystery still remaining. Because the undersea is an alien and dangerous environment, we are drawn to it by a simple fascination with the idea of being there. The 1989 expedition that filmed the wreck of the *Titanic* was staged chiefly to publicize an unmanned diving system designed to create the sensation of 'being there' without getting wet.

Previous page: Auguste Piccard's *Trieste* shortly before a test dive in August 1953.

Exploring from the Surface

Although men have dived in the sea since the beginning of history, early divers cannot really be called undersea explorers. Their incursions were short, only for as long as they could hold their breath, and they are better seen as early undersea workers.

The objectives of undersea exploration are to describe and understand the ocean waters, the seabed and the earth beneath. The activity embraces a wide range of scientific disciplines including marine biology, oceanography, and geophysics. The real undersea explorers are the people engaged in this work.

The first major voyage of undersea exploration was completed in 1876 when the British naval vessel *Challenger* returned from a thousand day survey covering 68,000 miles, the equivalent of three global circumnavigations. Her chief task was to search for deep-sea life but she also brought home valuable physical and chemical studies and the first depth measurements of the deep ocean.

Some 50 volumes of scientific results and findings were published by the *Challenger*'s scientists after their return. Forty of the volumes were on the voyage's zoological discoveries and these are still an important source for such studies today. An idea of the scale of the work involved can perhaps be gauged from the fact that the expedition and the preparation of the subsequent reports cost the British Admiralty £200,000 in the prices of the time.

Challenger's interventions below the surface of the sea were all unmanned. Her operations involved lowering sampling and measuring devices into the sea and were to set the style for many of the expeditions that followed her. Although in recent years the work of undersea explorers has been helped by improvements in communications, information technology, navigation and the use of satellites, its basic nature, observing, recording and analysing, remains unchanged.

This slow exploration is utterly dependent on machines. Measuring instruments are fixed to permanent structures in the ocean or carried on board ships, and for most purposes it is not necessary to send people underwater. Yet it would be wrong to ignore the efforts of the pioneers who first braved the dangers of the deeps. Their determination and courage in opening up the undersea has been enormously valuable. Not only has it helped to increase our knowledge of the oceans, it has, perhaps more importantly, extended our understanding of ourselves.

Below: The Reverend George Garrett, a clergyman from Liverpool, England, built this submarine, the *Resurgam* in 1879. Garrett is shown with two assistants and his young son who was drafted into the crew because he was able to work in the confined internal spaces. Although the submarine functioned it was not a great success.

Entering the Undersea

Archaeological evidence shows that divers were active as early as 4500 BC. By 3200 BC diving was widespread and by 2500 BC the Greek diving industry was supplying sponges throughout the known world. Without any kind of effective aids, these early divers went to depths of at least 100 feet (30m). Even so, because they could not stay down for long periods of time, they were unable to engage in systematic exploration.

Free divers use no aids. In Japan modern women pearl divers can go to depths of 150 feet and remain underwater for up to five minutes. While performances like these show that free diving is not quite as limited as the imagination might suggest, dives of such long duration and to such depths are extremely hazardous.

Mention was made in the first century AD of the use of hollow reeds as a breathing tube, or snorkel. These were the first aids used to extend a diver's capability but advances beyond this would not come for many hundreds of years.

Although the sixteenth century was an age of invention in diving, most of the devices designed then could never have worked because they were based either on long snorkels or on leather bags full of air. Divers cannot suck air through a snorkel longer than about two feet because human chest muscles are not strong enough to 'work against the pressure of water at greater depths than that, and to overcome the buoyancy of a large air bag, divers would have to carry so much ballast that they would be unable to move across the sea bed.

Bells, Chambers and Submarines

The first really effective advance over free diving came with the diving bell. The first of these is thought to have been designed by the Italian Guglielmo de Lorena. His device supposedly allowed a diver to remain underwater for up to one hour and seems to have been used to locate treasure galleys in a lake near Rome in 1531. Another claimant to this 'first' is an experiment at Toledo in Spain in 1538 in the presence of the Emperor Charles V in which at least the principle of the diving bell seems to have been successfully demonstrated.

A simple diving bell is an open-ended chamber that is lowered into the water open end downwards, so trapping air in its upper end. A diver can remain inside the bell, or work outside and return, breathing the trapped air until it is exhausted. Because the air inside it is compressed, a bell can only be used down to about 66 feet.

A bell supplied with air from the surface can reach much greater depths than this. The first such bell was used in 1689 and was invented by a versatile Frenchman called Denis Papin. Papin experimented in a variety of areas, many of them connected in general terms with pumps and other pressure vessels. He produced ideas for early types of steam engine (which did not work properly) and invented the pressure cooker (which still works very well). He also co-operated with the Dutch scientist Huygens in the design of air pumps. The pumps of the day, when used in diving, could only force air down to about 70 feet but Papin's principle was sound and opened the way for further advances to be made. Another early pioneer was the astronomer Edmund Halley who produced a diving bell design in 1717. His device used a clever system of bringing air down to the divers in barrels and he also claimed that dives of one and one half hours at 60 feet were easily accomplished.

Although bells are clearly useful and were widely used throughout the nineteenth century for underwater construction, to go really deep a diver must be sealed in a pressure-tight chamber. Early attempts to make such chambers from wood resulted in at least two deaths, an Englishman John Day in 1774, and a Spaniard named Cervo in 1831. Day was a ship's carpenter and achieved one successful dive with his machine. His contribution to submarine design was the use of large boulders hung from external bolts as ballast. His second dive, in Plymouth Sound on 20 June 1774, was disastrous. His wooden hull was probably crushed by the pressure at around 130 feet. Lord Sandwich, the First Lord of the Admiralty, happened to be present and organised rescue attempts but these were unsuccessful.

The first workable chamber was built from steel by a Frenchman, Ernst Bazin, in 1865 for use in a treasure hunt. It was lowered to a record depth of 245 feet (72m). By 1875 a similar chamber had an air supply that could sustain a diver for 50 hours. With the pressure and air problems solved, further substantial progress was possible. In 1930 the American zoologist William Beebbe and the engineer Otis Barton produced their bathysphere. This was a spherical steel vessel, just under five feet in diameter, and in 1934 Beebe set a new record for deep diving of 3028 feet (923m).

Bathyspheres hang on long heavy cables. There is a

Below: A medieval manuscript depicts a type of diving bell supposedly being employed in the time of Alexander the Great.

Above: Beebe's bathysphere is unloaded at Bermuda before his dives in July 1934.

Left: Barton (left) and Beebe with the bathysphere during their series of dives in 1934.

constant danger that the cable will break while the depth to which they can be lowered is restricted by the weight that can be handled by a winch. Of course, if a cable does break, then any divers down below cannot be helped.

The Swiss scientist Auguste Piccard, already well known for his exploits in high altitude ballooning, took a new direction in undersea work with bathyscaphes, chambers that could dive and resurface by themselves using weights and a buoyancy tank (containing gasoline, which is lighter than water). His first vessel was built in Belgium in 1946-8 but was damaged in trials off the Cape Verde Islands. Rebuilt to an improved design, Piccard took this device past 4000 meters (13,284 feet in fact) off Dakar in February 1954. Meanwhile Piccard had also designed another vessel, the *Trieste*, which was launched in 1953. The *Trieste* made various successful dives but was acquired by the US Navy in 1958 and a new cabin fitted. On 23 January 1960, piloted by Piccard's son, Jacques, and Lieutenant Don Walsh, *Trieste* reached the record depth of 35,810 feet (10,916 meters) in the Mariana Trench. The deepest part of the Mariana Trench is the deepest part of any ocean at 36,200 feet (11,034m).

Whereas bathyspheres and bathyscaphes are vehicles of exploration, submarines were designed as weapons of war but have also contributed to the technology of undersea exploration and done some exploring themselves. An Englishman William Bourne first wrote of a submersible boat in his *Inventions and Devices* in 1578. There is no evidence that Bourne ever built his design which was essentially a boat-shaped hull decked over and sealed to make it watertight with a hollow mast for breathing. The chief technical interest is in the inclusion of a form of ballast tank, leather bags which would fill with water to submerge and be squeezed empty by screw presses. The increased buoyancy of the craft then caused it to surface.

The first recorded use of any submarine in war was the *Turtle*, built by Yale graduate David Bushnell for use in the War of American Independence, which unsuccessfully attacked the British warship *Eagle* in September 1776. Various designs from a series of inventors followed during the nineteenth century and by the end of that

century the military submarine had taken on a recognisable modern form. The first such design is usually credited to an Irish-American John P. Holland whose *Holland* was bought by the US Navy in 1900 but the French *Narval* designed by Maxime Laubeuf also went into service at the same time.

Until much more recently military submarines have done little exploring but military requirements have done much to inspire improvements in underwater rescue techniques and equipment. The advent of nuclear power made other developments possible. 'Conventionally powered' boats are really 'submersibles' capable only of limited underwater endurance before resurfacing or at least raising a snorkel tube, but with nuclear power a 'true submarine' capable of long underwater voyages became practical.

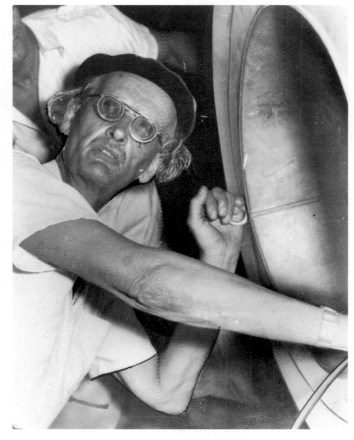

Left: Auguste Piccard inspects his bathysphere after it had been damaged in trials in November 1948. The apparatus to raise the vessel had broken down after it had been lowered unmanned to a depth of some 1500 meters.

Below left: Auguste and Jacques Piccard board the *Trieste*.

Below: Jacques Piccard (right) and Dr Andreas Rechnitzer, one of the senior scientists on the project, after they had taken the *Trieste* to 5700 meters in November 1959.

The world's first nuclear powered submarine was the USS *Nautilus*. Launched in 1954, she set various records in her early voyages but in 1958 she caught the world's imagination with a voyage under the North Pole under the polar ice. Since then the growing fleets of nuclear submarines of the world's major navies have often operated under the Arctic ice, on occasion surfacing in the gaps or leads between the ice floes. It is a sad reflection on the progress of exploration that the information gained by such voyages has largely remained subject to military secrecy when environmentalists and others believe that it could have wider value.

Modern undersea research vessels are hybrids between bathyscaphes and submarines. The US Navy possesses a small, nuclear-powered research vessel very similar to a standard submarine while deeper diving research vehicles employ pressure spheres and ballasting systems that are closer in lineage to bathyscaphes.

Helmets, Suits and Air Lines

The earliest known clear mention of a form of diving helmet is in *De Re Militari* by Vegetius, published in the early part of the sixteenth century but, even long before that, the Greek philosopher Aristotle had given vague descriptions of equipment for passing air down to divers. The first diving suit to give a diver the freedom to walk the sea bed was devised in 1715 by an English inventor named Becker. His divers, dressed in leather suits with air hoses attached, were supplied with air by pumps at the surface. Since Becker's pumps were not able to force air below twenty feet, his idea was of modest use. A contemporary of his, John Lethbridge, also produced a suit, without any air lines, being instead a barrel-like outfit with a glass observation port and leather covered sleeves. Wearing this a diver could supposedly take enough air to last 30 minutes down to 30 feet and Lethbridge is reported to have become wealthy as a result, although this seems unlikely.

Further improvements were made by the German inventor Kleingert at the very end of the eighteenth century. His divers submerged and surfaced by carrying and releasing lead weights and breathed in through a tube leading to the surface while a second tube carried foul air away from the helmet. Helmet diving was finally perfected by the German Augustus Siebe. He first devised an 'open' diving dress in which a metal helmet was filled with air from a pump on the surface, any surplus escaping around the bottom of the helmet as it might from a diving bell. This gave the diver considerable scope provided he was able to remain upright but if the helmet was tilted it would quickly fill with water and the diver drown. Siebe was aware of these problems and in 1830 he produced his first 'closed' diving suit where the helmet is fitted with an air regulating outlet valve. Various refinements by Siebe and others have followed but Siebe's suit was so safe and efficient that it became known as the Standard Helmet Diving Suit.

When air compressors developed sufficiently to allow helmet divers to start going to greater depths the medical

Left: A modern reconstruction of David Bushnell's *Turtle*, the first submarine employed in war. Bushnell's brother had been the operator of the vessel on its trials but he became ill, probably because of the poor breathing arrangements, and the first war mission was performed by one Sergeant Ezra Lee.

Below: Submarines and other underwater devices employed during the American Civil War.

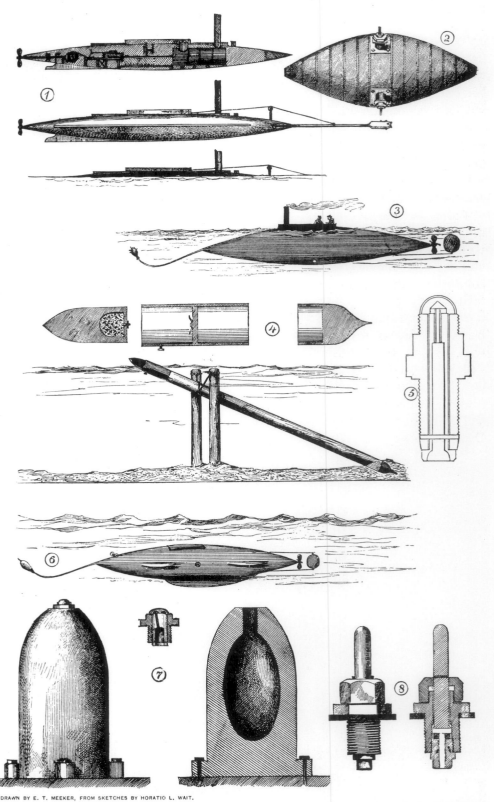

DRAWN BY E. T. MEEKER, FROM SKETCHES BY HORATIO L. WAIT.

1. CONFEDERATE TORPEDO-BOAT "DAVID." 2. CONFEDERATE TORPEDO. 3. CONFEDERATE TORPEDO-BOAT, AS DESCRIBED BY A REFUGEE. 4. CONFEDERATE SPAR-TORPEDO. 5. FUSE OF A BARREL-TORPEDO FOUND IN THE ST. JOHN'S RIVER. 6. CONFEDERATE SUBMARINE TORPEDO-BOAT, AS DESCRIBED BY A REFUGEE. 7. CONFEDERATE VOLCANO-TORPEDO. 8. CONFEDERATE TORPEDO-FUSE.

Left: The French submarine *Narval* established the important principle in submarine design of having one propulsion system (in this case a steam engine) for surface operation, and rechargeable batteries driving an electric motor for underwater.

Below & bottom: Not until the nuclear-powered *Nautilus* were the basic principles of the *Narval*'s design to be seriously challenged.

problems associated with deep diving, principally 'the bends' and nitrogen narcosis, began to be discovered. Addressing these problems led to research that would revolutionize industrial diving.

The air we breathe is a mixture mainly of oxygen and nitrogen. Our lungs dissolve these gases into the blood which carries them around the body to be absorbed by body tissues. As a diver is subjected to increasing pressure, more of these gases are absorbed. When a diver surfaces rapidly the release of pressure causes the nitrogen to form bubbles just as the gas in fizzy drinks makes bubbles when the cap is unscrewed. Nitrogen bubbles can obstruct blood vessels, disrupt the heart or damage nerve tissue. The condition, known as 'the bends', is extremely dangerous and painful and can be fatal.

When divers surface slowly, the nitrogen is able to dissolve into the blood and be expelled through the lungs. Decompressing in this way is a slow business, the deeper

a diver has gone, the longer it takes. Coming up from 1000 feet (300m) takes eleven and one half days.

Nitrogen narcosis is a second danger. At about 100 feet (30m), nitrogen absorbed in brain and nerve tissue causes a condition known as 'raptures of the deep'. Extreme cases result in loss of consciousness while the milder effects include intoxication. To a diver making life or death decisions the condition is potentially lethal.

Nitrogen narcosis is prevented by replacing nitrogen with helium in a diver's gas mixture. After the Second World War deposits of helium were discovered in the United States (helium is a by-product of uranium mining) making the use of this helium-oxygen breathing gas (heliox) a practical proposition. One amusing but significant consequence of breathing this helium-oxygen mixture is the 'Donald Duck' effect. Helium has different properties when passing over the vocal chords which result in distortions of the voice which can make telephonic communication so difficult that equipment to decode the distorted voice has to be supplied.

When people first realised that decompression was the answer to the bends, it was believed that the longer divers remained under pressure then the longer they would need to decompress. Very long decompression times therefore made prolonged deep diving impractical. In 1957 a US naval researcher, George Bond, discovered that if divers stayed under pressure for about 24 hours, then their required decompression time stopped increasing. Bond's discovery led to a new diving technique, saturation diving.

Beginning in 1962, the French 'Conshelf' and the US

Above: Pisces III, a modern industrial submersible.

Left & right: As well as his role in the design of the first effective Scuba system and his well known television programs on various aspects of undersea exploration, Captain Cousteau was also involved in experiments in living at depths for long periods. Views of his 1963 work on 'Pre-Continent No.2' are shown.

'Sealab' underwater living experiments demonstrated that saturation diving was viable. A new industry was born. Modern industrial diving operations in offshore oil fields combine helmet, bell and saturation diving techniques to allow divers to work for sustained periods at great depths while living, off shift, in comparative comfort.

SCUBA, Access to the Undersea

The ultimate dream of underwater freedom is to roam unfettered through the sea, but to do this divers must carry air with them – they need a Self-Contained Underwater Breathing Apparatus or SCUBA. A number of cumbersome but workable approaches to SCUBAs were made during the nineteeth century but only one of these is of real significance.

The Rouquaryol-Denayrouze apparatus, 1867, was not really self-contained since its low-pressure air reservoir was kept supplied from the surface. Its really significant feature was a device that supplied divers with air only when they breathed in, what would now be known as a demand valve. Other apparatuses supplied air constantly, wasting most of it.

The first effective, fully independent SCUBA was constructed in 1942 by Captain Jacques-Yves Cousteau and Emile Gagnan for the French Navy. Their success came from bringing together high-pressure air cylinders and the Rouquaryol-Denayrouze demand valve which, in spite of its success, had been ignored by other inventors.

Cousteau and Gagnan's apparatus provided the basis for all subsequent aqualungs. Used extensively by underwater researchers, workers and sportsmen since the early 1950s, it is the device which turned diving into a mass activity, giving inexpensive access to the undersea.

Major Events, Year of Undersea Science, 1989

New data on the different rates of water mixing in the Southern and Northern oceans could lead to more effective climatic monitoring during 'greenhouse-effect' global warming.

Increased understanding of the interaction between oceans and atmosphere led to a reduction in estimates of the sea level rises expected during global warming.

The discovery that dead whales on the ocean floor support their own miniature local ecosystems for up to five years, like oases of life in a sterile landscape, led to revisions of theories concerning the distribution of life through the deep oceans.

Five ships contributed 300 ship-days of observations of the North Atlantic Bloom, the oceanic equivalent of spring. The study helped understanding of the behavior of carbon dioxide in the atmosphere.

Dolphin deaths in 1987 and 1988 on the East coast of the United States were attributed to naturally occurring poisons associated with algae.

Studies in Western Australia gave unprecedented insights into dolphin social life which showed similarities with the social organisations of chimpanzees.

The drilling ship, *Joides Resolution*, recovered material from the oldest – Jurassic Period – part of the Pacific Ocean floor. This ended a twenty year search for the Jurassic Pacific and will contribute to the understanding of continental drift.

The British research vessel, *Charles Darwin*, completed a three year voyage with a detailed study of sea temperatures, salinity and currents in the Western Pacific. A new Japanese research vessel, *Hakuho Maru*, began her first voyage.

Space Exploration

by Tim Furniss

Our method of exploring space is quite unique. We do not actually have to go anywhere. The Earth is traveling around a star we call the Sun. The Sun is spinning around the outer edge of a galaxy we call the Milky Way. The Milky Way is traveling through the Universe. The Earth is therefore, in a sense, itself a spaceship. So, even the earliest man was a space traveler, exploring the wonder of the night sky with just his eyes. Man soon became familiar with the comings and goings of the moon and its phases, working out that the lunar cycle was 29 days. He grouped the stars into constellations. Other 'stars' seemed to wander about the sky but at the time it was not realized that they were planets. Events like eclipses of the sun and the appearance of comets were, not unnaturally, seen as harbingers of doom.

At the time, the Earth must have seemed to Man to be at the center of the universe and also flat. The Greek astronomer Aristotle is often credited with the first realisation that the Earth was round, in about 400 BC. Four hundred years before him, however, the prophet Isaiah had written in what later became part of the Holy Bible, that God hung stars 'over the circle of the Earth'. In the first century after Jesus Christ, the Roman elder, Pliny worked out that the tides of the sea were caused by the moon. Gradually, too, the assumption of the Earth's place at the 'center' of the Universe was being questioned.

In the 16th century, the Polish astronomer Nicholas Kopernicus published his theory that the Earth went around the Sun, together with other planets. In 1609, an astronomical revolution occurred when the Italian Galileo Galilei looked at the heavens through what was probably the first telescope. He saw craters on the Moon, rings around the planet Saturn, moons round Jupiter and the crescent of the bright planet Venus.

Being able actually to see other worlds in space inspired many writers to imagine what they were like and whether creatures lived on them. The most famous of these writers was Jules Verne, whose classic *From the Earth to the Moon* was published in 1865. Although science fiction, it was amazingly prophetic.

Previous pages: The second man on the moon photographed by the first – 'Buzz' Aldrin, July 20th, 1969.

Above and left: The founders of modern astronomy. Nicolas Copernicus (left), a Polish cleric, was the first to propound the theory that the Earth and planets moved round the sun – a total contradiction of the accepted beliefs. Galileo Galilei (above) pursued a series of astronomical experiments which convinced him in 1632 that the Copernician view of the universe was correct.

His manned space capsule, *Columbiad*, was launched to the moon by a space gun from a point not far from where the Kennedy Space Center, Florida is today. The capsule also splashed down in the sea at the end of its journey from the moon. Apollo 11, which made the first manned landing on the moon 104 years later, was launched from the Kennedy Space Center and its command module, called *Columbia*, splashed down in the Pacific at the end of the mission. To cap it all, Verne's astronauts also floated in weightlessness.

First Stages

Jules Verne was not the first person to think of a space rocket, however. The Chinese were firing rockets in the 13th century, using a propellant that we now know as gunpowder. Legend has it that Chinaman Wan-Hu was launched in a chair-like craft propelled by 47 rockets. The first 'astronaut' disappeared! Rockets were used in war in Europe in the 19th century. Briton Sir William Congreve developed solid fuel rockets which were used during the Napoleonic wars.

By the beginning of the 20th century the fantasies of space travel and the reality of rockets were infused with the theoretical knowledge and calculations needed to make space exploration possible. The Russian theoretician Konstantin Tsiolkovsky is described as the 'father of spaceflight'. In 1903, he published the fundamental

Left: A Chinese woodcut with a rather optimistic idea of how to carry men through the clouds.

Below: Galileo's use of the telescope finally provided visual proof that Copernicus' theory of the universe was right. The telescope was invented, apparently by chance, around 1600 and was vital as the instrument that proved the complicated mathematical theories of Galileo and his successors.

mathematical laws of rocket propulsion. Coincidentally, this was the same year that Orville Wright went airborne at Kitty Hawk. An American physics professor, Robert Goddard, developed a liquid fuelled rocket which made its first flight in 1926. This type of rocket was regarded as more efficient than solid propellant vehicles. The theoretical and practical work of a Rumanian teacher called Herman Oberth inspired the formation of rocket groups in many countries, including Germany.

The German *Verein fur Raumshiffahrt* (Society of Space Travel) was established in 1927 and within ten years was developing large liquid fuelled rockets at Peenemünde on the Baltic coast with military funding. Dr Wernher von Braun, a young engineer at Peenemünde, spearheaded the development of the 14 ton A4 rocket which was to make the first flights into space. He dreamed of launching science satellites around the Earth

and of manned space stations. The A4 made the first successful flight into space, to an altitude of over 50 miles, on October 3rd, 1942. By this time, however, it was not a vehicle for space exploration but for war. It was called the V2. After the Second World War, the German rocket technology was transferred both to the USA – to where von Braun moved – and the Soviet Union, to be merged with technologies already developed in these countries. By the early 1950s both countries were flying regularly into space on brief journeys carrying scientific payloads, some containing small creatures such as mice and dogs.

In 1955 the Soviet Union and USA both announced that the next stage of space exploration was near – the launch of the first Earth satellite. By August 1957, the Soviet Union had launched the first Intercontinental Ballistic Missile (ICBM). The launch of the first satellite was just two months away. It was to cause a shock.

Above: Before man could dream of exploring the heavens, he first had to devise a means of leaving the ground. The first motor propelled flight was made on December 17th, 1903 by Orville and Wilbur Wright.

Far left: Dr Robert Goddard, one of the pioneers of theoretical space exploration. Goddard (1882-1945), was a theoretical scientist as well as a practical engineer, who believed that rocket propulsion (*left*) was the way to the upper atmosphere. When the USA began the space race in earnest, the scientists of the 1950s recognized their debt to Goddard.

Going

It seemed that no one else had taken any notice of the Soviet Union when it said in 1955 that it would launch an Earth satellite within two years. Sputnik 1, was duly launched on October 4th, 1957 and shocked the world. To the USA, the fact that Sputnik was launched on the propulsion stages of a military rocket it could not match was a greater shock than the appearance in the sky of the wandering, bleeping satellite that marked the birth of the Space Age.

During 1957-61, the Soviet Union completely over-shadowed the USA in space. Sputnik 2 carried the first space traveler, a dog called Laika. Lunik 1 missed a planned moon impact and became the first spacecraft to become an artificial planet. Lunik 2 became the first artificial object to hit the moon, in September 1959, and Lunik 3 a month later, took photos which gave the Earth its first ever glimpse of what was on the far side of the moon.

The drama continued on April 12th, 1961 when cosmonaut Yuri Gagarin became the first man to enter space, orbiting the Earth once inside his spherical space capsule, Vostok 1. He was dubbed the Columbus of the Space Age. Although the USA performed similar feats, they were eclipsed simply because the Soviet Union did them first. The Soviets also used larger spacecraft, launched on more powerful rockets. These were necessary because they had not mastered the technology of miniaturization.

On May 25th, 1961 US President John F Kennedy changed the future of the Space Age by committing his country to landing men on the moon by 1969. He wanted to prove to the Soviet Union just which country was the technological leader in space. It was naturally assumed that the Soviet Union had the same goal and wanted to get to the moon first. Kennedy was also committing America to spending over $25 billion in eight years. The Apollo moon program was ironically completely to over-shadow the applications and achievements of US unmanned satellites. These satellites included the first weather, communications and navigation spacecraft which have

become part of today's age of high technology. As a result of the prominence given to the moon missions, when the Apollo goal was met in 1969, people were to question the value of exploring space at all.

The apparent competition between the Soviet Union and the USA in the 1960s was dubbed the Space Race or the Moon Race and dominated the era, contributing to the unique personality that earned the decade the description, the Swinging Sixties.

Above: Taken in 1948, this is one of the earliest photographs of Earth produced by a camera attached to an Aerobe rocket fired to an altitude of 57 miles.

Left: The Soviet Union was the first to experiment with sending living creatures into space. The dog Laika proved that an animal could survive the stresses of the launch, and for seven days her biomedical data was monitored from Earth. Laika was also the first casualty of the space race. Sputnik 2 could not be recovered and Laika died when her air ran out.

Below: In 1961 Yuri Gagarin became the first man to orbit the Earth, in a flight that lasted 108 minutes.

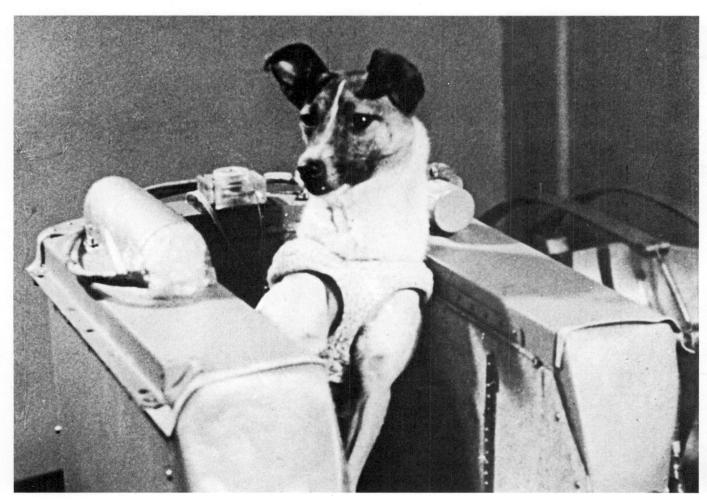

The Moon

In 1957, the Sputnik 2 space dog Laika proved that a living being could survive the stresses of being launched by a rocket into the weightlessness of Earth orbit. Yuri Gagarin confirmed this for humans in April 1961. The acceleration forces on a spaceman could be as great as ten times that of Earth's gravity. Weightlessness did not prove an unbeatable hazard either. It took a while for some spacemen to get used to weightlessness but eventually it became a comfortable and enjoyable environment in which to travel.

Spacecraft were also pressurized against the vacuum of space. As another precaution Gagarin and later spacemen wore pressure suits. Laika had been unfortunate in that her air ran out in six days. In any event, she could not have come home because her capsule was not fitted with a heatshield to protect it from the heat generated by the high speed re-entry into the Earth's atmosphere. Gagarin's Vostok capsule was protected by a heatshield and another hazard of spaceflight could be overcome.

With this pathfinding mission accomplished by Gagarin, the first US astronauts were launched, Alan Shepard, the first American in space and John Glenn, the first to orbit, flew aboard Mercury capsules in 1961-62. Enough confidence had been generated by these flights to proceed towards the manned moon landing goal. The next tasks were to find out whether a craft could land on the moon and where it would be best to land. It was also necessary to develop the technologies required for manned flights to the moon, which included rendezvous and docking maneuvers.

Unmanned US moon scouts were launched. Ranger 7 took the first close-up photos of the moon as it plummetted towards a destructive impact in 1964. Surveyor 1 made the first soft landing on the moon in 1966, proving that a spacecraft would not sink into moon dust. The same year the first Lunar Orbiters were launched. Altogether, three Rangers, six Surveyors and five Lunar Orbiters successfully reconnoitered the moon. The Americans confidently chose a possible 20 Apollo-manned landing sites.

At the same time, the Soviet Union launched Luna spacecraft but with less success, although Luna 9 did survive a semi-soft landing and returned the first pictures from the surface in 1966, followed closely by Luna 10 which became the first spacecraft to orbit the moon.

America's plan to land men on the moon involved the launch of two connected spacecraft. A combined Apollo command and service module and a lunar module would be launched. After the lunar landing and exploration, the lunar module would take off from the moon and rendezvous and dock with the command and service module in lunar orbit for the return journey to Earth.

Below & left: Alan Shepard was the first American in space. In May 1961, a month after Gagarin's trip, he piloted the spacecraft Freedom 7 on a 15-minute suborbital flight, reaching an altitude of 116½ miles.

Left: During the 1960s, the US space program was geared to fulfilling Kennedy's promise. This picture shows Surveyor 3 in 1967, one of a series of unmanned probes sent to assess the feasibility of landing a manned spacecraft on the surface of the moon.

Below: The Soviet Luna 9, the first spacecraft to achieve a soft landing on the moon. Launched in January 1966, Luna 9 transmitted the first television pictures from the surface of the moon.

To prepare for the moonflights, America launched ten two-man Gemini missions in Earth orbit to master rendezvous and dockings and to test other systems and maneuvers. Flights lasting longer than those planned for Apollo were to be made, as well as the first walks in space outside the spacecraft.

In June 1965, the spacesuited Ed White became the first American to spacewalk. He had followed the Soviet Union's Alexei Leonov, who performed the first spacewalk in March 1965 from Voskhod 2. In December 1965, the separately-launched Geminis 6 and 7 performed the first space rendezvous, featuring four astronauts, Frank Borman, James Lovell, Wally Schirra and Tom Stafford. Borman and Lovell's mission lasted nearly two weeks.

Gemini 8, under the command of Neil Armstrong, made the first space docking with an Agena target rocket in March 1966. This was a simulation of the vital maneuver in lunar orbit during Apollo. Later Gemini missions featured spacewalks lasting longer than two hours and engine re-boosts using the Agena targets' engines. On the Gemini 11 mission in September 1966 two crewmen reached a record altitude of 850 miles. They were high enough to see clearly the curvature of the Earth.

During the Gemini program, in 1965-66, no Russian was launched into space. Although there were initial plans to race America to the moon, these were shelved by the Soviets as technically and financially impossible. They did not entirely disregard the moon for potential future missions after Apollo had been there, however. America did not know at the time that it was racing itself to the moon and in its rush got careless. The first three Apollo astronauts, practising for an Earth orbit test flight, were killed in a spacecraft fire in January 1967. They included the veteran spacewalker, White, and Gus Grissom, who had become the second American in space in

1961 and the first spaceman to make a second journey into space, aboard Gemini 3 in March 1965. Due partly to the need to meet Kennedy's 1969 goal and to a conviction that Russia could beat them to it, America launched Apollo 7 and Apollo 8 in 1968. The pace was getting quite frantic. Apollo 8 became the first manned spacecraft to travel to another body in space when it entered orbit around the moon. At Christmas 1968, the world watched and listened in awe as astronauts Borman, Lovell and William Anders sent back TV pictures of the moon and recited words from Genesis.

Two more Apollo tests were flown in March and May 1969, by Apollo 9 in Earth orbit and Apollo 10 around the moon. All was ready for the lunar landing attempt. By the time Apollo 11 was launched on its historic mission on 16 July 1969 to land the first men on the moon, there was already a slight sense of anti-climax, since this was the third manned flight to the moon.

On July 20th, 1969 the Apollo 11 lunar module, *Eagle* touched down at Tranquility Base with seconds of fuel to spare. Later, Neil Armstrong became the first man to walk on the moon, reciting these words as he placed his left boot into the lunar dust: 'That's one small step for man, one giant leap for mankind.' He did not say 'a man'.

He and Buzz Aldrin, watched live by an enraptured TV audience of over 30 million people all over the world raised a flag and laid out some experiments. Soon, they were taking off to join Michael Collins in the command module, *Columbia* for the flight home. After their return to Earth the three astronauts set off on a glorious but frantic world tour. At the same time, the budget axe was falling and several Apollo landings were cancelled.

It had cost $25 billion to get Armstrong on the moon. The Russians had not been in the race after all. The moon rocks the astronauts brought back revealed interesting

Left: The ill-fated crew of Apollo 1. Virgil Grissom, Edward White II and Roger Chaffee were in the module undergoing a simulated launch on January 27, 1967 when a fire broke out in the spacecraft. In the five minutes it took rescuers to reach them, the three men died from asphyxiation, the first fatalities of the US space program.

Below: Edward White II was the first American to walk in space. This photograph was taken from his craft Gemini 4, in June 1965.

but not startling information. Many people were wondering what all the fuss was about, particularly as the next missions mostly went off like milk runs. Apollos 12, 14, 15, 16 and 17 made landings in 1969-72, with Apollo 13 aborting its flight in 1970.

America had proved its point repeatedly and interest in space was waning. Apollo was a politically motivated program to get to the moon as quickly as possible. That science was taking second place on Apollo was illustrated by the fact that of the 12 men who eventually walked on the moon, 11 were test pilots and only one, Jack Schmitt, flying the last Apollo, was a geologist. Little consideration was given to what to do after the Apollo moon landings. Although Apollo was very expensive and its origins were political, it was an impressive demonstration of just what Man can do. Apollo also amassed a list of vital statistics: 12 men spent 160 man-hours on the moon, covering 60 miles on foot and using roving vehicles; 2196 samples of rock were collected, weighing a total of 850 pounds. The samples were divided into 39,000 pieces and distributed to scientists in 19 countries. The samples actually did not tell us much about the moon that we did not suspect before and although they kept scientists busy for years, the lunar laboratories were eventually closed.

During Apollo, the American space agency NASA had been used to almost carte blanche mega-budgets. NASA needed them to stage such technological orgasms as Apollo. After Apollo NASA announced optimistic plans for a huge space station, a Space Shuttle and eventually manned flights to Mars possibly by 1986. Instead budgets were cut severely and NASA came down to earth as the Apollo euphoria waved. The space station was axed. A cut price Shuttle was authorized and there was to be no race to Mars. Manned spaceflight never seemed quite the same again.

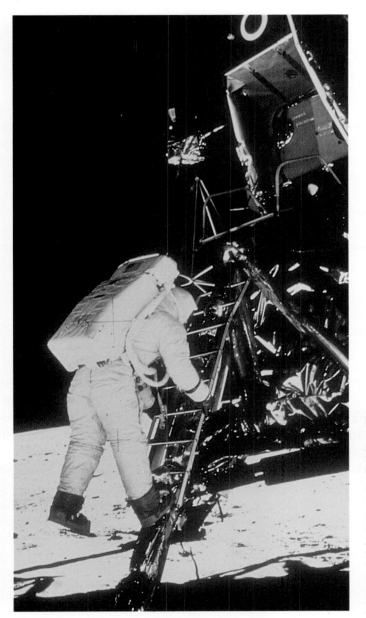

Left & below: The giant leap for mankind, July 20, 1969. Apollo 11 left Earth on July 16th, 1969, and 102 hours later the *Eagle* landed on the moon's Sea of Tranquillity. Mission commander Neil Armstrong (armed with a camera) was the first out of the craft, followed 20 minutes later by Edwin Aldrin, whose initial comment was 'Magnificent desolation'. They collected 44lbs of rocks, set up a solar wind experiment and returned safely to Earth on July 24th.

The Planets

Contrasting sharply with the Apollo program was the extraordinary success of several unmanned spacecraft that ventured much farther than the Moon – to the planets. The first successful planetary explorer was the US Mariner 2, which reached Venus in December 1962. Such was the comparatively rapid progress of unmanned space exploration, that by December 1990 every planet in the solar system except Pluto had been explored. Halley's Comet was also added to the interplanetary conquests by the European spacecraft *Giotto* in March 1986. These spacecraft played a major role in dispelling ideas of life in the solar system.

The enigmatic planet Venus is shrouded in thick cloud and the surface cannot be seen. Because of its size and proximity to the Earth, Venus was dubbed Earth's sister planet. There were even romantic notions that Venus was covered with lush jungle-like vegetation. Mariner 2 flew past Venus sending back information revealing that the temperature of the planet might be a lot hotter than people suspected.

In October 1967, the Soviet Venera 4 spacecraft ejected a capsule into the planet's atmosphere which descended beneath a parachute, with hopes of reaching the surface. The capsule was subjected to enormous atmospheric pressure and very high temperatures. About 27km above the surface it probably broke apart. Readings transmitted from the doomed capsule suggested that the surface temperature was about 500 degrees C and the atmospheric pressure up to 75 times that of Earth's. Thoughts of manned visits to Earth's sister were soon abandoned!

By January 1971, a sufficiently strengthened Venera 7 had survived and reached the surface. Venera 9 and 10 followed in October 1975, returning the first photographs. These were transmitted to the first Venus orbiters acting as data relay spacecraft which re-transmitted the signals to Earth. The photographs revealed a stark desert with flattened, eroded rocks. Later spacecraft returned the first color photos. Soviet and American radar mapping orbiters revealed the stark, parched lands of Venus on a large scale. Images featured huge plateaux the size of continents, deep canyons and many extraordinary geological features.

Another fly-by of Venus was made by Mariner 10 in 1974. Mariner was en route to three fly-bys of Mercury, the closest planet to the sun, in 1975. Photographs from Mariner 10 showed that the hot planet Mercury was remarkably like the Moon.

Early observations of the planet Mars through telescopes were misleading. Observations of what were thought to be canals inspired stories about intelligent life on the so-called Red Planet. During the Space Age, Mars was regarded as the most exciting planet to explore. In July 1965 the US Mariner 4 was the first successful Mars probe. It passed by the planet and took several black and white images, one of which clearly showed a stark, cratered surface and definitely no sign of life.

The spectacular success of Mariner 4 ironically disappointed the romantics. Their hopes were further jolted by Mariner 9, the first spacecraft to orbit the planet, in November 1971. Its image revealed a geologically-active and spectacular planet of canyons and volcanos. Again, no sign of life was detected. Mariner 9 also snapped the first photos of the potato-shaped, pockmarked Martian moons Phobos and Deimos.

There were still hopes that some form of life could be found on the barren, cold surface of Mars. The US Vikings were sent to find out. Arriving in July and September 1976, the Vikings made the first Martian soft landings. Surface pictures revealed a stony red desert. An in-house laboratory on each Viking sampled the surface

Below: The space probe Pioneer 10 is raised into the space simulator chamber. It was launched in March 1972 to conduct the first fly-by of Jupiter, and then to continue into deep space. It transmitted over 300 photographs of Jupiter in November 1973, and in 1987 left the solar system.

Bottom: Photographic proof that Mars really is a red planet. This was transmitted by Viking 2, which landed on Mars on September 3rd, 1976.

but showed no signs of life. Despite this, Mars remains the number one target for an eventual manned expedition. It seems that Man will not be convinced until he has seen for himself.

The next planet from Mars is the giant Jupiter. This was explored for the first time by Pioneer 10 in December 1973. This remarkable American spacecraft was the first to cross the asteroid belt. It revealed a deadly radiation belt around Jupiter as well as taking close-up pictures of the most famous Jovian feature, the Great Red Spot. Pioneer 11 followed a year later and after its fly-by of Jupiter, went on to explore the next planet Saturn in September 1979. To reach Saturn, Pioneer 11 had used the gravitational pull of Jupiter as a 'sling-shot' to divert its flightpath. The spacecraft discovered a new ring system and a new moon around Saturn. Both Pioneers were the first spacecraft to leave the solar system. Pioneer 10 is heading towards the constellation of Taurus, and Pioneer 11 towards the center of our galaxy. Just in case they are intercepted, the spacecraft carry plaques with a message.

These show diagrams of a man and a woman, the solar system and its position relative to 14 pulsars to indicate where the Pioneers came from.

Jupiter and Saturn were also the targets of the remarkable Voyager spacecraft launched by the USA in 1977. Voyager 1 reached Jupiter in March 1979 and Voyager 2 in July the same year. They showed that the giant planet had a ring system and several more moons than at first thought. Extraordinary photographs were returned of the four major moons of Jupiter, including Io. This incredible, sulphurous moon has active volcanoes spewing out debris hundreds of miles into space. If these photos had been obtained in 1969 they would have been greeted in awe by the public. However, the public had become so blasé about space exploration by 1979 that the Jupiter encounter was curiously unheralded.

Sling-shot maneuvers sent the Voyagers on to Saturn which was reached in November 1980 by Voyager 1, and in August 1981 by the second spacecraft. More moons were discovered. Close ups of the ring system showed it

Below: Jupiter's innermost moon, Io, photographed from Voyager 1 in 1979. The circular feature in the center is the active volcano Prometheus. Io is the first body in the solar system (besides Earth) where volcanism has been confirmed.

was made up of thousands of ringlets, comprising small particles of rock and ice. Voyager 1 was pushed out of the solar system by the gravitational effect from Saturn. In the case of Voyager 2, this was used to place it en route for yet another planet, Uranus, in January 1986. The remarkable Voyager 2 was then slung towards Neptune, which it reached in August 1989.

Voyager 2 completed the greatest ever voyage of exploration. It had traveled billions of miles across space, yet even from the distant Neptune – at the time the farthest planet in the solar system – returned spectacular photos. These particularly featured the Neptunian moon Triton, which was described by scientists as the most extraordinary world in the solar system.

Voyager 2's earlier fly-by of Uranus in 1986 had preceded by just four days the *Challenger* space shuttle disaster which killed seven astronauts on January 28. Inevitable comparisons were made between unmanned and manned spaceflight. Voyager 2, 4.5bn kilometers from Earth, relayed spectacular vistas of Uranus. These images were made up of radio signals which traveled 2 hours 45 minutes across the solar system to receiving dishes on Earth. Meanwhile, four days later at just 49,000ft above the Kennedy Space Center on the planet Earth, seven humans lost their lives attempting to make a routine flight into mere Earth orbit.

Voyager 2, of course, was programmed to take certain photos at specific times. If there is something on one of the Uranian moons that would reveal a secret of the Universe, then we will never know because Voyager did not have eyes and a brain like a human. It took what pictures it was commanded to take. By contrast, Apollo 11 would have crashed on the Moon had it been unmanned. Armstrong saw that *Eagle* was heading into a rock strewn crater and would have tipped over and he accordingly intervened and diverted his computer-controlled landing. Other Apollo missions were also saved by the presence of man on board.

Above left: The Uranian moon Ariel was first seen by the English amateur astronomer William Lassell in 1851. This picture was taken by Voyager 2 in 1986.

Above: Voyager 1's journey to Saturn greatly increased scientific understanding of the planet. Voyager passed within 63,000 miles of Saturn on August 25th, 1981.

Beyond the Solar System

The remarkable Voyagers may be en route out of the solar system but they will not reach the stars for thousands of years. Voyager 2 will pass within 0.8 light years of the bright star Sirius in 358,000 years time. For the present, exploration of the stars, galaxies and other astronomical phenomena can only be made by telescopic observations. The Earth's atmosphere acts like a filter of light. It is rather like lying at the bottom of a swimming pool trying to look out. Taking a telescope out of the atmosphere into space improves things enormously, as the first space observatories proved.

Astronomers have discovered more about black holes, pulsars, quasars and other phenomena using Earth orbiting observatories. The first major space observatory was the Orbiting Astronomical Observatory (OAO) in 1972. The Hubble Space Telescope, deployed by the Space Shuttle in 1990, is returning extremely exciting photos despite an imaging system problem because of manufacturing errors that caused NASA much embarrassment when this was first discovered.

Starships are obviously out for the immediate future. Capt Kirk and the *Enterprise* will have to continue to be consigned to the realms of science fiction. What of manned flights to the planets? It seems highly likely that a manned expedition to Mars will be mounted in around 2020. There will be several hazards, including the gigantic costs and long periods of weightlessness and isolation involved. A trip to Mars and back could last two years. In preparation for the long periods of weightlessness and isolation involved, the Soviet Union has flown several long duration flights in Earth orbit. These have been made aboard space stations, such as Mir. Cosmonauts Vladimir Titov and Musa Manarov stayed up for a record 366 days in 1987-88. The American record of just 84 days was achieved by three astronauts aboard the Skylab space station in 1974.

Return to Earth

One of the ironies of space exploration is that in going out, 'where no man has gone before', we have been able to look back towards the Earth and see it as it is really is in the vastness and blackness of space: a tiny but beautiful blue planet; a fragile sphere dependent on the sun for energy and light and a tenuous atmosphere for life.

When the first photos of the Earth taken by the Apollo astronauts as they traveled to and from the Moon were released, the people of the Earth could see for the first time what the privileged space traveler could see. It generated in many people the same feelings as in the Apollo astronauts themselves. The Earth and Universe could not just have happened. They were created by a being surpassing our understanding. That some of the first words spoken from the moon were 'In the beginning, God made the heaven and the Earth', seemed very apt.

The view of the fragile planet Earth in deep space, with no national boundaries marked out, emphasised the fact that the human race is one. Yet despite this there are wars, conflicts and terrorism. There is extraordinary inequality in the conditions of life. Some people starve while others gorge themselves. Pollution ravages the environment and has now even pierced our protective atmosphere's ozone layer. The view of Earth from space has become a symbol for the Green environmental movement. If the Earth is a spaceship then its life support system – and its crew – need to be managed carefully. Our exploration of space has shown that Man could conceivably fly to one of the planets but not much farther. Our view of the Earth as a result of space exploration shows that Man could perhaps be better off looking after his home planet.

Below: This view of Earth from space was one of the simplest, yet most awe-inspiring achievements of the space program.

Select Bibliography

A full bibliography of exploration would fill many volumes. Listed below are only the major works consulted during the preparation of this book.

General

Delpar, Helen, ed., *The Discoverers*: McGraw Hill (New York), 1980
Newby, Eric, *The World Atlas of Exploration*: Mitchell Beazley, 1975
Reid, Alan, *Discovery and Exploration*: Gentry Press, 1980
Time-Life, eds., *The World's Wild Places* (many volumes): Time-Life Books (Amsterdam), 1973/4
Tourtellot, Jonathan, ed., *Into the Unknown*: National Geographic Society (New York), 1987

Chapter 1

Cameron, Ian, *Lodestone and Evening Star*: Hodder & Stoughton, 1965
Cary, M. and Warmington, E.H., *The Ancient Explorers*: Methuen, 1929
Fox, Robin Lane, *Alexander the Great*: Penguin, 1973
Gaubert, H., *Necho et le Circumnavigation d'Afrique*: Geographia (Paris), 1955
Mirsky, Jeanette, *The Great Chinese Travellers*: Allen & Unwin, 1965

Chapter 2

Ashe, Geoffrey, *Land to the West*: Collins, 1962
Beaglehole, J.C., *The Exploration of the Pacific*: A. & C. Black, 1947
The Journals of Captain Cook: Cambridge University Press, 1967
Bellwood, Peter, *The Polynesians*: Thames & Hudson, 1984
Bougainville, L.A. de, *Voyage autour du Monde . . .* (Paris) 1771
Bradford, Ernle, *Southward the Caravels*: Hutchinson, 1961
Brebner, John, *The Explorers of North America*: A. & C. Black, 1933
Cameron, Ian, *Antarctica*: Cassell, 1974
Magellan: Weidenfeld & Nicholson, 1974
Christie, E.W. Hunter, *The Antarctic Problem*: Allen & Unwin, 1971
Golder, Frank A., Tr. and Ed., *Bering's Voyages*: American Geographical Society (New York), 1922/5
Graham-Campbell, J., *The Viking World*: Lincoln Press, 1989
Landstrom, Bjorn, *Columbus*: Allen & Unwin, 1967
The Ship: Allen & Unwin, 1961
Prestage, Edgar, *The Portuguese Pioneers*: A. & C. Black, 1933
Sharp, Andrew, *The Discovery of the Pacific Islands*: Clarendon Press, 1960
The Voyages of Abel Tasman: Oxford University Press, 1968
Stackpole, E.A., *The Sea Hunters*: Lippincott (New York), 1953
Whales and Destiny: Lippincott (New York), 1972

Chapter 3

Blunt, Wilfred, *The Golden Road to Samarkand*: Hamish Hamilton, 1973
Cornell, T. and Matthews, J., *Atlas of the Roman World*: Phaidon Press, 1982
Doughty, Charles (ed. H.L. Macritchie), *Arabia Deserta* (2 vols.): Bloomsbury, 1989
Harrisson, Tom, ed., *Borneo Jungle*: Lindsay Drummond, 1938
Mason, Kenneth, *Abode of Snow*: Diadem Books, 1987
McGrail, S., *Ancient Boats in North West Europe*: Longman, 1987
Phillimore, R.H., *The Historical Records of the Survey of India*: Dehra Dun (India), 1945
Thesiger, Wilfred, *Arabian Sands*: Longman, 1959
Yu, Anthony C., *The Journey to the West*: University of Chicago Press, (Chicago) 1977
Wessels, C.J., *Early Jesuit Travellers in Central Asia*: M. Nijhof (The Hague), 1924

Chapter 4

Baker, Samuel, *The Albert N'yanza*, 1866

Burton, Richard, *The Lake Regions of Central Africa*, 1860
Caillié, René, *Journal d'un Voyage à Temboctou et à Jenne dans l'Afrique Central* (3 vols.) (Paris), 1830
Gibb, H.R.A., ed., *The Travels of ibn Battuta*: Hakluyt Society II, 1958-71
Hall, Richard, *Lovers on the Nile*: Collins, 1980
Stanley: an Adventurer Explored, Collins, 1974
Hibbert, Christopher, *Africa Explored*: Alan Lane, 1982
Huxley, Elspeth, *Livingstone and his African Journeys*: Weidenfeld and Nicolson, 1974
Lander, John and Richard, *Journal of an Expedition to Explore the Course and Termination of the Niger* (3 vols.), 1832
Livingstone, David, *Missionary Travels and Researches in South Africa*: 1857
Narrative of an Expedition to the Zambezi and its Tributaries, 1865
Moorehead, Alan, *The Blue Nile*: Hamish Hamilton, 1962, *The White Nile*: Hamish Hamilton, 1960
Walker, Eric, *The Great Trek*: A. &. C. Black, 1938

Chapter 5

Billington, Ray Alan, *Westward Expansion*: Macmillan, 1960
Brebner, John, *The Explorers of North America*: A. & C. Black, 1933
Brogan, Hugh, *Longman History of the United States of America*: Longman, 1985
Cowes, Elliott, *History of the Expedition under the Command of Lewis and Clark* (4 vols): (New York), 1893
Delanglez, Jean, *Life and Voyages of Louis Jolliet*: Institute of Jesuit History Publications, (Chicago), 1948
Elliott, H.W., *An Arctic Province: Alaska and the Seal Islands*, 1886
Heiderich, C.E., *Explorations and Mappings of Samuel de Champlain*: York University (U.S.), 1976
Innes, Hammond, *The Conquistadors*: Collins, 1969
Karamanski, Theodore J., *Fur Trade and Expansion*: University of Oklahoma Press (U.S.) 1953
Madariaga, Salvador de, *Hernan Cortes, Conqueror of Mexico*: Hodder & Stoughton, 1941
Meinig, D.W., *Atlantic America: 1492-1800*: Yale University Press (U.S.), 1986
Morison, Samuel Eliot, *The European Discovery of America*: Oxford University Press, 1971
Newman, Peter C., *Company of Adventurers*: Viking, 1985
Prescott, William Hickling, *The Conquest of Mexico*, 1843
Stuart, R. and Ashton, R., *The Discovery of the Oregon Trail*: Charles Scribner (New York) 1935

Chapter 6

Agostini, Alberto De, *Trent anni nella Terra del Fuoco*: Societa Editrice Internazional (Turin), 1955
Bates, Henry W., *The Naturalist on the River Amazon*: Dent, 1969
Bingham, Hiram, *Inca Land: Exploration in the Highlands of Peru*: Houghton Mifflin (New York), 1922
Fitzgerald, Edward, *The Highest Andes*: Methuen, 1899
Garcilaso de la Vega el Inca, *Royal Commentaries of the Incas*: University of Texas Press (U.S.), 1966
Hemming, John, *The Conquest of the Incas*: Macmillan, 1970
The Search for El Dorado: Michael Joseph, 1978
Humboldt, A. Von. *Personal Narrative of Travels to the Equinoctial Regions of the New Continent, 1794-1804*, trans. H.M. Williams, 7 vols., 1814
La Condamine, C.M. de, *Relation abrégée d'un voyage fait dans l'interior de l'Amerique meridionale* (Paris), 1745
Mason, Alden, *The Ancient Civilisations of Peru*: Penguin, 1957

Chapter 7

Colwell, Max, *Whaling Around Australia*: Angus & Robertson, 1970
Eyre, Edward John, *Journal of Expeditions of Discovery into Central Australia . . . and to King George's Sound*, 1845
Feeken, E.H.J., and Spate, O.H.K., *The Discovery and*

Exploration of Australia: Nelson, 1971
Flinders, Matthew, *A Voyage to Terra Australis . . .* (2 vols.) 1814
Hastings, P., ed., *Prospero's Other Island*: Angus and Robertson, 1963
Leichhardt, Ludwig, *Journal of an Overland Expedition . . . from Morton Bay to Port Essington*, 1847
Moorehead, Alan, *Cooper's Creek*: Hamish Hamilton, 1963
Simpson, Colin, *Adam in Ochre*: Praeger, 1953
Plumes and Arrows, Angus and Robertson, 1963
Stuart, John McDouall, *The Journals of John McDouall Stuart . . .* 1864
Sturt, Charles, *Two Expeditions into the Interior of Southern Australia*, 1833
Taylor, N.H., *Early Travellers in New Zealand*, Oxford University Press, 1959

Chapters 8 and 9

Amundsen, Roald, *The South Pole* (2 vols.): John Murray, 1912
My Life as an Explorer: Heinemann, 1927
Byrd, Richard Evelyn, *Antarctic Discovery*: Putnam (New York) 1936
Little America: Putnam (New York), 1938
Cook, Frederick, *Through the First Antarctic Night*: C. Hurst, 1980
My Attainment of the Pole, Polar Publishing Co., 1911
Debenham, Frank, ed., *The Voyage of Captain Bellingshausen to the Antarctic Seas, 1819-21*
De Long, G.W., (ed., Emma De Long) *The Voyage of the Jeannette*, 1883
Dufek, George, J., *Operation Deep Freeze*: Harcourt Brace (New York), 1957
Dumont D'Urville, S.J.C., *Voyage au Pôle Sud et dans l'Oceanie sur les corvettes l'Astrolabe et la Zelée . . .* (Paris), 1841-54
Fisher, J. and M., *Shackleton*: James Barrie, 1957
Freuchen, Peter, *The Book of the Eskimos*: A. Barker, 1961
Fuchs, Vivian and Hillary, Edmund, *The Crossing of Antarctica*: Cassell, 1960
Gerlache de Gomery, Adrien de, *Quinze Mois dans l'Antartique*: Brussels, 1902
Hearne, Samuel (ed., R. Glover), *A Journey from Hudson's Bay to the northern ocean for the discovery . . . of a North West Passage*: Macmillan, 1958
Herbert, Wally, *The Noose of Laurels*: Hodder & Stoughton, 1989
Huntford, Roland, *Shackleton*: Hodder & Stoughton, 1985, *Scott and Amundsen*: Hodder & Stoughton, 1979
Kirwan, Laurence, P., *A History of Polar Exploration*: Penguin, 1962
Mackenzie, Alexander, *Voyages . . . through the Continent of North America to the Frozen and Pacific Oceans*: Radisson Society (Canada) 1927
Mountfield, David, *A History of Polar Exploration*: Hamlyn, 1974
Nansen, Fridtjof, *Farthest North*: Constable, 1897
In Northern Mists: Heinemann, 1911
Nordenskiold, Nils, (trans. A. Leslie) *Voyage of the Vega round Asia and Europe*, 1885
Nordenskiold, Otto, *Antarctica*: Hurst & Co., 1977
Owen, Roderic, *The Fate of Franklin*: Hutchinson, 1978
Peary, Robert E., *Northwest over the Great Ice*: Methuen, 1898
The North Pole: Hodder & Stoughton, 1910
Rae, John, *Narrative of an Expedition to the Shores of the Arctic Ocean, 1846 and 1847*: T. & W. Boone, 1850
Ross, James Clark, *A Voyage of Discovery and Research in the Southern and Antarctic Regions*, 1847
Scott, Robert F., *The Voyage of the Discovery*: John Murray, 1929
Scott's Last Expedition ed. L. Huxley: Smith Elder, 1913
Shackleton, Ernest, *The Heart of the Antarctic*: Heinemann, 1911
Veer, Gerrit de, *The Three Voyages of William Barents*: Hakluyt Society LIV, 1876
Wilkes, Charles, *Narrative of the United States Exploring Expedition 1838-1842*: Philadelphia, 1845

Index

Page numbers in italics refer to illustrations.

Aboriginees, 203-4, 210, 215-21, 223
Abrue, Antonio d', 224
Advance (American ship), 245
Adventure (English ship), 60
Africa, 14-20, 24-5, 90 95, *97-122*, 98-123; collision with Europe, 202; Europe/India sea route, 39-41; Greek and Roman imperialism, 72, 98, *99-100*; South, 57, 106-19
Aguilar, Geronimo de, 128
Al Hariri: *Magamat*, *24*
Al Idrisi: world map by, *24*
Alaska, *64-5*, 65-7, 145, 230-1, 238; Imperial Russia, 155-7, 160, 254
Alberquerque, Afonso de, 42
Albert, lake *see* Luta Nzigé
Aldrin, Buzz, *287*, 294
Aleutians, mountains and islands, 65-7, 155-7, 231, 254
Aleuts, Indians, 65, 126, 231, 236
Alexander the Great, 20-3, *21-2*, 72, 83
Alexandrina, lake, 216
Allumette, lake, 143
Almagro, Diego de, 180-2, *183*
Alsea, river, 62
Alvarado, Pedro de, 133
Amazon, 94, 174, 177, 185, 189-93, 198
Amazon, river, 174, 180-1, 183-4, 190
American continent, 43-5, *53*, 53, 126-99; before Columbus, 14, 32, 36-7, *238*, 230; Pacific/Atlantic link, 45, 58; separation from Asia, 65-6, 128
American Fur Company, 164
American Indians: Central, 43-4, *126-7*, 126, 128, *130-2*, 131-1; North, 38, 53, 65, 126, 133-68, *158*, *161*, *163*; South, 126, *174-8*, 174-84, *180-1*, *192-4*, 192-9, *see also* Aleuts: Aztecs: Incas
Amsterdam 231 (Dutch ship), 204
Amundsen, Roald, *244*, 244, 248, *263*, *272*, 260-6, 275
Anadyr, river, 231
Andes, 15, *173-5*, 174-82, 185-6, 189-97, *195-9*
Anson, Admiral George, 209
Antarctic Circle, 60, 68, 256, 260
Antarctic (Swedish ship), 262-3
Antartic Peninsula, 254, 260, 262-3, *274*
Antartic Treaty (1961), 275
Antartica, 28, 53, 57, 65, 68-9, *213-75*, 254-75; separation from Australia, 202-3
Appalachians, mountains, 135-6, 150, 157
Arctic, 28, 66-7, *67*, 154, *230-51*, 230-51; British exploration, 57, 65, 232-3, *236-44*, 236-44, *251*; Dutch exploration, 49, *232-3*, 233-4
Arctic Circle, 36, 66, 185
Arctic Council, *230*
Arctowski, Henryk, 260
Aristotle, 21, 282, 288
Arkansas: river 146, 168
Armijo, Antonio, 170
Armstrong, Neil, 293, 294, *295*
Arrian (historian), 22
arrows, poisoned, 103-4, 116, 122-3, 192
Ashley, Henry, 164
Asia, 8-11, 14, 20-5, 28-30, 43-4; discovering separation from America, 65-6, 128; prehistoric, 14, 126, 202
Assassins, Valley of, *79*, 79
Astrea (Spanish ship), 186
Astrolabe (French corvette), *256-7*, 256-7
astronomy, *11*, 20-2, 25, 28, 32, 45, 58, 288
Atacama Desert, 178-9, 182, 189-90
Atahualpa, Inca emperor, 133, *180*, 180
Athabaska, lake, 237
Atka (American icebreaker), 275
Atkinson, Thomas, 88
Atlantic islands, 23, 32-6, 39-40, 43, 186-7, 281; South Georgia, 61, 256, 170-1; South Orkney, 68, 256; South Shetlands, 68, 254, 256, 270-2, *see also* Bahamas: West Indies
Atlantic Ocean, 53, 60-1, 67, 154; before Columbus, 18, 23, 25, 29, 32-46; North Atlantic Bloom, 285; Pacific link, 46, 50, 61, 65, 138
Atlas Mountains, 72, 101
Atrevida (Spanish ship), 168
Augustus, Roman Emperor, 25, 72-3
Aurora (British ship), 268
Australia, 24-5, 52, 59-60, *64*, 68, *201-23*, 203-23; first European sighting, 55; prehistoric, 14, 202; studies of dolphins, 285; Torres Strait, 49, 60
Ayala, Poma de: manuscript of, 178
Ayres Rock, Australia, 223
Aztecs, 126-33, *127*, *130-2*
Azuraza, Enea de: miniature by, *40*

Back, George, 242
Back (Great Fish), river, 238, 243
Baffin Bay, *229*, 245
Baffin Island, 37, 239-41
Baffin, William, 240
Bahamas, 32, 34, 43
Baja California, 133, 138
Baker, Samuel and Florence, 90, 115-18, *116*
Balboa, Vasco Nunex de, 127-8, *128-9*
Baltic Sea, 23, 65, 75-6, 230
Banks, Sir Joseph, 59
Baranov Island, 155, *156*
Barcoo, river, 220
Barents Sea, 232
Barents, Willem, 49, *233*, 233-4
Barrow, Cape, 238
Barth, Heinrich, *105*, 106
Barton, Otis, 279, *280*
Bass, George, 212
Batavia (Dutch Ship), 205-6
Batavia, Indonesia, 50-2, *51*, 60, 204-5
Bates, Henry Walter, 192-3, 222
bathyspheres, 279-80, *281*
Baudin, Charles, 55
Bauer, Ferdinand (artist), *214-15*, 214
Bazin, Ernst, 279
Beagle, HMS (English ship), *190-1*, 190-1
Bear Island, *232*
bears, 90, 154, 161, 164; polar, *67*, 235, 241
Beaufort, Francis, *230*
beavers, 53, 138, 143-5, 150, 154, 239
Becknell, William, 168
Beebbe, William, 279, *280*
Belgica (Belgian ship), 260-1
Belle Isle, Strait of, 55, 139
Bellingshausen, Thaddeus von, 254, 256
Bellwood, Peter (historian), 30
Bengal, Bay of, 24, 87
Berchervaise, John, 254
Bering Sea, 156, 187
Bering Strait, 14, 66-8, 231, 236, 244, 248, 254
Bering, Vitus, 65-7, *66*, 155, 231
Beringa island, 66-7
Bidwell, John, 170
Bierstadt, Albert: painting by, *168*
Bigham, G.C.: painting by, *160*
Billington, Ray Allen: mission stations, 168
Bingham, Hiram, *196*, 196-7
birds, 25, 32-3, 37, *55*, 101; collecting/classifying, 90, 94, 192, 199, 224; evolution, 32-3, 191; penguins, 60, *260*, 262
Bishop, Iain, 199
Bismarck Archipelago, 50-1
bison, 126, 137, 146, 154-7, 161
Black Hills, S. Dakota, 164
Black Sea, 18, 20, *21*, 22, 75-6
Blaxland, Gregory, 215
blindness, 113, 186, 218, 221; snowblindness, 21, 196, 239, 262
Blue Mountains, Australia, 215
Blue Mountains, Oregan, 170, 215
Bojador, Cape, 39-41
Bolivar, Simon: Humboldt, 190
Bona Confidentia (British ship), 232
Bona Esperanze (British ship), 232
Bond, George (naval researcher), 284
Bonpland, Aimé, 189
Boone, Daniel, 135, *157-8*, 157-9, 164
Boothia, Gulf of, 239, 242
Borman, Frank, 293
Botany Bay, *59*, 59, *206*, 209
Bougainville, Louis Antoine de, *8*, 55-6, *57*, 208, 224
Bourne, William: submersible boats, 281
Boyd (whaling ship), 226
Bradford, Ernle: Henry the Navigator, 41
Bradford, William: painting by, *35*
Bradford, William (Pilgrim Father), 152
Brahmaputra, river, 85, 87
Bransfield, Edward, 254
Braun, Dr. Wernher von (engineer), 290
Brendan, Saint, 32-4, *33*
Britain, 23, 36-8, 58, *72*, 72, 121, 138
Brogan, Hugh: *History of the United States of America*, 159
Brouwer, Hendrik, 204
Brown, Robert (botanist), *214*, 214
Bruce, James, *111-12*, 111-12
Brule, Etienne, *143*
Brunner, Thomas, 225
Buanaventura (legendary river), 166
Buddhism, 73, *75*, 76, *84*, 84, *86-7*
Burke, Robert, *201*, 216-17
Burnett, Peter, 170
Burton, Richard, *112-14*, 113-15
Bushnell, David (submarine designer), 281
Byrd, Richard, *272*, 273-5

Cabot, John, *53*, 53, *58*, *138*, 138, 239, 244
Cabral, Pedro Alvares, 42
Caillie, René, *102*, 104-5, *105*
Calcias (tribe), 83
California, Gulf of, 133, 137
California (New Albion), 58, 62, 138, 156, 160, *169*, 278; Death Valley, *165*, 166
California trail, 168, 170
Callao, Peru, 48, 186-7, *205*
camels, 89-90, 102, 105-6, 127; in Australia, 216, 221-2, *222*
cannabis (*hash-hish*), 79
cannibalism, 149, 236, 239, 243, 245; Maori, 226; "riverside cannibals", 122-3
canoes, 103-5, 116, 147, 154, 161-2; bark, 143, 145, 236-8; pirogues, 161; Polynesian, 30
Cao, Diego, 41
Cape Cod, Massachussets, 38, 151
caravels, *39*, 39-41, 43, 98
Cardenas, Garcia de, 137
Carib Indians, 43-4
Caribbean, the, 28, 34, 43-4, *52*, 135, 174; sugar, 154
Carpentaria, Gulf of, 52, 214, *217*, 217, 221
Cartier, Jacques, 53-5, *54-5*, *139-40*, 139-42, 153 239
cartography, *28*, 28-9, 45, 48, *55*, 58, 60, *64*, 65-6; aerial surveying, 157, 261, *273*; Africa, 99, 116, *120*, 121-2; Asia, 86-7, 92, 95; Australasia, 214-15, 221, 225; early exploration, 18, 22-3, *24*, 25; establishing Earth's shape, 185; Matteo Ricci's maps, *84-5*; N. America, 138, *152*, 156-7, 160, 163; polar regions, 238, 240, 242-3, 254-8, 261-3, 273; S. America, 185-7, 190, 192, 198; Vinland map, 37-9, *38*
Carvajal, Gspar de, 184
Caspian Sea, 73, 75-6
Cecilia (American brig), 68-9
Central Mount Sturt, Australia, 217
Chad, lake, 72, 99, 103
Challenger (British naval vessel), 278
Challenger (space shuttle), 298
Champlain, lake, 142-3
Champlain, Samuel de, 55, *141*, 142-3
Chancellor, Richard, 232
Chang Jiang, river, 25
Charbonneau, Toussaint, 161
Charles Darwin (research vessel), 285
Charles II: King of Great Britain, 144-5
Charles III: King of Spain, 186
Charles IV: King of Spain, 188-9
Charles, lake, *134*
Charles V: Holy Roman Emperor (Charles I of Spain), 45, 279
Chatelaine: *Atlas Historique*, *101*
Chelyuskin, Cape, 231, 235
Chesapeake Bay, Maryland, 127, 148-50
Chile: "Vales of Paradise", 177-8, 183
China, 15, 42, 44, 79-84, *80-2*, 88-9, *89*, 141; early history, 72-7; Great Wall of, 24, 72-6, *74*, *80*, 81-4; Han dynasty, 24; Ming dynasty, *25*, *78*; search for Europe through America sea route, 138, 141-2
Chobe river, 119
Christianity, 39, 43, 48, 83, 94, 118, 168
Chukchi, nomadic tribe, 231, 235-6
Church Missionary Society, 226
Churchill, river, 154, 237
Cibola, Seven Cities of, 136-7
Clapperton: Hugh, *103-4*, 103
Clark, William, 159-61, *161*, 171
Clearwater, river, 162
coal, 82, 88-9, 157, 161
Coetree, W.H.: sketch by, *107*
Colenzoo, William, 226
colonization, 20, 22, 35, 38, 44, 230; Africa, 39, 57; America, 43, *54*, 55-7, 133, *135*, 148-54, 168-71; Australasia, 57, 206, 209-10, *211*, 221, 225
Colorado Desert, 170
Colorado, river, 137, 138, 166
Columbia, Command module, 289
Columbia river, 162-3, 166, 170
Columbus, Christopher, 15, 24, 28, 43-5, *45*
Comogre, Indian chief, 127
Confucianism, 25
Congo, river, 118, 121-3
Congreve: Sir William, 289
Conibear, Frank: beavers, 144
conservation, 94, 123, 198-9
"Conshelf" diving experiments, 284-5
Cook, Capt. James, *10*, 15, 28-32, 58-65, *60*; Australasia, 59-61, *63*, 203, 206-8, 224-5, *226*
Cock, Dr. Frederick, *10*, *240*, *247*, 247-8, 260-1
Cook Inlet, Alaska, 155, 157
Cooper's Creek, 216
Copernicus, Nicholas, *288*, 288
Coppermine, river, 236-8, 242
coral, 24, 59, 278; sea, 34
Coronado, Francisco Vasquez de, *136*, 136-8, 148
Coronation Gulf 236, 238
Cortes, Hernando, 128-33, *129-30*, *132*
Cousteau, Cap. Jacques-Yves, *284-5*, 285
Covilhao, Pedro de, 94-5
Craterus, 20
Croker mountains (mythical range), 241
Cross, Cape, Namibia, 41
currents: Agulhas, 98; Benguela, 20, 41; Guinea Drift, 20; Gulf Stream, 234; Mozambique, 20; north equatorial (Canary), 17, 39, 98; Peruvian, 189; polar, 250, 254
Cuzco, 177-8, 180-1, *182*, 196

da Gama, Vasco *see* Gama: Vasco da
D'Albertis, Luigi, 224-5
Daly, river, 221
Dampier, William, *53*, *205*, 224
Daniell, Samuel: painting by, *108*
Danube basin, migration from, 20
Darius, King of Persia, 21
Darling, river and basin, 215-16, 219
Darwin, Charles, 65, 94, 190-1
Davis, John, 240
Davis, John (New England sealer), 68-9, 256
Davis Strait, 240
De Agostini, Alberto, 197-8
de Gerlache, Adrien, 260-1
De Long, George Washington, 248, *249*, 250
De Niza, Marcos, 136
De Soto, Hernando, *133-4*, 133-8, *136*
Dease, Peter Warren, 238
Debenham, Professor Frank, 23
Denakil (tribe), 95
Denham, Major Dixon, 103
D'Entrecasteaux: Bruni, 55, 225
Descubierta (Spanish ship), 186
Detroit, river, 145
Dezhnev, Semeon, 231
Dias, Bartolemeu, *40*, 41
Diderot, Denis: people of Tahiti, 56
diet: Africa, 119; Australasia, 219; early land exploration, 21-2; early sea voyages, 32, 50, 59; polar regions, 241, 246, 250-1, 263-5, 268, *see also* starvation
Dilolo: lake, 119
Discovery (English ship), 61-2, *62*, 65, 240, 261
disease *see* ill health
diving, 278-85, *279*
Dnieper, river, 76
doldrums, 28
Dombey, Joseph (botanist), 186
"Dona Marina" (Aztec slavegirl), 128-9
Donnaconna (Huron chief), 141
Donner, George and Jacob, 170
D'Orville, Father Albert, 83-5
Doughty, Charles: *Arabia Deserta*, *95*, 95
Drake, Charles Tyrwhitt: painting by, *113*
Drake, Sir Francis, 49, *57-8*, 57-8, 68
Drakensberg Mountains, 106, 108, *109-10*
Drygalski, Erich von, 261
D'Urville, Jules Dumont, 225, 256-7, 260
Dutch East India Company, 49, 51-2, *53*, 204

Eagle (British warship), 281
Eagle (lunar module), 294, 298
Eannes: Gil, *40*, 40-1
East India Company, 58
Edward Bonaventure (British ship), 232
Eendracht (Dutch ship), 49-50
El Dorado (mythical land of gold), 49, 183-4
Elias, Mount, 66
Elizabeth 1, England, 40, 57-8
Ellesmere Island, 245, 246, 247
Elliot: *Alaska and the Seal Islands*, 155
Emin Pasha, *122*
Encyclopaedia Britannica: deep water voyaging, 29
Endeavour (English bark), 58-9, *59*, 206, *209*
Endurance (British ship), *268*, 268, *275*
Entrecasteaux, Bruni d', 55, 225
Erebus (bombship), *243*, 243-4, *258*, 250-60
Erebus, Mount, 260
Eric the Red, 36, *37*
Eriksfjord, Greenland, 37
Eriksson, Leif, 37, 37-8
Ermillon (French Ship), 139
Eskimos, 37, 231, 236-47, 250
Euphrates, river, 21
Eurasia, 25, 60, 66, 72-95, 102, 231; *see also* Asia: Europe
Europe, 14, 18, 20, 22-5, 35-6; collision with Africa, 202; sea route to India, 42; spread of plague, 39; transporting fish to, 53
Evans, Cape, *266*
Everest, Mount *71*, 84-5, *90*, *92-3*, 92
evolution: theory of, 94, 190-1, 193
Eyre, Edward John, *11*, *218*, 218

Fairchild monoplane, *273*, 273-4
Farewell, Cape, 36, 225
fauna: Africa, 17, 103-4, *104*, 116, 119, 123; Arctic, *67*, 67, *230*, 230-1, 234-5, 239-41; Asia, 89-90, 94; Australasia, 8, 25, *55*, 203, *208*, 214, 285; Galapagos, 190-1; N. America, 126, 154, 161, 163, 166; S. America, 190, 192-3, 199, *see also*

birds: reptiles: fish: camels: bison: bears: whales
Fedchenko, Alexis and Olga, 88-9
fish, 32, 34, 185, 189, 199; Arctic, 230; cod, 153-4, 230, 239, 254; Grand Banks, Newfoundland, 53, 138; Great Bank, New England, 153-4; Great Barrier Reef, 203; poisonous, 49; salmon, 155, 162, 230
Fisher, H.A.L.: European intellectual revolution, 82
FitzGerald, Edward, 195-6
Flateyiarbok (saga), 37
Flattery, Cape, 208
Flecker, James Elroy *The Golden Journey to Samarkand*, 8
Flinders, Matthew, 212-14, *213*
floatplanes, 225
flora: Africa, 41, 119; Asia, 88-9; Australasia, 59, 203, 214; evolution of, 174; N. America, 163, 166; S. America, 174, 186-7, *187*, 189, 192, *199*, 199, *see also* rain forests
Floyd Bennet (monoplane), *273*, 273-4
Forrest, John, 218, 223
Foveaux Strait, 225
Fox, river, 146
Fram (Norwegian ship), 250-1, 263-4, *265*
France, 22-3, 32, 36-8, *37*, 138
Francis I: King of France, 139
Franklin, Sir John, *230*, 236-9, *242*, 242-3, *244*
Freycinet, Louis Claude de Saulies de, 55
Frobisher, Sir Martin, *236*, 236, *239*, 239-50
Fuchs, Vivian, *271*, 272-3
Fundy, Bay of, 151
fur trade: American, 157, *160*, 164, 168-70; French, 53-5, 138, 142-6, *144-5*, *147*, 154; Russian, 67, 155, *156*, 157, 231; Viking, 75, *see also* seal hunting

Gagarin, Yuri, *291*, 291-2
Gagnan, Emile, 285
Galilei, Galileo, 288, *289*
Gallus, Aelius, 73, 94
Gama, Vasco da, 24-5, *41-2*, 41-2
Game Preservation Department, 123
Gandon, P.: painting by, *55*
Ganges, river, 75, 78, 85
Garcas, Father Francisco, 137
Garrett, Rev. George, *278*
Garry, Cape, *242*
Gaspé Bay, New Brunswick, *139*, 139
Gauss (German ship), 261
Genghiz Khan, 76-8, 80
Geographical Society of Paris, 105
Gerlache, Adrien de, 260-1
Gerlache Strait, 69, *274*
German Society of Space Travel (*Verein fur Raumshiffahrt*), 290
Gibraltar, Straits of, 18, 23, 29
Gibson Desert, 222
Gila, river, 138
Giles, Ernest, 8, 223
Gill, S.T., *221*
Gjoa (Norwegian ship), *244*, 244
glaciers, 88; Beardmore, 268; Humboldt, 245; Rongbuk, 92; Satan's, 263; Skeleton, 272
Glazunov, Andrey, 157
Glenn, John, 292
Goddard, Prof. Robert, *290*, 290
Godin, Louis, *185*, 185
Goes, Bento de, 83
gold, 15-17, 20, 24, 48-9, 75-6; African, 102, 111; Australasia, 205, 223, 225-6; N. American, 67, 88-9, 126-30, 133, 135-8, 157; S. American, 44, 58, 181; undersea, 278
Golden Seahorse: (Dutch ship), 204
Gomes, Diogo, 41
Good Hope, Cape of, 18, 20, 25, 58, *69*, *107*
Goodman: *Explorers of South America*, 192
Gosse, William, 223
Gottfried: *Newve Welt*, *205*
Graham, W.W., *9*, 90
Grand Canyon, *137*, 137
Grand, river, 146
Grand Hermyne (French ship), 139
Grant, James, 114
Gray, Charles, 216
Great Australian Bight, 204
Great Barrier Reef, 59-60, 203
Great Bear Lake, 238
Great Dividing Range, 220
Great Fish (Back) River, N.W. Territories, 238, 243
Great Fish River: S. Africa, 41
Great Lakes, 143-6, 154, 230, 237; Erie, 145-6; Huron, 143, 145, 146; Michigan, 136, 146; Ontario, 146; Superior, 145, 150
Great Salt Lake and Desert, 166, 170
Great Sandy Desert, 222
Great Slave Lake, 236, 237
Great Trigonometrical Survey of India, 86
Greek legends *Illiad* and *Oddyssey*, 20
Greeley, Major Horace: NY: *Tribue*, 170
Greely, Adolphus Washington, 245, 248
Greenland, *32*, 32, 36-9, *37-8* 145; aerial survey, 273; Arctic exploration, 236, 239-40, 245-7, 280
Gregory, Augustus and Frank, 218, 221
Grenville, Richard, 148
Griper (British brig), 241
Grissom, Gus, 293-4
Groseillers: Medard Chouart Sieur de, *144*, 144-5
Grueber, Father Johann, 83-5
Guardafue, Cape, 17
Guinea, Gulf of, 20

Hakuho Maru (Japanese research vessel), 285
Hall, Charles Francis, 245
Halley, Edmund, 279
Hanbury-Tenison, Robin, 94
Hansa (ship), 248
Hansen, Lt., *263*, *264*
Harmony (Dutch ship), 204
Harrison, Tom, *60*, *94*, 94
Hearne, Samuel, 154, *155*, 236
Hecla (ship), 241
Heemskerk (ship), 51
Henderson, Richard, 157
Henry the Navigator, 39-42, *40*
Henry VII, King of England, 138, 239
Hensen, Matthew, 246-7
Herbert, Wally, 248
Herjolffson, Bjarni, 37
Hero, (American ship), 254
Herodotus, 18, *19*, 111
Heyerdahl, Thor, *16*
Hicks, Lieutenant, 206-8
Hillary: Sir Edmund, 72, *270*, 272
Himalaya, the, 14, 21-2, 28, 72, 75, 83-92, *84*, *86*, *90*, 193-5, *see also* Everest, Mount: Hindu Kush
Hindu Kush, 21-2, 75, 77-8 83, 90
Hinduism, 78, *84*, 85, *86*, *91*
Hochelaga (Montreal), 55, *140* 141-2
Hedgers, W., *107*
Hodgson, Maurice: Hearne and Matonabee, 236
Hukule'a (ship), 32
Holland, John P., 281
Holland (submarine), 281
Holy Island (Lindisfarne), 36
Hoorn (ship), 49-50
Horn, Cape, 50, 57-8, 68, 186, 198
Hoseason Island, 69
Huang He river, 25
Hubble Space Telescope, 298
Hudson, Henry, 236, 240
Hudson, river, 234
Hudson's Bay Company, *144*, 145, *154*, 154-7, 164-6, 236-9, 243
Humber, river, Canada, *143*
Humboldt, Alexander von, *10*, 88, 190; painting by, *189*
Humboldt, river, 17-9
hunter-gatherers, 14, 126, 174, 176-7, 236

Ibn Battuta, 101, 102, *106*
Ibo (tribe), 104
ice: barriers, 60, 65, 240, 254, 259-64, 268; embedded vessels, 241-3, 250-1, 261; pressure ridges, 246-7; sea spray ridges, *266*
ice floes, 235-7, 243-5, 260, *268*, 268
icebergs, *35*, 246-8, 254, 257-9, *258*, *275*
Iliamna, lake, 157
ill health, 8, 20-1, 59; Africa, 103-5, 108, 111-13, 116, 119; America, 131-5, 149, 163, 184-6, 192, 195-6; Australia, 216-19; Polar regions, 231-4, 240, 243, 246, 261-8; undersea, 282-4, *see also* blindness: scurvy: starvation
Illinois, river, 146-7, *148*
immarama, 32
Incas, 15, 133, *176*, 177-81, *178*, *181*, 193-7
incense, 15-17, 20, 73, 126
Inconstant, river, 166
India, *28*, 39, 44, 57, 75-7, 83-8, 95, 202-3; discovery of, 24-5, 41-2; slaves from, 21
Indian Ocean, 24-5, 53, 60-1, 68, 88, 98, 218
Indians *see* American Indians: Carib Indians
Indonesia, 25, 28, 42, 49, *51-2*, 51-3, 60, 204-5
Indus, river, 21, 22, 72, 75, 85
insects, 90, 94, 189-93, 209, 225; and disease, 108, 111, 123, 174, 186; fleas and spread of plague, 39; living off, 123; locusts, 95; mosquitoes, 35, 111, 143, 160, 175; termites, 174, 199
Intercontinental Ballistic Missiles (ICBM), 290
International Geographical Congress (1895), 260
International Geographical Year (1957), 272, 275
Intrepid (British ship), *230*
Inuit (tribe), 230-1
Investigator (British ship), 212-14, 244
Ionides, Constantine, 123
Ireland, 32, 36, 38
Irizar, Capt., 262-3
Isbjrn (ship), 32
Islands, Bay of, 225-6
Issus, battle of, *21*
Issyk-kul, lake, 90
Ivan the Terrible, 232
ivory, 15-17, 22-4, 37, 75, 236

Jacquinot peak, 254
James Caird (ship), 270-1
James, river, 149-50
James, Thomas, 240
Jamin, Paul: painting by, *14*
Jan Mayen Island, 32, 35, 234
Japan, 25, 44, 48-9, 66, 76-7, *79*
Java, 14, *25*, 76-7, 206
Jaxartes, river, 21
Jeanette (American ship), 248, *249-50*, 250
Jefferson, President Thomas, USA, 159-60
Jesuit explorers, *83*, 83-5, 111, 137-8, 144-6, 192
jewels, 24, 58, 82, 127, 135; pearls, 127, 135
Jhelum, river, 22
Johnson, William, 86
Joides Resolution (drilling ship), 285
Joliet, Louis, *125*, 145-8

Kaiser Wilhelm II Land, 261
Kakadu National Park, Australia, *203*
Kalahari Desert, 119
Kalulong, Mount, 94
Kamchatka Peninsula, *63*, 65-6
Kamrasi (African king), 116
Kane, Elisha Kent, 245
Kara Kirghiz (tribe), 88
Kara Sea, 234
Kayak Island, 66
Kayopo (tribe), 199
Kelsey, Henry, 154
Kennedy, President John F.: USA, 291, 294
Kennedy Space Center, 289
Kerguelen Island, 51, 61
Keynes: J.M.: English overseas investment, 58
Khan of Tartary, 8-11
Khublae Khan, 25
Kievan Russia, 35, 76-7, *77*
King George's Sound, 214
King, John, 216-18
King William Island, 238, 243, 245
King's Mirror (10th Century), 8
Kinthup, Pundit, 87, 88
Kirina, Mali, *106*
Koko Nor, lake, 84
Kolyuchin: Gulf of, 235
Kongur, Mount, *89*
Korakorsyk, Pyotr, 157
Kristensen, Henning, 193-4
Kublai Khan, 25, *80*, 81-2, *82*, *85*
Kun Lun mountains, 84, 86, 90
Kuril Islands, 66
Kwipak (Yukon), river, 157

La Condamine, Charles-Marie de, *185*, 185, 192
La Salle, Rene-Robert Cavalier, Sieur de, *146-8*, 146-8, 171
Lachlan, river, 215
Lady Alice (steel boat), 121-2
Laika, (dog in spae), *291*, 291-2
Laing, Alexander Gordon, 8, 104
Lancaster Sound, 240, 242
Lander, Richard, 103
Lassell, William, 298
latitude, 22-3, 86, 185, 240
Laubeuf, Maxime, 281
Le Griffon (French ship), 146
Le Maire, Jakob, 49-51, 224
Le Testu, Guillaume: map by, *57*
Lederer, Dr. John, 150
Leichhardt, Friedrich, 218-21
Lena, river, 231, 250
Lena (ship), 235
Leptis Magna, 101
Lesneur: sketches by, *55*
Lethbridge, John, 282
Lewis, Meriwether, *159*, 159-61, *161*, 163, 171
Limpopo, river, 120
Lindisfarne (Holy Island), 36
Linné, Carl von (Linnaeus), 186
Linschoten, Jan Huygen van: *Navigato ac Itenerarium*, *25*
Lioness (Dutch ship), 204
Lisiansky: drawing by, *65*
Little Abbai River, 112
Livingstone, David, 90, 115, *118-21*, 118-21, 218
Looes, Wouter, 206
Lorena, Guglielmo de, 279
Los Tres Reyes (Spanish Ship), 204
Louis XIV, King of France, 147-8
Louisiana Purchase, 157, *159*, 160
Lovell, James, 293
Lualaba (Congo) River, 118, 121-3
Luta Nzigé (Albert), lake, 115-18, 121
Lytzen, Carl, 250-1

Macarthur, John, 218
McCormick, Dr. Robert, 259-60
Macdonnell Ranges, 222
MacGregor, William, 225
Mcholy-Nogyi, Laszlo, *68*
Machu Picchu, *175*, *192*, *194*, *197*, 197
Mackay Alexander, 238
Mackenzie, Alexander, 154, *155*, 171, 236, 237-8
Mackenzie, river, 242
McMurdo Sound, *261*, 261, 264, 275
Macquarie, river, 215-16
Magdalena, river, 127, 177, 189
Magellan, Ferdinand, 8, 28-9, 43, 45-8, *47-8*, 57, 60, 197
Magellan, Straits of, 46, 49-50, 57, *190*
Mahabharata: The, 85
Malaspina, Alessandro, 186, 187
Manarov, Musa, 298
Manco Inca, 181-2, 196, 197
Mandeville: John de: *Travels*, *28*
Manuel, King of Portugal, 42, 45
Maoris, 59, *225*, 225, *226*, *227*
maps *see* cartography
Maranon, river, 178
Margarita islands, 184
Marigold (English ship), 57
Marquette, Father Jacques, *125*, *146*, 146
Marsden, Rev. Samuel, 226
Maternus, Julius, 99, 103
Mato Grosso, 192, 198
Matra, James, 209
Matthew (ship), 239
Maule, river, 179, 182
Mauritius (Dutch ship), 204
Mawson, Douglas, 254
Mayas, *126*, 126, 128-9, 131, 133
Mayflower (English ship), *151*
Mecca, *24*, 84, 94, *95*, 102, 113
Mediterranean, sea and region, 18-24, 39, 73, 98
Melville, Herman: *Moby Dick*, 210
Melville Sound, 241-3
Mendana, Alvaro de, 48
Mendoza, Diego de, 133 *195*
Meneses, Jorge de, 224
Mentuhotep, Pharoah of Egypt, 16
metals, 23, 53, 88, *223*, *278*; copper, 22, 145, 237, 278, *see also* gold: silver
Mexico, Gulf of, 135-6, 146, 278
Miller, Arthur Jacob, *162*
Mir Khustau Dehlavt: miniature by, *22*
Mir (space station), 298
Mirnyi (ship), 256
missionaries, 48, 83-5, 113, 118, *121*, *145*, 168, *184*; New Zealand, 225-6; S. America, 192, 198
Mississippi, river, *125*, 126, 136, 142, 145-8; Great Falls, 161
Mississippi valley, 135, 146-7, 168
Missouri, river, *136*, 159-64; major tributaries, 161, 163
Moctezuma, Aztec king, 129-30, *130*, 130
Moller (Russian ship), 156
monsoons, 17, 20, 92, 98
Mont Réal, 141
Montgomerie, Thomas, 86-7
Moorhead, Alan: *The White Nile*, 114
Moors, 36, 43, 101, 104-5
Morocco, 99, *100*, 101
Morse, Eric, 144
Mortes, Rio das, 199
Moscosco: Luis de, 135
mountaineering, 86, 90-2, 193-8
Mozambique Channel, 20
Munster, Sebastian: map by, *140*
Murchison Falls, 116-17, *117*
Murchison, river, 206
Murray, river and basin, 203, 215, *216*, 219
Murrumbidgee, river, 215-16
Muscovy Company, 232
Muslims, 41, 48, 72, 77, 94-5, *95*, *102*
Mutesa, King of Buganda, 114

Nain Singh: Pundit, *87*, 87
Namib Desert, 20
Nansen, Fridtjof, 23, 248, *250*, 250-1
Napo, river, 184
Narval (French submarine), *283*
NASA (US space agency), 295
Nautilus (nuclear submarine), 282, *283*
Navigatio Sancti Brendani, 32-5
navigation, 22, 28, 31-2, 39, 45, 58, 185; instruments, *11*, 30, 39, *60*, 214; space technology, 291
Nazca lines, *174*, 195
Necho II: Pharoah of Egypt, 18, 20
Negro, river, 193
Nelson, river, 154
Nepal, 83, 86, *87*, *90*
Neptunes (aeroplanes), 275
Nero, Roman Emperor, 99
Nestorian christians, 83, 83-4
New Archangel harbor, *65*
New England: USA, 67-9, 151, 210
New Guinea, 14, 60, 203, 224, 225
New Plymouth, 151, 153
New Siberian Islands, 251
New South Wales, 207-8, 212
New York Herald, 121
New Zealand, 29-31, 52, 57-9, 61, *64*, 225-8
Newby, Eric, 43, 164, 170
Newcastle Waters, Australia, 217
Newfoundland, *29*, 53-5, *57*, 58, 138-9, *139-40*, 151, 239; fog bank, 32, 35; L'Anse aux Meadows, 38
Newport, Christopher, 150
Ngami, lake, 119
Niagara, river, 146
Nicolet, Jean, 138
Niger, river, 41, 103-6; Bussa Rapids, 103
Nile, river, 15-18, 103, 111-12, *115-16*, 121; discovering the source, 25, 99, 111-18; Tissiat Falls, 112
Nina (ship), *43*, 43
Ninle, river, 72
Nonsuch (English ship), 145
Nootka Sound, Vancouver, 62, *63*

Nordenskiold, Baron Nils, 234-5
Nordenskiold, Otto, 262, 262
North America, 52, 55, 65, 126-71, 126-71, 174
North Carolina, 148, 157, 158
North East Passage, 231-6
North Pole, 10, 114, 240, 245-8, 246, 247, 248; flying over, 272, 273, 273; submarine exploration, 282
North West Companay, 237
North West Passage, 15, 64, 187, 232, 236-44, 259
Novaya Zemlya, 49, 232-2, 234-5

Oakover, river, 223
Ob, river, 231
Oeussant: Isle d' (Ushant), 23
Ohio river, 126, 157
Operation Deepfreeze, 275
Orange, river, 106
Orbiting Astronomical Observatory (OAO), 298
Orellana, Francisco de, 183-4, 180, 192
Orinoco, river and basin, 177, 189
Ortelius: Orbis Terrarum, 64
Orville, Father Albert d', 83-5
Ottawa, river, 143, 146
Ottoman Turks, 39, 83
Oudney, Walter, 103
Ovalle, Alonso de, 182
Oxus, river, 22, 75, 80

Pachacuti, Inca Emperor, 177-9, 197
Pacific islands, 29-32, 48, 52, 55-61, 130-1, 190-1, 256; Easter, 15, 29-31; Hawaii, 29-32, 62, 65; Los Tres Marias, 133; Marianas, 48, 187; Philippines, 48, 187, 203; Tonga (Friendly), 30, 51-2, 58, 61; Tuamotus archipelago, 46-50; Vanuatu (New Hebrides), 48-9, 226, see also Spice Islands
Pacific Ocean: Atlantic link 46, 50, 65 68, 241; early exploration, 25, 29-32; Mariana Trench, 281; reaching by overland routes, 128, 128, 162-3, 166, 170-1; research in, 285; searching for the "Southern continent", 60
Pakistan, 22, 24, 85, 88, 89
Palmer, Capt. Nathaniel, 254
Papin, Denis, 279
Papua-New Guinea, 49, 51-2
Park, Mungo, 103, 103
Parkinson, Sydney, 208
Parry, Capt. Edward, 141-2, 230, 236, 240-1
Parry Islands, 236
Patagonia, 186, 197-8
Patience, Cape, 268, 269, 270
Paulinus, Suetonius, 99
Peace, river, 238
Peary, Capt. Robert Edwin, 10, 114, 245, 246, 246-7
Peel Strait, 243
Peking, 14, 24, 76, 83, 83-5, 101
Pelgrom, Jan, 206
Pendleton, Capt., 254
Peo, Fernao do, 41
Periplus of the Erythraean Sea (First Century seaman's manual), 24
Persian Gulf, 24, 25, 41, 72, 76, 79, 94
Peter the Great, Russian Tsar, 65, 65
Petit, Nicolas: painting by, 55
Petite Hermyne (French ship), 139
Phillip, Capt. Arthur, 209
Piccard, Auguste, 277, 281, 281
Pigafetta, Antonio, 46
Pilgrim Fathers, 151, 151-3, 153
Pinta (ship), 43, 43
Pisces III (submersible), 284
Pizarro, Francisco, 133, 179-81, 182-3
Pizarro, Gonzalo, 183-4
planets, 58, 126, 288, 294-8, 296-9
Plate, river, 46, 186
Plenty, Bay of, 225
Pliny: tides, 288
Pocahontas, 149, 149
Point Hicks Hill, 208
Polaris (ship), 245
poles: celestial, 22, 259, 275; Inaccessibility, 275, see also 15-2 North Pole: South Pole
Polo, Maffeo, 79, 81
Polo, Marco, 15, 25, 72, 79-83, 81-2, 218
Polo, Nicolo, 79-81

Polyphemus (frigate), 120
Ponting, H.G.: photography by, 255, 266
Popocatepetl, mountain, 129
Possession Island, 260
Potomac, river, 150
prayer wheels, 84, 87
Prehevalski: Nicholas, 88, 88-90, 94
Prince of Wales Island, 66
Prince William Sound, 155
Princess Martha Land, 256
Punt, 15-18
Pytheas of Marseilles, 21-3

Quebec, 55, 58, 139, 141-2, 145-50
Queen Maud – gulf and mountains, 274238
Quetzalcoatl (Aztec god-king), 129-30
Quiros, Pedro Fernandez de, 48-9
Quitoo, 184-5, 185, 189, 192

Radisson, Pierre-Esprit, 144, 144-5
Rae, Dr. John, 236, 238, 238-9, 243
Rae Strait, 238, 242
Rai Bahadut Kishen Singh: Pundit, 86
rain forests, 92-4, 177, 185, 190, 196-9
Raleigh, Sir Walter, 148, 149
Raven, Capt. (sealer), 225
Rechnitzer, Dr. Andreas, 281
Red Sea, 13, 16-18, 24-5, 39-41, 73, 94, 111-12, 278
Reger, Johann: world map by, 28
Remington, Frederick, 164
reptiles, 94, 161, 166, 191-3; crocodiles, 50, 103-4, 116
Resolution (English ship), 60, 61-2, 62, 65, 244
Resurgam (submarine), 278
Retez, Ortiz de, 224
Ricci, Matteo, 84-5
Richelieu, river, 142
Ripon Falls (The Stones), 114, 115, 121-2
Roanoke Island, 148-9, 150
Rocky mountains, 126, 154-5, 161-70, 236-8
Rolfe, John, 149, 150
Rondon, Candido, 198
Roosevelt, President Theodore: USA, 198, 246
Roosevelt (ship), 247
Roper, river, 221
Ross Ice Shelf, 259-60, 261, 263-4, 268
Ross, John, 241-2, 244
Ross Sea, 268, 273
Ross, Sir James Clark, 230, 258-9, 259-60
Rouquaryol-Denayrouze apparatus, 285
Rousseau, Jean Jacques: people of Tahiti, 56
Rovuma, river, 120
Royal Geographical Society, 58, 87, 219; Danish, 240; expeditions sponsored, 94, 113-15, 119-21, 197-9
Rubruck, Friar William of, 8-10
Ruiz, Hipolito, 186
Russian American Company, expeditions sponsored, 67, 155-6
Ruwenzori (mountains of the moon), 113, 123

Sabine, Cape, 245
Sacajawea (wife of Charbonneau), 161-2
Sacrobosco, Giovanni de, 9
Sahara desert, 9, 20, 28, 39-41, 72, 95, 98, 101-3, 106
Sahure, Pharaoh of Egypt, 16
St. Cecilia (ship), 68-9
St. Clair, river, 145
St. Gabriel (Russian ship), 66, 67
St. Helena Bay, S. Africa, 20
St. Julian, S. America, 46, 197
St. Lawrence, river, 55, 58, 139-46, 237-9; Lachine Rapids, 143; Traverse Rapids, 58
St. Peter (Russian ship), 66, 67
St. Pierre, lake, 142
St. Vincent, Cape, 23
Saint-Hilaire: Auguste de, 192, 192
Saint-Mein: Charles de, 163
San Antonio (Spanish ship), 46
San Joaquin Valley, 166, 170

San Lucas (brig), 48
San Pedrico (Spanish ship), 204
Sanchez, Pedro, 138
Santa Maria (ship), 24, 43, 43-4
Santacilia, Jorge Juan y, 185
Sante Fe, 166-70, 168, 170
Santiago (Spanish ship), 46
Sargasso Sea, 28, 33, 39, 44-6, 53, 98, 138
Sarmiento, Mount, 190, 198
Saskatchewan, province and river, 154
Savannah, river, 135
Save, river, 17
Scandinavia, 23, 32, 35-6, 75-6, 140, 231-5, 250
Schirra, Wally, 293
Schouten, Willem, 49
scientific research, 20-3, 88-95, 157, 278, 290-1; Australasia, 214, 224-5; Eighteenth Century exploration, 55, 185-93, 197-9; geomorphology, 92-4, 198; magnetism, 39, 160, 192, 214, 241; meteorology, 88, 157, 192, 198, 251, 291; orography, 88, 92; polar regions, 240, 243, 253, 256, 261-5, 275
Scott, Robert Falcon, 218, 241, 244, 255, 261-6
SCUBA, 285
scurvy, 32, 42, 46-50, 55, 66, 105; Artic explorers, 234, 243-5, 261, 264; Australian explorers, 209, 218-19; preventing, 32, 50, 58-60, 186, 214, 241, 261
Sea Gull (American ship), 257-8
"Sealab" experiments, 284-5
seals, hunting, 67, 67-8, 155, 187, 225, 230, 254, 262, 270
Selous, Frederick Courtney: A Hunter's Wanderings in Africa, 123
Semyonov, Peter, 88-9
Senyavin (Russian ship), 156
Severn river, Canada, 154
Shackleton, Sir Ernest Henry, 268-72
Shark Bay, 52, 204, 223
Sharp, Andrew, 30
Shepard, Alan, 292, 292
Siebe, Augustus, 282
Sierra Leone, 41, 50
Sierra Nevada, 166, 167, 169, 170
Sierra Perija, 187
Silk Road, 24, 39, 80, 83
silks, 15, 24-5, 58, 76, 82
silver, 16-17, 22-4, 58, 75-6, 82, 168-70, 182, 183, 278
Simpson, Colin: Adam in Ochre, 204
Simpson Desert, 219
Simpson, Thomas, 238
Sinai Desert, 77
Sink, river, 170
Skylab space station, 298
Skytrains (aeroplane), 275
slave trade, 21, 39, 43-5, 75, 101, 102, 108, 113, 118-19, 121; Bantu slaves, 106; European slaves, 209; Florence Baker, 116; Livingstone's fight against, 118-20
sledges, 146-7, 236, 248, 261-4, 266
Smith, Jedediah, 164-8
Smith, John, 149, 149
Smoky, river, 238
Snake, river, 162, 170
Solimoes, river, 184, 192
Solu Khumbu, Namche bazaar, 91
South America, 32, 42-3, 46, 49, 49, 53, 68, 173-99, 174-99
South pole, 52, 57, 202-3, 244, 263-6, 271
spacecraft, 289, 292-8, 296
spacewalking, 293-4
Spain, 36, 43, 48-9, 179
Speke, John Hanning, 113-16, 115, 121
Spice Islands (Moluccas), 41, 45, 49, 52, 58-60, 232-4
spices, 16, 24, 49, 58, 82
Sputniks I and II (space satellites), 291-2
Stadler: aquatint by, 63
Stafford, Tom, 293
Standard Helment Diving Suit, 282
Stanislaus, river, 170
Stanley, Henry Morton, 120, 121-3, 122-3
starvation, 8, 46-8, 66, 73, 106, 119,

149, 184; Alexander's troops, 21-2; Australia, 216-19, 223; polar regions, 231-3, 236, 243, 250, 264-5, 268
Staten Island, S. America, 50
Stein, Aurel, 81
Strabo (historian), 23
Stuart Highway, Australia, 218
Stuart, John McDouall, 216-18, 218
Sturt, Charles, 215, 216, 218-19, 219
submarines, 279, 281-2, 282
Sudd, the, 99
Sumerians, 15, 15, 72
Sutlej, river, 85
Sydney, 203, 208, 208-9, 210, 214-15, 219, 258

Table Bay, 107
Table Mountain, 20
Tagus, river, 39
Takla Makan, 73, 77, 80, 83, 88-9
Tamerlane, 76-8, 78, 83
Tana, lake, 111, 112
Tanganyika, lake, 113, 113, 120, 121
Tapac-Ri plateau, 177
Taratai (ship), 32
Tartar Desert, 84
Tasman, Abel Janzoon, 49, 51-2, 53, 204-5, 224-5
Taupo, lake, 220
Taymr Peninsula, 231
Tebenkov, M.D.: Atlas, 156-7
Tehuantepec, Gulf of, 133
Tenochtitlan, 129-30, 130-1, 133
Tensift, river, 40
Terra Nova (ship), 255, 264, 266
Terror (bombship), 243, 243-4, 258-60
Tethys, Sea of, 202
Theron (ship), 272
Thesiger, Wilfred, 9, 72, 95, 95
Thetis (ship), 246
thirst, 101, 170, 218-19, 222
Thomas (slave-trader), 104
Tibesti Mountains, 95, 99
tides, 22-3, 163 288
Tien Shan mountains, 73, 75, 88, 90
Tierra del Fuego, 14, 50, 57, 60, 68, 174, 199, 258; exinct animals, 190; Martial Mountains, 198
Tigris, river, 15, 21, 72-3
Timbuktu, 8, 102, 102-6, 105
Timofeiev, Yermak, 231
Titanic, 278
Titicaca, lake, 177
Tititira Point, 225
Titov, Vladimir, 298
Topa Yupanqui, Inca emperor, 178-9
Torres, Luis de, 48-9
Torres Strait, 14, 49, 52, 60
Trans Antarctic Expeditions, 272
Tri Svyaltitelay (Three Saints) (Russian galliot), 155
Trichardt family, 06-8, 107, 111
Trieste (bathysphere), 277, 281, 281
Tristao, Nuno, 41
Tsangpo, river, 87, 88
Tsiolkowsky, Konstantin, 289
Tuareg (tribe), 8, 104-6
"Turk, the", 137-8
Turtle: submarine, 281, 282

Ulloa, Antonio de, 185
Ulloa, Francisco de, 133
Ultima Thule, 22, 23
Ural Mountains, 77
Urubamba, river, 193, 196-7
Uruguay (Argentine ship), 262-3
Urville, Jules Dumont d', 225, 256-7, 260

Vallard: map by, 54
Van de Velde the elder: Willem, 50
Van Dieman's Lands (Tasmania), 204
Van Rensburg family, 106-8, 111
Vancouver Island, 63
Vandals, 101
Veer, Gerrit de, 234
Vega (ex whaling ship), 235-6
Vegetius: De Re Militari, 282
Verein fur Raumshiffaurt (Society of Space Travel), 200
Verne, Jules: prophetic novel, 288-9

vessels, 18, 18, 23, 25, 25, 32, 73; Arab, 24, 39, 41, 79; Dutch, 50, 204; Egyptian, 15-16, 16, 101; lateen rigged sails, 29, 39-43, 43; for polar regions, 235, 250, 259-61; Polynesian, 29, 31-2, 225; Spanish, 43, 43, 9; two masted sailing, 48, 67-8, 130, 190; Viking, 29, 32, 35, 35; warships, 50, 58, 73, see also canoes: caravels:
Victoria, Australia, 210, 212
Victoria Falls, 97, 120
Victoria, lake, 114-16, 115, 121
Victoria, Queen: Great Britain, 118, 216
Victoria, river, 221
Victoria (ship), 46, 49
Victoria Strait, 242
Victorian Exploring Committee, 216
Vikings, 24, 29, 35-9, 37, 75-6
Vineland (land of Sagas), 37-8, 38
Virgin, river, 166
Volga, river, 76, 101
Voltaire: earth's shape, 185
Vostok (ship), 256

Walker, river, 170
Wallace, Alfred Russel, 94, 192-3, 193
Wallis: painting by, 30
walrus, 61, 67, 67, 75, 139, 155, 231
Warburton, Peter Egerton, 218, 221-3, 222, 223
Waterton, Charles, 192
Webber: paintings and drawings by, 31, 58, 62
Seddell Sea, 273
West Indies, 34, 34, 43-4, 128, 133, see also Bahamas
whales, 34, 50, 60, 67, 155, 230, 254; Southern rights, 209-10; undersea scientific research, 285; whalers, 209-10, 210, 225, 226
Whales, Bay of, 263, 273
White, Edward, 293, 294
White Sea, 232
Wilkes, Capt. Charles, 30, 67, 69, 256-61
Williams (British brig), 254
Willoughby, Sir Hugh, 232-4
Wills, William, 202, 216-17
Wilson, John, 215
winds: Antarctic, 254; development of the caravel, 39; north east trades, 98; "roaring forties", 41, 98, 204; south east trades, 20, 41
Winnipeg: lake, 237
Wisconsin, river, 146
Wood, Abraham, 150
Worsley, Frank, 270
Wylie (Aborigine), 218-19

Xenophon, 20, 21
Xingu, river, 199
Xun Jiang, river, 25

Yenisey, river, 231
York, Cape, Australia, 212
York, Cape, Greenland, 32
Young, Brigham, 171
Younghusband, Francis, 89
Yucatan peninsula, 126, 128, 133
Yukon (Kwipak), river, 157

Zambezi, river, 119-20, 123
Zeehaen (ship), 51
Zelée (ship), 256, 256-7
Zulus, 107, 110, 111, 119-20
Zurbrigen, Mattias, 195-6

Acknowledgments

Acknowledgments
The author and publisher would like to thank David Eldred for designing this book, Sue Robertson for the index, Nicki Giles for production and the editors for providing the captions. All illustrations were provided by the Bettmann Archive except for the following:

Ulrich Ackerman 156(bottom)
Archiv Gerstenberg 126(top), 131
Australian Picture Library 206-7
Axel Poignant Archive 1,
38(bottom), 54(bottom three),
58(top), 123(top), 208, 214(bottom),
215, 225
Bison Picture Library 39(bottom),
60(bottom), 139(top left),
141(bottom)
Bodleian Library, Oxford 216(top)
British Museum 151(top), 236
C.M. Dixon Photo Resources 21,
99(bottom)
E.C.P.A. 283(top)
The Freelance Photographers Guild
161(bottom)
The Granger Collection 40(bottom
left and right), 102(bottom),
104(top), 105(bottom), 144(top),
122(bottom), 123(bottom),
218(bottom)
David Hamilton / High Adventure

89(both), 92(top)
Bruce Herrod 87(bottom right),
90(top), 91(both), 93(both), 274(top),
275(top & bottom)
Hirmer Fotoarchive 23
Hulton Picture Company
20(bottom), 21(top), 204(top),
205(top right)
Institute of American History and
Art 162(top)
Library of Congress 131(top and
bottom), 132(bottom), 134(top), 135,
136(top), 138, 142(bottom),
143(both), 151(bottom), 158(bottom),
162(bottom), 182
The Mansell Collection 87(top),
122(top), 201(top left)

Ministry of Defence – Navy
282(top)
Tony Morrison, South American
Pictures 11(bottom), 174, 176(both),
185(bottom), 192(top), 193(top right)
National Maritime Museum 10(top
left), 50, 52(top), 60(bottom),
230(bottom), 231, 235, 237
National Archives 159(both),
170(top)
Peter Newark's Western Americana
282(bottom)
Public Archives of Canada 155,
239(top), 238, 240(bottom)
Royal Commission on Monuments,
Scotland 22
Royal Geographical Society 4-5, 6,

9(top right & bottom), 10(bottom),
59(top), 65, 86(both), p 87(bottom),
88, 92(bottom), 103(left),
189(bottom), 256
Irene Hinke Sacilotto 156(top)
Jerry Sieve 166-7
Smithsonian Institution 158(top),
224(bottom)
Mireille Vautior 165
Vickers Oceanics 284(top)
Weldon Trannies 203, 206 217,
219, 222(top), 223
Werner Forman Archive 105(top
right), 126(bottom)
Wiedenfeld Archive 76, 127,
197(both)
Winterthur Museum, Delaware 163